MURDER DONE TO DEATH
Parody and Pastiche
in Detective Fiction

by
John Kennedy Melling

The Scarecrow Press, Inc.
Lanham, Md., & London

SCARECROW PRESS, INC.

Published in the United States of America
by Scarecrow Press, Inc.
4720 Boston Way
Lanham, Maryland 20706

4 Pleydell Gardens, Folkestone
Kent CT20 2DN, England

Copyright © 1996 by John Kennedy Melling.

British Cataloguing-in-Publication Information Available

Library of Congress Cataloging-in-Publication Data

Melling, John Kennedy
Murder done to death : parody and pastiche in detective fiction /
by John Kennedy Melling.
   p.   cm.
Includes bibliographical references and index.
1. Detective and mystery stories, English—History and criticism.
2. Detective and mystery stories, American—History and criticism.
3. Burlesque (Literature). 4. Parody in literature. 5. Murder in
literature. 6. Death in literature. 7. Imitation in literature.
8. Intertextuality. I. Title.
PR830.D4M45   1996   823'.087209—dc20   95-15442

ISBN 0-8108-3034-5 (cloth : alk. paper)

∞™ The paper used in this publication meets the minimum requirements of
American National Standard for Information Sciences—Permanence of
Paper for Printed Library Materials, ANSI Z39.48-1984.
Manufactured in the United States of America.

To Mother and Barbara

Contents

Acknowledgments	vii
Foreword, by Colin Wilson	ix
1. Early Days and Differences	1
2. Books in the Mirror	29
3. The Crowd of One Man	112
4. . . . Is Another Man's Pastiche	136
5. P & P . . . in 3-D	210
Bibliography	260
Index	267
About the Author	282

Acknowledgments

As an avalanche must start with a single pebble, so more than a dozen years' research commenced when my mother and I were staying with Barbara Miller in the elegant Blackheath Village, and I bought in a charity shop a copy of MURDER BY PASTICHE, and it is with gratitude I can record the encouragement I have received from that day forward.

First, my mother thought it was more exoteric and less esoteric than I believed, and therefore of more value than some other literary projects. Then Barbara Miller, with her great experience on stage, television and film of crime and detection suggested the title MURDER DONE TO DEATH, which I immediately secured by writing a monograph so titled in 1979.

After a couple of years through family bereavement, Gwendoline Butler encouraged me to revise, finalize and submit the manuscript.

JOHN KENNEDY MELLING

Foreword

When Dr. Watson made a list of Sherlock Holmes's salient characteristics, he noted: "Knowledge of sensational literature—immense. He appears to know every detail of every horror perpetrated in this century." The same comment could be applied, without change, to the author of this book—the difference being that when Holmes met Watson in 1881, there was very little sensational literature to know. It seems incredible that the very word "detective" had been in use only since 1853, when Dickens introduced Inspector Bucket (in *Bleak House*) as a "detective officer." It is true that the first great detective, Poe's August Dupin, had made his bow in "The Murders in the Rue Morgue" twelve years earlier. But Dupin stood unique and alone until he was joined by Inspector Bucket, then by Sergeant Cuff of *The Moonstone* by Wilkie Collins in 1868, then by Emile Gaboriau's Lecocq in the following year. It was five years after Holmes had met Watson that the first best-selling detective novel made its appearance in Australia—Fergus Hume's *Mystery of a Hansom Cab*. But of course, it was the partnership of Holmes and Watson (beginning in 1887 in *A Study in Scarlet*) that launched the detective story on its spectacular career as perhaps the most widely popular form of literary entertainment. Jacques Futrelle's "thinking machine" Professor Van Dusen, Chesterton's Father Brown, and Ernest Bramah's Max Carrados soon expanded and added variety to the genre.

But even here, long before the Golden Age of the detective story in the 1920s, we can already see an emerging problem. The writer has to find a detective who is, in some basic way, quite unlike Sherlock Holmes. So Futrelle invents a kind of mad professor whose logical powers are so formidable that they become absurd (he learns chess in an afternoon, then beats the world champion), Chesterton decides on a mild and slightly comic little priest, while Bramah is forced to create a blind detective. You could say that Sherlock Holmes had condemned the detective story to becoming a parody of real police work—which Collins and Gaboriau had done their best to portray before Holmes came along. And until the appearance of Simenon's Maigret, most detective stories remained parodies.

So it could be said that *Murder Done to Death* is, in fact, a history of the detective story. It is undoubtedly—as the reader will soon perceive—one of the most comprehensive and informative that exists.

And who is the author of this remarkable work—which will surely find a place on the bookshelf of everyone who is interested in the "horrors perpetrated in this century," whether fictional or nonfictional? He is, as I shall show in a moment, himself a detective of some ability. But first, to the more straightforward biographical details. John Kennedy Melling is a theatrical historian who has always made a living as an accountant. I have known him—and indeed been one of his clients—since 1956, and have often had reason to bless his name, since my finances, like those of most writers, are usually in a state of indescribable chaos.

In the summer of 1956, my first book, *The Outsider,* became a wholly unexpected best-seller, and after it had gone through half a dozen impressions in a few months, my publisher, Victor Gollancz, told me it was time my affairs were placed in the hands of an accountant. When I asked why, he explained that a writer can claim all sorts of allowances—from typewriter ribbons to the heating and lighting in his office—and that this would greatly reduce my tax burden. Accordingly, I went one afternoon to the offices of an accountancy firm off the Strand, and was directed up to a room at the top of the building with a superb view over London's rooftops. There, a slim, rather good-looking young man dressed in a pin-striped suit, and whose age was obviously not much greater than my own (I was twenty-five at the time), jumped to his feet and said: "Colin Wilson? I'm delighted to meet you. I am an Outsider." Although I had become rather wearily accustomed to this greeting in the past six months, I must admit that on this occasion it made me smile, since I found it difficult to imagine anyone who looked less of an "Outsider."

In fact, I soon came to realize that John Melling had more of a title to that description than the majority of the aspirants I had met.

Foreword

He had become an accountant because he was good at figures and because his father had been an accountant. Yet there was obviously a sense in which his heart was not quite in it. He was interested in people, in art, in gastronomy, in the theatre and cinema, in the history of the City of London. And in crime—real and fictitious. (He acquired some of his encyclopedic knowledge of detective novels as the editor of the Black Dagger editions of crime reprints.) Moreover, he greatly preferred working with writers, artists, and actors rather than with businessmen. His employers were at first delighted, since they found these bohemians more trouble than they were worth, and were glad to delegate the task to someone who enjoyed it. But when it became clear that John Melling, in spite of his artistic proclivities, was also a formidably efficient accountant, they decided to promote him to a position that would involve far more work in factories. John immediately resigned and set up his own company of accountants, in which his clients were chosen from the arts. I, naturally, moved with him, for I had already discovered the enormous advantages of having an accountant. Nearly forty years later—and in spite of his "official retirement"—he is still my accountant. More important, he is one of my oldest friends.

I owe a great deal to John. It was he who—when we were walking one day on the cliffs near my home in Cornwall—commented that the natural successor to my *Encyclopedia of Murder* and *Encyclopedia of Modern Murder* would be an *Encyclopedia of Unsolved Mysteries*. He expressed himself as perfectly willing to collaborate with me on it. I pigeonholed the idea at the time, but a year or two later, looking for a project on which I could work with my eldest son, Damon, I wrote to John asking if he would mind if I "stole" his idea. Since he had suggested it, I regarded it as his intellectual property. With typical generosity, he replied that as far as he could remember, it was my idea, but that obviously, I would be welcome to it in any case.

Now in fact, he made a number of excellent suggestions, which I was delighted to seize upon. One was the mystery of the Isleworth Mona Lisa—the Leonardo painting discovered in Bath just before World War I, which is almost certainly the original painting of "La Giaconda." Another was the mystery of whether Dillinger was actually killed by police officers in Chicago in 1934, or whether another man was killed in his place. But the third mystery concerned someone I had never come across—a mysterious writer called Harry Whitecliffe.

John first heard about Whitecliffe when he received a letter from a French author named Françoise d'Eaubonne, who in turn had come across it in a book called *Nouvelles Histoires Magiques* by Louis Pauwels and Jacques Bergier, the authors of the 1960s best-seller *Le Matin des Magiciens*. According to Pauwels and Bergier, Harry Whitecliffe was a young writer who achieved celebrity in the early 1920s with a book of essays, another book of parodies of Oscar Wilde, then with a play called *Similia,* which had four hundred performances in the West End and then toured England. Whitecliffe grew tired of celebrity and vanished to Dresden, where he became a publisher of rare books. In October 1924 he became engaged to a beautiful young woman named Wally von Hammerstein. Then he disappeared again. More than a year later, Wally received a letter from him, signed "Lovach Blume." Blume was a sadistic mass murderer who had committed suicide in the condemned cell in Berlin, after being caught in his hotel room standing over the corpse of a prostitute—his thirty-first murder in Berlin. Blume confessed that he was Harry Whitecliffe, and that his terrible secret was that he felt a periodic compulsion to kill and disembowel women. He had left London after killing nine prostitutes in the early 1920s. Wally was so shattered by this revelation that she entered a nunnery.

Françoise d'Eaubonne wanted to know more, so she contacted the British Society of Theatre Research, who advised her to write to "the theatre historian John Kennedy Melling," which she did. What she wanted to know was, Did Harry Whitecliffe really exist, or was he the invention of Pauwels and Bergier—who had ignored her letters on the subject?

A glance at various reference books on the theatre revealed that there had been no playwright called Harry Whitecliffe and no play called *Similia.* Then what about a series of Jack the Ripper–type murders in London in the early 1920s? When John asked me about this, I said that I was fairly certain that the murders had never taken place. John checked with Scotland Yard and crime historian Joe Gaute, who supported my view.

At this point, most theatre historians would have assumed that the whole story was nonsense, and given up. But John has a persistency and an obsession with detail which makes him a good accountant. *Similia* sounded not unlike *Salome,* so he approached another friend, Thelma Holland, the widow of Oscar Wilde's son, Vyvyan Holland. She could find no mention of a book of Wilde parodies among her late husband's papers. But she was an Australian by birth, and "Lovach Blume" had told Wally von Hammerstein that he had been born in Sydney of a German father and a Danish mother. Thelma Holland advised John to write to the Mitchell Library in Sydney.

Incredibly, the Mitchell Library was able to trace a Blume who had been sentenced to death in Dresden in 1922. His given name was not Lovach but William. William Blume *had* been a celebrated literary figure—not in London but in Dresden. His translations of British plays had been produced with success in theatres along the Rhine. He had founded a private press in Dresden which had printed limited editions. And he *had* committed several murders in Berlin, including one in the Adlon Hotel—and attempted another in Dresden.

There was one minor difference. Blume had killed postmen, not prostitutes. In those days, postmen often carried large sums in money and postal orders, which they delivered to consignees in their homes. Blume, it seemed, made a quick fortune by murdering and robbing postmen in the postwar chaos of Berlin. Interrupted on one occasion by his landlady while attacking a postman, he cut her throat and moved to Dresden. There he set up the Dorian Press, translated plays, and became something of a literary celebrity. He called himself Harry Whitecliffe, and invented stories about his success as a playwright in London.

Unfortunately, all the civic records in Dresden were destroyed by the Allied bombing in World War II, so we shall probably never know the whole truth about William Blume. Did he actually become engaged to Wally von Hammerstein? Did he write a play called *Similia,* which was presented in Germany? All we know for certain is that when his money ran out, he decided to replenish his coffers by murdering another postman. This time the crime went wrong; he was interrupted by the tenant of the house as he waited on the porch with two revolvers. He fled, tried to shoot pursuing policemen, and was captured when the revolvers misfired. In prison he attempted suicide, confessed to his other murders, and was—we assume—executed.

Presumably Pauwels and Bergier came across a garbled version of the story many years later, and published it in their *New Tales of Magic* in 1978. They probably heard it from some survivor of the 1920s—in which case, it seems probable that their informant has since died. So unless the whole story can be traced in some Dresden newspaper file, the strange history of Harry Whitecliffe will presumably never be known. But John Melling's detective work has made it clear that it is one of the strangest tales of our century.

Now that he has "retired," I am hoping to persuade John Melling to settle down and write the definitive history of the detective story. Whether he does or not, *Murder Done to Death* will remain perhaps the most erudite and fascinating contribution to this delightful—if minor—branch of literary history.

—Colin Wilson

1. Early Days and Differences

"Parody is a young man's job; pastiche is for the older man."

"Parody is written with bitterness; pastiche with affection."

"If you find the proper names are distorted, it's parody; if the names are still the same, it's pastiche."

Three popular differences between parody and pastiche—and all equally wrong. Perhaps a better definition is that by Ellery Queen in *101 Years Entertainment: The Great Detective Stories,* written in 1941: "A parody is a burlesque imitating some serious work; a pastiche is usually a serious imitation in the exact manner of the original author."

There are various meanings to "parody" in dictionaries and literature, ranging from a "burlesque imitation" to a "composition in which the characteristic turns of thought and phrase of an author are mimicked and made to appear ridiculous, especially by applying them to ludicrously inappropriate subjects" (*Shorter Oxford Dictionary*). Brewer quotes Hippomax of Ephesus of the sixth century B.C. as the Father of Parody, the term being derived from the Greek *paroida* (*para,* "beside"; *oide,* "an ode"—hence, an ode perverting the meaning of another ode).

Dr. Thomas Arnold (1795–1842), the headmaster of Rugby, advised boys to follow his example by never reading parodies, "as they suggested themselves to the mind for ever after in connection with the beautiful pieces which they parodied." The seventeenth-century writer Père Montespan held that the essence of parody was the substitution of a new and light for an old and serious subject, and the free use (or misuse) of the expression of the author parodied, while Lord Francis Jeffrey (1773–1850), the editor of the *Edinburgh Review,* in his review of *Rejected Addresses* subtly and acutely differentiated among various forms of parody, distinguishing between mere imitation of externals (personal imitation) and that higher and rarer art which brings before us the intellectual characteristics of the original. Other writers and critics give whole or partial explanation in their own writings.

The term "parody" in current form dates back to 1598, but has had varying interpretations. In 1745 it was used to mean "to compose a parody on"; by 1801 it meant something was "little better than a parody of" the original; by 1830 it implied a travesty; and by 1875 it was used as a verb again, as to compose a parody.

So much for the somewhat classical interpretations ranging back into history, well before the genesis of the detective story. "Pastiche" is of a much later vintage. We have already had reference to "burlesque" in connection with parody, and in the nineteenth century burlesque was an established type of theatrical entertainment. Madam Vestris, the celebrated actress-manager and player of what were termed "breeches" parts, or *travesti* roles, could stage *Don Giovanni in London,* interpolating somewhat inappropriately her popular song "Cherry Ripe" to public demand, and London's famous Gaiety Theatre could stage such classics as *Cinder Ellen* (1891), *Monte Christo Junior* (1886), *Carmen Up to Data* (1890), by George R. Sims and Henry Pettitt, with glamorous actresses in the male leads, as with the British pantomime tradition—but not as in the American form of "burlesque." At this same period pastiche also became popular, the term dating from 1878, from the earlier term *pasticcio* (1752), in turn coming from French, Italian, and German, a "pasta," "paste," "pastos," sprinkled or salted, or a barley porridge, leading to the dictionary definitions of medley, jumble, hotch-potch, farrago, or a composition in literature, music, painting, or design, perhaps made up from bits of other works or imitations of another's style. Detective fiction, or literature generally, is not the only art to be the target of both parody and pastiche, then and now, but it is the former whose development we must now consider before we can see how parody and pastiche have formed fresh channels and deltas.

This is not, of course, anywhere near the first attempt to analyze these two categories. An excellent comment was in the preface, by that master of both arts, Jon L. Breen, of his *Hair of the Sleuthhound,* published in 1982, subtitled "Parodies of Mystery Fiction," but containing pastiches as well in the twenty-two chapters, each with a short, neat introduction. In his preface he gives some American dictionary definitions of "parody," lists some nonmystery anthologies, and stresses some of the differences (e.g., humorous variations of a detective's name), but he too points out that the obvious, well-known definitions mentioned above are not always definitive. One interesting comment he makes, and also quotes Nathaniel Benchley thereon, is of parody as a form of literary criticism. (Occasionally, dramatic critics write their entire reviews as parody.) We shall consider Breen's subtle and witty book, and his work generally, again, both his short stories and full-length novels.

In his *Theatrecraft,* published by Marc Europe in 1986, Nigel Forde, a broadcaster, author, and poet, wrote in chapter 6, "Writing":

> The best form of literary criticism is also the best fun: it is parody, by which I mean the conscious imitation of somebody else's style. There is also another form which goes under the name of parody, where certain words of the original passage are replaced by others, in order to poke fun, as in Lewis Carroll's version of "Twinkle, twinkle, little star":
>
> Twinkle, twinkle, little bat!
> How I wonder what you're at!
> Up above the world you fly,
> Like a tea-tray in the sky.
>
> But this is not really parody at all; it is properly called burlesque. It is extremely tedious unless it is exceptionally well done, in which case it is only fairly tedious. Parody, however, is an art because, to do it well, the writer has had to understand how the mind of the original writer works, and that requires a great deal of knowledge and a large amount of sympathy if not love. Parodies done in spite are often too extreme and unconsidered—more of a scream than a statement—but to write a good parody makes you ask all the right questions: What image would he have chosen for that? What would he have thought of that? Are those words in his vocabulary? and so on. A good parody should be easily mistakable for the real thing. It is instructive and enjoyable to try writing a famous scene in a play in the style of three or four different playwrights.

There are two other terms used to describe works in this survey. The first has also been mentioned in connection with theatre—

"burlesque" — which is both a playful or jocular composition, and a deliberate exaggeration in mockery, as with women taking men's roles in otherwise straight drama. The other term frequently used for books and films is "spoof," a term coined by the great English comedian Arthur Roberts (1852–1933) for the hoaxing game he invented, hence something bogus, but now used in the sense of a joke or send-up or, of course, a form of parody.

For another and earlier distinction I am indebted to author Peter Lovesey, with whose books we shall be concerned later. In 1985 he was a guest at Rheims of 813, the French association of crime authors and fans, became a member, and receives the journal *813*. In no. 14, December, 1985, he kindly sent me, was the article *Les Parodies Du Roman Policier* by Regis Messac, from *La Revue Belge,* vol. 2, no. 2. (April 15, 1930): the author specifies: "On ne pastiche que les auteurs qui en valent la peine; c'est presque un titre de glorie que de figurer dans un receuil de *A la Manière de* . . . De même, un genre littéraire n'obtient les honneurs de la parodie que lorsqu'il jouit d'une existence definie, d'un cercle de lecteurs assez vaste, en un mot, de la popularité." The main subjects of this long and interesting article are several parodies of Sherlock Holmes and his methods (including two plays), Stephen Leacock, Mark Twain, the French favorite Fantomas, and A. A. Milne's *The Red House Mystery,* with its secret passage in the library.

Another pertinent comment from the French comes in *Le Compagnonnage,* by Dr. Bernard de Castéra, in 1988: "La parodie, l'imitation ne sont pas necessairement des moqueries. Elles peuvent être le signe d'une profonde admiration."

Yet another interesting comparison by August Derleth was quoted by Richard Lancelyn Green in the introduction to his 1985 collection, *The Further Adventures of Sherlock Holmes,* consisting of what are both sequels and pastiches, two of which — by Derleth and Julian Symons — we shall consider in Chapter 4. Although the thousand or more parodies and pastiches of Holmes can be only lightly touched upon here, Green, son of writer Roger Lancelyn Green, has a neat collection, with apt quotes and facts. The Derleth comment on his splendid Solar Pons pastiche was that he did not follow the "ridiculing imitation designed for laughter," preferring the "fond and admiring one less widely known as pastiche." Other stories in Green's book include an Arthur Whitaker story once thought to be by Doyle, and others by Vincent Starrett, Stuart Palmer, creator of Miss Hildegarde Withers, and the winner of a competition.

It was said by a leading American detective fiction historian and critic, Howard Haycraft, that we could not have detective stories before we had detectives, but that has been described as too facile a comment, because the actual terms "detective," and the art of police "detection," are much older, going back many years. Two early trends are Samuel Johnson, the great lexicographer (1709–1784), described by novelist Tobias Smollett (1721–1771) as "that Great Cham of literature," and the early crime novel *Things as They Are; or, The Adventures of Caleb Williams* (1794) by William Godwin (1756–1836), the father of Mary Wollstonecraft Godwin (1797–1851) who was the wife of poet Percy Bysshe Shelley and herself the writer of the classic gothic novel *Frankenstein* in 1818. Historians quote the biblical stories of Susanna and Judith, and Voltaire, as well as the private police forces of the London Docks and London Magistrates, before the official foundation of British police forces in the early nineteenth century, but deduction, in the sense of Poe's "ratiocination," is now generally accepted, and the five famous short stories written between 1841 and 1844 by the American Edgar Allan Poe (1809–1849), "The Mystery of Marie Roget," "The Murders in the Rue Morgue," "The Purloined Letter," "The Gold Bug," and "Thou Art the Man," a quintet first selected by the detective story writer Dorothy L. Sayers (1893–1957). Poe was affected by drink and drugs, so surprise and skepticism were expressed about such a writer and editor being able to produce such analytical and deductive short stories, but it has been established that these were written in the period when he was free from those effects. His detective is the egregious chevalier C. Auguste Dupin, who goes out only at night, and can follow through a logical line of thought psychologically in his companion walking silently beside him—admittedly a man whose thought processes he would naturally know better than a stranger's, which is not to detract from the feat.

In his biography of Phineas T. Barnum, a great American showman and circus owner, titled *Humbug,* Harris has an interesting comment, that America was then ripe for such men as Poe, Richard Adams Locke, and Barnum, who were all adept at exposing hoaxes and setting up hoaxes themselves, while American literature was thus ready for any problem solving, such as Poe's ratiocination.

Various authors wrote detectives stories during the next two decades, establishing continuation of the genre, including Wilkie Collins (1824–1889), Charles Dickens (1812–1870), and others, until the Southsea (near Portsmouth) doctor who wrote short stories while awaiting patients for *Strand Magazine* gave impetus with the birth of Sherlock Holmes. Arthur Conan Doyle (1859–1930) wrote his first Holmes novel, *A Study in Scarlet,* in 1887, and the first short story in the *Strand*—"A Scandal in Bohemia"— for the July 1891 issue. He was to find his Holmes stories brought him more fame than his practice, war service, historical novels, and political and occult activities, much as did Arthur Sullivan find his collaboration with William Gilbert in the Savoy operettas (themselves definite parodies) outclass his "serious" operas, hymns, and oratorios, and Dorothy L. Sayers's Wimsey stories more famous than her poetic translations and excellent religious play *The Man Born to Be King*. Colin Wilson has an apt comment here. His books have encompassed so many different fields, including detective stories. In his early philosophical book, *The Strength to Dream* (1962), in references to Poe's and Jules Verne's detailed work, he notes "the imaginings have a certain authority." (This can be seen also in Poe's detective stories, as well as in the Sherlock Holmes stories, which are clearly related to them.)

At this time, it must be remembered that police forces were not popular, because of their alleged paramilitary basis, and a nonexistent bias against the working classes, so strong indeed that a police constable killed in England while endeavoring to control a mob had his death recorded as justifiable homicide. Hence these first fictional detectives tended to be amateur, or nonprofessional, often scoring off the Scotland Yard detectives, as with Holmes.

A variation of the amateur sleuth's operations is the gothic novel, with honorable roots as far back as Horace Walpole and Mary Wollstonecraft Shelley, a genus still very popular with writers and readers today. Donald Westlake neatly described it: "A Gothic is a story about a girl who gets a house." Gwendoline Butler has pointed out that Jane Eyre is a typical gothic tale. Invariably the heroine sets out to solve the murder mystery herself, goes off into cellar, marsh, attic, forest, or whatever, alone, then has to be rescued by the hero or the police. "Had I but known . . ." is the invariable phrase used, to christen it the Had-I-but-Known school. Ogden Nash in his poem on the subject, "Don't Guess, Let Me Tell You," ends: I wouldn't have bought it had I but known it was impregnated with Had I But Knowns. Isaac Asimov comments in "The Three Goblets" in *The Union Club Mysteries* (1984) on mystery writers giving "brains and insights" to the Holmeses, Poirots, and Wimseys as opposed to the "Scotland Yard bunglers," to which another of his clubmen retorts that the Applebys and Leopolds are the "public hirelings" solving "the most difficult and subtle crimes." "In fact, the police procedural is now much more popular than the old-fashioned Philo Vance bit."

Charlie Chan comes in for some peculiar comments in a book described as "A Social History of the Crime Story," *Delightful Murder,* by Ernest Mandel (1984), written from the Marxist viewpoint, and with certain errors of both type and thought. On one page, Chan is described as the only classic sleuth not from the upper class. Later, with Maigret and Ellery Queen, he appears as the "transitional figure" from the private sleuth to the police detective, but with little support from the department. Still later, Chan, Philo Vance, Ellery Queen, Perry Mason, and Nero Wolfe are hardly different from the classical Alan Grant of Josephine Tey (1897–1952), Roderick Alleyn of Ngaio Marsh (1895–1982), among a long list of policemen. Finally, "Lord Peter Wimsey's humour, Charlie Chan's apologetic sing-song, or Ellery Queen's eccentricities" are esoteric qualities not thought by the author to command their old following—a statement unsupported by the reissue of both books and films featuring this individualistic trio.

This tendency had increased partly as a result of a sensational bribery scandal in which some high-ranking and successful senior Scotland Yard officers had been involved and convicted. Notable exceptions, however, had been Charles Dickens with his creation of Inspector Bucket of the Detective, in *Bleak House* (1852–1853), based on Inspector Field, about whom he also wrote some laudatory magazine articles stemming from his own enthusiastic support; Wilkie Collins's Sergeant Cuff was based on Inspector Whicher, who had solved the Constance Kent murder case, and the obtuse Superintendent Seagrave based on the real Inspector Foley, in *The Moonstone,* published in 1868, of whom more anon. (An interesting side effect, not always noticed, is that so many detectives had anapestic names: a two-syllable given name and a one-syllable surname—such as Sherlock Holmes, Sexton Blake, Dixon Hawke, Ferrers Locke, Philo Gubb, Philo Vance, Charlie Chan, "Father" Brown, Nelson Lee, Parker Pyne, Nero Wolfe, Harley Quin, Gervase Fen, Jason Love, Dixon Brett, Daisy Bell, Falcon Swift, Martin Track, Kerry Drake, Colwyn Dane, Stanley Dare, Carfax Baines, Gordon Fox, Abel Link, Derek Clyde, Panther Grayle, Kenyon Ford, Vernon Bead, Martin Dale, and Matthew Helm, from the 1890s to the 1970s, across the whole field.) In his introduction to one edition of Agatha Christie's sensational and surprising *The Murder of Roger Ackroyd* (an "acroidal" book, according to H. R. F. Keating), the journalist Torquemada comments first on the respectability brought by "the lighthearted labours of three men" before World War I—Dr. Austin Freeman's *The Red Thumb Mark* (1907), G. K. Chesterton's *The Innocence of Father Brown* (1911), and two years later, E. C. Bentley's *Trent's Last Case*—after which he comments the war years increased the reading of John Buchan and Edgar Wallace "thrillers" and the "shockers" since a corpse or two more or less didn't seem to matter. It is in this introduction that he states he traced eighty-five clues and indirections in Christie's book.

An early recognition of the boring aspects of detailed police procedures came from Victor L. Whitechurch (1868–1933) in *Murder at the Pageant*. At the beginning of chapter 3 he referred to "that meticulous routine work which is so little known to the general public and bears such a minute part in modern detective fiction." In the first paragraph of chapter 5 he mentions dull, routine police work: "To write the real, complete story of any crime however interesting in itself, its detection and its result, would be to weary the reader intensely."

After World War I came the two decades known as the Golden Age of the detective story—from 1920 to 1940—when so many great authors flourished, like Agatha Christie, Dorothy L. Sayers, Ngaio Marsh, Margery Allingham, G. K. Chesterton, John Dickson Carr, John Creasey, and H. C. Bailey in Britain, and Erle Stanley Gardner, Dashiell Hammett, Jonathan Latimer, Earl Derr Biggers, and Raymond Chandler in America—to name just a few among many famous names. World War II brought a taste for more violence, realism, and harshness to the postwar writers. Other developments had been the psychological novel, more "why" than "whodunnit," to be followed by the police procedural, in which a team of police detectives solved various cases simultaneously, as would be the case in real life, rather than a single talented sleuth.

H. R. F. Keating in his interesting analysis *Murder Must Appetize* has noted that the hero detective became a brand label, indicative of the usual quality expected and received when any trademarked or hallmarked product is bought. The detective story has been likened to a modern version of the morality or mystery play ("mystery" referring to the guilds, or *métiers,* which presented the individual scenes), in the sense of the evildoer being discovered and punished, good triumphing over evil in the end—the Protestant ethos—which helps to explain why the genre was not so popular in police states. G. K. Chesterton (1874–1936), originator of Father Brown and first president of the Detection Club, said *In Defence of Detective Stories:* "No one can have failed to notice that in these stories the hero or the investigator crosses London with something of the loneliness and liberty of a prince in a tale of elfland, that in the course of that incalculable journey the casual omnibus assumes the primal colours of a fairy ship." The link between morality plays and the later fairy tales (although based on stories of antiquity) is stressed. Raymond Chandler (1888–1959) has his immortal line in *The Simple Art of Murder* (1950): "But down these mean streets a man must go who is not himself mean, who is neither tarnished nor afraid," and again following a Chesteron quote, notes: "When a policeman is made out to be a fool, as he always was in the Sherlock Holmes stories, this not only deprecates the accomplishment of the detective but it makes the reader doubt the author's knowledge of his own field." We have seen how the amateur or nonprofessional sleuth was at that time (1901) frequently scoring over the official detectives, a trend that continued.

Sherlock Holmes was frequently indifferent to the culprit's punishment by law, but the malefactor's downfall has a comforting feeling. In his book *Justice and the Press,* John Sefton, in the chapter "The Need for Scapegoats," comments that in Edmund Wilson's world nobody is guiltless or safe, and there is relief when the murderer is caught because "he is not, after all, a person like you or me. He is a villain—known to the trade as George Gruesome—he has been caught by an infallible Power, the supercilious and omniscient detective, who knows exactly where to fix the guilt."

The trend toward realism, in literature as in the theatre, cannot be wholly successful; for example, detective story writers strive to get their facts correct on such matters as ballistics, fingerprints, or forensic science, as these steadily evolve (in all probability the Jack the Ripper murders in the East End of London in the 1890s might have been solved had, say, the science of fingerprints been more advanced), but even if in a police procedural novel or television program much of the tedium and detail can be shown, too much detail would slow the narration to complete boredom.

This brief survey is not intended to be a full history of detective and crime fiction, just a list of landmarks, as there are many historical surveys of the genre, in whole or in part, to some of which reference will be made, and many of them listed in the Bibliography. Some universities offer courses on detective fiction, and in an interview with the writer for the *Poisoned Pen* magazine (vol. 6, no. 3 [1985]), Walter Gorski, a psychologist and leading police authority in America on hostages, hijacking, and the use of deadly force, stated that detective fiction in selected cases is used in the training of police officers.

Dr. Gorski, incidentally, drew my attention to an erudite book by Stefano Tani, published in 1984 by the Southern Illinois University Press, entitled *The Doomed Detective,* described as the "Contribution of the Detective Novel to Post-Modern American and Italian Fiction." Tani traces the rise of the anti-detective novel upturning the traditional detective formula, and splitting the future course into three—innovation, deconstruction, and metrication—an esoteric treatment in which he can make certain brief observations on the emergence of parody and self-parody. It is natural for all forms of popular culture to be analyzed in depth, and this has been happening to the detective story at least since the 1970s, and even earlier in the case of Sherlock Holmes. One writer in the excellent American University journal *Clues* in the 1980s pointed out that the popular television police lieutenant, Kojak, played by Telly Savalas, was a tribute to the Greeks as an ethnic minority, although his expensive tailor-made suits did not sit lightly on a lieutenant's pay.

Dr. Tani deals with such titles as the international success *The Name of the Rose,* by Umberto Eco, to which we shall turn again

Early Days and Differences

under parody; Pynchon's *Crying of Lot 49;* and Nabokov's *Pale Fire*. Dealing with detective story authors he says they "cling to the conventions of the British style (P. M. Hubbard) peppered with self-parody," that Italian authors have been slow to adopt detective stories as they "favored an ironic and parodic approach over indulgence in the murder of any gruesome aspects of the narrative," that Giallo of the 1930s had "a taste for the parodic and comic sides of the foreign genre." His other comments of an academic yet thoughtful nature are, for example, that the names of characters in Jorge Luis Borges's *La Muerte y la Brujula* (Death and the Compass, 1942), "seem to parody the self-destructive detective-murderer duality that is the pivot of the story," that another author, like Calvino, parodies the ending and the solution, for example, in *Se una Notte d'Inverno un Viaggiatore,* and, on a less cerebral note, that Silas Flannery "parodies" Sean Connery in Borges's book. This serious book does underline the popularity and prominence of detective fiction in England, America, and northern Europe, but certainly treats it as a serious branch of literature and culture, which Dorothy L. Sayers feared not to be the case.

It might have been expected that the first signs of parody or pastiche would have been from the onset of humor, which is not necessarily regarded as appropriate in the detective story. In later years the comedy-thriller made its appearance as book, film, and stage or television play, and some, as we shall see, altered the entire course of the subject. The first parodies, however, appeared as early as one year after the Holmes story in 1891. Robert Barr wrote the "Adventures of Sherlaw Kombs," in the *Idler,* a magazine edited by Jerome K. Jerome and himself. In this story, later titled "The Great Pegram Mystery," Dr. Whatson recounts admiringly his idol's miraculous, but completely incorrect, deductions of the missing financier shot in the Scotch Express. The story was reissued in 1979 by the Aspen Press of Colorado, which four years earlier had also republished the second parody of Holmes, which was "The Adventures of Picklock Holes" by Rudolf Chambers Lehmann, in *Punch,* the British humorous magazine, in 1893. Here Dr. Potson again recounts the brilliant, incorrect deductions of the Great Detective, interspersed with delightful non sequiturs such as "A day or two after . . . I happened to be travelling . . . through . . . Bokhara." Holmes has proved the main target for parody and pastiche to such an extent that more than one thousand examples have now been written. With such a vast and growing number, it is obviously impossible to deal with all Holmes's parodies and pastiches in depth, especially as there are many volumes devoted to specific parts thereof, so this study is intended to deal only with those examples which amplify the subject to a greater degree, as with the two pioneers quoted above.

In this survey of the early years of development, and pioneer parodies, we can now consider a short story which Julian Symons in his introduction to the *Penguin Crime Omnibus* referred to as "a parody of detective work such as Wilkie Collins's *'The Biter Bit.'*" This first recorded humorous detective story was part of Collins's *The Queen of Hearts,* published in 1859, and consists of a series of letters between Chief Inspector Francis Theakstone and Matthew Sharpin, concerning a robbery at 13 Rutherford Street, Soho (a cosmopolitan district in the West End of London). Yatman, a stationer who has had a career of ups and downs, lives over the shop with his wife, and a lodger, Jay, and has had his savings stolen. The pompous Sharpin, with friends in high places, has been wished onto the chief inspector, who assigns him to solve the robbery. Sharpin takes lodgings with the Yatmans, suspects Jay, bores two holes in the wall connecting their rooms—one for his eye, and the other for his ear—follows Jay to a mysterious assignation with the two detectives he has demanded as backup, only to find Jay attending a wedding. After following Jay, and writing meticulously and unnecessarily detailed reports, Sharpin is taken off the case; Sergeant Bulmer resumes it to discover promptly that Mrs. Yatman, adored by Sharpin, is the thief of the two hundred sovereigns to pay her secret dressmaker's bill. Yatman forgives her, and Sharpin disappears in a huff. Interesting to note that Collins and Dickens were great friends, sharing Dickens's amateur theatricals, Dickens encouraging Collins to write his type of novel, and Collins giving Dickens the example to start the unfinished whodunnit, *The Mystery of Edwin Drood* (which Poe could probably have solved), and then Collins going on to pen what is the first parody of detective fiction. We shall see later that Dickens himself again used parody, both of style and of living persons, in his own writings.

The other early parody is Edgar Allan Poe's short story "Thou Art the Man" (1844), satirizing writers of crime stories. The narrator tricks one Goodfellow by what Dorothy L. Sayers described,

Early Days and Differences

in her introduction to the first *Great Short Stories of Detection, Mystery and Horror* (1928), as "a repulsive kind of jack-in-the-box" into discovery of the murder. She stressed, however, that this story established two traditions: false clues by the murderer and the "solution by way of the most unlikely person."

The similarities between Collins's and Dickens's literary careers were marked. Dickens admired his friend's stories of crime and detection, and attempted them himself. They both wrote about social evils, although Dickens's accounts were usually just after necessary reforms had started. They shared an interest in amateur theatre travels. Collins followed Dickens's lead in novel writing. Just as Dickens wrote nonfiction articles on the police of London and elsewhere, Collins in fact wrote several stories and books with crime and detection, as well as *The Woman in White, The Moonstone,* and *The Biter Bit. The Law and the Lady* (1875) was based on the trial of Madeleine Smith. *No Name* (1862) had a woman detective, and several short stories had a crime motive. Both of course parodied the new detective story.

After this brief survey of the early years and development, we shall turn to the main section, of books. Parody will cover both persons and mores, including literary styles; mass parody will cover the highlighting of more than one style of detective simultaneously. Before pastiche will come a survey of group efforts, where a handful of writers combine to write one book in parts to make a whole. There is a section on what may be termed do-it-yourself, covering dossier-style books, books and picture-type puzzles, and mystery and murder weekends in England and America.

Then will come sequels, where authors take over another's characters or plots, and finally, children's books of detection written by authors normally in the adult market. The section on the visual will cover—naturally—theatre, films, and television productions, including plays, sketches, and so on.

An early volume of parody was *A Century of Parody and Imitation,* edited by Walter Jerrold and R. M. Leonard, published in 1913 by Oxford University Press, for a copy of which I am indebted to Joy Wilson, wife of Colin Wilson. It has some interesting comments and pieces. In the prefatory note is quoted the remark of Isaac D'Israeli, father of the great Benjamin Disraeli, "Unless the prototype is familiar to us a parody is nothing"—

rather like watching a stage impressionist impersonating someone unknown to his audience. Another quotation is from Owen Seaman on imitations: "The lowest, a mere verbal echo, to the highest, where it becomes a department of pure criticism." The book covers the period from 1812, and there are four parodies of E. A. Poe's poetry, one of them, "Chateaux d'Espagne," having a touch of relevance to our theme. Describing a visit to the Haymarket Theatre, soon after the Lord Dundreary success, written by Henry Sambrooke Leigh (1837–1883):

> I was doubtful and uncertain, at the rising of the curtain,
> If the piece would prove a novelty, or one I'd seen before.
> For a band of robbers drinking in a gloomy cave, and clinking
> With their glasses on the table, I had witnessed o'er and o'er.
> Since the half-forgotten period of my innocence was o'er;
> Twenty years ago or more.
>
> Tell me who, then, was the maiden, that appear'd so sorrow laden.
> In the room of David Garrick, with a bust, above the door?
> Quoth my neighbour, "Nelly Moore."

The footnotes identify Nelly Moore as an actress famed for playing at the Haymarket with Edward A. Sothern as Lord Dundreary (1861/62), and T. W. Robertson's play *David Garrick* was produced in 1864.

Most of the parodies and pastiches, with or without the thousand on the Sherlock Holmes list, concern themselves with the written word rather than the visual entertainment, which forms the subject of a later chapter. We must first consider just what elements in the detective or crime story are available for this treatment.

As has been pointed out by many historians, the elements of a 'tecker, as detective stories are known in the book trade, are normally a victim (particularly of murder, which is the usual crime offered and expected), a detective with or without a partner, and a murderer or other criminal, occasionally with an assistant villain. Rules and regulations have been prescribed by various bodies or individuals. The Detection Club of England, founded in 1928 by Anthony Berkeley (A. B. Cox, Anthony Berkeley Cox, and Francis Iles, 1893–1970), today has each newly elected member processing in, surrounded by candle-holding members, to take a solemn oath on an illumined skull that no unfair tricks shall be played on the reader, such as unsuspected twins, Chinamen, unknown poisons, etc. Ronald A. Knox (1888–1957), priest, don, member of the Detection Club, critic, editor of *Detective Fiction,* and author of such detective novels as *The Viaduct Murder* (1925), listed in 1929 in *The Best English Detective Stories* of 1928, which he coedited, his own ten rules to be followed by fair-playing authors. S. S. Van Dine (Willard Huntington Wright, 1888–1939), author of the Philo Vance books, listed his own "Twenty Rules for Writing Detective Stories" in an article in 1928 for the *American Magazine.* Their rules included, for example, not letting the detective possess or acquire information or clues kept back from the reader, not letting the detective prove to be the criminal, and so on. Obviously these rules are sometimes broken; for example, the detective has proved to be the murderer, and not all writers follow the scrupulous example of Ellery Queen in ensuring that every clue is mentioned, however lightly.

A lesser-known observation from S. S. Van Dine is in the foreword he wrote for *The Mystery Puzzle Book,* by Lassiter Wren and Randle McKay (undated, but obviously from the 1920s or 1930s), a copy of which was given me by an old friend, John Fisher, a TV producer, member of the Magic Circle, and author of many books on magic, show business, and Lewis Carroll. After commenting on the reader being given a series of clues to solve and arrange, Van Dine comments: "But there is another vital element that enters into the type of puzzle which we call the detective story; and that is the appeal of the actual material of which the puzzle is fabricated." He explains the fascination crime has for the reader, as has achieving the solution, bearing in mind that most of the puzzles in that book are based on actual cases. "He has, perhaps (by projecting himself into the realities of crime), a sense of having achieved something not only mentally, but ethically, worthwhile." This brings us back to the Protestant ethos of solving crime, even at second hand or by surrogate, and seeing right triumph and evil put down.

S. S. Van Dine, in his "Twenty Rules for Writing Detective Stories," listed as number 3: "There must be no love interest in the story. To introduce amour is to clutter up a purely intellectual experience with irrelevant sentiment. The business in hand is to bring a criminal to the bar of justice, not to bring a lovelorn couple to the hymeneal altar." This rule was gradually and inexorably chipped away—even Marlowe married—and film and television sleuths regularly fall into amours, or more often affairs, with suspects or clients.

A crime story can be written from various viewpoints. The author can write in the first person as the sleuth—amateur or professional—as happened so often in the gothic novels, or the Had-I-but-Known school, where the narrator's full thoughts are described en passant. One must be particularly careful, if the narrator is to be the criminal, that nothing is said to mislead the reader deliberately—Agatha Christie was most punctilious in this. It can be written from the viewpoint of the detective's assistant, his Dr. Watson, admiringly, and bemusedly, and finally overwhelmed with amazement. The author can write with omniscience as he manipulates his actors on the stage of his own choice, but even here he can write from either a subjective or an objective viewpoint—that is, as things appear to a character or as they should or could appear to him. The reader can thus be the detective, in a literary or practical sense, or his assistant; he will not usually be able to cast himself as the killer, except in the type of book called "inverted": the reader knows the criminal, and perhaps the crime also, and the story unfolds psychologically, showing the whyfor and whether the criminal will get away with his crime.

There is a situation where the narrator may prove to be the murderer, a situation described by H. R. F. Keating as "acroidal." We shall consider a fantastic permutation thereon by Cameron MacCabe. Michiko Kakutani, a *New York Times* critic, writing there on January 15, 1984, "Mysteries Join the Mainstream," comments on Jorge Luis Borges and Alain Robbe-Grillet and their unexpected denouements. "In Mr. Borges' *Death and the Compass,* the detective winds up as the murderer's final victim, realizing that the pattern he had discerned earlier existed only in his own mind. In Mr. Robbe-Grillet's *Erasers* the detective and the murderer turn out to be the same person."

There are certain rules under which the genre must flourish. Obviously there must be criminal, crime, and detective. Equally obviously there must be a solution with the good triumphant and the evil conquered and preferably punished. We may now see a likeness, as with the western, to the original morality or mystery play, based on biblical themes, like the carpenters and the building of

Early Days and Differences

the ark on the floats making up the religious processions round the towns. Similar carnival processions still take place today in Britain and Europe. The element of morality in detective fiction has always been stressed—Erik Routley even titling his book *The Puritan Pleasures of the Detective Story*—as representative of the Puritan ethos. Detectives should not be criminals, nor should they really fall in love. Detective stories did not seem to thrive in police states, like the Soviet Union. Psychologists think readers prefer the detective stories as confirming (that is, strengthening) their beliefs in law and order. Comparisons can be made with medieval knights, killing dragons or villains, rescuing damsels in distress, dispensing justice, and bestowing protection. In a *New York Times* article, "Super Thrillers and Superpowers" (February 19, 1984), Robert Larchman adds a postscript: "In a somewhat simpler and less cynical era, private eyes like Sam Spade and Philip Marlowe satisfied another fantasy, that of prevailing against heavy odds."

It has been said that every detective story should teach the reader something about something, to interest him; this can be taken to excess. When the author was the British Broadcasting Corporation's only radio crime book critic in 1984/85, one murder story set in the mountains proved to have so much technical data on mountaineering as to make up a separate textbook, while others have had masses of commercial, sports, accountancy, racing, etc., data to confuse readers, especially those not necessarily sharing the interests—although books based on show business, radio, theatre, films, or festivals never seem to fall into this trap. Crime stories can be set in any milieu—country houses, universities, schools, theatres, fashion houses, football stadia, police stations, jungles, the nineteenth century—or the eighteenth, or even the fifth B.C.—on any of the five continents. Detectives can be from all walks of life—professors, private eyes, drunks, schoolboys, natives, heiresses, dilettantes, merchants, crime writers and correspondents, or homemakers—and they can follow any available trials of thought they prefer—ratiocination, scientific deduction, forensic science, psychology, psychic research, trial and error, or even blundering guesswork—any combination is allowed so long as the reader's attention is held against boredom or indifference. Every one of these factors is capable of parody and pastiche, of whatever format, so long as the target can be recognized, even if a clue may be needed.

In the Golden Age arose the phenomenon called by the Americans the age of silly-assery, in which so many private sleuths appeared to be amiable idiots, with sharp brains, puerile patter, and often monocles: Sayers's Lord Peter Wimsey, H. C. Bailey's Dr. Reggie Fortune, S. S. Van Dine's Philo Vance, Anthony Berkeley's Roger Sheringham, perhaps Christie's Captain Hastings, Leslie Charteris's Saint, Margery Allingham's Albert Campion, et al. What or who started this trend? Jane Austen, perhaps. Certainly Philo Vance was an early example, appearing in 1926 in *The Benson Murder Case* and oft quoted as an original, but five years earlier had appeared a book of short stories, *Call Mr. Fortune.* Against this can be quoted Edgar Wallace's 1908 *Angel Esquire,* in which a teetotal, card-playing detective betrayed distinct traces of silly-assery to advantage. It is significant that the finest exponent on television, radio, and audio books of both Lord Peter Wimsey and P. G. Wodehouse's silly ass, Bertie Wooster, has been the same actor, Ian Carmichael. Recent research into the origins of Blandings Castle, Wooster, and his man Jeeves by Norman Murphy indicates Wooster was based on an actor, light comedian, society entertainer, and Gilbert and Sullivan star, George Grossmith. The most convincing contender and the earliest is the creation of Baroness Orczy (1865–1947); her detectives included the Old Man in the Corner (Bill Owen, 1905), Lady Molly of Scotland Yard (1910), and Patrick Mulligan (*Skin O' My Tooth,* 1928), but in 1905 came her immortal creation, the aristocratic dandy who could disguise himself as a sans-culotte to save the French aristos from Mam'zelle Guillotine—Sir Percy Blakeney, Baronet—to say nothing of her *The First Sir Percy: An Adventure of the Laughing Cavalier* (1921).

To summarize and clarify, therefore, our approach mentioned above, parody of individuals, detectives, living or literary persons involved parody of mores, genre, the methods, literary styles, or even social life depicted.

Mass parody is that in which more than one detective is satirized. The next section will survey pastiche, including those books written as tributes to the period or style. Group efforts are where six or more authors wrote a book together, taking the story on by stages, sometimes in each others' literary styles. The reader and his efforts to solve the problems include a do-it-yourself format, dossiers, books, murder games, puzzles and competitions, which include film and murder weekends, where one pays to join a house

Early Days and Differences

party or train to take part in the action with professional actors. Sequels will cover authors who carry on, usually with permission, the characters of other writers who may have died or ceased writing. Books for children are written by authors normally writing for an adult readership—both detective stories for children and books outside the genre.

Finally, parody, mass parody, and pastiche occur in theatre, films, and television.

We have already mentioned the emergence of humor in detective fiction, and the effect we might expect it to have on future development, from comedy-thrillers, as they were performed. This is undeniable on the three-dimensional versions—plays, films, and television productions—but humor in the written tales has proved a slight dichotomy. The rules have always leaned against the introduction of humor, as have many practitioners. For example, William Somerset Maugham (1874–1965), a playwright whose elegant classic comedy *The Circle* ranks with Wilde, Sheridan, and Congreve; doctor; intelligence operator; novelist and essayist—he created Ashenden, *The British Agent* (1928), filmed by Alfred Hitchcock in 1936 with John Gielgud in the lead; he wrote a penetrating essay, "The Decline and Fall of the Detective Story" in *The Vagrant Mood* (1952), in which he stressed, "I look upon the introduction of humour in a detective story as mistaken, but I see the reason for it and with a sigh accept it." Raymond Chandler (1888–1959), creator of the great "private eye," or PI (private investigator) Philip Marlowe, in 1950 wrote an excellent essay, "The Simple Art of Murder," in which he commented: "It is not a very fragrant world, but it is the world you live in, and certain writers with tough minds and cool spirit of detachment can make very interesting and even amusing patterns out of it. It is not funny that a man should be killed, but it is sometimes funny that he should be killed for so little, and that his death should be the coin of what we call civilization." Thomas E. Williams in the American University journal *CLUES* (vol. 1, no. 1 [Spring 1980]), wrote an article, *"Martin Beck: The Swedish Version of Barney Miller Without the Canned Laughter,"* and said: "However, the commercialism of various plots interwoven in the story line, which struggles to be *au courant,* rings with the familiarity of a television situation comedy, *Barney Miller,* where the situation is a New York City police precinct and the comedy struggles to be relevant. In *Barney Miller* there is no detection, only laughs caused by characterization with the supposition that policemen are human beings who have foibles." (Martin Beck is, of course, the Swedish detective created by Maj Sjöwall and Per Wahlöö, hero of a series of well-written books, at least one of whose cases has been filmed.) A team of French authors, both of detective stories and analytical surveys, Boileau-Narcejac, wrote in 1975 *Le Roman Policier,* of which one chapter is entitled "Les Francs Tireurs." They had no comments on parody and pastiche (and indeed very few analysts so far have), but they did deal with such authors as Exbrayat, with his sleuth Imogene whose exploits verge on the hilarious; Pierre Very, who has striven to extend and rejuvenate the detective novel; and they conclude with, "Reste à se moquer ouvertment de lui, à travestir victimes, criminels, detectives, enquête, en joyeuse, cavalcade, en carnaval, échevels, avec grosses têtes, lazzi contrepetteries, rigolade énorme." The reference to "lazzi" would indicate the particular trick, or tricks, that each clown makes peculiarly his own in circuses throughout the world—for example, Achille Zavatta, in France, with his mime of eating the entire menu listed on the sandwich board he carries; the English Grimble and his pagoda balancing on a unicycle; and the tricks of diving into a pool or eating an imaginary bag of grapes, as described in Dorothy L. Sayers's Lord Peter Wimsey story, *Murder Must Advertise,* based on an advertising agency in which she herself had worked, and whose staircase I discovered.

Pierre Very, born in 1900, wrote "Murder on Parnassus: The Literature of the Future," in the April 1935 issue of *Living Age*; he and Georges Simenon are the only French writers listed by François Fosca in *Histoire et Technique du Roman Policier.*

Just as some crime writers also wrote children's mystery stories, as we shall see later, so other writers wrote outside their milieu. Edgar Wallace (1875–1932) had humor in his Sanders of the River tales; Sydney Horler (1888–1954), creator of Tiger Standish, author of more than 150 books under three pen names, also wrote humorous romantic P. G. Wodehouse–style books; and James Hadley Chase (a.k.a. Raymond Marshall, James L. Docherty, Ambrose Grant, real name, René Raymond), who wrote many tough books and stories (one of which will be considered in the last chapter), such as *No Orchids for Miss Blandish* (1932) and *Lady—Here's Your Wreath,* could also write a very funny book, *Miss Shumway Waves a Wand* (1949), involving a woman who can become two, float in the air, and transform her opponents, a wolfhound that suddenly starts talking, and various hilarious events before nearly everybody lives happily, very happily, ever after.

Julian Symons (1912–1994) was president of the Detection Club until 1985, was a founder-member of the Crime Writers' Association and its chair in 1958/59, a critic, and author of detective stories and analytical studies. In *Bloody Murder* (1972, reissued and revised 1985; American title, *Mortal Consequences*), he said in the first edition: "Successful comic crime stories, short or long, are rare. One turns away with a shudder from the many Holmes parodies and from such collections as Sir Basil Thomson's stories about Mr. Pepper." In the second edition he changed the wording after "Holmes parodies" to "and with not much more cheerfulness from the conscientiously crazy detective stories of the English Pamela Branch and the Americans Craig Rice and Elliot Paul." It is perhaps interesting to note that when Rice's *My Kingdom for a Hearse* was criticized by Julian Symons in the British *Sunday Times,* the quotation at the back of her *The April Robin Murders* was: "By the only genuinely funny crime writer. . . Wildly more comic in bits, and most readable throughout!"

H. R. F. Keating, who was installed as president of the Detection Club on Wednesday, November 6, 1985, at the Café Royal, London, edited *Whodunnit?* described as a "Guide to Crime, Suspense and Spy Fiction," in 1982. His own contributions included a comprehensive twelve-page introduction in which he analyzed the entertainment value of crime and other fiction, the strengthening of the Protestant ethos, and the comparison of the type of crime fiction published—Le Carré to Christie—today's scene, yesterday's period scene, commenting, "For every can't-put-it-down there is a laugh-aloud (or, combining crime and humour being a particularly difficult art, there are at least a handful of laughter-makers)."

Perhaps we should glance at some "genuinely" or otherwise comic detective stories. Pamela Branch (1920–1967) mixed her mystery and farce quite irreverently; for example, in *The Wooden Overcoat,* published in 1951. The Asterisk Club flourished in Flood Street, in London's fashionable Chelsea district, near the river Thames, consisted of acquitted murderers, and took its name from Tennyson's "Ye, against whose familiar names not yet / The fatal asterisk of death is set." The club battles with two innocent families next door as they endeavor to dispose of two unwanted corpses, of Bengi Cann and Lilli Cluj. The families are helped by a limp-wristed ballet dancer who complains at one point, "No matter what Caryl Brahms might say, a bullet or any other form of violent death in the ballet was frowned upon by the management. It was crude, rude and lewd." (The reference is of course to Caryl Brahms and S. J. Simon's ballet murders, *A Bullet in the Ballet* and *Six Curtains for Stroganova*.) Mr. Beesum, an inappropriately named rat-catcher, is also involved.

Craig Rice (1908–1957) wrote a string of first-class detective stories under various names (Daphne Sanders, Michael Venning); ghosted as George Sanders, an English Hollywood film actor, and Gypsy Rose Lee, a famous, witty, ecdysiast; wrote nonfiction surveys of crime; had her books filmed; and herself wrote such film scripts as for Michael Arlen's *The Falcon*.

Elliot Paul (1891–1958) we shall also consider later, but his *The Mysterious Mickey Finn; or Murder at the Café du Dome,* written in 1939, for example, is marked by a natural zaniness that pervades even his chapter headings ("The Sound of a Great Amen"), and the names of his characters (Dinde, or M. Crayon de Crayon, and Fakir Yenolob—"boloney" spelled backwards), and with a surge of plot complications that never lets up.

Some final examples from each side of the Atlantic: Donald Westlake, born in Brooklyn, writes under five noms de plume, including Tucker Coe, and his titles themselves are witty, such as *The Fugitive Pigeon* (1965). His books are full of ludicrous situations but with that element of logic, once shrewdly noted by composer, musicologist, and conductor Constant Lambert in his book *Music: Ho!* when he stated that the films of the Marx Brothers were pure surrealism. In England the detective story writer David Williams (there is another novelist, and a journalist, of the same name) was formerly the spokesman for the entire British advertising profession as the head of a leading agency; when he left that world he commenced writing, and a dozen novels involving his merchant-banker detective Mark Treasure (often compared with John Putnam Thatcher) are marked by an aristocratic, polished sense of humor and the ridiculous, combined with realism and with no inaccurate police activity. He has twice served on the committee of the Crime Writers' Association, and we shall survey his characters below. When I interviewed him for the *Poisoned Pen* magazine he had some interesting facts both on his writing

Early Days and Differences 23

and, as we shall see, on how (and on whom) he based some of his characters.

Further irreverent treatment of a murder mystery, again with ballet dancers but plus volatile Russians, came from Caryl Brahms and S. J. Simon, who wrote *A Bullet in the Ballet* in 1937 (later adapted as a BBC radio play), followed by *Six Curtains for Stroganova.* The Ballet Stroganoff presented *Petroushka, Ajax, Gare du Nord,* etc., at London's Collodium Theatre (collodion is a gluey substance) when Anton Palook as Petroushka is shot; the body is removed before Inspector Quill arrives ("You cannot have a body in *Ajax* and anyway the *decor,* it is different"). Other shootings seem to accrue to this ballet; the Russians all behave eccentrically and with eccentric names like Marius Pilaff, Pavel Bunia, Volti-Subito the conductor—all in the usual hilarious manner of all the books of this pair of writers. They later wrote a short story, *A Bishop in the Ballet,* about a false bishop trying to smuggle drugs through the ballet company, plus some very surrealistic comic novels with titles like *No Bed for Bacon* and *Don't, Mr. Disraeli,* in which previous and contemporary events and persons are linked together in a way that clarifies why Stroganoff can act eccentrically but to him completely logically. As the great English actress Ellen Terry said, "To be eccentric you must first find the centre."

After all these examples, how can humor be part of the recipe, or prescription, for murder mysteries? It can, according to Howard Haycraft, in the chapter "The Rules of the Game," subheaded "The Puzzle Element," in his book, *Murder for Pleasure,* published in 1941. He quotes the "recipe" given by B. J. R. Stolper in *Scholastic* (October 22, 1938):

½ Sherlock Holmes
¼ P. G. Wodehouse
⅛ sheer adventure
⅛ anything you know best

When I started reading detective fiction at school during the Second World War, with my mother, we received from my father vast numbers of paperback books from various publishers, the authors including Jonathan Latimer, born in Chicago, a screenwriter for such films as *The Glass Key* (second version), Perry Mason television scripts, and his own humorous books with titles like *The Dead Don't Care, Headed for a Hearse,* and *Murder in the Madhouse,* well-written puzzles but happy, and later turned into films. Significantly such lightness of touch in English stories seemed to come from an aristocratic milieu, such as Lord Peter Wimsey, Margery Allingham's royal-connected Albert Campion, Dr. Reggie Fortune (by H. C. Bailey) — all related to P. G. Wodehouse's immortal Bertie Wooster, and Frank Richards's classic school stories of St. Jim's and Greyfriars.

In *Snobbery with Violence,* a slightly left-wing analysis showing great research and knowledge by Colin Watson, came this comment: "That the public continued to consider this sort of thing enormous fun is proved by the sustained success of the Aldwych farces, in which Ralph Lynn was the perennial embodiment of Silly-assery, by the popularity of P. G. Wodehouse's Bertie Wooster stories, and, not least, by the politic sense of fashion that prompted writers such as Dorothy L. Sayers, Margery Allingham and even Anthony Berkeley Cox to endow their detective with an air of fatuity." We shall see later that this class of sleuth, peculiarly English, is indeed parodied, and it will help if we recall that the Aldwych farces were those presented regularly at London's Aldwych Theatre, written by Ben Travers with consummate ease and success, and who told me just a year or so before he died in his nineties, "Your knees don't matter as long as your mind is active." He himself had great interests, wrote a successful modern Aldwych farce (*The Bed Before Yesterday*) just before he died, stood on his head every day, and was a teetotaler. Ralph Lynn played in all the stage farces and film versions, wore a monocle, had immaculate timing, and was the typical aristocratic Englishman until well into his seventies. Ian Carmichael played both Wooster and Wimsey on BBC television and in audio books. In 1981 I took German novelist and poet Renata Rasp, daughter of Germany's greatest actor, Fritz Rasp, to see three plays in succession at Plymouth, Devon: the farce *Not Now, Darling,* in the stellar cast of which appeared my friend Barbara Miller, who suggested the title of this book and the previous monograph; comedy *Caught in the Act;* and Agatha Christie's *Black Coffee,* with Patrick Cargill, and asked for her comments and first impressions. She said the men had the best roles, that the men's roles could be interchanged, and, "Why did Cargill play Poirot like you, John, like a typical

Englishman in P. G. Wodehouse?" (to whose books I had recently introduced her). I told her these impressions were all correct, and indeed Cargill did interpret Poirot as a 1930s dandified Belgian comedian.

Do writers always know they use parody and pastiche? Many with whom I corresponded in the researches for this book, after my original monograph, denied at first any such claims, although revising their opinions later, as subsequent chapters will seek to show. Some authors, however, have been quite precise and adamant about their nonuse of either form.

Exbrayat's books about his sleuth, the irrepressible Imogene, are hilarious, and at first reading in French seem to come within our terms of reference. But no; in 1982 his publisher wrote to me stating categorically that neither parody nor pastiche was present in any of Exbrayat's work. Exbrayat, like Berkeley Gray, chooses titles of wit and fun; for example, *Ne Vous Fachez Pas, Imogene* or *Mortimer, Comment Osez-Vous?* Berkeley Gray, who was also that prolific author for boys, Edwy Searles Brooks, chose titles for his hero, Norman Conquest, known as "1066," like *Mr. Mortimer Gets the Jitters.*

Still, in France, in correspondence that same year with the elegant and erudite Hélène de Monaghan, whose detective stories are marked by skill, originality, and interest to win some prestigious awards, she answered my query by writing, "Je n'ai jamais pour mon part utilisé ne la parodie ne la pastiche. (Tant ou moins voluntairement car inconsciemment il est possible que chacun de nous sait un pastichan ou un parodein qui s'ignore!)"

Margaret Millar, one of America's greatest crime writers, visited London in 1984, and when I interviewed her for my BBC crime book review slot, and asked her the same question, her answer was prompt—she *never* used parody herself, but her late husband, Ross Macdonald had—perhaps a reference to "The South Sea Soup Company" featuring Herlock Sholmes or the autobiographical strain in several of his crime books.

Further proof of this argument comes from Marsha Daly's biography, *Telly Savalas* (1975), chapter 8, "Kojak: Fame, Fortune and Girls at Last," when she recounts how Abby Mann wrote *Justice in the Backroom* based on the Wylie-Hoffert New York murders in the 1960s, later fictionalized as *The Marcus-Nelson Murders,* with Telly Savalas as the detective in the CBS pilot, followed by the series in the fall of 1973. Played for realism, save for occasional slips and some criticism of the exterior sets, with Lieutenant Kojak giving police academy lectures, it became a hit for CBS and Universal. Daly comments: "Although Lt. Theo Kojak was conceived as a Polish cop, Telly soon let his own Mediterranean heritage emerge. The important factor was to play Kojak for his ethnic pride; whether it was Greek or Polish was of secondary importance." She also quotes Roger Rosenblatt in the *New Republic* comparing Kojak with Sam Spade or Lew Archer as running against the current, but unlike them in that their backgrounds are sketchy and irrelevant, not unlike the "WASPS who hired them," whereas Kojak does not belong to society and has a complete family background which his audience can share. Oddly enough, parody came into Kojak when Savalas was asked to help the government savings bond drive, and Daly recounts how the team made a twelve-minute, $38,000 satire, showing him arresting crooks, getting them to buy bonds—but all the crooks had Italian names, which would have upset another minority. The film was withdrawn.

One feature-length Kojak film, *The Summer of '69*, not only referred to him as the only cop in 1977 wearing three-hundred-dollar suits, but showed him rebelling against his superiors in the aggressively negative manner of the antiestablishment and the "right man" approach combined.

So, a writer may be adamant against such devices, or have adopted them unknowingly, or easily recognized them in others, or know how to stop short of parody. Frederick Dard is one of the highest-selling authors in France or elsewhere; his San Antonio stories have sold more than a hundred million copies. Boileau-Narcejac in *Le Roman Policier,* in the section "Les Margineaux" in chapter 7, "Les Frances-Tireurs," comments on his careful use of the bizarre and colorful background, never distracting the reader's attention and curiosity, "Dard, en effect, même quand il pousse le burlesque jusqu'à l'extravagance, a toujours soin de jouer sur le mystère." So perhaps these will be the clues as we look at a selection of various authors. One analyst described the witty, hard-boiled tales of Jonathan Latimer as "parodistic"—of what was not explained.

(Meanwhile, to put parody and pastiche into perspective, let us ponder the remarks of Commissioner of Police R. J. McGuire at the Crime Writers' International Congress of New York, as reported in June 1978: "While James Bond made love to numerous women my people delivered 46 babies. While Nero Wolfe tended his orchids, the missing persons squad looked for 18,396 people and found 17,476 of them.")

Parody can almost be unconscious. In *The Last Laugh,* a novel written by Paul Denver in 1963 and published with his short story "No Pictures for Cathy," he is writing about two private eyes: Mike Power of New York and John Lester of Los Angeles. On the first page of the former story he writes of Major Barling, a client (and the name Barling is used in both stories). What he needed, he thought, was a tall, tough, but reasonably presentable private investigator, who did not have whiskey on his breath before lunch, and remembered to take his hat off on entering a room. This is an obvious reference to investigators like Marlowe with a bottle of whiskey in the desk drawer or filing cabinet. Only in a couple of brief phrases does Denver incidentally write in the manner of Raymond Chandler but without the wisecracking humor.

In chapter 6, part 2, Power calls on the missing daughter's husband, whose Filipino houseboy answers the door. "I told him my name and calling and showed him one of my embossed cards to prove it, the one without the crossed Lugers rampant," a clear reference to Marlowe and his cards, and later Robert B. Parker's Spenser.

It is not only authors who find it difficult at times to recognize parody for what it intrinsically is. In 1986 an American private eye series made its first appearance on British television. In the usual search for a new formula, a man and a woman were teamed, the woman being the boss. The lack of originality was not only proved by other television series, but by going back to Mr. and Mrs. North, created by Frances and Richard Lockridge in 1940, and filmed and televised, and Hammett's Nick and Nora Charles. There was a certain amount of predictable humor and weird or absurd characters in the somewhat confused pilot episode, which was rewarded by one British television critic gushing admiringly, "It's pure parody, with over-sexed appeal."

There was a unique quote in the *MWA Handbook* for 1956, in Sam S. Baker's "Words from a Master" concerning a lecture by Dashiell Hammett (1894–1961) and the reference "by writing one that would break practically every mystery rule. The detective would fall in love with a woman who would turn out to be a murderess; he'd live with her, then turn her in. The villain would be fat, another would have at least a touch of homosexuality. Says he didn't know whether the story would have much chance for publication, but he'd have fun. The story was *The Maltese Falcon*." This classic story, filmed three times, once in the incomparable Humphrey Bogart–Mary Astor–Sydney Greenstreet version, is invariably accepted as it stands without any suspicion of the author's subtle parody. Hammett's clinical summary is analogous to a fifty-word synopsis of *Hamlet* as a melodrama. Any clever parody can be accepted unquestionably as the real thing, or object parodied—for example, Sandy Wilson's parody 1920s musical *The Boy Friend,* and that that also applies to *The Maltese Falcon* is emphasized by the comment in her autobiography *My Story,* written in 1959 by Mary Astor, who played Brigid O'Shaughnessy (or Miss Wonderly) in the definitive 1941 Warner Bros. version. After praising John Huston's adaptation and first-ever direction and the happy spirit in the team, she adds significantly in chapter 10: "The picture was a completely new conception of the gangster movie; it was the story not of hoodlums but of a group of evil though intelligent people playing for very high stakes." She goes on to explain her role as an unscrupulous, crooked woman, who lied and changed her name at will, in this classic, well-presented film that met all criteria triumphantly. In one of the editions, Hammett's introduction states that most of the crooked characters, including Gutman, were based on criminals he had shadowed or arrested when he was a Pinkerton's operative; Gutman was the villain, Seth Gutman in Hammett's unfinished novel *The Secret Emperor,* the heroine of which was Tamar Gutman; Gutman inspired a radio series, *The Fat Man,* from 1946 to 1950, the fat detective being named Brad Runyon, and this in turn led to a 1951 Universal film, *The Fat Man.*

In 1932 Hammett was invited by his publisher, Alfred Knopf, to write an introduction to a book by Walter Brooks, titled *Freddy the Detective,* which was a parody of detective stories—a task which Hammett did not appear to approach avidly or promptly.

2. Books in the Mirror

It is not unknown for detective and mystery story writers to interpolate subtle, sly, or even blunt comments on their own craft in their own books—sometimes even on themselves. A small selection from some of the great names will illustrate this.

Margery Allingham (1904–1966) created the inimitable Albert Campion with his valet Magersfontein Lugg; aristocratic, of mysterious antecedents, as we shall see, intellectually brilliant, yet with all the casual inconsequence of Bertie Wooster, with the same social background. In *Mr. Campion and Others* (1939), the writer comments ironically: "Petronella was not easy to find. She was neither dancing at the Berkeley nor dining at Claridge's. He looked in at the ballet and did not see her, and it was not until he remembered the Duchess of Monewden's Charity Ball at the Fitzrupert Hotel that he found her." The Berkeley is an original luxury hotel then situated off Piccadilly, Claridge's an equally elegant hotel in Mayfair off New Bond Street, the ballet presumably referred to the Royal Opera House, Covent Garden, with its crush bar (although there would be others), Monewden might be a weak pun implying a narwhal or overpowering society hostess, and there is no leading West End hotel the Fitzrupert, named after any illegitimate son of Prince Rupert (1619–1682). As a matter of interest, his two illegitimate children were Dudley Bard (mother, Francesca Bard) and Rupert Hughes (mother, Margaret Hughes). A clear picture of the social scene in London's Mayfair in 1939 is given, however, and commented on by Colin Watson (1920–1984) in his *Snobbery with Violence*.

Delano Ames's book titles give an indication of their humor, such as *She Shall Have Murder* and the 1950 *Corpse Diplomatique,* set in the Victoria Pension in Nice, with the murder of a blackmailer, a second death, and continual twists and turns as each guest becomes suspect. Jane and Dagobert Brown are the debonair sleuths, like the Norths or Charleses. Near the beginning Dagobert suggests Jane write a book with the title *Corpse Diplomatique,* and at the end, she is doing just that. Writing in the first-person singular, as Jane, she starts chapter 9 after her motor accident by hinting the official account ought to take over; she comments that a confession would not be allowed by any other reader to be taken as final "seeing that the book was only two-thirds finished," even if she used the confession as a dramatic chapter ending—as Ames does.

Colin Watson draws attention to a play, originally presented in the West End of London with John Gielgud, later Emlyn Williams, as the headmaster, *Forty Years On,* based on a public school, by Alan Bennett, one of the quartet who made up *Beyond the Fringe,* an amusing, sophisticated, unusual entertainment presented at the Fringe of the Edinburgh Festival. He refers to Sapper, John Buchan, and Dornford Yates—all decidedly English writers whose crooks, spies, and enemies were naturally foreigners; so as he shows they still must be in any good spy stories—taking precedence over the various heroes and villains he mentions en passant: "rootless intellectuals, alien Jews and international pederasts who call themselves the Labour Party"—descriptions which have come to the fore again in yet more spy scandals.

Yet John Buchan, Lord Tweedsmuir (1875–1940), author and diplomat, has one character comment to Richard Hannay in *The Three Hostages,* published in 1924, of his dislike of detective stories: "I've another objection to the stuff—it's not ingenious enough, or rather it doesn't take account of the infernal complexity of life. It might have been alright twenty years ago, when most people argued and behaved fairly logically, but they don't nowadays"—and this is at the very beginning of the Golden Age of the art.

In 1946 R. T. Campbell wrote *Bodies in a Bookshop,* in which several actual London bookshops are mentioned, including Lewis and Zwemmer, as well as other London landmarks like the ABC Café, Southampton Row, the Arts Theatre Club (still operating), Marchmount Street and Bernard Street in the WC1 area, the internationally known umbrella shop in New Oxford Street, and the Fitzroy Public House (there is a Fitzroy Hotel in that area, in Fitzroy Street). The well-known sculptor Nina Hamnett, also featured in Anthony Powell's novels, appears.

Hamnett (1890–1956), friend of the famous, from Modigliani to Gertrude Stein, from the Sitwells to Dylan Thomas, was a sensational name in bohemia from her naked dances in Paris before World War I to her later leadership of Soho and "Fitzrovia" in London and Paris; she was as well known for her private life as for her own excellent likenesses of celebrities and the great artists who portrayed her in their own work, from sculpture to memoirs, novels, and paintings.

A character comments, "I know you're a marvel—sort of combined Sherlock Holmes and Sexton Blake." A few pages later, Professor John Stubbs complains: "I don't like easy cases. I'm a reader of thrillers and I like those that I can't guess till I'm more than half way through."

R. T. Campbell was the nom de plume of novelist, critic, and poet Ruthven Todd, according to the blurb on the 1984 American edition, and although apparently the author of a dozen detective stories, several books never got published. Max Boyle explodes, "Damn it all, sir, you yourself object to the detective story where all the cards are not placed properly on the table." The professor is compared with Chesterton, while Boyle compares himself to an unsatisfactory Watson, "not suitably astonished when he produces the solution like the rabbit from the conjuror's topper."

Other books by Campbell, all also dated 1946 and also published by Westhouse, were *Adventure with a Goat, Apollo Wore a Wig, Take Thee a Sharp Knife, The Death Cat,* and *Swing Low, Sweet Death,* with *Unholy Dying* being dated 1945.

In John Dickson Carr's *The Eight of Swords,* written in 1934, a Dr. Gideon Fell adventure, Morgan, a thriller writer seen in action is also Tournedos, described as an author of more esoteric books.

Raymond Chandler, born in Chicago but educated at the English public school Dulwich College, created the hard-boiled Philip Marlowe, named after a school house. He frequently gave him subtle or mocking lines against the craft of crime writer and profession of private eye. For example, in *The Big Sleep* Marlowe says, "I'm not Sherlock Holmes or Philo Vance," and in *The Lady in the Lake* tells Mrs. Fallbrook, mysterious visitor to a murdered man's house, that he *is* Philo Vance, an unemployed lawman acting as a part-time collector for car loans.

Edmund Crispin was the nom de plume of Robert Bruce Montgomery, who combined esoteric detective fiction and crime book reviewing for the *Sunday Times* with composing music for such films as the peculiarly British comedy *Carry On, Nurse*. We shall consider his detective hero, the Oxford don Gervase Fen, in the section devoted to real-life characters, but meanwhile he has commented wryly on detective fiction in the Fen books. In *The Gilded Fly* (1944), set in about 1940, Fen comments: "That's all very well in a detective novel, where it has to be put in to camouflage the significant things—I must say I think some more entertaining form of camouflage might be devised." Sir Richard roused himself acerbically. "Really, Gervase, if there's anything I profoundly dislike it is the sort of detective story in which one of the characters propounds views on how detective stories should be written. It's bad enough having a detective who *reads* the things—they all do." Later, when a character tells Fen he has followed all his cases, Fen retorts that that's more than Crispin's readers do. In *Love Lies Bleeding* (1948), a character says no one could make a novel out of Fen's cases.

The erudite and amusing Michael Innes, of whom more anon, had a character say: "Exactly—a real detective. There is a very good man whose name I forget; a foreigner and very conceited—but, they are thoroughly reliable"—an obvious reference to Agatha Christie's Hercule Poirot.

Philip Macdonald, crime author and Hollywood screenwriter for Mr. Moto and Charlie Chan, in 1924 in his first and most famous novel created Colonel Anthony Ruthven Gethryn, who comments in *The Noose* (1930): "Expect it comes from reading too many detective stories. My subconscious ego—monstrous brute—wants to identify itself with Lecoq and Rouletabille and Gore. They all hold their tongues till page three hundred and four. They've got to, or no one'd read about them." Lecoq is the detective of Emile Gaboriau (1833–1873), Rouletabille of Gaston Leroux (1868–1927), and Colonel Gore of Lynn Brock, Alister McAllister, and playwright Anthony Wharton (1877–1943).

In *The Rasp* (1928), a character turns out to be E. Tennel, author of books about Carlton Howe, prince of investigators, and Colonel Gethryn speaks of Howe.

Ngaio Marsh (1899–1982) started writing detective stories in the 1930s, and in one of her early Roderick Alleyn (named after a public school) books, *Death in Ecstasy* (1936), Chief Detective Inspector Alleyn is discussing the murder in the freakish, fringe church with reporter Nigel Bathgate, who suggests he pretends to be halfway through a detective story, which Alleyn counters would be full of very red herrings out of season which he would follow, but does say: "It depends on the author. If it's Agatha Christie, Miss Wade's occulted guilt drips from every page. Dorothy Sayers' Lord Peter would plump for Pringle, I fancy. Inspector French would go for Ogden. Of course Ogden, on the face of it, is the first suspect."

Ellery Queen, another erudite aristocratic example of silly-assery, went in for subtle self-parody—like Chandler, in *The Spanish Cape Mystery,* written and promptly filmed in 1935 with Donald Cook as Queen and Gay Usher as his father. Queen was influenced by Philo Vance. In this film of a series of murders at Spanish Cape, California, the blundering, pompous local sheriff taunts Queen, before the latter takes any part in the enquiry, as "Philo Holmes," "Sherlock," and "Philo"; of course, Queen solves the mystery smoothly. An interesting touch, reminiscent of the short stories, is that just as he is leaving for vacation with Judge Macklin, played by Berton Churchill, his father telephones him to solve the mystery of valuable stolen diamonds, with thief and shopkeeper in his office, and Ellery finds the gems and proves the thief's guilt in a matter of minutes on obvious details. In *The Player on the Other Side* (1963), chapter 12, "Divergent Attack," part 2, "Middle Game," a chain of murders based on chess and religion, Queen refers to "clever coots" in detective stories, "especially mine . . . and Rex's, and John's, and Miss Christie's, and other practitioners of the delightfully improbable."

Clayton Rawson (1906–1971), editor, magician, and creator of the Great Merlini, magician-detective, wrote *The Footprints on the Ceiling,* a Merlini mystery, in 1939. After the inspector has referred to Ellery Queen, Philo Vance, and Archie Goodwin, Merlini answers on a case "that a clam is twice as informative as any of those gentlemen up until chapter twenty." This story was made into a Mike Shayne film three years later, starring, as usual, Lloyd Nolan as Shayne.

In June 1984, over lunch at the now defunct Press Club in London, where Edgar Wallace was honored by a special room and chair, his daughter Penelope, a writer and chair of the Crime Writers' Association in 1980/81, when asked if her father had ever indulged in parody or pastiche, immediately referred me to his *Big*

Foot. The quotes she mentioned are both of a tongue-in-cheek nature over detective fiction. " 'In fact I *knew* she hadn't come this mornin'.' Farraby was staggered. 'That's deduction,' said Sooper complacently, 'deduction an' logic. Maybe it's psychology too.' 'But how did you know that she hadn't come this morning?' insisted Jim. 'Because Latimer phoned me an hour ago,' was the calm reply. 'That's proper police work: havin' a man on the spot an' getting him to phone. *And* deduction—I deduce that he's telling the truth.' " The second quote from Sooper (Police Superintendent Patrick J. Minter) on theory versus practice: "When th'ry gets into the ring with fact, he takes the count in the first round. Here's a big fact—death by violence. To sit around in a comfortable armchair an' play a fiddle an' th'riize is one thing; to come up against the smell of blood an' general nastiness is another."

So, even the most illustrious crime writers occasionally have their tongues in their cheeks to satirize or make gentle fun of their craft.

Will the Real . . . and the Real . . . ?

Authors always disclaim any connection with their own characters, although living persons have been immortalized in literature, from Shakespeare's Malvolio, Shylock, Polonius, and Don Armado on. At times there is an obvious element of parody, even affection, and similarly some authors put themselves into their heroes. We shall survey a representative selection.

Under both parody and pastiche real persons have detective activities ascribed to them, including Aristotle, Dr. Samuel Johnson, and Robert Browning, inter alia. An outstanding example which is too modern to ascribe to either, and where a leading figure is the actual sleuth and not just a witness (as in Kaminsky's stories) is in the books of Elliott Roosevelt, son of President F. D. Roosevelt. *Murder and the First Lady* (1984) and *Murder at Hobcaw Barony* (1986), feature his own mother, the great Eleanor Roosevelt, solving the mysteries. The former concerns English aristocrats involved in murder and gambling; the latter is set in Bernard Baruch's estate in South Carolina. His 1989 title, *Murder at the Palace,* had his mother at Buckingham Palace during World War

II, when an equerry to King George VI is murdered, and one of the suspects is Sir Alan Burton, from Scotland Yard, with whom the First Lady had previously worked.

The series included *The Hyde Park Murders* (1985), an ingenious idea involving reality based on firsthand knowledge of the White House, similar to but not quite the same as the clever detective stories by Margaret Truman, daughter of former president Harry S Truman, whose titles include *Murder in the White House* (1980), *Murder on Capitol Hill* (1981), *Murder in the Supreme Court* (1982), *Murder in the Smithsonian* (1983), *Murder on Embassy Row* (1984), and *Murder at the FBI* (1985) — one of which even mentioned precisely an antique dealer in historic Blackheath, a London village. A similar list of titles came from "Diplomat," John Franklin Carter (1897–1967), journalist, diplomat, and friend of FDR, such as *Death in the Senate* (1933), and *The Corpse on the White House Lawn* (1932), based on the 1929 Christmas Eve fire there.

Steve Allen, a leading American television interviewer and personality, neatly placed himself in the role of an investigator of a murder — on a Steve Allen TV show, in his 1989 title, *Murder on the Glitter Box*. While he is guest hosting for two weeks on the Terry Cole television show, a subject, Hal Hoaglund, is killed by drinking poisoned vodka. A second murder; credible descriptions of putting on a TV show; inviting the suspects (a former interviewer, a producer, an ex-wife, a president, a comedienne, a driver) to dinner at the famous Chasens' — Allen has himself commenting that it never happened with Hercule Poirot that *he* was accused. There is witty dialogue and well-drawn characters. Of course, a television studio, like a theatre, is a favorite venue, a closed community with all the glamour, which is why so many such stories are set on film sets, TV studios, and theatre and opera stages — for example, one of the stories in the *Murder, She Wrote* series, the famous 1960 French story *Ten Million Witnesses,* and Patricia McGirr's 1951 *Death in a Million Living Rooms* (British title, *Die Laughing*).

Margery Allingham's detective, as we have seen, was the great Albert Campion, related to royalty. It was believed that the model was the prince of Wales who became king of England on the death of his father, King George V; in less than a year, and before he was even crowned, he abdicated, as he wished to marry an American divorcée, Wallis Warfield Simpson, which was constitutionally impossible for a monarch in a country with an established church. Another parody of that time was sung at English preparatory schools, long before the days of Tom Lehrer:

> Hark, the herald angels sing,
> Mrs. Simpson's pinched our King.

He then became the duke of Windsor. As prince of Wales he had been very popular and was a leader of fashion in England and on the Continent. He might well have been a model for Campion, but it is reported that in an interview Margery Allingham said that her model "became king of England" when his brother abdicated. Following constitutional law, the next brother, the duke of York, succeeded unexpectedly. He had a stutter, which would have been a distinct bar to royal life, but he overcame this splendidly and had a successful reign, strongly supported by his wife, until his sad death brought his daughter to the throne as Queen Elizabeth II. His personality would seem to be more apt for Campion.

Erik Routley, in his *Puritan Pleasures of the Detective Story,* comments on Margery Allingham's 1948 *More Work for the Undertaker,* which features Inspector Charles Luke, whom he thought was based on the poet Charles Williams, who died in 1945, and whose description and method of speech tallied completely save for a difference in height.

Robert Barnard's books have a keen sense of humor. For example, in *Death in a Cold Climate,* he states there is no resemblance between his characters and the living, except for the professor at Tromsö—at the time of writing he was himself a professor at Tromsö. Another of his books in Britain was *Unruly Son* (published in 1978) and in America *Death of a Mystery Writer.* In it Sir Oliver Fairleigh-Stubbs, Bart., is a top writer, living in the West Country of England, three miles from Bracken New Town, a pundit on whom press and radio can call for an opinion on anything, whether he knows or not. For example, the famous BBC radio program, *Any Questions?* is described as one on which he appears. His books are studded with wine lore, with such titles as *Death in the Dukeries* or *The Frightened Footman.* He is murdered with poisoned rare wine. Barnard explained that his author was modeled on Evelyn Waugh, who did live in the West Country, was a pundit, and like the fictional writer was severely criticized after his death. One interesting anecdote concerns Barnard's writer, who is invited to a neighbor's for lunch—neighbors who are pathetically scrounging advice—when they get it from Sir Oliver it is, "Sack your cook!" I told Barnard that in one of the biographies of Waugh is the incident of a young man who came to stay with him for the weekend and brought just black tie, or dinner jacket (tuxedo), only to find a formal, white-tie (tailcoat) function had been arranged. He apologized to Waugh (because he could have inquired first), to receive Waugh's magnanimous forgiveness, saying, "Sack your man!" Barnard had not heard of this, but realized such a rejoinder was very typical of Waugh. The anecdote is told of other celebrities.

Crime writers are favorite targets for murder, judging by such titles as *The Murder of a Mystery Writer* by John Hawk, written in 1929, and Eric Heath's *Murder of a Mystery Writer* twenty-six years later.

James Barnett was a commander in the Metropolitan Police, holder of the prestigious QPM (Queen's Police Medal), then on retirement turned to writing, and has served on the committee of the Crime Writers' Association. His books include the fascinating *The Head of the Force,* where the commissioner of the Metropolitan Police is found decapitated as a prelude to a national mystery. In his *Backfire Is Hostile* appears a Labour prime minister who is modeled on a certain leading Labour politician, and Barnett also wrote that his book is intended to be a parody of social conditions, and he wondered if writers had any unconscious personal parodies, a similar comment to Hélène de Monaghan above.

Nicholas Blake was the nom de plume of Cecil Day Lewis (1904–1972), the Poet Laureate from 1968 to 1972, broadcaster, author, and critic, and, as Blake, creator in seventeen books of Nigel Strangeways, amateur detective and nephew of an assistant commissioner of Scotland Yard. His adventures were against the backgrounds of Blake's own life, and were based in the earlier books on Blake's friend, W. H. Auden, the poet (parodied in Dylan Thomas's and John Davenport's *The Death of the King's Canary*) who in later years resembled more Blake himself, in gradual transmogrification similar to Sir Henry Merrivale's.

John Dickson Carr and Carter Dickson created several outstanding detectives, and of them it is fair to select Dr. Gideon Fell as based on G. K. Chesterton. Their physical descriptions tally, and their psychology—for it was Chesterton who commented he wore an Inverness cape and carried a swordstick in the hope that one day he might be able to rescue a maiden in distress. Another Carr sleuth, and again an outstanding character, is Sir Henry Merrivale, Bart., some say based on Winston Spencer Churchill, a great British prime minister and war leader, while others believe that the character is built up, not from Churchill, but gradually developing his traits as the years pass.

Colonel March of Scotland Yard, who was played in 1953 on American and later British television by the English actor Boris Karloff, was created and based by Carr on his friend John Rhode (1884–1964), himself the author of many detective stories featuring Dr. Priestley, and as Miles Burton, Desmond Merrion, and whose real name, very appropriately from one nom de plume, was Major Cecil John Charles Street. In *The Hungry Goblin* (1972), Carr used Wilkie Collins as an amateur detective. As Carter Dickson in 1941 he wrote *And So to Murder,* an amusing (in the P. G. Wodehouse manner) detective story set in an English film studio at "Pineham" (a cross between Pinewood and Boreham). Monica Stanton's first book, a passionate novel titled *Desire,* causes chaos in her rectory home; as her aunt continually complains, "If only Monica had written a nice detective story." The studio hires her to adapt William Cartwright's detective story *And So to Murder* (based obviously on Samuel Pepys's repeated diary entry, "And so to bed"), while Cartwright is to adapt her romance for the screen. When he criticizes her hero and her femme fatale heroine, she ripostes that his books' "silly little murders" are "nasty, footling little tricks that would never work in a thousand years." Cartwright's earlier book, *The Doctor's Pleasure,* around homicidal Rodman Teriss MD of 1882, had been filmed with the suburban street and a complete Teriss house, with a story device of vitriol down a speaking-tube, and this proves the first murder attempt against Monica Stanton on that very set. Later, after reading masses of detective novels she criticizes his treatment of a clergyman so strongly in one of his books he feels himself "lucky he escaped being burnt at the stake," another light touch in this clever Sir Henry Merrivale story.

Vivian Butler has pointed out in his *Durable Desperadoes* that Leslie Charteris's character of Monty Hayward in the Saint story *Getaway* (1932) is based on Percy Montague Haydon, born in

1895, the controlling editor at Fleetway Amalgamated Press, for the immortal *Gem, Magnet,* and *Thriller* boys' magazines; as Charteris makes him say, "And I've been editing this kind of stuff all my life," a charming and obviously genuine tribute.

G. K. Chesterton himself created an outstanding detective, the Essex Catholic priest Father Brown, and based him on a real-life friend and priest, Msgr. John O'Connor; a book was published in 1937, *Father Brown on Chesterton,* on their conversations and Chesterton's conversion to Roman Catholicism.

Agatha Christie (1890–1976) is undeniably the top name in detective fiction, and although she indulged but a little in parody, one of her detectives was novelist Ariadne Oliver, believed to be a caricature of herself. In *Elephants Can Remember,* published in 1972, she says "A speech! No, of course not, you know I never make speeches . . . Several other people who *like* doing it will be making speeches and they are much better at it than I could be . . . Now it's alright with words. You can write words down or speak them into a machine or dictate them. I can do things with words so long as I know it's not a speech I'm making." Christie served as president of the Detection Club, before Julian Symons, and was so shy and retiring she insisted that another member should make all her presidential speeches for her.

We have already considered Edmund Crispin's Oxford don detective, Professor Gervase Fen. In *The Puritan Pleasures of the Detective Story,* Erik Routley states how surprised he was to learn who was the original of Fen. David Williams, a crime author, went to Oxford, and Gwendoline Butler was at Lady Margaret Hall, Oxford; in addition, her late husband, Lionel Butler, was an Oxford don before becoming vice principal of St. Andrews University, then principal of Royal Holloway College of the University of London. Butler, who also writes as Jennie Melville, is the author of more than fifty modern and Victorian detective stories, romances, and gothic tales, and has also served on the CWA committee. Both she and Williams believed Fen to be a mixture of Lord David Cecil and Professor Nevill Coghill, a Chaucer scholar and cowriter of a famous musical, *The Canterbury Tales,* and who recorded for me a detailed account of his approach to and development of Chaucer research just before he died. It is only fair to mention that Lord David Cecil's son, Jonathan Cecil, an eminent English actor, famed for, inter alia, playing Captain Hastings to

Peter Ustinov's excellent Hercule Poirot, told me his father was unaware of this comparison. Williams also mentioned that some believe Fen to be based on crime writer Michael Innes, author of the Appleby stories, who also writes under his own name of J. I. M. Stewart and who served as a professor in Australia as well as at Oxford. Williams mentioned another Oxford don alleges he himself is the original of Fen.

Gwendoline Butler had put me in touch with Professor Lord Strang over the query as to the original musician in Crispin's *Love Lies Bleeding,* and Lord Strang in turn advised me to speak to Peter Oldham of Cardiff University, to whom *Buried for Pleasure* was dedicated. On the telephone Monday, February 24, 1986, Oldham pointed out that the obituaries of both Edmund Crispin and Will G. Moore, English tutor of St. John's, quoted the latter as the physical model for Fen, with his hair sticking out behind his head, which theory seems most accepted to date.

Kenneth Fearing (1902–1961) wrote such outstanding books as *Dagger of the Mind* (1941) and *The Big Clock* (1946), in which a megalomaniac publisher, Earl Janoth of Janoth Enterprises, commits a murder and has his own reporter seek the missing witness, who *is* the reporter. The film from Paramount in 1948 called his magazine *Crimeways.* Fearing had worked on *Time* magazine and is believed to have based his group and magnate on that magazine and its publisher, Henry Luce.

In November 1985 at Oxford with Gwendoline Butler to found an Oxford Chapter of the CWA, attended by Elizabeth Ferrars, I asked her about her detective, Professor Andrew Basnett, and she replied that he was based on both her husband and herself.

Dr. Richard Austin Freeman (1862–1943), author and specialist, invented the "inverted" detective story, in which the murderer is known at the outset, and created the doctor-detective John Evelyn Thorndyke, modeled, he indicated, on Professor Alfred Swaine Taylor, an authority on jurisprudence.

Robert Lee Hall took Benjamin Franklin (1706–1790), an American writer, scientist, and statesman, as his sleuth, chronicled by his "Watson," Nicholas Handy, in 1795 on Franklin's visit to England (where for a time he lived near the present Charing Cross Station), first in *Benjamin Franklin Takes the Case* (1990), followed by *Benjamin Franklin and a Case of Christmas Murder* (1991).

Nick and Nora Charles, the lighthearted husband-and-wife team created by Dashiell Hammett (1894–1961), played on screen by William Powell and Myrna Loy, and named as the Thin Man series (although the Thin Man was a victim in the first film), was obviously based on Hammett himself and Lillian Hellman, a playwright and his friend for thirty years.

Peter Lovesey has written some excellent Victorian detective stories featuring Sergeant Cribb and Constable Thackeray, who are the opposite sides of himself, respectively the optimistic and pessimistic. Inspector Jowett, the less likeable, is based on a man of today.

William J. Palmer set his 1990 novel *The Detective and Mr. Dickens* in 1851, and his sleuths were Dickens and Wilkie Collins.

The year 1993 was the centenary of the birth of Dorothy L. Sayers on June 13, 1893; it was marked by several commemorative events. The Canterbury Festival, scene of her 1937 religious play *The Zeal of Thy House,* commissioned Gwendoline Butler and the present writer to deliver a joint lecture on October 14, in the Theodore Room in the Cathedral Cloisters, under the title "The Wimsey-Sayers Engagement." Among the topics falling to this writer's share were Sayers's incorrect comments about monocles and the present locations of the poison cupboard in *Strong Poison* (1930) and the circular staircase from *Murder Must Advertise* (1933). The existing owners of the properties were most cooperative with, in the instance of the staircase, allowing Butler to be recorded walking down several times and myself screaming heartily. The other main topic was the original of Lord Peter Wimsey. By now there were several biographies and critiques of Sayers published, with analogies drawn between Eric Whelpton, John Cournos, and a later Balliol man. One writer commented, however, on Sayers's "Greyfriars" attitude to public school life, and that Wimsey was based on the character of Arthur Augustus D'Arcy at St. Jim's (Wimsey was originally to be in a Sexton Blake novella, in the Sexton Blake Library). The creator of St. Jim's was probably the world's most prolific author—of more than one hundred million words—Charles Hamilton (1876–1961). He created St. Jim's in 1906, in *Pluck,* then a year later in the weekly magazine *Gem,* and another year after that, Billy Bunter and Greyfriars School for another weekly magazine, *Magnet* (both read assiduously by this author and his father). Hamilton's noms de plume included Frank Richards, Martin Clifford, Owen Conquest, Hilda Richards, inter alia. In his autobiography in 1952, republished ten years later, he stated he based "Gussy," the Honorable Arthur Augustus D'Arcy, on C. Maurice Down, who had joined Amalgamated Press about 1904, publishers of the various magazines, who in 1921 became editor of *Magnet, Gem,* etc., and the *Holiday Annual,* his own invention, until 1940. The elegance, monocle, Bertie-Woosterish sayings all show the links to prove the genesis of Wimsey, on whom another literary sleuth was to be based in 1935 for a girls' magazine. Sexton Blake is the detective hero of many millions of words from a huge stable of authors, and although Sayers later spoke somewhat disparagingly of him, it did not deter her from editing a Sexton Blake feature in the *Evening Standard* newspaper on November 23, 1936.

Georges Simenon's immortal Superintendent Jules Maigret is based on Charles Chenevier, but we shall see later a surprising aspect of his creation.

Dorothy Simpson is a very talented detective story author, and has been a very active CWA committee member; her policeman, Inspector Luke Thanet, is of her county of Kent. I discussed her detective's personality with her, and she explained he was how she imagined herself acting and thinking if she were a man. One of her books won the Silver Dagger for 1985, presented to her at the awards dinner on May 1, 1986.

In November 1983 I gave a lecture on the "Story of the Detective Story" to a club in the Lambeth area of London, and afterward a J. W. Cooper approached me to say his uncle was the original of Edgar Wallace's Mr. J. G. Reeder, a Superintendent Charles Crocker. His description of his uncle tallied with the famous Wallace delineation, including muffler, coat, and flat-topped bowler or derby, still worn during the last war by Winston Churchill, for example. I contacted the Metropolitan and City of London Police, obtained copies of the relevant papers of, respectively, the superintendent and Detective Inspector Crocker; we agreed the Met superintendent tallied with Cooper's family background. Whereupon I wrote for Penelope Wallace's *Edgar Wallace Society Newsletter* an article on our discoveries. She told me that Percy Hoskins, former chief crime reporter of the English *Daily Express* newspaper had thought the original might have been a police officer named Wallace, but she agreed this new claimant seemed correct.

So we see some of the originals of great fictional sleuths, from Sherlock Holmes onward—indeed, Holmes has been likened to the famous Dr. Bell, an analytical professor under whom Doyle studied, and the author himself has been described as the man who was Holmes—he has also been described as the man who was Watson, and the physical outlines do certainly tally. Indeed, in 1993 two detective novels were published with Doyle as a sleuth. (It will be recalled he had been active, like Erle Stanley Gardner, in taking up cases of apparent injustices, in particular the Edalji animal maiming case and the Oscar Slater false recognition.) One book was *Photographing Fairies* by Steve Szilagyi, starting with a 1920s American photographer named Castle approaching Doyle with alleged photographs of fairies from a country policeman; Castle takes up the inquiry when he won't touch them. (Doyle had been involved in the notorious alleged fairy photographs taken by two small girls.) In *The List of 7,* by Mark Frost, young surgeon and psychic investigator(!) Doyle is lured into a trap set by satanists on Christmas Day 1884, only to be rescued by Queen Victoria's secret agent. The author was cocreator of *Twin Peaks,* a famous 1990s esoteric television serial seen in America and Britain.

We can look now very briefly at some of the villains, and other characters in crime stories. Let us start with a mystery man who intrigued a leading French writer, and caused the present author many hours of interesting research, only partly successful.

In 1981 Colin Wilson received a letter from Françoise d'Eaubonne, an eminent French writer on ecological and feminist topics and a novelist. She asked if he could help trace an English playwright of the 1920s whose name might have been Harry Whitecliffe, a parodist of Oscar Wilde. He fled from England before several murders were traced to him, settled in Dresden, founded the Dorian Press, then again vanished, only to write to his new fiancée from the condemned cell in a Berlin jail before committing suicide, having been found guilty of yet more murders. Wilson passed the letter on to me, because of the theatrical import. I wrote in vain to every source mentioned, visited Paris twice to meet d'Eaubonne, and tried fruitlessly many times to contact a French journalist who had written about Whitecliffe. Thelma Holland, the daughter-in-law of Oscar Wilde, suggested writing her native Australia, where "Whitecliffe," or Lovach Blume of Berlin, had family connections—and surely, the *Argus* of August 8, 1922, reported the capture of Wilhelm Blume, a cultured murderer, who had founded the Dorian Press in Dresden. Was there a Whitecliffe first? When d'Eaubonne published her book it was a novel, *A La Limite des Ténèbres* in 1983, stating that vigorous inquiries had failed to prove Whitecliffe's work. Wilson has published this essay in several of his crime anthologies, and concludes that Blume, a murderer in Germany but not in England at all, had fantasized many of these details of his earlier life.

Colin Wilson around 1960 introduced me to a guest—a quiet, highly respectable young man—on whom he based his enigmatic mass murderer in his first fiction book *Ritual in the Dark,* a tale of a modern Ripper-style killer in London.

Aldous Huxley used the famous Greenwood poisoning case as the basis for *The Gioconda Smile.*

Dorothy Uhnak's police procedural *The Investigation* (1977) appears to be based on the Alice Crimmins kidnapping in New York.

Mario Puzo appears to have based his *Godfather* Luca Brasi on Larry Gallo.

Mary Rinehart's 1914 *The After House* was based on the 1896 case of Captain Charles Nash, his wife Laure, and August W. Blomberg.

Charles Dickens based his short story "Hunted Down" (1859) on the famous poisoner Thomas Griffiths Wainwright—and we shall see later this is not the only criminal to be metamorphosed into one of his books.

Waldo Lydecker, the elegant, powerful man-about-town in Vera Caspary's famous *Laura* (1943), made into an equally gripping film the next year, was apparently based on Alexander Woollcott, critic and wit, who also became *The Man Who Came to Dinner,* with another character based on Noël Coward, in play and film.

With Poe's "ratiocination" in his own books and deductions of others, like Dickens, it was inevitable that he would himself appear as a sleuth in the books and stories of other authors. John Dickson Carr's story *The Gentleman from Paris,* later filmed as *Man with a Cloak* (MGM, 1951), has Poe, played by Joseph Cotten, anonymously averting a robbery. Many other films featured Poe, but one other novel is the 1978 *Evermore,* by B. and D. Stewart, involving Poe with the two Mayerling deaths in the Viennese woods of Crown Prince Rudolf and Baroness Vetsera (the hunting lodge is now run as a tourist attraction by nuns, with an altar where the bed used to be). Jay Robert Nash, author of many useful, detailed handbooks on crime and criminals has written that Demetrios, in Eric Ambler's *The Mask of Demetrios* (American title, *A Coffin for Demetrios;* 1939), was based on a millionaire international financier, Sir Basil Zaharoff, and that Gutman, the mysterious fat man in Dashiell Hammett's classic *The Maltese Falcon* (of which more anon), was based on A. Maundy Gregory. Sydney Greenstreet was outstanding in both films made.

There is, however, an interesting contradiction. In 1985 as a new member of the CWA committee I suggested an award to outstanding world crime writers. Chair Antonia Fraser backed me, and Gwendoline Butler suggested a Diamond Dagger, which Cartier, international jewelers, agreed to provide for ten years—a dagger piercing a book to be held for a year, with a diamond tiepin or brooch for each holder. Eric Ambler was the first recipient at the awards dinner at Armoury House, the historic London headquarters of the Honourable Artillery Company, England's oldest territorial regiment. On May 1, 1986, as toastmaster, I had the chance to ask Ambler if he had based Demetrios on Zaharoff, as stated in the American book. His reply: "Nonsense." After he had written the book, he was told of a Greek financier living in Paris—so this disposes of Nash's theory unequivocally. The investiture was filmed by BBC television for the *Omnibus* program documentary on Ambler.

Francis Iles, who was also Anthony Berkeley (1893–1971), wrote *Before the Fact* in 1932, and there is a character in the book obviously designed to be Dorothy L. Sayers, "fitted with a volume control like the wireless." Howard Haycraft called this book Iles's "masterpiece" with the "internally terrifying portrait of the murderer." It was filmed for RKO in 1941 by Alfred Hitchcock, as *Suspicion,* with Joan Fontaine as the wife, Cary Grant as her mysterious husband, Cedric Hardwicke, Nigel Bruce, and May Whitty.

In *Murder Plus Six,* John Bingham in 1951 pays tribute to his publisher Victor Gollancz by naming one character Gollancz.

The Gentleman from Chicago by John Cashman referred to Dr. Thomas Neill Cream.

Arnold Rothstein, (1882–1928) a leading American gambler and criminal, was Damon Runyon's the Brain in that 1937 haunting short story, *The Brain Goes Home*, and Wolfsheim in Scott Fitzgerald's classic *The Great Gatsby*. A character based on him was shot by Clark Gable in the 1934 film *Manhattan Melodrama*, showing at the Biograph Theatre, Chicago, on July 22, 1934, after which the man the FBI claimed was John Dillinger was shot — a matter in some doubt. Damon Runyon (1880–1946), to be considered in Chapter 5, created a gallery of immortal New York crooks in his stories written in the historic present so vividly that E. C. Bentley was right that his one past tense stands out like a beacon; one character later, a Bob Hope film success, was the Lemon Drop Kid, based by Runyon on Swifty Morgan, a friend of comic Joseph Everglades Lewis, the film hero of Frank Sinatra's *The Joker Is Wild*.

S. S. Van Dine's first book, *The Benson Murder Case* (1926), featuring dilettante Philo Vance, told of a murder victim found in West 48th Street, New York, on Friday, June 14 (which would have to have been 1929), minus teeth and toupee. This was based on the unsolved murder of wealthy Joseph P. Elwell, womanizer and bridge expert, on Friday, January 1, 1920, at 244 West 70th Street — minus teeth and wig. *Elwell on Bridge* and *Elwell's Advanced Bridge* had been written by his wealthy wife, Helen Darby, who had left him in 1914 after ten years' marriage, to his three mansions (the one in New York with a "seduction chamber" for his innumerable conquests), race-horse stable, objets d'art, yacht, five autos, and wealth. He died after an evening at dinner and the theatre, shot within sight of passers-by between the postman's call at 7:10 or 7:30 A.M. and the housekeeper's arrival at eight o'clock. Holding one of the morning's letters, in a chair backing the wall, killed by a .45 gun never traced, shot at an upward angle, he was dressed in wrinkled pajamas, no fit state for a megalopsychic like Elwell to be seen, especially by women. The book was filmed in 1930 with William Powell playing Vance. Alexander Woollcott wrote about the case, Anthony Abbott, or Fulton Oursler, lived in the same block, and Edmund Pearson stated that Van Dine and Woollcott were once alleged to be his own pseudonyms. In *Masterpices of Murder,* chapter 16, on the case he wrote: "Only experts like Messrs. Alexander Woollcott and S. S. Van Dine will be familiar with Sir John Hall's work, and as it has been solemnly asserted in print that the names of both Mr. Woollcott and Mr. Van Dine are but pseudonyms of the writer of this book, the circle is very much narrowed."

It is generally recognized that Josephine Tey (1896–1952) based her famous story *The Franchise Affair* (1948) on the eighteenth-century kidnapping case of Elizabeth Canning, but it is not so quickly realized that it is also founded on the famous eighteenth-century murderer Nurse Brownrigg, perhaps the first exponent of the English crime of child battering combined with indifference of official local authority.

Another crime story based on a true crime, as an example selected from many, is Jean Potts's *Go, Lovely Rose* (1954), which is based on the killing of housemaid Rose Harsent, in Suffolk, England, in 1902. This was a lesser-known murder on May 31/June 1 at night in Providence House, Peasenhall. William Gardiner was accused; the inquest was held on June 3; the trial at Ipswich County Hall opened on November 7. The retrial on January 21, 1903, at the same venue again resulted in the jury not being able to agree, so the Crown dropped the case.

Authors may parody sleuths, victims, their friends, or public figures, and sometimes more than one person at a time is under the microscope. We have seen that crime writers, perhaps the most sociable and least jealous writers, join clubs and attend seminars, so what more natural a target for a painstaking author with a sharp eye?

A complete industry has been built up writing biographies and "real-life" background data designed to "prove" the existence of fictional sleuths. Literally hundreds of books have been written about Sherlock Holmes, with titles like *Sherlock Holmes: Fact or Fiction?* by T. S. Blakeney (1932). Some authors have written a series of books on various aspects of Holmes's life, home, and cases, seeking to prove the derivations of the names and cases taken by Doyle. Two excellently produced books were published by Paulette Greene of New York, a rare-books specialist on crime and criminal subjects. One book was titled *Sherlock Holmes: Rare Book Collector* (1981), by Madeline B. Stern, and was a detailed analysis of all the books in Holmes's library, those mentioned by name, with editors traced where possible, and those titled from the author's indications. Lord Peter Wimsey has had the honor of books about his private life. One in hardback and paperback was called *The Wimsey Family* (1977) and was written by C. W. Scott-Giles, Fitzalan Pursuivant of Arms, from Dorothy L. Sayers letters; it not only gave convincing particulars of his family arms and of the dukes of Denver, but of his family history. A very different tack was taken by *The Lord Peter Wimsey Cookbook,* written in 1981 by Elizbeth Boyd Ryan and William J. Eakins, and published by Ticknor and Fields of New Haven and New York. All meals, snacks, and drinks are divided into "Breakfasts," "Lunches," "Teas," "Dinners," "Suppers," "Drinks," with full quotes from books and stories, wine, today's equivalents, and California wines—but with no references to specific poisons or to horseradish poison—and it all makes a very good cookery book as well, and ideal for staging a nostalgic or period party. Wimsey, like Bond, did make the occasional gourmet lapse, like calling a Rhône wine a claret, but this elegant book avoids solecisms. Lord Peter's genesis has been considered above, and it has been thought his address in Piccadilly, 110a, in London's West End, was half the number of Sherlock Holmes's 221b Baker Street apartments, the precise location of which has been proved in a definite article written by Bernard Davis, former actor, secretary of the Dracula Society, chair of the Sherlock Holmes Society, whose friendship began after I impersonated Davis on the television game *Tell the Truth.*

An unusual and rarely seen book is *Papers Relating to the Family of Wimsey,* edited by "Matthew Wimsey," a pseudonym, privately printed in 1936 in an edition of around five hundred copies, illustrated, prepared by Dorothy L. Sayers and Helen Simpson, for the friends of the former as a humorous gesture, and not for sale.

Can this machine be reversed? Apparently, because real-life American top detective Raymond Schindler took a hint from *The Hound of the Baskervilles* and used a dog for a collaborator in his efforts to save the life of a poor Negro in one of his many famous cases.

The list of books and films based on true incidents and characters would be shown as wide indeed, so a few general examples will suffice here. Joan Fleming's 1966 *Midnight Hag* (based on the strangling in Holy Trinity churchyard, Stratford-upon-Avon, on Shakespeare's birthday, April 23, 1954, of Olive Bennett) is one, and *The House Without the Door* (1942) by Elizabeth Daly (1879–1967) (based loosely on the Dorothy Arnold Case) is another. On film Al Capone can be seen as the theme of *Key Largo* (1948), *Scarface* (1932), or *Little Caesar;* Dillinger for Humphrey Bogart's *Petrified Forest* and *High Sierra;* Siegel, Luciano, Crowley, Moran, O'Connor, et al. for other films, and real gangsters actually taking part in Hollywood films themselves from 1912 to 1928. Truth is stranger than fiction—or is it fiction, anyway?

All in League Together . . . ?

Peter Antony is the pen name of the Shaffer twins, born 1926, Peter and Antony, each of whom has acquired fame as an author and playwright. They combined their talents to write three detective stories in the 1950s, featuring a private sleuth, Mr. Verity, who lives in a Sussex cottage, friendly with Inspector Rambler, and they both belong to the Beverley Club, to study crime as an art form. *The Woman in the Wardrobe* (1951) is a locked-room mystery; *How Doth the Little Crocodile?* (1952) has the Beverley Club asking Verity to solve the murder of two of its members; and *Withered Murder* (1955) has a victim killed in a room a few feet away from an unknowing secretary.

Anthony Boucher, William Anthony Parker White (1911–1968), critic, editor, author (also as H. H. Holmes, the name of a famous American murderer), wrote *Rocket to the Morgue* in 1942, which is set among science fiction writers and their fans, in which "Boucher himself appeared in a minor role," commented one critic.

Agatha Christie created her own crime writers' club in her 1966 Poirot case, *Third Girl,* when in chapter 2 Ariadne Oliver rings Poirot: "It is the annual dinner of our detective authors' club; I wondered if you would come and be our guest speaker this year." This is the story which starts with Poirot's own researches, on the first page—"He had finished his *magnum opus,* an analysis of great writers of detective fiction. He had dared to speak scathingly of Edgar Allan Poe, he had complained of the lack of method or order in the romantic outpourings of Wilkie Collins, had lauded to the skies two American authors who were practically unknown, and had in various other ways given honour where honour was due and sternly withheld it where he had considered it was not . . . the vast amount of reading he had had to do"—and he throws some books on the floor.

Anthony Berkeley Cox (Francis Iles, 1893–1971) had a tongue-in-cheek approach to his craft even in *Jumping Jenny* (1933), where Ronald Stratton wrote detective stories "because it amused him to do so," and Roger Sheringham, based on a man known to Cox, attends the fancy dress party where the sister-in-law is killed, Great lengths are gone to to switch the blame, and the parodic denouement involves a moving chair. *Trial and Error* (1937) has doomed-to-die Todhunter (*Tod* is German for "death") on trial deliberately for this murder of unpleasant actress Jean Norwood, based on Pellizzioni's murdering the Englishman Harrington in 1866, when another Italian, Mogni, pleaded self-defense and H. Negretti, of a famous optical instrument firm, led the inquiries. Todhunter dies before his execution. The league parody, however, is his *The Poisoned Chocolates Case* (1929), based on his short story "The Avenging Chance." In *Modern Fiction Studies,* vol. 29, no. 3 (Autumn 1983): 479, from "Detective Story to Detective Novel," Thomas M. Leitch commented, *"The Poisoned Chocolates Case* presents a club, obviously modelled on Berkeley's own Detective [*sic*] Club, whose members act as armchair detectives in attempting to solve a murder whose facts are set forth in 'The Avenging Chance.' Each member refutes the previous member's solution and offers his own. The seven solutions offered include Berkeley's original, but this time it is wrong." A lady samples a poisoned box of chocolates, and Sheringham's own Crimes Circle undertakes the inquiry. The fourth answer of the club was that in the short story—and one of the wrong ones in this parody of writers, detectives, and the Detection Club itself, of which Cox was a founder.

The six members of Sheringham's Crimes Circle are Sir Charles Wildman, KC; Mrs. Fillder-Fleming, playwright; Morton Harrogate Bradley (formerly Percy Robinson), detective story writer; Sheringham; Alicia Dammers, author of *Flesh and the Devil;* and the diffident Ambrose Chitterwick (whose surname might indicate a chattering wiseman). Their solutions have differing interpretations of facts and of witnesses' statements, and the case references range from Lafarge, Molineux, and Dr. Wilson, to Christine Edmunds, Carlyle Harris, Tawell, and Horwood. "This satire on detectives, mystery writers, and the Detection Club is often cited as the best novel signed by Berkeley."

Robert L. Fish's *The Murder League* is a very different club, in fact it is a mystery authors' club, opposite what was the Amberford House, now a twenty-story office block, across "Pomfret

Street" to "Swan's Park" where the nursemaids take their charges (probably a reference to Hyde Park or Kensington Gardens). The Detection Club's first premises were, until 1931, at 31 Gerrard Street, near Shaftesbury Avenue, in the heart of the London theatre district. The three founder-members, now ignored by the younger writers, are Clifford Simpson (tall), Tim Briggs (with tiny face and wizened body), and William Carruthers (with a shock of white hair, broad face, portly stomach, who was a police reporter as a young man, and who wrote *Bloody Dagger* in 1926). These descriptions could almost apply directly or inversely, to G. K. Chesterton and Anthony Berkeley, Detection Club founder-members. They think up ten brilliant murders, so clever that the police calculator is ten murders out, fall down on the last, and are "helped" by a ruthless counsel, but all live very happily after. Their organization, advertised in the *Times* as the Murder League, is picked up by the police computer as the length of road from London Bridge, in the City of London, to "Chamberley Street," three miles along the bank. Fish writes a clever parody, gently mocking the police, and the highly ingenious efforts of the three murder plotters, with a new lease of life from their teamwork, and the parody stays at the same high level throughout. The play based on this book will be considered in Chapter 5 below.

Although there are over a thousand parodies and pastiches of Sherlock Holmes, which rules out a wholesale listing, among those most worthy of mention are the Sherlock Homes parodies written by Fish under his own name (he also writes as Robert L. Pike and A. C. Lamprey, other marine connections): "Homes" and his assistant "Dr. Watney" live at 221b Bagel Street, and the first volume of short stories, *The Incredible Schlock Homes,* was published in 1966, and the critics have praised the stories as among the best parody-pastiches of Holmes.

Val Gielgud (1900–1981) was head of BBC radio drama for thirty-five years, brother of actor John Gielgud, and a skilled novelist and playwright, his books including *Death at Broadcasting House* (1934), filmed soon after. *Death in Budapest* (1937) recounts the murder of an opera singer during a performance, witnessed by a convention of professional detectives "as well as several fictional sleuths," one of the first such novels. The investigating detective is Inspector Simon Spears. B. M. Gill wrote *Seminar for Murder,* wherein Detective Chief Inspector Tom Maybridge lectures in October 1985 at the annual weekend seminar of the Golden Guillotine Club, criticizing amateurs somewhat too strongly after reading the last six crime novels for the award that evening. Of course, such organizations as the CWA in Britain hold these seminars with visiting lecturers of this caliber, and forensic scientists and crime writers do get together to their mutual benefit. The morning after Maybridge's lecture, the president of the club is found dead in bed with a note pinned to the bedhead "Fault this murder, Detective Chief Inspector Maybridge if you can." A second brutal murder and the crime writers find themselves necessarily involved, before the case is solved and he finds fault again. This book was published after murder and mystery weekends became popular in Britain and the States.

Two other examples can be briefly considered. Shannon OCork's *The Murder of Muriel Lake* had the eponymous heroine choosing the annual convention of Writers of Mystery to announce her divorce from fellow writer Jonathan Pells, but hours later she is dead. Charlaine Harris's 1991 title *Real Murders* has her heroine, Aurora Teegarden, known to her friends as Roe, preparing an excellent speech to the Real Murders Society of Lawrenceton, Georgia, but a club member is killed in a reenactment of the crime she selected and worse still, it appears, she is to be the next victim.

In 1955 Brett Halliday (1904–1977)—Davis Dresser—wrote Michael Shayne's twenty-fifth case, *She Woke to Darkness*. Up to chapter 10, it is written in the first person as Halliday, or some chapters are the actual manuscript that is the elusive key to the puzzle. Various real-life characters take larger or smaller parts in the story, including Ellery Queen, Dorothy Gardiner, Ed Radin, and Clayton Rawson.

Mike Shayne in fact came to the aid of Halliday who met Elsie Murray at the 1953 MWA dinner in New York, read her manuscript about a woman mixed up in a murder, and found she had been murdered after he left. Thus Shayne was to solve the mystery in the manuscript and the murder simultaneously, while Halliday had been made away with by the killer. The manuscript, titled *She Woke to Darkness,* recounts the earlier case as an unfinished story, and Ed Radin takes a leading part in saving Halliday.

An unusual sidelight in Halliday's writing came in *Murder*

Cavalcade, the MWA 1946 anthology. In the section "Fact-Fiction," described as "the newest step in the telling of crime stories" in combining fiction with the ring of truth, Michael Shayne, "the first established imaginary detective to join the files of true crime cases" solves the "Million-Dollar Motive," first appearing in *Master Detective,* the theft of a million dollars from a New Orleans brokerage firm, a murder, and the trap for the killer-thief.

The line dividing parody and pastiche is at times both faint and wavering, as we have seen, which is the reason for separate sections on real life, puzzles the reader has to solve himself, continuations of another author's series, and subsections such as this. We shall see some authors regard their books as a tribute to the Golden Age of detective stories rather than parody or pastiche. The next novel in this subsection involving both crime writers' organizations and (therefore) real persons was specifically described in a letter from this author, dated April 9, 1984, as neither a parody nor a pastiche, nor is the detective a pastiche on Dashiell Hammet's *Black Mask* writings. This author is the versatile and prolific short story expert Edward D. Hoch, and his first book had the fascinating title in 1970 *The Shattered Raven.* It recounts how ex–private eye turned detective story author Barney Hamet is present at the MWA awards dinner where television news commentator Ross Craigthorn is about to speak on receiving the Reader of the Year Award when he is shot—by the microphone. Many famous writers have what Hoch called "nonspeaking parts," such as Ellery Queen, Rex Stout, Clayton Rawson, Robert Fish, Joe Gores, and Larry Treat at the dinner, and others are also mentioned. The disclaimer states, "Because many living people and actual places are mentioned by name," all events, characters, etc., are of course fictitious. A precise touch is the way in which authors are mentioned—Clayton Rawson attending a craft meeting addressed by Ernie Hutter of *Alfred Hitchcock Mystery Magazine,* Mike Avallone handling the lighting cues at the dinner, Rex Stout posing for pictures as the president was at home in Montana. There are many literary clues, especially "Raven"—more popular in crime fiction than Hamet and his journalist assistant Susan Veldt realize.

Edward Hoch also indicated his short story "The Spy at the Crime Writers' Congress" (*Ellery Queen Mystery Magazine* [November 1976]) and "Murder at The Bouchercon" (*EQMM* [November 1983]), featuring the crime writer Barney Hamet in the latter, and real-life crime writers as extras in both.

Another prestigious award ceremony to be the scene of a murder mystery was *Murder at the Academy Awards,* a 1983 title from Joe Hyams. The Academy Awards in Hollywood are the annual bestowal of the statuettes nicknamed "Oscars" for every aspect of international filmmaking, a glittering occasion compèred very effectively for many years by Bob Hope. (The British equivalent is the BAFTA [British Academy of Film and Television Arts] awards ceremony.) Another book in which the Academy Awards ceremony played a significant part was the 1959 *Black Is the Fashion for Dying* (or *The Mink-Lined Coffin*) by Jonathan Latimer (the witty crime writer and Hollywood scriptwriter of *The Glass Key,* etc.). His hard-boiled stories frequently featured PI Bill Crane, some of them duly filmed, the others included this present book, in which slipping, hated, vicious film star Caresse Garnett is murdered on set during filming. One suspect is the clever, ruthless studio head Karl Fabro, due for his second Oscar. At the ceremony, Jack Benny, the master of ceremonies Bob Hope, Red Skelton, Doris Day, Danny Kaye, Jerry Lewis, Tab Hunter, and Kim Novak are all taking part in the platform action; Edith Head receives an award for best costume design in black-and-white photography; but when Fabro is due to receive his Oscar from Kim Novak, a trick is played on him that one cannot visualize the ceremony stewards allowing, even though it was on radio not television in 1957.

We have already seen Robert Barnard's gift for parody; in 1987 he wrote *Death in Purple Prose,* in which his sleuth Superintendent Perry Trethowen escorts his romance novelist sister to the biennial conference at Bergen, Norway, of WARN—World Association of Romantic Novelists. With tongue-in-cheek reference to publishers Bills and Coo (an obvious disguise), the writers, mainly British and American women, with their own reference book, find themselves in a web of petty blackmail, casual amours, and bitter rivalry between the British Amanda Fairchild and American Lorelei Le Neve (or Zuckerman). Finally an inexplicable murder, followed by yet more secrets, includes the interesting theory, à la Sexton Blake, of ghost-writing of a heavy output. The book is described as a "hilarious send-up of the world of romantic fiction"; Barnard knows Scandinavia and understands the world of literary conferences.

So, Crime Writers' is not the only conference selected as a murder scene: *Sweet, Savage Death* by Orania Papazoglou (Jane Haddam), and *Die for Love,* by Elizabeth Peters, both in 1984, feature murder at romance novelists' conferences in the States. Papazoglou wrote another murder story with a literary background in 1985, *Wicked, Loving Murder,* and Peters wrote other titles with literary or bookish backgrounds, for example, *The Seventh Sinner* (1972) on archaeology (her doctorate subject from the University of Chicago), and she is also Barbara Michaels, the romance novelist. In contrast to her crime stories, convent- and Vassar-educated Papazoglou's 1986 book, *Sanctity,* was a drama of three young women entering as novitiates the mother house of the Order of the Society of Mary, whose secrets and desires mount to an overwhelming psychological climax for the convent and themselves.

Michael Innes (1906–1995) and John Innes Mackintosh Stewart are names synonymous with quality we shall be considering— appropriately enough, as they are the same man. As Michael Innes, he wrote a series of high-quality detective stories, with literary allusions, vocabulary, and erudition comparable with Ellery Queen and Edmund Crispin, his detective starting as Inspector John Appleby and ending as Past Commissioner Sir John—a career paralleled by Francis Gerard's Inspector, later Sir, John Meredith. In 1973 he wrote a spoof, *Appleby's Answer,* which featured a club rather like the Detection Club, to a meeting of which is traveling Priscilla Pringle when the action starts. She is the author of *Vengeance at the Vicarage, Revenge at the Rectory, Murder in the Cathedral* (*sic*), and the meeting at the Café Royal was the Diner Dupin, the annual dinner, the crooks colloquium, on the top table a letter rack with envelope (as in "The Purloined Letter") and with a stuffed orangutan or gorilla (the actual Detection Club has a famous illuminated skull used for declarations); the chairman at the meeting was Miss Barrace, one diner was Dr. Hussey, master of a Cambridge college, whose first story had been, predictably enough, about murder in a Cambridge college. The speaker was Sir John Appleby. Miss Pringle was worried about her encounter in the train with a man who disagreed with her writing and proposed a collaboration with his ideas, a suggestion disliked by many authors. He lived at Long Canings with two suspicious young men he is allegedly "cramming" for examinations, with sound effects and the like to gull any chance visitor. Later his meetings with Priscilla form the basis for blackmail, through edited tapes, and almost for her murder, but for Sir John and a goat. In *Murder in the Cathedral* the ironic touches include finding a revolver behind the reredos, and the missing cathedral plate in Canon Pantin's pantry, bearing in mind perhaps that a pantine, or pantin, is the French term for a pasteboard jumping jack.

Anne Morice's detective stories featured actress Tessa Crichton, married to a policeman, and have a knowledgeable theatrical background. Her *Dead on Cue* (1985), starts with, " 'Ever heard of the Alibi Club?' Robin asked. . . . The membership is restricted to forty, and they're all top flight mystery writers. It started with a bunch of old-fashioned classic detective novelists, but they're getting thinner on the ground now, so the umbrella's been extended to science fiction and so on. They have no premises of their own, but they meet informally four times a year for dinner in some Soho restaurant, whose name for the moment escapes me." (The Detection Club did start with classical crime writers, of course, and does meet a few times a year at the Savoy Hotel and the Garrick Club, a famous club for the arts, both in London's West End.)

We learn the Alibi Club's activities include selection of new members and requesting a Scotland Yard officer to address the gathering. One writer victim is taken ill at a meeting, and a classic tale unfolds involving copyright and plagiarism which rings true, and it is certainly not unknown in Britain for an unscrupulous author to endeavor to pass off another's manuscript as his own. Anne Morice had a subtle reference to a shy elected author who specializes in writing about most valiant men and women, unlike, say, Mickey Spillane portraying his own hero on screen.

Padder Nash is one of the three noms de plume of Alan Sewart, former police superintendent living in Yorkshire, an active member of the CWA, who uses his own career to add credence to the books which he produces regularly. *The Educating of Quinton Quinn* (1984) is a tale of murder at a crime writers' conference at a stately home, and to the knowing, there are many appropriate touches in the account of the police–crime writer attending the conference, helping his superior officer to solve the murder, but with the lordly proviso that his poor superior treat him, not only as a stranger, but with respect too. One character who is found fishing in the ornamental lake is named Alfred Hamley, a depiction of Alfred Manley. Wanley Stilson is Stanley Wilson. Lilian

Tuart is the real-life Vivianne Stewart, her Australian trilogy being really about South Africa. There are references to Easingwold, where Siwart lives, to Padder Nash himself in the action, and to Robert Hale, the publisher who brought out this book. One of the lectures for members is "The Living Novel" by the famous F. R. K. Heating, an obvious lead to H. R. F. Keating, president of the Detection Club, chair of the CWA (1970/71), author, critic, and historian.

These are some of the conference and club themes, and we shall see later some of the clubs specializing in problems for members and readers, like the Black Widowers, and other types including, for example, Robert Louis Stevenson's *The Suicide Club,* later filmed, but the postscript is a very ingenious short story involving living writers in a contest with more than a punch. "The Final Problem," the Prize-Contest Story to End All Prize Contest Detective Stories, by Bliss Austin, got an honorable mention in the Queen's Awards for 1946. Ellery Queen, Howard Haycraft, and Christopher Morley receive a short story from Hugh Ashton at Yale, with a cyanide cigar. Professor Moriarty is mentioned and described. Inspector Queen and Velie go to Yale, Old Haven, meet local policeman Moran; the carbon copy of the story is stolen, Ashton is murdered, there is an attempt on the sleuths, the inspector is killed by Colonel Moran disguised as Professor Moriarty, because Ashton had been blackmailing Moran over a notorious New York murder. A story that does leave the reader in a blissful quandary—but fortunately it didn't stop the flow of entries for competitions in future years.

These examples show the different ways in which writers depict their associations, both the more esoteric types like the Detection Club of England, and the larger organizations such as MWA (of America) and the CWA of Great Britain. Of course, in England greater care must be taken perhaps to avoid upsetting colleagues, but the actual activities written about are accurate. We shall consider later group activities where several members of a club combine to write a story among them, and under parody some do comment on fictional associations' members. In October 1985 I was asked by CWA chair Antonia Fraser to look after the public relations of the annual conference at Norwich in Norfolk. I took fellow committee member Gwendoline Butler to a local BBC afternoon live radio chat show, when the interviewer suggested a crime worked out by such a conference of top crime writers had a very good chance of success. To this our reply was, "Yes, especially with our ex-policeman authors—but unfortunately we would be the first prime suspects!"

Parody Per Se!

We shall find many more examples of parody than pastiche, and again alphabetical order of authors will prove convenient rather than an artificial classification, particularly as parody can take more than one form in the same book or short story. In general, the many parodies of Sherlock Holmes will be represented only by the more striking efforts, so the books and stories quoted will not, and cannot, reach the total in this category—such a catalogue would be a mere dictionary of parody rather than a survey of a trend.

Adrian Alington's 1939 book *The Amazing Test Match Crime* tells of surrealistic, parodic, and hilarious attempts to ruin the final test against Australia. The English captain is Norman Blood, the Australian Lethbridge (Bradman?), one bowler is Imp Bumper, two others are named Hugh and Crigh. There are parodies of Kipling and G. K. Chesterton, references to Deen Crunch (Dean Inge?), Red Queen cigarette cards (cf. Black Cat), Riviera writer N. Julius Guggleheim (E. Phillips Oppenheim), and dramatist R. B. Parsley writing a letter about time (J. B. Priestley). It is written in the historic present like Damon Runyon; there are attempts to kidnap Blood and to shoot the field from an airplane advertising products. The headings range from "Who Dies if England Lives Markley" and "Dogged Does It Gordon" to "I Am the Captain of My Soul Philpotts," and the gang of bad men rejoice in such names as Sawn-off Carlo and Ralph the Disappointment. Other characters are ex-cricketers S. P. Q. Marshbanks, R.S.V.P. Ratstock and Q. E. D. Majoribanks. Loamshire (the mythical county popular in cricket stories) is mentioned, the county shaped like an egg, and the red-and-white belt with the snake-shaped buckle was worn by every schoolboy and cricketer in the 1930s.

Alex Atkinson, author of the mystery *Exit Charlie,* a reference to theatre crime and parlance, was a popular *Punch* contributor, in the 1956 anthology of which was reprinted his "Chapter the

Last—Merriman Explains." The monocled, clownish Merriman is a parody of Carr's Merrivale, and the tale is very witty, full of crazy situations like Humphrey's repeated remarks, hitting Eleanor on the head, bringing down the chandelier, CI Rodd sleeping through it all, Humphrey throwing a lawn mower at Merriman, and a reference to 104 ways "of getting into a room with no doors on the inside and no windows on the outside."

In 1972 Michael Angelo Avallone, Jr., already mentioned as appearing in E. D. Hoch's *The Shattered Raven,* wrote *Shoot It Again, Sam,* a reference to the line allegedly but incorrectly credited to Humphrey Bogart as spoken to his pianist in the bar in the film *Casablanca* (later parodied in other films). He started each chapter with a line in Hollywood dialogue, and divided the text into two "books," each prefaced with a page of such dialogue. The president orders his series detective Ed Noon to accompany the body of a Hollywood hero, Dan David (obviously a parody on John Wayne), the son (Peter Fonda), and a former wife (Lauren Bacall), across the USA. In California the body sits up, Noon is captured by Chinese agents to replay *The Manchurian Candidate* (the famous novel and film), the surrounding brainwashers all made up to resemble Clark Gable, James Cagney, Peter Lorre, etc., to make him think he is Bogart playing Sam Spade; he is offered poisoned shoes, as featured in Ian Fleming's *From Russia with Love* (1964) so that he might later kick the American president to death. There is a strong element of surrealism in this book.

George Baxt can write both parody and pastiche, but this parody is a book written in 1968: *Topsy and Evil,* a reference to Topsy and Eva in *Uncle Tom's Cabin.* Characters are led by a black detective, dramatically named Satan Stagg (following the tradition, mentioned already, of two-syllable given names and one-syllable surnames), Topsy Alcott, with four girls described as her "daughters," Guru Raskalnikov (shades of Russian literature), a mention of the real-life financier Serge Rubinstein, and a mystery written in code on velvet wallpaper. Then comes a book, *In Cold Water* (presumably in opposition to *In Cold Blood*), by Peter and Robert Mouling, sons of Madeleine Cartier, a former Shirley Temple–like star, mentions of dancer Bojangles Robinson and film actor Hardy Kruger, followed by a mysterious cabaret star Ocelot and "her" connection with missing Pharaoh Love. There are further strange players, including Igor Isogul from Transylvania (with a reception where were served Bloody Marys and blood sausages), the murdered Sweet Harriet Dimple (perhaps a glancing memory of Bette Davis films) and Wera Shrdlu (a reference to the keys on a typewriter), Tara's Club of New York, Tramb Nicolu with dyed persimmon hair (from the Native American date plum tree?), and Flora Fleur in her sixties with her daughter Fauna, fourteen years younger—leading to the important quote, reminiscent of Orson Welles to "Rosebud," which is not what it ever seemed. It could be said that many of these are in-jokes, but the average reader should follow the literary names, the real-life personages, and the satirical touches right up to the dramatic finale. Baxt will be considered further in the section on pastiche.

E. C. Bentley (1875–1956) is a name famous in detective fiction, in humor, and in literature and criticism generally. Edmund Clerihew was the inventor of the "clerihew" poem, a past president of the Detection Club, following his friend G. K. Chesterton, author of *Trent's Last Case* (1913), the parody that became a classic instead, and two other books about Philip Trent, and was both editor and humorist as well. Bentley slyly introduces a character named Clerihew in one book; he is a know-all wine merchant who is an authority on wine corks. In the book *Parody Party* (1936), with illustrations by Nicholas Bentley, edited by Leonard Russell, appeared "Greedy Night," later reproduced in *The Faber Book of Parody* (1984), edited by Simon Brett, chair of the CWA (1986/87), who first drew my attention to it. This is a parody on Dorothy L. Sayers's *Gaudy Night* (1935), the Lord Peter Wimsey novel set in a women's Oxford college, a "gaudy" being a festival. Bentley's parody is witty, clever, and well constructed to underline the gentle absurdity—for example, the references to the Sotheby's auction sale, to furniture polish and Vichy water for breakfast, to the bishop of Glastonbury (a sacred hill in the West Country but not supporting a bishop), and his story of Topsy, his favorite sister. The Dermot bird, seemingly uninjured but the victim of foul play; Professor Bill Mixer, Spoopendyke Professor of Egyptology; the Fendlair motorcar; and Janus College (so called perhaps because it faced both ways), where there is a Front Quad, the Acuinas Club in the Senior Common Room, the Square leading to the Quad, then on to the Pateshull Quad. The Dermot bird proves to have died from "strong poison" (the title of the 1930 Sayers novel introducing Harriet Vane). We might expect some literary touches of humor, and true enough there is the remark, "Take the nasty breakfast away, I don't want any breakfast today," parodying Hilaire Belloc, and even a clerihew: "Lord Peter Wimsey may look a little flimsy, but he's simply sublime when nosing out a crime."

Incidentally, *Parody Party* has two other parodies nearly but not quite in our field, in Francis Iles's "Close Season in Polchester," guying Sir Hugh Walpole; and J. B. Morton (Beachcomber, the famous *Daily Express* humorist) with his John Buchan parody, "The Queen of Manikoe."

Anthony Berkeley (or Francis Iles) has already been considered in more detail over his classic mass parody *The Poisoned Chocolates Case,* but he did write a book parodying two elegant detectives: Dr. Reggie Fortune of H. C. Bailey (1878–1961), and Margery Allingham's Albert Campion, in *Top Story Murder* (1931). A year later he wrote *Murder in the Basement.* This last title starts with a body in the cellar and ends with a very ingenious answer.

A short but witty parody by Margaret Birns was published in *Murder Ink,* that most useful book of reference on all aspects of detective story writing and reading. Titled the "Maltese Duck Caper; or, Wild Goose Chase," it is a Mike Wrench (cf. Hammer) mystery "translated from the vernacular," all the slang carefully and overcarefully transcribed into hilarious academic English. It tells of Velma Wonderly (a Chandler touch, as well as Hammett), Fosco (Collins's villain in *The Woman in White*) with his gunsel Wilmer and their search for the statuette, a Maltese duck. Hammett's great Sam Spade story had been parodied on television, as well as being filmed three times.

In 1985 John Blumenthal wrote *The Case of the Hardboiled Dicks,* a parody involving New York private investigator Mac Slade, and the boiling of the sons of Mike Hammer and Philip Marlowe.

Jon L. Breen has already been discussed in the first chapter and will be considered in depth for his short stories in the section on mass parody, but he has written full-length detective novels, and the first was indeed a parody: *Listen for the Click* (1983; U.K. title, *Vicar's Roses* [1984]). It follows the classic formula but contains many subtle touches all through. Early on comes a mention of a John Rhode story in large print, and a quotation from Raymond Chandler's *Simple Art of Murder* on taking murder out of the vicar's rose garden. Stan Digby in downtown Los Angeles gets "an agreeable Archer-Marlowe feeling," detective Gaston Miles (two-syllable and one-syllable again) is Elton Gabriel Maxwell when unmasked as an actor. There is a description of a library full of detective stories, references to Sherlock Holmes, to "ghosts of Warren William, Basil Rathbone and Warner Oland," "Chandler Macdonald styled," the "Doyle or Van Dine Line" and the "Charlie Chan bit," and finally a summation, confrontation, and unmasking in the library. His detective is a racing commentator, and in his next book, *Triple Crown* (1985), the clues to the murders are based on various interpretations of esoteric horse-racing lore, but with a classic puzzle.

Jimmy Breslin wrote an obviously funny book, *The Gang That Couldn't Shoot Straight* (1969), that was later filmed. Ernest Mandel, in a Marxist analysis *Delightful Murder,* that seems to try to prove the detective story a bourgeois trait, refers to it as "a comic parody [that] should also be mentioned" under a list of anti-Mafia stories described as of a "pulp magazine type." Breslin's book has authentic touches of gang bosses meeting in restaurants, cars mined with bombs, plus many funny events. For example, a contract hit man is hired to administer knockout drops to huge black-clad gangster bodyguards at the restaurants; he gives them potent laxatives which he forces them to drink at gunpoint before casually rushing off to catch his train, leaving them indeed hors de combat on the men's room stairs. Meanwhile the fish truck used to kidnap the gangster is held up by a militant woman traffic warden, and aspiring gangster Kid "Sally" Palumbo loads his gun with the wrong ammunition. Father of a New York Mafia family, Anthony Pastrumo, Sr., known as Baccala, gets his wife to start his car each morning in case it is mined. A six-day cycle race, a romance, buying a young lion that kills one gangster, wrong disguises, a dwarf—all make a farcical story, with many statements of fact, and familiar sounding names (Palumbo/Columbo). It was made into an MGM film with Jerry Orbach, Leigh Taylor-Young, Jo Van Fleet, and Lionel Stander, with screenplay by Waldo Salt. Based on the Gallo gang war with the Profaci family, Joey Gallo is the fictional Kid Sally Palumbo. It was filmed near their President Street base, with Armando the Dwarf and the lion mascot. Joey Gallo became friendly with Jerry Orbach and his wife, Martha, so they spent Gallo's forty-third birthday party with the Orbachs, comedian David Steinberg and a girlfriend, and famed columnist Earl Wilson and his secretary at the Copacabana nightclub. At 4:00 A.M., April 7, 1972, Gallo was killed by a .38 caliber pistol near the door at Umberto's Clam House, in Chinatown–Little Italy, in traditional style.

Simon Brett's anthology has been mentioned. His own detective stories usually involve a hard-drinking, womanizing, not-too-successful actor named Charles Paris, and the locales of theatres, television studios, and festivals are always accurate, as the author was for a decade a BBC radio producer and has also been a television director, playwright, and stage director. Asked if he himself ever indulged in parody, he told me of one book intriguingly titled *Situation Tragedy*. It recounts a ruthless but sweet actress making her comeback after retirement, with her apparently harmless ex-actor husband, in a television play for West End Television, WET House, Lisson Grove. Her signature tune had been "I Dream of Dancing in Shimmering Stars," signifying a background of musicals. There are several murders among the television team, and Paris finds each is based on a murder in books by an unknown author. By the time he discovers who among the team is the author, he has not realized the book chosen for his own murder—but at the last minute he survives, to find a double death by the murderer again based on his own book. Brett has a very keen eye for show business and its characters, so much so that in one book two homosexual actors-manqués-turned-restaurateurs were recognized—as two different pairs. In *Situation Tragedy,* for example, when Paris is nearly killed by being pushed off the bleachers (seats for a television audience) and falls on striking stagehands, they immediately discuss whether they have grounds for damages for being involved, not for working but playing cards behind the scenes—and stop groaning when they haven't.

This 1983 book has some interesting touches, including the accidents; the murders of a personal assistant, scriptwriter, director (not mentioned in the blurb), and floor manager; the dame's dog being named Cocky after the late Charles B. Cochran, known as Cocky, famous for creating C. B. Cochran's Young Ladies, a great draw in many excellent West End shows; the Hampstead crime book collector Stanley Harvey, who never reads his purchases; and the chief clue, the vanity publisher—known as R. Q. Wilberforce—whose published books were titled *Death Takes a Tumble, Death Takes the Wrong Turning, Death Takes a Drive, Death Takes a Stand, Death Takes a Shortcut, Death Takes a Back Seat,* and the manuscript of *Death Takes the Honourable Course*—the titles which show Paris how each murder is being committed and how, to avoid discovery and disgrace for the fated pair, the car is deliberately driven to a planned clifftop accident.

Michael Butterworth comes into both parody and pastiche, and an example of the former is his 1974 *The Man in the Sopwith Camel.* Ernest Kitteridge is a nondescript bank clerk who indulges his Walter Mitty fantasies at night or when he switches off during the day by imagining himself at the controls of a Sopwith Camel, one of the most popular and efficient fighter airplanes for Britain in World War I, and one of the most sought-after to construct by airplane modelers between the two wars. On a night out with the newly promoted manager Norman Braithwaite on his last day, Kitteridge finds Braithwaite dead in the house of prostitute Gladys Grubb. After being made to bury the body, he assumes his identity as manager in Cambridge, desperately seeking to avoid being found out, aided by Gladys, while they try to rob a bank of £30,000. After various coarse adventures they succeed in Ireland, flee to America, get involved in more picaresque situations, ranging from wrong suitcases to a runaway morticians conference. Gladys is accidentally decapitated, and Kitteridge becomes a South Seas–type beachcomber, only to lose the money as hut wallpaper, before realizing his new happiness has driven the Sopwith Camel and its aerial dogfights away for good. Described as a black comedy, it is not a whodunnit; it is the small man parodying a criminal or war ace in humorous or bungling ways, akin to pure (or impure) comedy crime stories, poles apart from the Westlakes, Williamses, or Latimers. As Inspector Cockrill says in the film of Christianna Brand's *Green for Danger,* as with music hall and laughing gas, it is the impurities therein that make you laugh.

When *Murder, Mystery and Mayhem* was published by Collins in 1988, the author, Jennifer Carnell, was aged just sixteen. Described perhaps as a Miss Marple–type mystery spoof with a general murdered, or by the publishers as "this parody of an Agatha Christie murder mystery" (and they also publish Christie, with the undertaking never to let any title go out of print), this book can be compared with the latter's book *Ten Little Niggers,* filmed under all sorts of titles, in that the heroine, Esmeralda Fry, sets out from Felston in Sussex to spend New Year's Eve 1986/87 at the Waddington Castle Hotel, after the death of her father (Waddington sells board games like *Cluedo*). There are ten guests in the snowbound castle, with the telephone cut off, of course—a general, a woman, a journalist, his glamorous wife, a dotty vicar, a French onionseller, a maid, a butler, a porter, and Esmeralda. There are eight murders, and a happy ending; the style is reminiscent of Daisy Ashford's wonderful *The Young Visiters* (*sic*), the gothic air recalls *The Cat and the Canary*, and there is even the odd P. G. Wodehouse phrase.

We have already seen Raymond Chandler commenting satirically on crime writing, and he has another parodic touch in *The Lady in the Lake,* with a mysterious female character known as Chrystal Kingsley at one point, shown in the cast list as "Ellay Mort," the French *elle est morte* meaning "she is dead," or "she has died." Oddly enough, in *The Notebooks of Raymond Chandler* (1976), is a parody by him, and as there are so many parodies of him, perhaps this is the right place to note it. "Beer in the Sergeant-Major's Hat; or, The Sun Also Sneezes" parodies Ernest Hemingway's *The Sun Also Rises*. Written on August 7, 1932, it tells of jaded Hank cleaning his teeth gloomily, spreading toothpaste over upper lip (like an ambassador), eyebrows, and elsewhere; swallowing hard liquor, then falling asleep with his head on the cat (who licks off the toothpaste from his eyebrows), muttering, "She shouldn't have done it." In *Farewell, My Lovely* (1940) there are various continual gags about Hemingway, of whose talent Marlowe professes ignorance, and in his intriguing *The Simple Art of Murder* (1950) Chandler comments, "Hemingway says somewhere that the good writer competes only with the dead." By coincidence, it was Simon Brett who pointed out the cricket report in the *Times* in June 1986 by Miles Kington as a parody of Chandler's style; the following week his cricket report was à la Alice in Wonderland. Brett himself set a quiz at the CWA Annual Conference at Norwich, Norfolk, in October 1985, in which the answers made up the name of Raymond Chandler, and a report had to be written as a parody of him.

In his survey of clubland and well-educated heroes on both sides of the law, *The Durable Desperadoes* (1973), William Vivian Butler draws attention to a remarkable short story by Leslie

Charteris in his *Saint Errant* (1949). His hero, the Saint, vacationing in a mountain cabin, meets a typical film cast, including a mysterious young man, a villain who talks in the buttery voice of the actor Sydney Greenstreet (*The Maltese Falcon*, Count Fosco in *The Woman in White*) and is so addressed by the Saint—then the Saint is shot dead. He wakes up to find it is all a dream, until he makes inquiries about the young man, to discover it might be something psychic or time-warped. This is a very unusual story from Charteris, and one of those he wrote with hidden depths; the killing of a hero proving to be a dream sequence has been used in some Hollywood films, notably one with Robert Cummings.

The books of G. K. Chesteron (1874–1936) are frequently embellished with a philosophical-cum-religious-cum-occult touch, noticeable in the Father Brown stories, *The Man Who Was Thursday* (1908), an allegorical detective novel, the fantastic *The Napoleon of Notting Hill,* and the surrealistic first mystery in *The Club of Queer Trades.* In this 1905 book of short stories of unheard-of occupations (like the judge who invented a new alphabet language) is that accurate and delightful question of what you would think if you saw a public figure in the fountains of Trafalgar Square, in London's West End. A man like Lord Baden-Powell, British army hero and founder of the Boy Scouts, might do it for a dare; a judge, for example, might have gone mad.

It is just this differentiation in a book of four short stories published in 1930, *Four Faultless Felons,* which turns upside down the normal detective story. The four are "The Moderate Murderer," "The Honest Quack," "The Ecstatic Thief," and "The Loyal Traitor," each of whom tells his story to pressman Asa Lee Pinion of the *Chicago Comet* (an atmospheric name for a journalist—a sheltered wing, perhaps). Each has used his crime to benefit others, according to his own light—only the Loyal Traitor riding somewhat roughshod over others. As they explain, "The Truth is we have devoted ourselves to a new sort of detective story—or detective service if you like. We do not hunt for crimes but for concealed virtues." They refer to modern quotations as to, say, a painter trying to paint with both hands. In the first story, a tutor shoots to wound the governor of a colony to save him from being assassinated. Finally they make the bemused young American a member, because he also is misunderstood. There are echoes of the strange logic of *The Club of Queer Trades* and its members, and paradoxical morality, based on the religious principles activating Father Brown himself.

In her autobiography, Agatha Christie, in chapter 11 of part 9, the Queen of Crime Writers mentions writing (about 1930) *Partners in Crime,* a series of short stories, as her only effort in parody. Indeed, in her introduction to her second series of *Great Short Stories of Detection, Mystery and Horror* (1931), Dorothy L. Sayers commented: "In *Partners in Crime,* the same author has pleasantly burlesqued the detective-story, with results that are uniformly delightful if one refuses to be put off by the perpetual brightness of Tommy and Tuppence. Experiments like these are all to the good." We shall deal with this interesting and amusing book in the section on mass parody, but here we can perhaps look at another popular title, dating from 1942, *The Body in the Library.* In the foreword Christie refers to "certain clichés": the "body in the library for the detective story . . . highly orthodox and conventional library . . . wildly improbable and highly sensational body," and to having watched an unusual group of people in a south coast luxury hotel, identified as the Imperial Torquay. From this she built up a typically ingenious and surprising murder mystery, with first a garishly dressed body of a young woman in Colonel Bantry's stately home, followed it with another and with the secret-marriage idea she has used elsewhere to make a dramatic denouement.

Throughout the author has her characters make sly references to detective stories. Colonel Bantry chides his wife with, "It's that detective story you were reading—*The Clue of the Broken Match.* You know—Lord Edgbaston finds a beautiful blonde on the library hearthrug. Bodies are always being found in libraries in books." When Mrs. Bantry has called in her old friend Miss Jane Marple, she complains to her, "I mean, I thought they only happened in books." Energetic young sleuth Peter Carmody says, "Making fun of the police is very old-fashioned." (Raymond Chandler agreed with that comment, as we have seen.) Later Peter asks, "Do you like detective stories? I do. I read them all, and I've got autographs from Dorothy Sayers and Agatha Christie and Dickson Carr and H. C. Bailey." Miss Marple comments, "Of course, it was all very confusing, her being found in Colonel Bantry's library, altogether too like a book to be *true.*"

For a comment on this book we can turn to Professor Mary S.

Weinkauf's article "*Miss Jane Marple and Ageing in Literature*" in the issue of *Clues* (Spring 1980) devoted to the genre. "*The Body in the Library* is a particularly good example of Miss Marple's technique of associating previous episodes and people with the murders at hand. She even refuses to tell her friend who did the crime because she knows she will tell, just as she foreknew that Miss Partridge could embezzle the Red Cross funds."

Cyril Connolly was one of England's most distinguished literary critics, editors, and essayists, and in *Previous Convictions* he wrote a devastating parody on the James Bond saga, "Bond Strikes Camp," in which his Secret Service boss M sends him in drag to the Kitchener Club, where he meets the secretary Lolita Ponsonby (who is lesbian), and finally General Apraxin, who makes violent passes at him and who proves to be M himself in disguise. (Apraxia is the loss, due to brain injury, of the ability to manipulate objects.) Minor satirical touches include Bond's normal visit to the department to fit him up with not only the usual knives and guns but a woman's wardrobe, and Bond's final brush with an amorous taxidriver. Perhaps we can compare this with the Nick Carter story in which an American secret agent is fitted with a gun that fires when her pants are removed, and a BBC-TV parody by the two British comedians Ronnie Barker and Ronnie Corbett—"The Two Ronnies"—of the Roaring Twenties when Corbett in the James Cagney role enters the speakeasy as a chorus girl with two guns firing through "her" brassiere. There have been many parodies on Bond and his style, at some of which we shall be looking, but meanwhile we can observe en passant *Vengeance Is Black,* in which the hero is Dr. James Bond, an ornithologist and an unwilling spy.

We have already considered Edmund Crispin and his detective the erudite Professor Gervase Fen's identity and comments, and we will briefly reconsider *Love Lies Bleeding* because many of the characters are named after great church musicians and composers, including Stanford, Parry, Taverner, Tye, and Boyce, and beause of a disguised interview in the plot with a great English musician, either Vaughan Williams or Elgar.

Gwendoline Butler's introduction to Professor Lord Strang over this query brought the interesting answer from Lord Strang, who has been, inter alia, professor of philosophy at Newcastle University, and who now has retired to France, that Bruce Montgomery (Edmund Crispin) "seldom spoke of, or listened to, V.W. or Britten, in my experience," leaving Elgar, or more likely Walton, as the top choice, a name with which Gwendoline Butler agreed. On the telephone to Peter Oldham, mentioned earlier, at Lord Strang's suggestion, he thought the composer was an amalgam of Wagner, Rubbra, Vaughan Williams, and Montgomery himself.

Crispin's *The Long Divorce* (1951) is dedicated "To Pat and Colin Strang," and this mystery which starts on Friday, June 2, 1950, had Fen masquerading as a Mr. Datchery, recognized by one or two Dickens-reading characters only; the story involves a murder, suicide, and poison pen letters, has Fen's deductions and a cast list of strange names: Inspector Casby (from *Little Dorrit*, perhaps), PC Burns (Mark Twain's White Elephant Police Captain?), Mrs. Flack (a gossip in a 1961 book), Penny Polt and a cat named Lavender, which might recall Ruth Rolt and Lavender from Pinero's 1881 *Sweet Lavender*. The title comes from Shakespeare and Fletcher's *Henry VIII*, and refers to the murder weapon. I wrote to Mrs. Montgomery, widow of the author and herself a member of the CWA, but she did not reply and died some months later.

Marcel d'Agneau is the nom de plume of a writer living partly in Monte Carlo, and who wrote *Eeny Meeny Miny Mole* in 1980, a parody of *Tinker, Tailor, Soldier, Spy* (1974) and of author John Le Carré as well as of Len Deighton. The retired chief of the section is Grimly (as opposed to George Smiley, of course), with his sex-mad mother, Lady Grimly, Peter Hallam and his pedophilic friend Wendy, and the Russian Captain Crewk (Captain Hook with a crook) join references to Lily Tiger, Slightly, Croc, the Russian Tinkabelle (a Peter Pan-tomime), a sex change for the doctor, and eleven spies ousted with eleven more to follow. The department moves to Putney (a suburb in southwest London); the boss is known as the Stationmaster (the original title for the head of an individual railway station); there is an account of the Berlin Wall being smashed by the Russians; and Grimly gives a long explanation while in a coma—all exaggerated ad absurdum—but in all seriousness, the name d'Agneau, the French for "lamb," could be a pun on the first spy assignment.

In 1981 d'Agneau wrote *The Curse of the Nibelung,* the foreword signed as from Monte Carlo and London, and which was yet another Holmes pastiche. Lord Holmes of Baker Street, aged eighty-three, and Sir John Watson, eighty-seven, back at 221b, are called on, in 1939, by Winston Churchill, as First Lord of the admiralty, to visit Nuremberg's Wagner Festival, with an assistant, to investigate Dr. Laubscher's "chocolate." Active adventures, a disguised chocolate factory making Messerschmitt rocket planes, the voice of Moriarty as the German newscaster, and Holmes solving a murder at the Christmas house party make up an interesting story, embellished by a Red-Headed League of Irishmen radio-bicycling through France and coming to the rescue. There is even a footnote to another Holmes pastiche.

One humorous touch is using motor-propelled bathchairs to save them from drowning after shipwreck in the Channel. At the house party a German makes a denigratory remark about Poirot; Watson's comment is, "Poirot is quite impossible, Holmes, an upstart, uses your methods and claims them as his. Same with Father Brown, plagiarists all. There are so many who set themselves up as consulting detectives these days, bounders all."

We come now to that great English writer Charles Dickens—stage director, actor, journalist, editor, lecturer, who turned to the theatre more as his marriage broke down. He and Wilkie Collins admired each other's styles so much that they imitated them, hence Dickens's writing *The Mystery of Edwin Drood* at the time of his death. It has been noted that many of the social evils of which he wrote had already by then been corrected, or were in process thereof. He admired the police so much that he wrote about them frequently, sometimes, as we have noted, under assumed names—in fact, his eulogistic article about the members of the detective squad visiting his office was incorrect in that there were at that time more members in that department. There are at least two classic novels in which there is an element of parody. The first is *Bleak House* (1852), in which he created Inspector Bucket of the Detective, based on Inspector Field, and of course many other books have crimes, murders, constables, watchmen, or bailiffs mentioned. The present author gave a lecture, "Dickens and the Detectives," at the Annual Dickens Festival at Rochester, Kent, in 1983, afterward reprinted and summarized in the *Poisoned Pen,* listing these and comparing them with actual crimes and police activities. The element of parody is in his own style for the first thirty-two chapters in the third person, then of Esther in the first person for thirty-three chapters. We have already seen

Dickens used the Wainwright murders as the basis for *Hunted Down,* and similarly he used the real life murderer Mrs. Manning, a Frenchwoman, as the model of his murderer Hortense in this book. He attended the public hangings of the Mannings, and wrote a letter to the *Times* (though not on the date quoted in Forster's *Life of Dickens*) protesting against the public behavior at the hanging. Incidentally, it was noted that Manning's body seemed shrunken after hanging, whereas his wife's did not, but it was disclosed that she had been hanged in her stays, in a black satin dress, and black satin went out of fashion for twenty years thereafter. The cemetery Tom Tiddler's Ground was where now the office blocks of Kingsway and Aldwych stand in the west central business district of London.

His early parody came in *Oliver Twist* (1837–39), in chapter 13, where he introduces two Bow Street Runners, the forerunners of the new regular London police forces. Deliberately named Blathers and Duff, they produce differing but incorrect theories of the burglary apparently involving one Lankey Chickweed (chickweed is a weed eaten by fowl and caged birds). "Jacob's Island" and the Nancy Steps by London Bridge still exist. Ian Busby in *Bloodhounds of Heaven* (1976) has commented on Dickens's sparse use of detectives in his earlier books, adding: "Blathers and Duff, the Bow Street runners called to investigate Sikes' attempted burglary of the Maylies' house in *Oliver Twist,* are present for only a few pages of the action and are used simply to provide a comic interlude."

Friedrich Durrenmatt (1921–1990), a Swiss playwright, critic, artist, and author, can be considered here, from his acknowledged relation to parody and to Mandel's reference to one of his fictional detectives. There are four particular detective stories said to have a Kafkaesque quality. *The Judge and His Hangman,* first published in 1952 as *Der Richter und sein Henker,* refers to a first English edition by Jonathan Cape in 1954, although the present writer's copy is a Herbert Jenkins issue in that year. Inspector Barlach of Bern is in charge of the inquiry into the murder of one of his detectives, Schmid, and his framing by using another detective of the criminal he has sought for forty years. The references to judge and hangman are to him, not to the courts. *The Quarry* first appeared in 1953 and refers to November 1948; Barlach is now a commissioner, still seriously ill, and pursuing a criminal doctor in his Zurich clinic. Again the detective story is used as an allegory. *A Dangerous Game* (1956) has no detective in the story of the sales manager caught in a mock trial by retired lawyers. *The Pledge* (1958) is in the form of a retired Zurich police chief and federal deputy recounting to the narrator, who had just lectured on "the art of writing detective stories" in Chur, the account of his brilliant chief officer who wastes life and career trying to catch a child killer, whose identity is later casually given the chief by a dying aristocrat. In this story the chief comments to the narrator on the "fraud" in detective stories: "You build your plots up logically, like a chess game; here the criminal, here the victim, here the accomplice, here the mastermind. The detective need only know the rules and play the game over, and he has the criminal trapped, has won a victory for justice, ignoring 'chance' which ironically or paradoxically affects logic and scientific deduction."

In 1980 was written in Italian a novel that was to become a best-seller in many countries—*Il Nome della Rosa* (*The Name of the Rose*), by Umberto Eco. It follows the formula of the writer finding a book, based on a manuscript of centuries earlier, and the simple story is of an inquiry into crimes in a monastery by a specially appointed visiting brother; more crimes are discovered; a young brother acts as a gullible and suitably amazed "Watson"; and a dramatic conflagration is the finale. The book is actually a subtle study in parody, as borne out by the comments of critics and of the author himself. For example, the visiting brother is, significantly, William of Baskerville. Described by Eco, he has "perhaps seen fifty springs . . . His energy seemed inexhaustible . . . he moved backwards in moments of inertia, and I watched him lie for hours on my pallet in my cell . . . and I would have suspected he was in the power of some vegetal substance capable of reproducing visions." Julian Symons, in *Bloody Murder,* commenting on the Italian detective story wrote: "The detective William of Baskerville . . . owes something to Conan Doyle, in appearance and conversation as well as in name, but the book's elaborate periphrastical jokiness is more reminiscent of Borges, Nabokov, even of Baron Corvo." Tani, who has also dealt with the writers Symons lists, refers in his summing-up of this book in *The Doomed Detective* to "a somehow parodic protodetective," and when dealing with the riddle of the labyrinth in the library, solved by William, says it "is clearly a Borgesian parody," that the blind monk Jorge is a "parody of his illustrious namesake, Jorge Luis Borges, blind creator of erudite mysteries," and thinks the end of the book parallels a James Bond film finale. Some American editions of the book have the labyrinth on the cover in the same shape as the library itself (a maze or labyrinth often equals a detective problem), and it has been pointed out the murders are not by one man, but really in an apocryphal order. Eco himself wrote an article in *Encounter* magazine (no. 374, April 1985), entitled "Reflections on *The Name of the Rose,*" before his next book appeared. In it he said, "And since I wanted you to feel as pleasurable the one thing that frightens us—namely, the metaphysical shudder—I had only to choose (from among the model plots) the most metaphysical and philosophical: the detective novel." He has a subsection—"The Detective Metaphysical"—and in this he comments: "It is no accident that the book starts out as a mystery (and continues to deceive the ingenious reader until the end, so the ingenious reader may not even realise that this is a mystery in which very little is discovered and the detective is defeated). I believe people like thrillers not because there are corpses or because there is a final celebratory triumph of order (intellectual, social, legal, and moral) over the disorder of evil. The fact is that the crime novel represents a kind of conjecture, pure and simple."

Interesting is his use of "thrillers" and his denial of the Protestant ethos as to right over wrong, particularly when so many surveys have been taken as to the people who read crime, and why. (Interesting, too, in that his detective novel not only became required reading socially, but turned the genus into the most esoteric atmosphere—metaphysical, religious, psychological—almost as a form of parable, and first of all in Italian, not English.) The novel is long, convincing in its background, and even has a plan of the monastery at the beginning, as used to be the fashion. We shall see that crime in historic monastic circles is not unknown when we come to the titles in the pastiche section, and great care has to be taken by the authors to keep the social and scientific details from being anachronistic. A neat touch is when William puts on his spectacles, and gets a brother to make him a new pair, not the tubes of Samuel Pepys but a simple pair, almost as Galileo might have prescribed.

The funnies have produced various detectives whose exploits have spanned the years, and one with a distinct element of parody is Will Eisner's Spirit, which started in 1944, and was reissued in 1966 by Harvey Comics. The disembodied hero, who lives in a cemetery, is approached, for example, by an inventor who advises him that as Bond has bombs and Fink a cigar lighter, he should adopt his inventions, which compare with those many ingenious devices thought up by that secret British government department during World War II for secret agents. The Spirit casually flattens the inventor with his fist, leaving the latter trying to sell his inventions to UNK, a parallel to the UN or to the later "Man from UNCLE."

A remarkable parody occurred in the syndicated comic strip *Calvin and Hobbes* by Bill Watterson, from Monday, February 25, to Saturday, March 2, 1991. Calvin is the wicked, self-centered, but occasionally lovable, small boy with his familiar, Hobbes, a stuffed tiger that to him, of course, is alive. After playing baseball indoors and smashing a vase, Calvin goes into one of his Walter Mitty states: "I'm Tracer Bullet. I'm a professional snoop . . . Snooping pays the bills, though. Especially Bill, my bookie, and Bill, my probation officer." In Marlowesque wisecracks and reactions, he deals with a hysterical, tall brunette (his mother), her hired goon (his father), figures out "who trashed the dame's living room," but as the culprit was his buddy he closes the case in a very crisp, well-written, and well-drawn episode.

Something slightly different from the funnies was journalist Christopher Stevens's 1991 booklet, which he published himself, *In Black and White,* a thirty-two-page imitation tabloid of sex and murder, with a lesbian policewoman, and consisting of various stories of 350 words, which can be read in any order. His purpose was to get his book published as a first effort at a reasonable price (£1.95) in this unusual format to attract bookshops. Another variant was the 1930s *Bowery Murder* by W. K. Smith, written in the form of newspaper articles interspersed with notes. We shall consider below the dossier, three-dimensional format. There have been magazines devoted to a case, with all its reports, interviews, and photographs, the solution concealed at the end.

Marian Babson thought that one book might have given the original concept to the introduction of James Bond in *Casino Royale* in 1953. This was *The Man with the Scarlet Skull* by Gwyn Evans, published in the 1930s (no date of publication, although January 1935 is mentioned in the text). The hero is Quentin Ellery

Drex, known as QED, an ex–naval officer and scientist, living in Room 999 of the Cliffstone Hotel, on the London Embankment, with his own autogiro, gyroplane *Silver Hawk,* radio intercom, laboratory, viewing panels to every room in the hotel; he is Secret Service Agent 13, with a robot Alpha. The skull mark came from a fight with the tongs. QED stands for *quod erat demonstrandum,* or "that which was to have been proven," as the book implies. Agent 13 compares with Bond 007 (which Roger Bell has pointed out would have been known to Ian Fleming as the spy number of Elizabethan scientist John Dee). The Cliffstone Hotel is obviously the famous Savoy, which appears under various names in literature. E. Phillips Oppenheim (1866–1946) called it the Milan in his short stories "A Pulpit in the Grillroom" (1938) and "The Milan Grillroom" (1941), a reference to the maître d'hôtel's elevated chair and desk, and Arnold Bennett (1847–1931) had it in mind for his *The Grand Babylon Hotel.* Crime fighters with either apparently unlimited wealth or great scientific adjuncts were also popular in British comics and schoolboy magazines, and in the form of Batman, for example, in American funnies, films, and television. Flash Gordon could be a later comparison.

Paul W. Fairman wrote a short story in *EQMM* (no. 88, May 1960) titled "Wally the Watchful Eye." The editorial headnote was a reference to Ellis Parker Butler's creation of Philo Gubb, the correspondence school sleuth. Fairman's amusing seven-page tale consists of ten letters passing between John Hayden, president of the grandly named but very modest Watchful Eye Detective School, of the Parker Building, New York City (actually his furnished room at 121 Sixth Avenue), and Walter A. Watts of Lettyville, New York. The latter is enthusiastically taking the six lessons from the school, paying tardily therefor, while explaining how helpful they are in his attempts to prove his stingy grocer employer, Tom Barton, to be guilty of his wife Martha's "suicide" when he was out of town in Boston for two days. As Johnny Hayden gets hysterically anxious, he learns from Wally that his proof came from his girlfriend checking Barton's gas bills to show him too mean to let gas escape for the two days—which should give the school a great advertising point.

Andrew J. Fennedy wrote in 1977 a novel with the intriguing title *The Man with Bogart's Face,* dedicated to Hammett, Chandler, Bogart, Powell, and Tierney, the authors and film actors famous for the hard-boiled detectives, "Bogart" meaning Humphrey Bogart, who portrayed both Sam Spade and Philip Marlowe so brilliantly on screen. The book's characters include Mustafa Hakim, a Zachary Scott type; Zebra, a Sydney Greenstreet type; the search for the Eyes of Alexander sapphires, with Sam Marlowe, private investigator: "I Don't Sleep" (cf. Pinkerton's eye motif, and the nickname for PI, private investigator, as a private eye), with a second-story office, two rooms (toilet and kitchen) in the Larchmont 500 block near the corner of Larchmont and Beverley. Marlowe has changed his name by deed poll, and has had the necessary facial plastic surgery; he also buys a Luger and a derringer. There is a description of missing studios; a film man named Horst Borsht is killed; an assortment of crooks; a heroine; chases; and a dramatic finale aboard a yacht, with complicated explanations. The *Poisoned Pen* (Spring 1984 issue) referred to his writing and producing a 1980 film version of *Sam Marlowe, Private Eye*. A parody like this, well written and with plenty of authentic detail, needs a basic knowledge of crime books and films to appreciate the in-jokes.

Fennedy was the producer and author of the screenplay of the 1970 John Wayne film *Chisum,* the tale of a cattle baron in 1878 New Mexico calling in Billy the Kid to help his fight against crooked land-grabbers.

Elizabeth Ferrars, already mentioned above for her latest sleuth, the Professor, in a letter in September 1985 said she had written a short story for *Winter's Crimes* titled "Fly Said the Spy" (it will be recalled *I, Said the Fly* was one of her earlier successful books in detective fiction) and that she intended this short story as a parody on the spy story but that it was taken "quite seriously; very disconcerting." (In another field, Sandy Wilson wrote the musical *The Boyfriend* as a pastiche of the 1920s, but to most playgoers it is again the genuine article.)

The Case of the Radioactive Redhead may recall Erle Stanley Gardner's witty Perry Mason titles, or perhaps the more outrageous titles in Raymond Chandler's essay or those invented by P. G. Wodehouse. A Belmont paperback of April 1963 is marked "An original Erik March mystery published by special arrangement with the author." It deals with the Hollywood mystery of ten women in a pornographic film, one of whom may have stolen a radium bomb from a hospital used in one sequence (under guise of a "training film"), to be solved by Erik March, private investigator. He charges $1,000 a day plus expenses, has a "four-room Taj Mahal on Sunset Boulevard with a swimming pool in the downstairs lobby and a lavish private office" east of the boulevard, with teak walls, expensive furniture, and an efficient secretary. He is 180 pounds in weight, in his thirties, from a poor background, lives on Laguna Beach, yet tends to stammer when embarrassed, despite his amorous encounters with women. There are five deaths in all, very little sadistic detail, locales like a motel in Rosarito Beach, Mexico, some interesting details of Hollywood, some wisecracks, and a spectacular ending that leaves many of the problems unanswered. Indeed, part of the plot is incomprehensible in this strange literary style. It seems to parody Marlowe, a Norman Conquest (1066) type, and Hollywood. The author, apparently G. G. Fickling, also wrote *Naughty but Dead* about Vice Inc., based on a true Hollywood case. There is even a mistake on the colored cover.

We may recall Robert L. Fish's *The Murder League* and his other noms de plume, but we can regard here one of his short stories, which appeared in *Ellery Queen's Scenes of the Crime* (1981) "The Adventure of the Animal Fare," first published in 1977. This story of Homes of Bagel Street is a chapter of complete misinterpretations of every single clue connected with the circus, from Camels cigarettes to using CB radio terms on the waiter against a background reminiscent of Queen's own problems. The parody lies in the paradoxical logicality of these misinterpretations taken quite literally. Other examples will be considered in the section on parody en masse.

Nils-Olsen Franzen has been writing since the 1950s in Stockholm a series of spoof detective novels featuring Agaton Sax, an editor in the Swedish town of Bykoping, with such titles as *Agaton Sax and the League of Silent Exploders* (1956; UK, 1974) and *Agaton Sax and the Criminal Doubles* (1963). The former example is set in Brosnia-Merzogovina and the county of Kent in England, and features Andreas Kark with his steel-toed shoe containing his escape tools; an eccentric English lord, the seventh earl of Woolverwoolton; and the criminal Professor Anexogoras Frank. A veteran car rally makes for a hilarious chase sequence; a scientist is trying to invent a silent explosive; and finally, a discount on double rewards to the captors results in their giving rewards to each other. Sax proves himself a fantastic athlete and is accompanied by his dog. The latter novel tells of two crooks—Julius Mosca (echoes of Julius Caesar) and Octopus Scott—and their doubles—Absalom Nick from Chickenchester, and Charlie McSnuff, a window cleaner from Pimlico in London—to add to the confusion. Inspector Lispington from Scotland Yard, wholesale drugging by knockout drops, a great deal of double-talk, and Aunt Matilda (looking after the newspaper in Sax's absence) uses her knitting to clear matters up. This farcical series is not only a parody on "unbeatable" heroes like James Bond and others, but it expands the parameters of the traditional detective story—all in a language of childlike simplicity.

Timothy Fuller wrote *Three-Thirds of a Ghost* in 1941 as a humorous novel portraying various well-known Boston people, including author John P. Marquand (1893–1960)—creator of that likable and inscrutable Japanese sleuth Mr. I. O. Moto, played in films by Hungarian Peter Lorre—as the murder victim. (This novel is not to be confused with Helen McCloy's 1956 Dr. Basil Willing mystery *Two-Thirds of a Ghost*.) Some of Fuller's other quirky titles are *Harvard Has a Homicide* (1936), *This Is Murder, Mr. Jones* (1943), and *Reunion with Murder* (1941).

Superintendent Jules Maigret is one of the greatest figures in detective fiction. We have seen his original, and we see now the first of the parodies, always with obvious affection and respect. "Madame Maigret Mourns a Raincoat," appearing in that useful reference book *Murderess Ink,* is by Bartholomew Gill, author of such Inspector McCarr stories as *McCarr at the Dublin Horse Show* (1980). It is a gentle short story of Madame persuading Maigret to don his new suit, shoes, coat, etc., in honor of spring on March 17, St. Patrick's Day, and there is a reference to Gill himself or his inspector in Maigret's remarks. This story could almost be a pastiche in its treatment.

When Tom Girtin wrote what he described as "a Commercial Novel," *Unnatural Break,* in 1959, commercial (not subsidized) television in the United Kingdom was only four years old, and was still being parodied itself, so this book has an air of racy, fairly obvious, and easily digested humor. Every time a product is mentioned—such as Parker pens or Lifebuoy soap—an advertisement is reproduced as illustration. The story includes various actual London locations, such as Soho, an East End public house, a famous joke shop then standing in Holborn, etc. The action races round London with fake mediums and prostitutes, and the plot is of the theft of pornographic books from the Home Secretary, Sir John Henderson; the suspects who have visited his house include an actor-manager, Sir Roland Benson, Mother Euphemia (euphemism and euphoria?) whose order has connections at Passyle-Cruet, and Algerton Kingston-Soper, a TV actor. Charles Crispin and his daughter Shirley live at Tout Court; there are references to Girtin's other books, such as *Doctor with Aunts,* covering a porn volume; and the letters from the thief are signed like a drunken spider, so when Detective Inspector Marples, CID, aided by Sergeant Harbinger and pretty Sergeant Dorris Finchley (a suburb of London) with whom he has fallen in love, finds a drunken spider in a drawer of the commissioner of police, Robert Ewart Mortimer, who has always been on the spot as each crime occurred, we are not surprised to see the last advertisement is inserted by former inspector Bachelor seeking employment. Girtin, who wrote histories of some London city guilds also published *Death in the Loving Cup* (a City ceremony of friendship going back to Saxon times), in 1987, of murder at the 1965 election dinner of the Baizemakers' Guild, with an accurate background and details, the murder solved by an inspector and a constable.

Ron Goulart's short story "The Peppermint-Striped Goodbye" appeared in *Best American Detective Stories of the Year* in 1967, and had an accolade from editor Anthony Boucher: "It was also an unusually good year for parody and pastiche, to such an extent that I almost regret that I included only one specimen, Ron Goulart's acute and malicious mockery of Ross Macdonald." Ross Pewter's case involves millionaire Tro Bultitude (echoes of *Vice Versa*), wife Hazel Willow Whitney, a reference to Rachel Seeswand, and complicated business with guns, a missing son, a restaurant, and the sea. It was John D. MacDonald who wrote *The Deep Blue Good-By* in 1964, the first of Travis McGee's adventures, each with a color in the title, and Ross Macdonald, who created Lew Archer, from 1949, with the 1962 title *The Zebra-Striped Hearse*. Boucher's comment is just—it is an exquisite small parody.

Bruce Graeme is internationally famous as the creator of Richard Verrall, "Blackshirt," the gentleman criminal, in a series of novels continued by his son. In 1963 was published in Israel by

Bridbooks a paperback, *Almost without Murder,* described on the back cover as "almost a parody of an American gangster setting, and one of Bruce Graeme's slickest, quickest and most amusing stories." It tells of Terence O'Connor, a redheaded Irishman, ex-RAF, making his first postwar visit to New York, bearing a message from his aunt's neighbor to the head of a lingerie manufacturing company—so mysterious a message that the millionaire promptly disappears, leaving the hero to be chased, kidnapped, beaten up by thugs, but to be helped by the attractive receptionist Maureen O'Toole, daughter of police chief Captain O'Toole. Mysterious links of the UK business with a shipping company lead to the uncovering of widespread criminal activities. There are indeed no killings until the denouement and shoot-out in a deserted house. It is a nice, simple, fast story, almost like a film script, as the hero routs the gang with his fists rather than a gun, and with great panache.

Andrew Hall wrote in 1967 *Frost,* a parody of the spy story, again with many ingredients exaggerated to absurdity. Frost is Thomas Hinton Stern, a minor clerk in a ministry and son of a clergyman, who is being blackmailed over microfilm of St. Paul's Cathedral. Younghusband, a dentist, is the spymaster, one of the three spies who get killed after a chase. There is inefficient photography, and Younghusband's mistress, a thirteen-year-old nymphet blackmailer, Mercia Daphne Ann Forbes, full of hopelessness, and all fairly predictable.

Tim Heald is a novelist, journalist, and former chair of the CWA; in 1985 he wrote *Red Herrings* (also the title of the CWA monthly journal). His sleuth is Simon Bognor, and the murder is of a VAT inspector, which gets him off with a laugh right away. The village of Herring St. George seems peopled with crooks, including Dandiprat the butler (correctly referred to as a coin—it was a silver three-halfpenny piece), the Bhagwan Josht (a swami), and Chief Inspector the Earl of Rotherhithe (a dockland area of London) with his expensive car. One character comments, "It's like that Agatha Christie where they take turns stabbing the man on the train." "The Orient Express," said Guy. In September 1985 Heald stated he intended a parody of the genre and of the Orient Express. He thinks of specific scenes, say, in an Allingham novel or an episode involving a clergyman, which gave him his Rev. Barnwell Larch, the homosexual licensees of the public house, or

Lady Amanda Mandible (a mandible is a jawbone). A somewhat hapless hero adds to the chaos, of course, especially when he could be susceptible to the femmes fatales with camera-carrying escorts. Rather neatly the cover of this Macmillan book featured two red herrings in a block of ice. Typically English, and in the mold of a less sophisticated brand of the silly-assery mentioned earlier.

Ben Hecht (1893–1964) was a playwright (*The Front Page*, with Charles MacArthur), novelist, screenwriter (*Underworld*, etc.—he told how Al Capone sent henchmen to ask if his film *Scarface,* on the W. R. Burnett book, was based on Capone's life—when he denied it, saying it was on Dion O'Banion's, they assured him all was well, as they had already killed him). He published the first chapter of a detective novel, *The Whistling Corpse,* in *Ellery Queen Mystery Magazine* (September 1945; reprinted in Haycraft's *The Art of the Mystery Story);* he wrote it as for the women's magazines, with a dedication to eighteen women, including Wife and Mother. An unusual form of parody, as opposed to some English humorists' "now read on" summaries. Hecht's detective writing stretches from *The Florentine Dagger* in 1923 to *Hollywood Mystery (I Hate Actors)* in 1944.

O. Henry (William Sidney Porter, 1862–1910) wrote many volumes of immaculate short stories, among the best in that field. He essayed parody occasionally; in 1911, in *Sixes and Sevens* there were two Sherlock Holmes parodies, and the following year in *Rolling Stones* there were two parodies of François Eugène Vidocq (1775–1857), whose career as criminal, chief of police, and private detective was summarized in his *Memoires* published in 1828–29, and who was himself depicted by Honoré de Balzac as "Vautrin."

Headon Hill was the nom de plume of Francis Edward Grainger (1857–1924). He wrote for journals like *Woman and Home* mystery stories like "Guilty Gold" (1896), "The Queen of Night" (the same year), and "The Narrowing Circle" (1924), featuring male and female sleuths, plus excellent short stories. "Radford Shone" first appearing in the magazine, was in book form in 1908 and is described by one writer as a rare parody of Albert Campion and Reggie Fortune, although these two examples of silly-assery did not first appear until, respectively, 1929 and 1920.

In 1983 I asked Edward D. Hoch, a leading American crime short story writer, former MWA president, and critic, if he had ever written parodies or pastiche. In a letter dated November 22, 1982, he gave details of an ingenious pastiche, but went on, "At the same time it occurs to me that my series about Sir Gideon Parrot is a 'gentle spoof' of the Golden Age Mystery, especially the Christie-Carr type," kindly sending details of these first five short stories, published in *EQMM* in 1981, 1982 (twice), 1983, and in *Mike Shayne* (1983) with a copy of the first, "Lady of the Impossible" (*EQMM* [March 1981]), the headnote referring to the narrator's description as "a story out of the Golden Age as reading a gentle spoof." Vangi Hope, the lady of the impossible on New York radio, holds a dinner party forecasting her own death, the guests Sir Gideon Parrot (the *t* is silent), the narrator as Watson, prime suspect, the former husband, young lovers, least-suspected person, a priest, and an author. A scream in a locked bedroom, discovery of her stabbed body downstairs, a butler named Diener whom Parrot immediately eliminates as a fake, a young actor (*Diener* being German for "servant"), and a classic gathering with the police, Sergeant Nims ("nim" is an obsolete term for stealing), as the "slender, bird-like" Parrot solves the conspiracy. En route to the city the narrator compares it to a mystery novel he could have stayed at home to read, but Parrot retorts, "They don't write them like this any more"—a clever, charming, ingenious parody. We have considered Hoch again under parody en masse for his *The Shattered Raven*.

There are few cases of the occult in parodies, and one of that number was a short story by Clark Howard, in *Ellery Queen Mystery Magazine* (April 1984), "The Last Private Eye." Edward Land, a PI with an office in Melrose, California, with money owing in all directions, is approached by the head of Donlevy Petroleum to trace a missing daughter, the youngest child, Laura, who is in a religious commune in the Dos Rios section of Zachal Canyon. He finds every inmate claims to meet the idols of his dreams. He returns because the Mahatma would let him visit the great detectives of the past, the ones "a lot of people didn't even believe were real, like Nick Charles, Sam Spade, Charlie Chan, Ellery Queen, Philip Marlowe, The Saint, The Falcon." A strange blend of fact and either imagination or directed thought on the subject.

Fergus Hume (Ferguson Wright Hume), born in England in 1859 and died in Essex, England, in 1932, wrote 130 books, so his writing, like Doyle's spanned the reigns of Victoria, Edward, and George. His best-known book is *The Mystery of a Hansom Cab*, published in Melbourne in 1886, or 1887 according to some authorities. This best-seller has been described as the first parody of detective fiction, although he was confessionally influenced by Emile Gaboriau for this early novel. Parody seemed to surround him. In my ephemera collection I have a postcard with that title over an amusing picture. In the 1970s I was approached by an Australian professor researching Hume, and I asked him if William Black's *The Strange Adventures of a Phaeton* (1886) could have stemmed from Hume's just-published book, and he thought it possible. I read the copy belonging to my mother and found it an interesting and amusing account of a journey across England. Black also wrote *The Strange Adventures of a Houseboat,* on similar lines. In 1888 was published a parody by Walter Scott, in pictorial wrappers, *The Mystery of a Wheelbarrow; or, Gaboriau Gaborooed* by W. Hume Ferguson. Incidentally, I acquired a signed copy of his *Red Money,* addressed to his friends near our house, for he lived not far away, and found in it a letter to them, perhaps the last he wrote, saying he could not undertake the short bus journey to them as the vibration affected his heart.

We come now to Michael Innes again, as his alter ego of J. I. M. Stewart, and his book of short stories, titled from the first one, *The Man Who Wrote Detective Stories* (1959). Freddie Seston, a professor of fine art who writes detective stories like *Death Lies Dead* and *Dead on the Hour* as Hugo St. John, meets former fellow undergraduate Jonathan, a barrister, in Venice. Suddenly he learns a murder has been committed in Golders Green based on the method in his aristocratic *Death by Water*—a week before it is due to be published. The journalists and Inspector Cuff appear in Venice; "a detective story should be very much a matter of convention—tall story, you know, with something basically bizarre or fantastic to it." There are references to the plot of *Phèdre;* to make matters worse the dead man's stepmother arrives in Venice, followed by Cyril Loakes, who claims the plot came from his *Murder in the Nude,* published in 1921. It is finally decided Seston must have read this book as a young man, and subconsciously retained it. Some critics, including Howard Haycraft, have "felt that what had once been a successful attempt to fuse satire with the mystery novel had deteriorated into strained attempts at humour," in Innes's Appleby books, which first appeared in 1936, but this criticism would not seem right for this story, which underlines a basic problem for many fiction writers, including those who base their books on real-life crime cases. This narrative illustrates the buildup of panic for Seston as neatly as, if more gently than, in, say, some of the chases in *The Journeying Boy* and *The Secret Vanguard.*

Stephen Leacock, professor at McGill University and universal humorist, turned his attention to detective fiction and parody in at least two books of short stories: "Maddened by Mystery; or The Defective Detective" in *Nonsense Novels* (1911) and *Winsome Winnie and Other Nonsense Novels* (1922), plus another Holmes parody in an "Irreducible Detective Story" in *Further Foolishness* (1916). A typical Holmes story has a dog mistaken for the prince of Württemberg, with the archbishop, prime minister, and the countess of Dashleigh involved, the great detective changing disguises so quickly as to baffle his secretary, and finally appearing in the dog show, winning first prize, but having to be destroyed because his dog tax hasn't been paid. The other non-Holmes parodies in *Winsome Winnie,* are "Who Do You Think Did It? or; The Mixed-up Murder Mystery," of ten chapters, with a murder in a billiards room, various suspects, an editor, an investigative crime reporter, and a denouement involving a wooden-legged sailor. One character is named Transome Kent; a transom is a window crossbar, and a kent is a leaping or punting pole. "The Kidnapped Plumber: A Tale of the New Time" follows the formula of a group sitting around and the telling of a story of a bishop and a general kidnapping, with a happy ending. These are straightforward parodies of the classic format; the idea of a group sitting around telling stories has been popular from Victorian times right to the present, in both books and films.

Gillian Linscott was a playwright and journalist before becoming a BBC parliamentary reporter, for radio and television, and a crime writer. Her first two books were *A Healthy Body* (1984) and *Murder Makes Tracks* (1985). Linscott is a member of the CWA. Her hero is ex-policeman "Birdie" Linnit, with his girlfriend; his first adventure is of murder in a French nudist camp, where the body is hidden in a seaweed tank; his second takes him to an unfashionable Italian Alpine holiday resort with a party of schoolchildren learning to ski, where a millionaire is murdered. The suspects range from schoolboys to eccentric American religious fanatics. Linscott told me she always wrote of locales she knew firsthand; for example, she is a skilled skier who has actually successfully shot the terrifying "rifle-barrel" run Birdie had to do. At dinner in the Houses of Parliament in July 1986, however, she told me Birdie was deliberately designed as an exact antithesis to Lord Peter Wimsey—burly, tough, ex-cop, poorly educated, lacking in social graces and wine lore, rude, and nonaristocratic—an unusual inverse parody. A very professional, conscientious writer, with a keen sense of humor, she claims to be unwilling to lose face in life. By the time her third book came out in 1986, Linscott was promoted to BBC producer; *Knightfall* has Birdie working for an idealistic organization specializing in promoting Arthurian jousting and classic chivalry near historic Camelot and Glastonbury. A mélange of murder, robbery, and exhilarating "wrong-righting" whirls round him and his now tour-operating girlfriend until answer after answer settle gently on his battered, bemused, and very unsuspecting head.

Television scriptwriter Jeremy Lloyd wrote in 1973 *The Further Adventures of Captain Gregory Dangerfield,* "as told to Jeremy Lloyd by the late P. W. Arnold," a completely surrealist parody. Henry W. Potts of 69 Ranleigh Road, Streatham, a London suburb, is the author of the rejected *The Missing Detective* and is starting writing *The Game Is Up, Mr. Gates,* and the typewriter, originally belonging to the late P. W. Arnold, is in fact writing it for him. The sophisticated, well-dressed captain has incredible adventures in jungles, airplanes, Paris cabarets, with medieval warriors, glamorous women from his digs, men lodgers, bank managers, in a public house, in a bank, and so on, almost like a cliff-hanger serial in the cinema or a boys' magazine. The late author tries to take over Potts, who fights back to return to the safety of his own room in the with-one-bound touch of esoteric fighting blows learned from exotics, meeting half-dressed women explorers, Arabs, dancers, et al.—the book-in-a-book idea is a delightful mixture of two worlds—of fantasy with everyday life—not dissimilar to films or books, with dream sequences involving the day's meetings. Thus the reader or viewer is left unsure which is which, like the Chinese philosopher dreaming he was a butterfly.

Peter Lovesey is a former chair of the CWA and the author of many Victorian detective stories, with the two detectives representing, as we have seen, opposing sides of himself; certainly they are pastiche of the highest order, recognized by his winning the CWA Silver Dagger in 1978 for *Waxwork* and the CWA Gold Dagger in 1962 for *The False Inspector Dew*. In answer to my inquiry regarding parody as opposed to pastiche, he sent me copies of two contrasting pieces. "Arabella's Answer" is a short story in *Ellery Queen Mystery Magazine* (April 1984) and in the *Creasey Collection* (1985). It consists of a series of letters, a literary form since the seventeenth century, to Arabella from a sob sister from January 1878 to May 1885, regarding her courtship, marriage, widowhood, further courtship, and sudden death of the sob sister herself, Miss Gertrude Smyth. This is followed by the remarriage of Arabella, all couched in pure women's magazine language of that period—for example, advising of the delicate line between receiving condolences or compliments, plus the editorial note of the letters editor's sudden death, not unconnected with Arabella's disinclination to take the formal, conventional advice. *Swing, Swing Together* (1976) is a full-length book, the title taken from the Eton boating song, and the chapter headings taken from Jerome K. Jerome's great *Three Men in a Boat;* for example, "Original Use of Butter," "Respecting the Rules," "Down to the Thames." Very cleverly does Lovesey adapt the headings to his action—e.g., the butter for the windows for the midnight bath. His story fits the headings, with the murder of a tramp and a mysterious don, Bonner-Hill, Harriet Shaw being a witness, three men and a dog in a boat followed by Sergeant Cribb in unexpected finery. Various references to the Ripper and to Inspector Abberline (Detective Inspector Abberline of Scotland Yard exclaimed that Jack the Ripper had been caught when George Chapman was arrested) add to a neat conspiracy plot and a surprise ending. All the original locations in Jerome are mentioned, locks or hotels, and the finale with Harriet is very funny. This is an ingenious ploy to fit a parody to a detailed chapter-heading outline. In his article in *Murder Ink,* titled "Once upon a Crime," of the nineteenth century he wrote, "Even the most extravagant plots conform to historical truth." In 1985 Lovesey deservedly won the French Prix de Littérature Policiers.

During World War II I read with fascination and amazement a Cherry Tree Book paperback, *The Face on the Cutting-Room Floor* by Cameron McCabe (1937). The book contains, in order, an encomium from the series editor as "one of the best detective stories," a tribute to friends of 1935 "when Mr. McCabe's story broke," a warning to those who think themselves portrayed in the book as being open to libel by the author, explanation of "cutting-room floor" (where films are edited and cut in the studio), the novel, an epilogue by A. B. C. Muller as epitaph for Cameron McCabe, envoi from E. C. Bentley's *Trent's Last Case,* apologies, and list of quotations. This is a tale of the murder of the actress whose face is on the cutting-room floor, McCabe's arrest and acquittal, and the death of detective Smith. This is followed by Muller's proof that anyone (including McCabe) could be the killer, aided by McCabe après suicide, by Muller killing a girl on the last line. A brilliant parody with a double twist followed by another double twist; there are various clues scattered through the book as Adolf Benito Comrade (cf. dictators) Muller shows. In his epilogue he cleverly proves his points by quotations from reviews of the book (which he has not yet had published) by taking actual 1930s reviews, books, and periodicals, including Ernest Hemingway, Milward Kennedy, C. Day Lewis, and Cyril Connolly, inter alia. He selects some esoteric comments. "A synthetic and romantic modern toughness . . . like Hemingway, Hammett, Cain, McCoy, Fessier and . . . O'Hara . . . The critics cannot even agree on a definition of a detective story, or the duration of the Golden Age." The Cyril Connolly quote lists the only three 1930s detective stories, and in placing the Golden Age from 1918 to 1921 catalogues the later sleuths, including "Philo Vance and Peter Wimsey before they became parodies of themselves . . . Who now enjoys the famous solution-dinner that should occur at the end of every good detective story?" The Connolly quote goes on to complain of the "Van Dine five-card trick," and the "words-of-one-syllable crime of violence," presumably the hard-boiled school.

McCabe was Ernest Wilhelm Julius Borneman, and the 1981 American edition by Gregg Press, with an afterword by the author and editors, says the author wrote the book as a nineteen-year-old refugee, and was by 1981 a professor in Austria. Interestingly, Julian Symons in the first edition of his *Bloody Murder (Mortal Consequences)* has a sentence omitted from the second edition, after referring to McCabe's trial and acquittal: "It is then revealed that he was in fact the murderer, and at the end of the story he kills the detective, Smith, who was on his track."

Another strange, final thought: The eclectic quotes from Connolly and others mull over the composition of detective stories or thrillers, yet this paperback book is categorized on the front cover as a "thriller." (The same title was used in a 1993 novel by Stan Cutler for a Hollywood PI novel, completely unconnected with the earlier classic, and yet again in another genre.)

Australian-born Mark McShane (or Marc Lovell) lets his humor appear not only in his crime books but in their titles too, ranging from his famous *Seance on a Wet Afternoon* to *Ill Met by a Fish Shop on George Street, The Crimson Madness of Little Doom* to his 1969 parody *The Singular Case of the Multiple Dead,* in which a group of zany idealists decide to kill the Chancellor of the Exchequer over his proposed tax on theatre seats. Bloomsbury Group Junior consists of Jem Gate, Lady Madge Severn, Virginius Twyce, Jean Quin, and the five others who themselves get killed in the various attempts—Tony Zero, Relentable Cease, Minerva Droplet, Sid Fourpenny, and Pat Single. The elements include a fascist group, seduction, a gun, a suffragette, and love letters as the gang altruistically keeps killing, and trying to find a killer, while amusing similes are typical of the author's style (some of his other books have atrocious paronomasias, like *Apple to the Core*).

We come now to the second Maigret parody, in a very different vein from the first, in a short story by Vincent O'Connor in *Ellery Queens Anthology* (Fall–Winter 1979), "Just Like Inspector Maigret." George Drayton, age seventy-five, usually sits in a London square, and frequently it is Maigret he is reading, for example: "Maigret was moving quickly now. Each of the clues which had seemed so innocent before had become ominous as the great French detective linked them together." Drayton watches the occupants of the square, their activities, and their visitors, and is able to solve a crime. "George Drayton smiled. He had solved the Clarkson case and he had done it without moving from the bench in Knightswood Square. . . . Just like Inspector Maigret." This is not the only example we shall find in solving a crime by comparing it to an earlier case—and indeed the present author once helped the police solve a robbery by drawing on the advice of a famous fictional colleague.

Deviating slightly from the alphabetical list of authors of parody brings us to the genus of the much parodied, and Philip Marlowe and creator Raymond Chandler have been copied and parodied frequently. Indeed, he was himself quite taken with his element of self-parody, which he felt was not always recognized!

We have already seen Chandler's satirically getting Marlowe to refer to Philo Vance, and in *The World of Raymond Chandler,* by various leading authors, is an essay by T. J. Binyon, Oxford don, newspaper critic, and fellow member of the Gold Dagger Awards Committee of the CWA, titled "A Lasting Influence?" Among the influences he gives are John Bingham being affected in his own treatment of police, the works of Clark Smith, Peter Israel whose "hero" B. F. Cage in two books is definitely anti-Marlowe, and Andrew Bergman with his Jewish investigator Jack Le Vine who gets involved in Dewey's election campaign and meets Bogart and Richard Nixon in Hollywood. Ross Macdonald, John D. MacDonald, Thomas B. Dewey, etc., are among the authors influenced, as is, in a different way, Robert B. Parker, whose hero is Spenser, a Boston private eye, described by one English reviewer as "the most civilised and likeable private eye with the slickest dialogue since Marlowe," who is featured in more than a dozen novels. The first page of *Promised Land* has him redecorating his new offices after town planning's compulsory removal, and Parker's thought for him is, "I bet Philo Vance never painted his own office." Where a character like Marlowe has proved so popular with various cinema and television films and series, it is natural for parodies and, as we shall see, pastiches to follow as a tribute, and indeed Binyon does emphasize the pastiche of Spenser.

We have already met one scathing parody of James Bond, Ian Fleming's invention of the amorous and vicious secret agent who wins every adventure with monotonous regularity. Based partly on a man who later was retired on a Caribbean island, partly on Fleming's own service during which he learned of Dr. John Dee's number of 007, Bond was portrayed in several films, some made more than once, by actor Roger Moore (who was one of the television Saints of Charteris) and others, but perhaps exceeded by Jean Bruce's creation of his agent OSS 117, played on screen in some hilarious tongue-in-cheek films by Frederick Stafford (later to appear in Alfred Hitchcock's *Topaz*)—who else has propelled villains through windows twenty floors up by swinging from an operating theatre's overhead light, and used the table as a battering ram?

The Adventures of James Bond Junior 003 ½ (1967) by R. D. Mascott is a gentle parody; the boy, nicknamed 003 ½ by his school housemaster, as Bond's nephew, says, "But I wrote to him once. You know, as man to man. I thought, well, we had something in common." "And . . .?" "He sent me a sheath knife but he didn't really say much—not like he realised, I mean." The boy solves the Great Bullion Robbery at Beacon Hill on the borders of the southern English counties of Kent and Sussex, only to see the credit coolly taken by the pompous and not very efficient Sir Cuthbert Conningtower, former naval intelligence author of *Spies I've Espied* (a conning tower is part of a submarine, and "to con" is to trick, so the name is apt). Other parodies and spoofs of Bond have been attempted.

One of Alfred Hitchcock's anthologies, *Tales to Scare You Stiff,* edited by that excellent authority Eleanor Sullivan in 1969, contained the short story "Farewell, My Brother" by Theodore Mathieson (cf. *Farewell, My Lovely*). In this tale the character (Marlowe), age ostensibly seventy, overrules his literary father (Chandler). "Thanks to this writer, who for forty yeas has forced me, his Creation, to try to rival the exploits of such investigators as Nero Wolfe and Hercule Poirot. Farewell, my brothers." We have already seen another example of the somewhat Frankenstein-like principle of a character taking over the author's style and life in Jeremy Lloyd's book, and indeed the idea appears in many other media; for example, Sparky the Magic Piano teaching a little boy to play.

Mickey Spillane has parodied himself on American television shows, and has acted in films as himself, in a circus film with Clyde Beatty, *Ring of Fear* (1954), and as his own creation Mike Hammer in 1963 in *The Girl Hunters*. His tough private eye was in turn parodied by M. J. Monk in *Nasty Habits,* a novel on "nun-running" with a blonde disguised as a nun being advised to "kick the habit" in a sequence of puns and one-line gags to mirror Spillane's style. We shall find later Spillane has a literary output far removed from the sex-and-sadism school.

We have included but a few of the thousands of Holmes parodies (and pastiches), but yet another remarkable example is in *The Scarlet Thumb-Print* (undated) published by Skeffington & Son Ltd. in England and written by Guy Morton, listed as having written *The Burleigh Murders, The Ragged Robin Murders,* and *The*

Perrin Murder Case. He has a sleuth Konrad Roque, assisted by Markus Keene, known as Doc, and Mulcahy of the New York District Attorney's Office. They are seeking to solve in Nassau the apparent emergence of a master criminal known as the Kaffir, who always leaves a huge scarlet thumbprint, with the top apparently lopped of. Crooks are seeking lost diamonds; there are two murders and assumed identities, but Roque is aided by a remarkable assistant in Beerlock Bones the Great, whose card reads: "Mr. Henry J. Bohens, Criminal Expert, Operative 10,033 Universal Agency. Terms reasonable. Integrity guaranteed. Demonstrations upon request. Special rates for families." Bones is continually disguised, trying to solve the mystery of missing pop bottles, and, as a chubby, eccentrically dressed, thirty-year-old sleuth who diagnoses invariably wrongly, analyzing careers and interests, in the style of Professor Bell and Holmes, with detailed, logical, spurious, and incorrect diagnoses. He does help solve the mysteries. He is described in the synopsis: "The author has certainly struck a novel and entertaining idea in the introduction of a mad detective who, however, is sane enough to help the authorities in solving the mystery of the murders and discovering the criminals." Such an unusual role for a parodic Holmes (and Roque and Doc Keene—note Konrad Roque is the correct two syllable/one syllable name) justifies its consideration here.

William F. Nolan is an author of repute. After such titles as *Death Is for Losers* (1968) and *The White Cad Cross-Up* (1969), featuring Los Angles private eye Bert Challis, he wrote *Space for Hire* in 1971, a blend of science fiction and mystery, which won an MWA nomination for best paperback original. Sam Space, based on Warner Bros.' Bogart and Chandler is "Hammetized"— Sam's office is on Mars, he is visited by three-headed women, he travels down on the *President Agnew,* misses his return flight on the *President Reagan,* only to find after being killed the brain can be transplanted to a new body. A parallel is drawn with the play *Halfway to Heaven,* filmed as *Here Comes Mr. Jordan,* where a life is transferred to an appropriate body after dying accidentally and prematurely.

Frank Norman's partly autobiographical plays and novels of East London life have received praise from Raymond Chandler, and in 1981 he wrote *The Baskerville Caper,* the story of Sir Charles Baskerville of Baskerville Hall, Coombe Tacy, who bought Muddicombe, in North Devon in southwest England. Other ingredients include the butler John Barrymore (an ex-actor), flying saucers, references to Sir Harry Baskerville and Grimpen Mire, Giles and Margaret Stapleton who steal from stately homes, a reporter's car numbered PHY 64Q, a man in a deerstalker hat, Dr. Barnardo Holmes (Norman's other books frequently feature Barnardo's Homes for Children), Mirripit House, Lafter Hall, a dog called Tiny, and Ivor Frankland, who writes for the *Spectator,* an astronomer "son of the famous novelist and wit, Evelyn Frankland, wrote *The Decline and Fall of Rupert Goldsmith*" (another allusion to Evelyn Waugh). Ivor is bald with sparse ginger hair, long thin nose, "pair of gold-wire framed specs with spherical lenses," five foot eight inches in height, speaks with an impediment preventing his sounding his R's—a telescope shows a spider "spinning a web in the bwacken, two or three miles away on the moor." "Two miles, five hundred yards to be exact." Inspector Lestrade of Scotland Yard actually picks up a Luger with a pencil down the barrel to put it in a polyethylene bag in the time-honored tradition, while Ed Norton from a shabby office in Soho calls himself Philip Marlowe. This is not quite an exclusive Holmes parody; it is somewhat confused in the writing with a few loose ends, but an interesting, humorous effort rather out of Norman's usual writing.

In February 1954 Stuart Palmer (1905–1968) published "A Valentine for the Victim" in *American Magazine;* in the Green Door Mystery series of Pyramid Books in July 1964 it was *Cold Poison*—in the United Kingdom in 1954 and again in 1985 it became *Exit Laughing.* It is a Hildegarde Withers novel of murder in a cartoon animation studio featuring Peter Penguin, acknowledged by Palmer as a parody of Woody Woodpecker, the penguin a theme of Palmer's books. Two volumes of short stories were written in partnership with Craig Rice (1908–1957). *Cold Poison* gives an interesting perspective of a cartoon character dominating a studio complex and all its employees. Hildegarde Withers (portrayed by various actresses including Edna May Oliver on film and Eve Arden on U.S. television in 1971, UK 1984) was a combination of Palmer's high school teacher Miss Fern Hackett and Palmer's father. Palmer wrote film scripts for Bulldog Drummond, the Falcon, and the Lone Wolf.

We have already referred to Elliot Paul (1891–1958) and his

1939 book, *The Mysterious Mickey Finn; or, Murder at the Café du Dome,* and its witty chapter headings, like "Two Hearts That Cease to Beat as One, or to Beat at All for That Matter," and the eccentrically named cast, including M. Paty de Pussy and Dr. Hyacinthe Toudoux. The endpapers consist of a map of Paris highlighting the scenes of action when Homer Evans, an American living in Paris in a bohemian community, gets involved with spies, shootings, chases, bombs, gangs, a royalist conspiracy, fake paintings, much technical data, and esoteric clues such as a shot through a painting telling them to go to Frontville. Lighthearted, fast, wholesome, a comedy-thriller that holds the attention to the last page, following yet parodying the detective tradition.

In 1949 came a similar comedy-thriller, *Hugger-Mugger in the Louvre,* with Homer Evans, Miriam Montana, Dr. Toudoux, and others, but new characters included the Prefect, Philippe de la Chemise Farcie ("stuffed shirt"), ill-fated minister of beaux arts, Marquis de la Rose d'Antan, and a retired professor Zacherie de la Poussiere, whose Egyptological researches involve physical and mental dust indeed. This book comprises three kidnappings, murder, theft of a Watteau from the Louvre, a gang, and substitution of the body in a most involved and humorous plot, solved by Homer and Miriam again. Chapter headings are shorter and somewhat quieter—for example "Sock Filled with Sand and Joyce's *Ulysses*" or "Aurora, Pluvius and Cupid All Play the Field."

Yet another parody of Chandler, and a spoof which Chandler admired, was *Farewell, My Lovely Appetizer* by that great humorist S. J. Perelman. Perhaps not all the ironies are realized in Chandler's metaphors and similes, but it was certainly correct and appropriate for Perelman alone to write. A similar pun on "appetize" was in H. R. F. Keating's neat, short 1975 analysis *Murder Must Appetize* (cf. Sayers's *Murder Must Advertise*).

Bill Pronzini has written books about the Nameless Detective, many short stories, and has edited numerous anthologies, but in 1982 he wrote the fascinating *Gun in Cheek,* consisting of extracts from and analyses of detective and mystery stories, pieces which, upon analysis and a second look, contained a strong element of the ridiculous, either in the intrinsic meaning, the juxtaposition of the surrounding phrases, or the misreading. His sequel was *Son of Gun in Cheek* (1987).

Just as in pantomine, commedia dell'arte, or farce, it is the more outlandish characters who are outstanding, easily remembered, and frequently mimicked, so we return to what we saw was called silly-assery, and this time it is again Philo Vance. *The John Riddell Murder Case* marked as by John Riddell was written in 1930 by Corey Ford; its subtitle was *A Philo Vance Parody*—unusual, but following the remarks by Jon L. Breen and Nathaniel Benchley mentioned earlier, it is described as parody-criticism. John Riddell, a book reviewer, is found dead in a yawn with his feet gone to sleep, so, as his library is full of last year's best-sellers, Vance deduces he died of boredom. This parody does not follow Van Dine's rule of six letters in the title-name crime (Benson, Bishop, Canary, Garden, etc.), with the exception of the Gracie Allen Case.

Mike Ripley is a crime writer, television scriptwriter, and newspaper crime book critic. He is also a member of the Dorothy L. Sayers Society, which in 1991 published a paperback by various writers titled *Encounters with Lord Peter*. Ripley's contribution, which first appeared therein, was "Lord Peter and the Butterboy," a short story. The narrator drives "a delicensed FX45 Austin black cab," which breaks down on a wet Saturday evening in London. As he repairs it, a retired taxi driver tells him of the time he picked up Lord Peter in the 1920s. Wimsey's name for the cabdrivers was "Butterboys," after the American Yellow Cabs. The narrator realizes too late he has lost a scoop.

Robert Robinson is an English television critic and chair of television panel games. In 1956 he wrote *Landscape with Dead Dons,* a parody of the intellectual Innes and Crispin type of Oxford books. The clue is at the beginning; his sleuths are Inspectors Autumn and Dorcas (famous for good works); with a journalist named Bum they arrive at Warlock College, where dons include Christelow, Falal (cf. music), Undigo, undergraduates Dogg, Egg, Flower, and Archangel, porter Tantalum (an element unable to absorb water), Chaplain Bow-Parley (aptly named from the French), and the college clock is called Iscariot because it strikes thirteen at midnight. The women's college is Walpurgis Hall with a female porter who shaves, a coach named Pearl Corker, and an undergraduate named Balboa after the Brazilian nit. There are references to the vacancy for the Rockinge Chair, and a pornographic books dealer named Emmanuel Kant. Two murders stem from a newly discovered Chaucer poem, and the finale is a Keystone Kops chase of naked dons through Oxford after the killer.

The Murdered Cliché, a "Fantastic Thriller" by Joseph Samuel (1947), sets its tone by being dedicated to the Marx Brothers, and this zany, logical surrealism features M. Mercury Poitrine, the eminent detective clad in morning coat and hat, called in to investigate the peculiar murder of the host at a country house party at Elvers Towers (an elver is a young eel). The butler informs her ladyship, with whom he appears to be on vaguely intimate terms, that he has found her husband dead in the bathroom, his head in the bath. Inspector Crimble of Little Woppingham Police Force arrives in uniform, and thereupon the plot does indeed resemble a Marx Brothers film. The names are eccentric—Semolina Jackson the cook, guests Peggy Chumleigh, Jimmy Conker, Amos Boustead; the action is even more outré—when guests and staff queue up to visit the murder bathroom, the butler passes along like a cinema usher bearing a tray of chocolates and ices; the dialogue is subtly exaggerated—Amos Boustead refers continually to the Jews as did many 1930s heroes, but he confuses his terminology among "Jews," "juices," and "jujubes." There are references to happenings on "page 233"; characters go in and out of the back, front, and side entrances of the Jolly Roger public house as through a revolving door. Poitrine complains "he might have been working for E. Phillips Oppenheim or even William Le Queux in Monte Carlo . . . instead of slaving for Joseph Samuel." An ex-batman not recognizing his disguised officer as in Sherlock Holmes, puns, farcical patter, pages of philosophy, and a crazy reconstruction denouement that reverses the murder and could start the story all over again . . .

Tom Sharpe has written some topsy-turvy books, and in 1982 *Vintage Stuff* proved to be a parody of Bulldog Drummond, James Bond, and author Dornford Yates in a headlong tale of a tutor, pupil Peregrine, a countess, and a 1927 Bentley car.

Douglas Shea wrote the 453rd First Story in *EQMM* in 1976; it was "Advice Unlimited," and was selected for *Ellery Queen's Anthology* (Spring-Summer, 1980). It is a parody of letters to an author from fans, to Gihon Gore, of Chutney & Chivers, Inc., Publishers, Quentin Quarles, Editor, and to George Ohm. The increasingly complaining and threatening "fan" refers to the use as a murder weapon of Bees in *Brent's Last Case* and curare in *The Affair at Byles.*

Mike Shelley wrote in 1984 an original paperback published in Belfast called *The Last Private Eye in Belfast* which, like his *Madame Eddie's Chamber of Horrors* and *The Terror of Her Ways,* deals with bespectacled private investigator and alleged former British special agent Bernard Holland. Bernard Holland & Associates has only one employee, Herman, who joins the crooks and gets shot, and the former partner Dale Diamond (cf. Sam Spade) got killed while Holland was having an affair with his wife. The offices are on two floors on Ormeau Road; Holland prefers classical music; is married but unfaithful and is often in trouble with the police—one of whom loses his false teeth in a tough interrogation. Chapter headings are satiric: "Bedrabbled, Bothered and Bewildered" (cf. the *Pal Joey* song); "Play It Again, Gilfurphy" (cf. the nonexistent line in *Casablanca*). Holland is on the trail of buried stolen bank money on an island, pursued by Mr. Kaine's gang, a ruthless British intelligence agent Major Peppar, his own niece Faye Dunslaney, a mysterious professor steeped in crime (cf. Professor Moriarty), crooks operating alone—and a Japanese gang which scoops the pool. There is a wry reference to Philip Marlowe, and an amusing sentence to start chapter 4, referring to private eyes in hard-boiled detective stories: "After getting coshed once or twice, escaping from a sinking car or two, outwitting killer dogs, being betrayed by his well-stacked female confidant, and, during the quieter moments, tangling with the local cops, he finally exposes the drug-dealing politician or saves the small seaside burg from the mob, and all this seems to happen in three or four drink-sodden days." The parody is of both Marlowe-type books and corresponding films, California being reduced to Belfast.

One of the best ways to learn a foreign language is to read its well-written books, preferably those authors who read fast and easily, bearing in mind Dr. Samuel Johnson's dictum that easy reading is damned hard writing. The prolific mystery and detective fiction of Georges Simenon (1903–1989) comes well into that category, particularly the tales of Commissaire Jules Maigret, based as we have seen on the real-life Charles Chenevier. On one visit to Paris with Barbara Miller I was happy to see, near the famous Cirque d'Hiver (Winter Circus) we were visiting, the Boulevard Richard Lenoir where stands Maigret's flat. Many great actors have portrayed Maigret, including Jean Gabin and Harry Baur in French films, Charles Laughton in the 1949 RKO American film *The Man on the Eiffel Tower,* and Rupert Davies in the popular BBC-TV series in the 1970s. I had read the novel *Les Memoires de Maigret,* published by Presses de la Cité in 1950, enjoyed very much its accounts of Maigret's early meetings with that journalist Georges Sim, later Simenon, complaining wryly about Sim's remarks on his clothes and life. Julian Symons also picks up on this aspect, describing the *Memoires* as "this very witty book," even though it is "plausibly extending the myth of Maigret and stressing its artificiality."

Qui Etes-vous, Georges Simenon? an excellent pocket-sized Marabout Flash book written in French in 1959 by Leon Thoorens, refers to Thomas Narcejac's grouping of Simenon's books into publisher categories, including NRF psychology books, adding, "Il en est d'ailleurs de fort bons: par example *Les Mémoires de Maigret* où le personnage est ramassé, complète de façon étonnante." John Raymond analyzed the writer in a similar way in *Simenon in Court* (1968), with the three Maigrets: "The *Mémoires* are good reading in their own right.... The book is also admirable as a description of Maigret's relationship with his creator....

> 'Was it absolutely necessary to simplify *me*?'
> 'To begin with, it certainly was. The public has to get used to you ... All this is excellent fooling.'

Adding this prohibits the readers forming a fan club as with Holmes and other detectives, but establishes Maigret's yardstick for all his judgments.

I wrote an article for the Fall 1986 issue of the *Poisoned Pen* about my own correspondence with Simenon, and of course sent him a copy. I mentioned the "facelessness" of the famous Maigret statue, and the descriptions in the books, and I received a charming and helpful letter from him personally, dated January 14, 1987, in which he emphasized deliberately omitting descriptions of the features of Maigret or any other characters, to allow the reader's imagination full play, going on to say, "As it is, readers are often shocked to discover in a portrayal, for instance, a look that does not correspond to the figure they attribute to a particular character." An interesting confirmation of both style and statue, and typical of the thought Simenon has always given to all the books, including the *Mémoires*.

The style of this book is so different that I wrote to Simenon in Switzerland to ask if he was parodying his creation. In a friendly letter, dated September 27, 1982, he answered that it was "in no way a parody or pastiche of my Inspector . . . sort of autobiography . . . sentimental . . . grain of humour. You won't find, in any of my other books, a trace of pastiche, nor of parody." I confess I was still worried about the different speech rhythm, because some writers do not observe the different speech rhythms of their characters, and this difference was noticeable about Maigret's own account. I therefore wrote again, explaining tactfully my views, and received another detailed letter, this time from his secretary, dated very promptly October 20, 1982, saying, inter alia, "Mr. Simenon wrote this book while his mother-in-law was visiting the Simenon family for a rather prolonged period, and settling down to work . . . would have demanded too tight a concentration; he started writing gaily his encounters with Maigret, and this gave birth to 'Maigret's Memoire.' " When we recall the speed with which Simenon actually wrote his books after the study and research, we can see the marked effect this change of atmosphere would cause. I asked his secretary if the master would sign my copy of the French edition, and he wrote in November 1982 a lengthy, humorous, and warm, personal note in the book referring to Connecticut's distance from Paris. Perhaps every reader has a different interpretation of Maigret, and it has been noticed by author and lawyer Fenton Bresler that Simenon didn't "see" Maigret's face, and La Cour and Mogenson in their splendid illustrated book commented that the statue of Maigret did not show it either. (For the same reason André Tahon, a leading French puppeteer, of La Compagnie des Marottes, told me in Paris he does not put mouths on his rod puppets, so each viewer can supply the face he sees.)

It is impressive to see the trouble Simenon took to consider this request so thoroughly as to check his diaries of thirty years earlier, and to deal with it in depth and warmth. It was with particular pleasure in 1991, as editor of the Chivers Black Dagger Series of reissued crime classics I selected the 1955 novel *Maigret Tend un Piège (Maigret Sets a Trap)* and wrote the foreword. This novel was years ahead of its time in the account of Maigret and Professor Tissot collaborating in establishing the identity of the murderer of five women in the Eighteenth Arrondissement of Paris, long before psychological profiling became police practice. The psychological approach, accuracy of police procedure, and sense of atmosphere, degradation, or despair in all Simenon's books have taken him to the top of the world literary tree.

George R. Sims (1847–1922) was a prominent name in the literature of fin de siècle London, turning out plays, pantomimes, many volumes of short stories, dozens of articles, two volumes of detective fiction featuring a lady sleuth (both volumes, in 1897 and again in 1898, titled *Dorcas Dene, Detective*), poetry, etc. His favorite drink in London's parks in summer was sherry and lemonade long before the 1980s rediscovered it as an elegant beverage. In 1907 he wrote *The Mystery of Mary Anne,* but in 1890 he had already written *The Case of George Candlemass,* on the formula of Sir Arthur Strangeways answering personal advertisements in agony columns in newspapers because he wants to play detective. Julian Symons in the first edition of *Bloody Murder* describes the book as an "uneasy attempt to guy the whole form," but makes no reference to the book in the second edition in 1985.

Andrew Sinclair is a prolific author, his books ranging from fiction to a serious study of Prohibition, but in 1979 appeared *The Facts in the Case of E. A. Poe,* "edited by" Sir Andrew Sinclair, and apparently a manuscript originally by Ernest Albert Pons, formerly Ponz, a Jew living in Manhattan, who chooses the only psychiatrist in Manhattan named Dr. Charles Dupin, whose family is connected with the wine trade. Pons identifies himself with E. A. Poe, and revisits all the sites in his life, always blaming Dupin for his failures. Finally he barricades himself in his flat and is tricked by Dupin by getting Pons's colleague Miss Zimmerman to dress up as Rosa. Throughout are references, not just to venues, but to persons and events; for example, to M. Roget in Nassau Street, to "puzzles as well as in horror stories," such as Maelzel's Automaton Chess Player, to three Dupin stories, the winning of one hundred dollars from *Dollar Newspaper* for "The Gold Bug," and to "Thou Art the Man." It is not unusual to find stories of men, not always patients, assuming identities of others; for example, the 1935 film of *The Raven* had Bela Lugosi as a retired surgeon, Dr. Richard Vollin, an apparent "reincarnation" of Poe, with such Poe devices as the pit and the pendulum, who treats wanted man Boris Karloff to exact his revenge. Sinclair's book gives much background material of Poe's life as Pons seeks to establish his persona.

Nancy Spain was a newspaper journalist, critic, and author of books ranging from accounts of women's wartime service to a series of detective stories of a distinctly farcical nature, titles lurching from *Death Before Wicket, The Kat Strikes, Murder, Bless It, Poison in Play* (murder at a tennis tournament finals), to *Cinderella Goes to the Morgue* (1950; 1978, reissued as *Minutes to Midnight,* murder in a provincial pantomime in England at Christmas), all with a keen eye for credibility and atmosphere. Her sleuths are Miriam Birdseye, a forthright eccentric, sounding and looking like Hermione Gingold, the actress to whom at least one of the books is dedicated, and Natasha, beautiful ballet dancer (based on a Spain relation), ex-wife of nightclub owner Johnny Du Vivien, known formerly when a professional wrestler as "Ion Orr." When murder decimates the pantomime cast, Miriam and Natasha join the players with successful if unexpected results. Strange names appear—*Poison in Play* has a character named Piers Ghent. Miriam and Natasha invariably solve the ingenious murders. In the 1970s the present writer wanted to turn *Cinderella Goes to the Morgue* into a musical with composer Betty Lawrence. The agents granted a free six-month option, because Hermione Gingold had herself shown interest in the book. Ironically, they turned down our adaptation without even seeing it or hearing the music, and nothing has since been heard of any performance of this particular murder mystery, with its climax in a large department store a few days after Christmas.

Dylan Thomas's fame in matters literary lies in his poetry, such as "Do Not Go Gentle into That Good Night," and his plays including the poetic *Under Milk Wood,* based on a day in the life of the Welsh villagers of Llareggub (once again, try reversing the name), but with John Davenport he wrote *Death of the King's Canary,* first published in Britain in 1976 and in America the following year. It tells of the British prime minister having to appoint a new poet laureate, based on the biographies and specimen poems sent him, and this gives ample opportunity for parodies of the poetry of T. S. Eliot, W. H. Auden, inter alia. The poet laureate is, of course, the King's Canary. After the appointment of Hilary Byrd (*sic*) comes a vicious account of a party attended by many thinly disguised literary celebrities at Dymmock Hall, with horrible food, sickening company, blackmailing revenge, and fifty-one suspects. The chapter headings are frivolous: "Choosing the Canary," "A Gilded Cage," "Cat's Fugue," "Parliaments of Birds," "The Canary Sings," "Bird's Eye View," and "Night Birds." According to the cover it "makes many chapters deliberate parodies, full of clichés, of other detective-writers." Among those parodied are Augustus Johns, Cyril Connolly, Aleister Crowley (as Hamish Corbie), and Thomas and Davenport parody themselves as hard-drinking oarsmen.

The evil new poet laureate offering his unpleasant party for his rivals in all fields, with mice in aspic, swans, marijuana cigarettes, "aphrodisiacs," and narcotics to humiliate them before the press photographers, has many esoteric clues. When Corbie is made to dress up as a female fortune-teller he is called the Great Raven. The circus and fairground element in the courtyard recalls a nightmare sequence of Michael Innes. The aristocratic Lord Lacy with sisters Lucretia and Crystal is an inverted parody of the three Sitwells. The leading younger poet Wyndham Nils Snowden is W. H. Auden, sculptor Harry Bartatt (from the Yorkshire folk song) obviously Henry Moore, Oliver Fry the artist Roger Bacon, artist Hercules Jones is Augustus Johns, and Edmund Bell is Edmund Blunden. The magazine editor recalls the famous counterpart whose prediction for the highbrow did not please her glossy publishers. References to Dudley recall the restoration counterpart in court circles of Empson, etc., etc. The date is fixed by reference to the fall of Burma in World War II. The Alice-in-Wonderland murder of the host brings down the curtain.

Sir Basil Thomson, as one of the first leading Scotland Yard chiefs, wrote a serious textbook on his career, called *Queer People* (ca. 1922), but he also wrote humorous detective stories that did not always receive acclaim from the critics. Julian Symons in the first edition of *Bloody Murder* says, "One turns away with a shudder from the many Holmes parodies and from such collections as Sir Basil Thomson's stories about Mr. Pepper . . ." but as we have seen this target disappears from his second edition. Howard Haycraft refers to Thomson's work in both his books; in *The Art of the Mystery Story* (1946), Thomson is mentioned as producing in 1925 that rara avis, a comic detective, and in *Murder for Pleasure* (1941) he mentions the methodical Constable Richardson, and the ill-advised Pepper parodies.

Mark Twain (Samuel Langhorne Clemens, 1835–1910) brought crime and detection into his books as early examples of the genre, such as in *Life on the Mississippi* (1883) containing the first use in fiction of fingerprints, eleven years before the advent of his *Pudd'nhead Wilson*, but he too brought in parody. *The Stolen White Elephant, Etc.* (1882) in its title story parodies Inspector Blunt and his staff, while "A Double-Barrelled Detective Story" in 1902 parodied in a western the great powers of Fetlock Jones's uncle, Sherlock Holmes. *Simon Wheeler, Detective* was a satiric novel, unfinished at Twain's death, and not published until 1963. Naturally, even his straight detective stories were overlaid with the unique Twain humor common to all his books.

Murder! Murder! was the engaging title of a spoof detective story written in 1931 by Laurence Vail, ex-husband of both Kay Boyle and Peggy Guggenheim, a story in which the hero believes he has killed dozens of victims in Paris. Julian Symons in *Bloody Murder* described it as "often funny, equally often boring, a stylishly written curiousity."

S. S. Van Dine and his detective, of whom Ogden Nash wrote succinctly "Philo Vance /needs a kick in the pance," was parodied yet again, this time by Christopher Ward (1868–1942) in the *Saturday Review of Literature* (November 2, 1929; reprinted in Haycraft's *The Art of the Mystery Story*) with "The Pine Murder Case" by S. S. Veendam. The four chapters are dated, as in the Vance originals, but 1732, 1929, 1066, and 1444. There are references to Pants, to Detective Bogan being on the Elwell and Rothstein murder cases (the 1920 Elwell murder was the basis of the Benson Murder Case for Vance), and to the Dorothy Arnold disappearance (Dorothy Arnold was an heiress, educated at Bryn Mawr, of 108 East 79th Street, New York, who vanished inexplicably from the junction of Fifth Avenue and 27th Street at 11 A.M. on December 12, 1910), to Barker as the DA, and the "silly old Veendam." There are the usual weighty footnotes, for example to the author of Green, Canary, Mauve, and Beige Murder Cases as titles (unlike the original books which had the six-letter title word, as we have seen). This parody is listed in Haycraft's *Murder for Pleasure*. Rothstein is, of course, Arnold Rothstein, Mr. Big the Brain, gambler and financier, already mentioned in connection with Damon Runyon's and F. Scott Fitzgerald's depictions in their books.

We have noted above the original of Edgar Wallace's Mr. J. G. Reeder as Superintendent Charles Crocker. In the books Reeder's career is described as being with both the banks and the public prosecutor, and living in the Brockley area of southeast London, which his daughter Penelope Wallace says he knew so well from residing there himself. (Indeed, his very unusual *The Day of Uniting* [1926] is actually set in the beautiful southeast London village of Blackheath and in Greenwich Park, but it is very hard to pinpoint the actual mansion facing the heath from which much of the action stems and can be seen.) Margaret Lane in her biography *Edgar Wallace* categorizes the many books into those with intricate plots, those with a central character like Reeder even though the plots are intricate, racing, and one-off plots. She states the hero is usually a detective, like Mr. Reeder of the Public Prosecutor's Office, and the humor comes from minor characters, like petty thieves, "unless, as in the case of Mr. Reeder, the humour is supplied by the hero himself." It will be remembered that in one book, *Room 13,* J. G. Reeder, turns out to be his own predecessor Mr. Golden, and *Johnny Gray,* the "ex-convict," to be the inspector in charge of the office, which is somewhat confusing. Penelope Wallace answered my query by saying she thinks her father brought Reeder back as too valuable a character to lose. A parody on Reeder comes in the unexpected form of westerns. J. T. Edson is a prolific writer in this genre, creating various worlds of cowboys and rangers, living in Melton Mowbray in England, his readers able to join the J. T. Edson Society. Two paperback books feature him: *"Cap" Fog, Texas Ranger, Meets Mr. J. G. Reeder,* and the other, No. 104 in the same series, *The Return of Rapido Clint,* which we shall now examine. Cap Sergeant Fog leads the hunt by Company Seven of the Texas Rangers for the killer named the Chopper, escaping from Fort Worth. Fog is Rapido Clint, and his team consists of Rita, Sgt. Mark Scrapton (Comanche Blood), and Sgt. Ranse Smith (Alvin). They travel to London where a contract is out for Reeder, as a prominent London gang leader tries to earn Mad John Flack's Encyclopaedia of Crime (mentioned in Wallace's *Terror Keep*), promised by Olga Flack to the killer of her father's murderer. There are additional references to the Wallace stories, sometimes in voluminous and factual footnotes; for example, to Chief Inspector Oliver Rater, the "Orator"; we learn of Jeremiah *G*olden getting the KCB (Knight Commander of the Order of the Bath); and Jeremiah Golden Reeder has three nephews: Jason *G*rant, Major John *G*ray, and James *G*arfield, all of whom can play their uncle in disguise. A character, Mark, refers to *Underworld Nights* by Charles Raven, and there are mentions of Major John Grant, and of "Major John Gray," whose rarely used surname was Reeder. There are some discrepancies in these Reeders and Goldens in the apparent superhuman killings that occur, and there is even a somewhat anachronistic Polish joke in this otherwise ingenious book.

We have already considered briefly David Williams, along with Donald Westlake, in the comments on detective fiction writers with a distinct sense of humor. I interviewed Williams for the *Poisoned Pen* (vol. 6, no. 3 [Fall 1985]), and he disclosed that unlike Agatha Christie, for example, basing Miss Marple on her own grandmother, he constructed some of his characters on actors playing the roles. We can see that Ralph Richardson was the goofy judge in *Murder for Treasure;* in *Copper, Gold and Treasure,* one character was Alec Guinness playing the part. His first six books had "Treasure" in the title, Mark Treasure being the merchant banker who solved the murders in strange, elegant, and unusual surroundings in the first twenty-four hours before the arrival of the official police, in a manner often compared to John Putnam Thatcher. He thought that subconsciously inevitably, but consciously not at all, he might put something of himself into Treasure, who is based on Robert Hardy playing the role. Hardy, like Williams an Oxford graduate, is perhaps most famous for his portrayal of Winston Churchill on stage and television, and is also, as I found when writing another book, an authority on the medieval longbow and the battles in which it was used. The wife in the books is an actress, and is based on an English actress playing the role. Williams loves the Golden Age of detective fiction and his parody or spoof thereof, *Treasure by Degrees* (1977), was based on a university college. One character, who is not so innocent as she seems throughout, is based on an actress playing the part— and the actress was Margaret Rutherford, famous for her individual, if not ideal, screen portrayals of Miss Jane Marple. In *Unholy Writ,* Williams confessed he based the financier-chairman on a real-life individual.

A strange mixture of cartoon characters and humans was in Gary Wolfe's *Who Censored "Roger Rabbit"?* (published by St. Martin's Press, New York, in 1981). Roger Rabbit and his wife Jessica, Roger's doppelganger who is partner to author Eddie Valiant, and another double for Jessica all get mixed up with humans Eddie, the De Greasy Brothers syndicate, Rocco, and Dominick; Rocco lived with Jessica Rabbit and got murdered. There are cartoon and real police, balloons of speech appear as in strip cartoons (some get the Maltese Falcon, others get Rabbits); a missing teakettle is a genie's lamp; there is a parody of Eddie Valiant entering his Los Angeles office to avoid waylaying (office rent, $300 per month); there is confusion between getting rabbits and Maltese Falcons; a child star, baby Herman; cartoons racket Lewd, Crude, and In the Mood by Sid Sleaze—all add up to an amusing, surrealistic amalgam of Hollywood, parody, cartoon, and fantasy.

A report in MWA's *The Third Degree* by Shannon OCork in her "Whispers" said that the Disney Studios had selected this as the 1987 Christmas feature film, to be directed by Robert Zemeckis as a mix of live action and new animation techniques (a mixture proved successful in Uncle Remus and Gene Kelly films), written by Lowell Gantz and Babaloo Mandell, and with producer Steven Spielberg, but with the title changed to *Who Shot Roger Rabbit?* By 1988 the £25 million spectacular, animator Oscar-winning Roger Williams, was titled *Who Framed Roger Rabbit*.

The Big Bow Mystery (The Perfect Crime): A Story of Crime by Israel Zangwill was published in 1891, and my own small black-bound copy is described as "published by the Detective Story Club Ltd. for Wm. Collins' Sons & Co. Ltd." I spoke to the then-longest-serving Collins executive, who told me this was the predecessor to the famous Crime Club with their outstanding logos of gun and knife (the black editions have the menacing-man logo) and that prices were sevenpence in 1907, one shilling and sixpence in 1922, three shillings and sixpence in 1927, and one shilling in 1928 (predecimalization rates), and my copy would be 1929. Zangwill (1864–1926) was English, the son of a Russian Jewish émigré, and this book has been described both as a parody and, in Symons's first edition only of *Bloody Murder* as "much more like a parody than has been acknowledged." Also described as the first full-length locked-room mystery, it tells of Mrs. Drabdump, of 11 Grover Street, Bow (a district on the east side of London), victim Arthur Constant, BA, near neighbor ex-detective Grodman whose *Criminals I Have Caught* is in its twenty-fourth edition ghosted for him by Denzil Cantercot, Edward Wimp of Scotland Yard, Peter Crowl, Tom Mortlake, and even W. E. Gladstone the Liberal prime minister. This mystery is of a man found dead in a locked room by Grodman, a murder for which Mortlake is arrested and reprieved without Grodman's dramatic, self-confessing visit to the home secretary, much to Grodman's disgust. Yet another strangely named character in this very readable short book is a Queen's Counsel named Spigot. The book has been filmed twice, first in 1928 as *The Perfect Crime* and then in 1946 as *The Verdict* with Sydney Greenstreet and Peter Lorre, who appeared together in many classic crime films, including *The Maltese Falcon* and Eric Ambler's *The Mask of Demetrios*.

From Sword to Distaff

David Williams's depiction of a "creator" of Miss Marple as a "chief suspect" is not the only indication of parodying female sleuths, and there are a few examples to complete this chapter. To start with, Is the remark true in a book surveying lady detectives that Jemima Shore, the creation in some half-dozen books and a British television series of Antonia Fraser, is a parody of American "private eye" jargon? Fraser, professional historian, broadcaster, and member of a famous literary family, was chair of the CWA for 1985/86, and the committee was assisting her in some of the functions in her year of office. On March 9, 1985, she was definite that she could not understand it all; it didn't make any sense to her as she certainly did not parody either PIs or their jargon—and furthermore, she did not approve of those two authors of that book *The Lady Investigates* disclosing the plots of her own books, all of which are still in print. In another conversation, on July 1, 1985, asked if it was true Jemima Shore, her television investigative sleuth, was based on the British Joan Bakewell, she answered that the true basis was the American Barbara Walters, a friend of hers; she noticed at lunch people kept coming to Walters for advice. Later she made Shore a Cambridge graduate, unlike herself at Oxford, and included some traits of Joan Bakewell. I pointed out the similarities between Shore and her creator: they are both honey-colored, very attractive, drink white wine, and speak in very similar voice rhythms.

In the second edition of his *Bloody Murder* Julian Symons said in 1985, speaking of homosexual detectives, "One awaits the first Lesbian PI." He was wrong; she had appeared six years earlier in David Galloway's *Lamar Ransome Private Eye*. Galloway's second book, *A Family Album,* has two strange errors, based on a set of photographs, with a blurb for his next offering describing it as a "loving parody" of the tough Chandler detective novel (involving Howard Hughes, the Andrews Sisters, Busby Berkeley, and a cast of thousands). A book about any American city does presumably involve a cast of thousands; the Andrews Sisters are heard on a radio at one point; Howard Hughes's impact is fleeting; and Busby Berkeley proves enigmatic, as we shall see. Ransome is the lesbian, which causes occasional witticisms, like her saying, "Guess it brings out the man in me," ringing her woman friend with Bogart-style patter, and having a black homosexual secretary named Lavender Trevelyan. Her office is in the Cahuenga Building, with a competitor at the back of the block, obviously meant to be Marlowe. The date is fixed by references to the Dionne quints' ninth birthday (they were born May 28, 1934); there are parody's usually crop of characters with peculiar names like Blanche Framboise (white raspberry), Yvette Laflamme, Sebastian Tropes (figure of speech; "to trope" meant to insert tropes or liturgical interpolations into ecclesiastical chants from eighth- or ninth-century Byzantine time), Brand Brockaway, and Holmes Woolcott who has a son Alexander. One address is Loma Drive— surely not the loma, a membraneous fringe? One gun is a Mauser 7.65, but the surprise is the killer, Rigsby Riley, described as a great dance director, whose first film success was a Paris sequence; presumably this is a parody of Busby Berkeley, whose career was in the theatre from 1920 to 1930, who choreographed the film *Whoopee* in 1930, and directed and choreographed *She Had to Say Yes* in 1933. There is a spectacular finale in a film studio in this somewhat uneasy story.

By the 1990s there were several lesbian detectives, including Ellen Hart's Jane Lawless, and Randye Lordon's PI Sydney Sloane. Mabel Maney's Cherry Aimless, in one novel, *The Case of the Not-So-Nice Nurse,* is described as a parody of the best-selling sleuth Nancy Drew.

In 1942 psychologist William Moulton Marston devised a master (or mistress) foe against the forces of evil, to rival Batman, and so Wonder Woman made her appearance in the comic strips, later to become a popular television series in America first, then England. The series has been attacked by such outstanding writers as Frederick Wertheim for its alleged lesbian slant. Wonder Woman is a primly bespectacled office operative, whose alter ego is apparently not guessed by colleagues or enemies (except for one enemy who carried out the popular cinema trick of unsuspectedly occupying and manipulating bodies and minds). She goes into action by removing her glasses and spinning round into a technicolored leotard and indulges in spectacular leaps by careful use of trampolines. Even in the television series, the comic strip element is maintained by shots of, say, "Back at Washington H.Q." References are made to her activities in the 1940s and to links with a romance in some other galaxy.

A TV film, *The New Original Wonder Woman,* was made in 1975, featuring Lynda Carter, and with William Moulton Marston's character; the story is of a princess, a mother, and her daughters in a Devil's Triangle island, plus an American pilot, another from Germany, a long-range German fighter-bomber, spies, plus comedian Red Buttons.

In 1984 Lynda Carter, who had played Wonder Woman on television, took the lead in another television series, *Fifty-Fifty,* with the former lead of *WRKP in Cincinnati,* Loni Anderson, as the two private eyes who seek their ex-husband's killer and take over his detective agency, although the previous careers of Carole Stanwyck and Sydney Kovak were photographer and musician. Carol (Carter) and Syd (Anderson) first meet at the funeral of their joint husband, find they inherit not only his detective agency but his heavily mortgaged mansion, but they live there with their joint mother-in-law Jeanie, played by Eileen Heckart. They portray the partners as intelligent, energetic young women, yet glamorous enough to appear as models when investigating piracy of fashion designs in one episode, "Fashioned for Murder." Like Michael Underwood's sleuthing female solicitor, they do not try to "go it alone," or to be "had I but known," but liaise with a representative of the local police, one Lieutenant Vronski. The series, which had a ninety-minute pilot followed by sixty-minute episodes, is owned by a delightfully named company, Partners in Crime. Of course, female sleuths glamorous or forbidding, have been prevalent from the earliest days of Lady Molly of Scotland Yard, to Nancy Drew, to the Norths, to Miss Marple (could her St. Mary Mead, nicknamed Mayhem Parva, have got its nickname from J. J. Conington's Sir Clinton Driffield 1929 story *Nemesis at Raynham Parva*?). *Fifty-Fifty* scripts have touches of humor, are well written, but not in general parodic, although the late joint husband's given names were Raymond Dashiell.

English author Susan Moody also decided to have a female answer to a male ego, this time James Bond, in several books, including *Penny Black, Penny Dreadful,* and *Penny Post* in 1984 and 1985. Penny is a six foot, well-educated, very well dressed woman, daughter of a black ambassador and a white English aristocrat, and with an old Etonian boyfriend. Her attitude is amoral: while righting wrongs and foiling the ungodly, she invariably has an affair with some man she meets, and shares her boyfriend's profits in stealing antiques, sometimes even from those she has helped. Susan explained on the telephone on May 8, 1985, that it was intended as a parody of Bond; why should men have all the fun with bed-hopping? It was intended to be amusing. Penny gets furious if she meets those who don't seem to share her own somewhat liberal views; her menus and clothes, apart from a paucity of underwear, are described in detail, and certainly the writer has a keen eye and ear for atmosphere and setting.

Michele B. Slung, in her introduction to a book of tales of female sleuths *Crime on Her Mind* (1975), refers to the trend since 1961, and "the female parody of superagent James Bond as manifested in Modesty Blaise . . . now passes as Bond." Emma Peel of *The Avengers* is another; as we shall see there have been stories about various women sleuths in different studies, from Eileen Dare, Nelson Lee's assistant, to actual policewomen on cases, like Gwendoline Butler's or Dorothy Uhnak's. Created by Peter O'Donnell as a newspaper strip cartoon in 1962 for England, then featured in one film and several books, Modesty Blaise is apparently a waif, yet well educated, head of a crime network, then retired to become a freelance operative with sidekick Willie Garven, for British intelligence, reminiscent of radio's Peculiar Lady in Blue. She has various lovers and is a keen fighter, described as a sex object with guns, the Nailer, weapons concealed in a roomy chignon and brassiere, (see below) the trick of surprising men by stripping (one would hardly think a professional so deterred), and yet complains about one particular gun because it does not fit in with her somewhat prominent breasts. Modesty and Garven succeed in routing the various gangs, however large, much like Bond. An interesting endorsement to Slung's bracketing of Blaise with the parodied Bond is in *Le Roman Policier* by Boileau-Narcejac, PUF (1975): "Ici, le sentiment céde le pas à la sensation, comme il arrive toujours quand on demande au lecteur de se changer en voyeur. A la limite, il n'y a même plus à sentir mais simplement à regarder. C'est alors le règne de James Bond ou de Modesty Blaise, sur un monde terrifiant et pueril."

Apart from the newspaper comic strip and the film with Monica Vitti, CWA member Peter O'Donnell has written a series of books about Modesty, including *Modesty Blaise, Sabre-Tooth, I, Lucifer, A Taste for Death, The Impossible Virgin, The Silver Mistress,* and *Pieces of Modesty,* inter alia. Her career has built up from a waif to a successful criminal gang leader to a wealthy adventuress now on the side of British intelligence. She and Willie Garven can take on, defeat, and kill a complete gang of individualistic criminals, like Bond and, again like Bond, with amazing technical devices like those given to British spies and airmen in World War II (compasses in buttons, etc.). A "Kongo" (small, adaptable, defensive weapon) concealed in her chignon, gas spray gun in lipstick, aerial wire in a brassiere, and Willie having false shoe welts and a false skin layer with a miniature transmitter are just some ingenious examples with the aid of which a score of gangsters may be wiped out. There is no romance between the two, who have their own dalliances. The locales, ethos, and swift action are all in the Bond style. Peter O'Donnell now lives in Brighton on the Sussex coast and for thirty-five years had an office above a famous press watering hole, El Vino's, in Fleet Street.

The last story in the distaff section is a fitting end to this chapter on parody. In *Ellery Queen's Masks of Mystery* (1979) appeared a story by Rod Reed with the eye-catching title of "Give Me Lib, or Give Me Death." Imagine a robbery at the United Notions (*sic*) the manufacturers of Monotony (*sic*)—then imagine a team of women sleuths, all listed in the preamble: Boston Blondie, Nora Woof, Simone Templer, Hillary Quinn, Goldilock Holmes, Samantha Shovel, Micheline Hammerlock (described in the actual story as Hammer), Charlotte Chin, Hercula Parrot, May Gray (who does not get a mention in the story), Violet Pantz (who is another absentee in the text), plus in the text but not in the preamble, Miss Motto.

This roll call of the great names of detective fiction is a dramatic outburst to general parody, both of men and women sleuths, and leads on to parody en masse, in two parts.

One section deals with writers who parody two detectives in the same book or short story (sometimes writing different parts in the appropriate literary styles), as when two detectives are involved on the same case. The other treatment is that popular in England in the 1930s and again just after World War II, when six authors combined to write a single detective story, carrying on the narrative and clearing the problems left by the writer of the preceding chapter, creating new puzzles for the next chapter writer, yet still keeping a logical, homogeneous whole.

Parody by the handful—shooting down several targets simultaneously, grapeshot in the dark!

3. The Crowd of One Man

The writer who wishes to parody more than one detective can approach the problem from opposing directions. A story with two detectives? Separate books with a different sleuth? A league or club, like those in the preceding chapter? We shall even find one writer who combined nine different forms of pastiche in a sparkling entity, in the appropriate section below.

An example of the first is the 1930s story in the British *Wild West Weekly* in which Sexton Blake went out West to meet the millionaire rancher, Kit Carson, and to hunt a mysterious masked horseman who robbed on the Robin Hood principle and outwitted all the local lawmen. Blake deduced that Carson and the masked rider were one and the same because, as he explained to Carson, he always dressed in white from head to foot, the rider always similarly in black, and you learned always to suspect such contrasts.

One man who made an industry of parody is Jon L. Breen, whose *Vicar's Roses* has already been noted. In *Hair of the Sleuthhound* (1982) he wrote twenty-two stories which swept the board in every category. His introduction had the excellent comment on parody and pastiche quoted in the first chapter. More stories have been published in *EQMM,* and all the major writers have been under fire: McBain, Marric, Arthur B. Reeve, Dick Francis, Christie, Ellery Queen, J. D. MacDonald, Ross Macdonald, Earl Derr Biggers, S. S. Van Dine, E. D. Hoch, the last gothic, etc., etc.

In *Dear Dead Days* (1974), edited by Edward D. Hoch, appeared "The Austin Murder Case: or, The Talkie Murder Case" (note the six-letter names), set in 1929, when actor Jack Austin is killed at a screen fancy-dress party, with a clue of spectacles—an imitation Harold Lloyd is among the guests, as are Eugene Pallette, and Tom Mix. There are the usual learned footnotes, and when Markham, Van Dine, and Philo Vance attend, the last is in Douglas Fairbanks Sr.'s black pirate garb.

Breen's work is always enlivened by humor; when Charlie

Chan is asked why he has no moustache, his reply is that he leaves that to Swedish actors. Some stories are perhaps more pastiche than parody, but we shall only consider some representative examples here.

"The $106,000 Mud Bunny" parodies Dashiell Hammett (1894–1961), with the Transcendental Detective agency, and a mud bunny smashed in a character's pocket—one of the crooks rejoicing in the name of Con Crete. The target is of course the Continental Op and the $106,000 Blood Money.

Breen's Ed McBain parody starts with the usual lyrical, "The City is a female," with Steve Berella.

"The House of the Shrill Whispers" is a parody of John Dickson Carr, and starts off with a list of cases solved, which are summarized as "a rumored seal, a rocked loom, a rooked lamb, an impossible chrome, a miracle pabulum and a sealed groom," and goes on to refer to real people, to committing the crime himself, but objecting to a secret passage.

"An Evening with the White Divorcées" also appeared in Ellery Queen's 1976 *Veils of Mystery,* where Breen is referred to as the "foremost parodist and pastichist in the mystery field," and in Queen's *Anthology* (vol. 39, Spring-Summer, 1980). A parody of Isaac Asimov's Black Widowers, meeting at the Garibaldi Restaurant, with parody guest Calvin Souse, artist Grimaldo Moreno not Mario Gonzalo, attorney Godfrey Catalana as Geoffrey Avalon, it "spoofs both the Black Widowers and their creator."

"Champoux Versus Joshua," in Ellery Queen's *Faces of Mystery* (1978, dated 1973) has Pierre Chambrun manager of a luxury hotel in New York, the Beaumont, becoming Henry Champoux, and Judson Philips's (as Hugh Pentecost) other hero John Jericho metamorphosed into Job Joshua, in the affair of the murder at the Hotel of Doug Gooder, Sr., chairman of the Bleeding American Hearts, at the annual dinner, with much byplay with fancy dress and weapons before the denouement. Doug Gooder must have been a "do-gooder." Amusingly, a crime bookseller's catalogue had an item of letters between a literary agent, Jacques Chambrun and author Michael Harrison.

One final example from the book *Hair of the Sleuthhound* and the magazine *EQMM* is "Frank Merriwell's Greatest Case; or The Daring One-Hander." *The Adventures of Frank Merriwell* was a famous American dime-novel-hero cinema serial, popular in England in the 1930s for children's Saturday morning cinema clubs. This story of murder on the sports field, with commentary, is duly solved; in one reprint, however, at the end is a key showing the derivations of several players' names: Greystoke is Edgar Rice Burroughs's Tarzan; Wayne is Bruce Wayne, Bob Kane's Batman; R. Grant refers to Clark Kent, Superman; L. Grant refers to Walter B. Gibson (Maxwell Grant) and his creation Lamont Cranston, the Shadow; Reid is Britt Reid, publisher of the *Daily Sentinel* in Fran Striker and George W. Trendle's *The Green Hornet* radio, screen, and comic strip series.

Breen's parodies and pastiches are always written in the correct styles, and his touches of extravagance always in keeping, as the quoted examples show, and the mad logicality adds to the credibility of his storytelling, like the surrealism of the Marx Brothers, as composer Constant Lambert wrote. This is borne out by his foreword in *Hair of the Sleuthhound*, and his other books already listed.

We have already mentioned Simon Brett, chair of the CWA in 1986/87, with his *Faber Book of Parodies,* parody *Situation Tragedy,* and later his pastiche *Murder in the Title*. In 1986 came his *The Wastepaper Basket Archives* with three pieces therein, which brings him also into the mass parody genre. "From Raymond Chandler's Wastepaper Basket" comes a two-page excerpt from a "lost" Marlowe story, in which the sleuth is interviewed by a tough businessman and his glamorous secretary. The usual laconic Marlowe wisecracks annoy the man (Marlowe's card "with the tommygun in the corner" upsets him "as if I'd shoved last week's cheese sandwich up his nose"), and when Marlowe reports Darnley Bombeck had hired him to find his missing daughter, the other offers to pay him not to find her. Marlowe quotes his rates: "A hundred down as retainer—that's when I'm working with strangers. Then twenty-five a day, plus expenses."

"That include the car?"

"Eight cents a mile."

The rhythms of Chandler's dialogue and descriptions are authentic and witty. "From Agatha Christie's Wastepaper Basket" comes a canceled last will and testament with estate complications. The long-lost nephew from Australia, Eric—or his illegitimate brother Henry the solicitor—or my housekeeper Winifred Caister, daughter of my doctor Marmaduke Dobbington—or her father "but only if he is reconciled with his estranged wife Daphne"—or if Daphne doesn't survive "the police should be called and after Marmaduke's arrest"—the long suffering nurse, Betty—but if she should "die in suspicious circumstances"—here the holograph will is torn across—a typical Christie mystery.

"From Charles Dickens' Wastepaper Basket" comes a transcription of the actual chapter 23 of *The Mystery of Edwin Drood*. A description of a dusty early summer morning in London—dust everywhere—a mysterious veiled lady walks from the docks to a dusty sad hotel "at the dingy end of Cheesemaker Street," her head, her hands, her face, concealed, as the dusty fat boy takes her to a dusty small room. Then the large sunbrowned hands with the strange Moroccan ring remove the veil from the strong, heavy-browed, sad face as she smilingly murmurs to the mirror, "Welcome back to England, Edwina Drood."

Brett displays a knowledge of his authors, their rhythms and meters, and of the purpose of parody vis-à-vis its original to good effect.

Leo Bruce picked on the formula of a country copper who solves complicated murders despite the presence of intelligent professionals, amateurs, or senior police officers. In 1936 he wrote *Case for Three Detectives,* published by Geoffrey Bles, concerning the murder of Mrs. Thurston in a locked-room mystery. In come three famous detectives—"one had probably been staying in the district, another was a friend of Dr. Tate's, while a third, perhaps, had already been asked to stay with the Thurstons."

Lord Simon Plimsoll has three Rolls-Royce cars, a valet named Butterworth, and is staying at the local inn, was first heard of ten years previous (*Whose Body?* by Dorothy L. Sayers had been published in 1923), wasn't a day older, and had a Jack Hulbert chin (Hulbert was a leading light-comedy actor of the British cinema and West End stage, famous for his debonair song and dance, acting, and his long chin). The second sleuth is a curious little man, M. Amer Picon, with an egg-shaped head (*amer* means "sharp"; *picon* could be "pike"; *Amer Picon* is a strong French drink). The third detective is a small human pudding, Monsignor Smith, with parcels and a green parasol.

The parody runs throughout: Plimsoll finds a rope in the cistern; Picon asks if it was there earlier, so Smith fishes out a second rope. Plimsoll has the first solution, Picon the second, finally comes

Smith's—until Sergeant Beef produces the correct answer, rather in the manner of *Murder by Death,* to be considered in the show business chapter. All three detectives use the correct language of Wimsey, Poirot, and Brown—for example, Msgr. Smith uses metaphysical terms.

While considering the Leo Bruce stories we can ponder an interesting paragraph by R. F. Stewart, in his analytical study ". . . And Always a Detective." Dr. Routley in his *The Puritan Pleasures of the Detective Story* describes a book by Christopher Bush entitled *Case for Four Detectives,* in which the feverish activities of Holmes, the modish clubmanship of Wimsey, the indolent sedentary reasoning of Poirot, and the obscure and oracular epigrams of Father Brown are beaten by the village policeman. Stewart claims this is one of the mistakes in Routley's study, in that *Case for Three Detectives* (1936) has been confused with Christopher Bush's 1951 *The Case of the Fourth Detective,* which has his usual title the case of and the two normal sleuths of Ludovic Travers and Superintendent Wharton of Scotland Yard. Bruce's is yet another book that parodies Fortune and Campion, plus the three main targets, and has such strange clues as the unseen car.

In 1951 Bruce wrote *Case for Sergeant Beef,* No. 847 in the Penguin paperback series. There is an early reference to "Lord Simon Plimsoll and M. Amer Picon and them." Beef comments that his biographer, his Watson, would do better if Plimsoll were on the scene again. In this book, which Haycraft describes as "determinedly humorous" in his *Murder for Pleasure,* appear Constable Watts-Dunton (Watts-Dunton was the name of the poet who cared for the ill Algernon Swinburne in his villa at Putney), Wellington Chickle, Inspector Chatto, and Jack Ribbon—all deliberately strange names in the style of Dickens and P. G. Wodehouse.

The mysterious Wellington Chickle refers in the eighth entry in his diary to some new books from Bumpus, "among them some detective novels by a writer new to me—Leo Bruce. He relates the investigations of a certain Sergeant Beef through an observer called Townsend." Chickle is found by the pair of sleuths reading Beef's fifth case, but Beef still complains of Townsend, when Chatto does not know him. "Now if I was Lord Plimsoll or Monsieur Amer Picon, or Mr. Albert Campion, or one of them, you'd know of me quickly enough, wouldn't you?" The case has some ingenious contrasting theories of the death, with Beef agreeing with the police, and telling Townsend that the desired last-chapter surprise is unprecedented in detective fiction for even hardened readers: the police "suspect" guilty.

A neat tribute to Sergeant Beef comes in Francis Gerard's *Golden Guilt* (1940). Gerard's literary output is considered elsewhere, but suffice it at the moment to say that many of his titles were alliterative (*Fatal Friday, Emerald Embassy*), his sleuth rises from Inspector John Meredith to Brigadier Sir John Meredith, ex-commissioner, before Michael Innes's Sir John Appleby and all his books, starting in 1936 and going on to the 1950s, and including some historical titles, are well written and ingenious. Gerard was born in 1906, of a famous French family, lived in London, continued three of Edgar Wallace's Sanders of the River books, served in the Essex Regiment, which comes into the 1952 *The Mind of Sir John Meredith,* and like, John Dickson Carr, left a socialist England—to live and die in South Africa. In *Golden Guilt* Meredith's sergeant, and later batman, is Matthew Beef, who is annoyed at his cousin's cockiness "over 'is last case . . . and his more famous cousin, Sergeant William Beef, who had so signally put the amateur detectives in their place in the case which had made his name, and which had been chronicled by Mr. Leo Bruce under the heading of *Case for Three Detectives*." Beef couldn't beat his cousin at darts and comments, "I mean, look at William's handling of that there case where there was a murder but there wasn't no corpse. Just sheer luck, that's what it is, just sheer luck." Meredith shook his head. "I think you're a bit prejudiced, Beef. I read that case very carefully, and it was more than luck; I thought your cousin handled the thing quite brilliantly." Elsewhere in this book: "I'm not really trying to behave like a detective in a book," Meredith said, "but you know the more I read detective fiction the more I realise that the detective heroes are quite right to behave as they do and keep their mouths shut until the *dénouement*."

A further stage in Beef's career is stated in "Death in the Garden," a short story originally appearing in the London *Evening Standard* newspaper, and collected into *The Evening Standard Detective Book,* published in 1950: "And now he had retired from the Force he was gaining a reputation as a private investigator." This particular early case, told by an unnamed narrator, concerns Beef as a constable doing gardening to supplement his income before he married, at the Mill House, in his village of Long Cotterell "in one of the home counties"—a case he solves from the heat given to his crop of mustard and cress.

Leo Bruce also created another contrasting detective, Carolus Deene, but his own writings were exhaustive, as he was in fact Rupert Croft-Cooke (1903–1979), whose books range from a comprehensive survey of Madeira wine, *A Book of Madeira,* to excellent books on the circus, biographies, and novels.

We come now to the acknowledged Queen of Crime Writers of all time, Agatha Christie (1890–1976), a president of the Detection Club of England, and romantic novelist Mary Westmacott. In her autobiography, *Agatha Christie,* in chapter 2 of part 9, she recalls writing around 1930 *Partners in Crime,* short stories in the manner of twelve differing detectives, recalling writers thereof as Austin Freeman, Freeman Wills Crofts, and Sherlock Holmes, inter alia. In my original monograph *Murder Done to Death,* published in 1979, I mentioned having bought from a specialist English crime bookseller, Dr. Camille Wolff, a delightful Collins sixpenny paperback having a charming, humorous art deco colored cover of the two sleuths in evening dress, accompanied by a bloodhound, with twelve chapters covering nine cases of Tommy and Tuppence Beresford's detective agency. The later paperback, by Pan Books, had twenty-three, the earlier Collins containing chapters 1 to 10, and 23 only; as these are separate cases, they read like short stories.

Tommy and Tuppence Beresford appeared in *The Secret Adversary* (1922), *Partners in Crime* (1929), *N or M?* (1941), *By the Pricking of My Thumbs* (1968), and *Postern of Fate* (1973). The first was filmed in Germany in 1928 as *Die Abenteuer G.m.b.H.,* directed by Fred Sauer, featuring Eve Gray. *Partners in Crime* features them as partners in a London detective agency, and each case is solved according to whichever detective story on the office shelves Tommy has just been reading, hence the writer's reference to three authors. Others parodied or mentioned are the Old Man in the Corner; Austin Freeman's blind investigator, Thornley Colton, whose cases are recorded by Clinton H. Stagg; Father Brown; Christie's Hercule Poirot; and Carl Petersen and Bulldog Drummond (*Blindman's Buff,* based on Colton, has the villain dispatched in a duel of spectacular explosiveness, very like those aimed by Petersen at Drummond).

G. C. Ramsey in *Agatha Christie: Mistress of Mystery* (1967) comments: "Mrs. Ariadne Oliver, as we have mentioned, satirises lady detective writers; and the young adventurers Tommy and Tuppence Beresford parody Poirot in one of this author's favourite short stories: 'The Man Who Was No. 16,' which one takes to represent *The Big Four*—squared. This last story in *Partners in Crime* shows clearly that Christie intends never to fall into the most deadly of all authors' traps—that of taking oneself and one's work too seriously." In appendix C he refers to this last short story again: " 'The Man Who Was Number 16' (the famous satire on Poirot and his methods)."

The Big Four (1927) is a Poirot story of the gallant Belgian with his "twin" Achille and Captain Hastings versus the powerful Chinaman, American millionaire, influential Frenchwoman, and the "Destroyer," Number Four, the man of many disguises who kills the syndicate's enemies—or tries to. Chapter 1 has the prophetic heading, "The Unexpected Guest." Poirot makes many deductions with "the little grey cells" in this action-packed story.

That excellent vade mecum *Murderess Ink* (1979) by Dilys Winn, a companion to *Murder Ink,* has an interesting comment in the essay "Till Death Do Us Part": "As snappy with a retort as Nora Charles (though not so stylish), as wildly imaginative as Pamela North (though not so accident prone), Tuppence in one series of short stories, *Partners in Crime,* represents Christie's only excursion into satire. Tongue in cheek, she and Tommy solve cases in the manner of Dr. Thorndyke, Sherlock Holmes, the Old Man in the Corner and even Poirot himself! Actually, Tuppence plays the great detectives' sidekicks in each instance, a role she disdains in her own sleuthing."

The "only excursion into satire" or parody could be disputed as we have seen Ariadne Oliver parodies Christie, and *The Body in the Library* was intended as a gentle parody of the genre.

Partners in Crime became a British television series, but one from which all the parody was washed away. For example, the story in which a missing woman is sought, and where she was found in a private clinic seeking to lose excess weight, was the Sherlock Holmes parody. "Man in the Mist" (the Father Brown parody) had Tommy dressed as a Catholic priest, with no adequate explanation, solving the murder of a famous actress in the fog (the titled man to whom she was affianced; the longhair poet, her earlier love?) but it turns out to be the policeman (not the postman), a former husband, met by Tommy in the fog near the actress's gate. I queried this lack of emphasis with David Crosse, a British stage and television actor, stage director, and adapter of Christie plays for the stage himself, and in a letter dated December 21, 1983, he agreed he had missed and forgotten the parody supposed to be the prime purpose of the stories. When the series was sold to ARD/Degeto Films (Frankfurt), *Stage* newspaper of June 21, 1984, described it as, "two detectives with a taste for the high life and the bizarre." A sad case of missing the point in adapting and directing.

Another Christie 1936 book and subsequent play with parodic tones is *Cards on the Table,* in which the mysterious Mr. Shaitana invites four Christie sleuths—Hercule Poirot, Ariadne Oliver (who wrote *The Body in the Library*), Colonel Race, and Superintendent Battle—plus four suspects from earlier crimes—Dr. Roberts, Mrs. Lorrimer, Major Despard, and Miss Meredith. A murder takes place in this mysterious gathering—of Shaitana himself—so the four detectives have to decide the guilty party from knowledge of the prior crimes, present facts, and the methods of playing and scoring bridge. Four different theories emerge (two squared this time?), and there are dramatic final events before Poirot's denouement.

When the play was adapted by Leslie Darbon for the Vaudeville Theatre, Poirot and Race were deleted, another seven characters were added, and the date was "Summer, 1935." Two interesting touches of the rare Christie parody: *The Mirror Crack'd from Side to Side* (1962), title taken from Tennyson's "Lady of Shalott," dedicated to Margaret Rutherford, was based on the glamorous Hollywood actress Gene Tierney's autobiographical recounting of her lost baby through meeting a fan with German measles; and Seeley Regester's 1867 *The Dead Letter,* deducing character from handwriting, is said to be satirized by Christie in her 1936 novel, *The ABC Murders,* later filmed.

In 1976 Desmond Cory wrote a long short story called "The Story of Stumblebum the Wizard." Three wizards under training see a murder by a princess and are called to give solutions at the Court of Enquiry. The first two wizards had their eyes shut, but they gave technically clever, directly opposite, and logical expositions: the first came from Dick Thorn, listed as Thorn Dick, and was very precise; the other was casual yet surprising from Perry the Mason; and the reports were in contrasting literary styles. The third wizard had his eyes open, but nobody believed his story and merely tried to prove him wrong—neat little parody on theoretical solutions from the experts, and a denigration of eyewitness reports.

Cory is an English writer who started in the spy genre with his Johnny Fedora, then changed in 1970 to psychological stories, one of which, in 1977, had obvious parodic leanings, according to H. R. F. Keating, in his chapter 7, "New Patents Pending," in *Crime Writers,* a 1978 BBC publication he edited, issued in conjunction with a BBC-TV education series: "to the books of Desmond Cory, such as *Bennett* in which he exploits every trick of illusions, down to a fake list of 'other books by' in advance of his title-page, to make the reader think about the supposedly secure bases of his world" (you may recall the famous mystery play with the convincing, yet false, curriculum vitae of the "actors").

We shall be considering August Derleth (1909–1971) under pastiche, for his creation of that great London detective Solar Pons, with his assistant Dr. Lyndon Parker, in a series of volumes of short stories and full-length cases. Derleth was the founder of Arkham House, and Mycroft and Moran, author, critic, anthologist, editor, and promulgator of science fiction in America. One of his short stories comes into this present section: "The Adventure of the Orient Express" appears in *The Chronicles of Solar Pons* (1965). Dr. Parker is traveling across Europe by train in 1938, sharing his compartment (or private cabin) with an enigmatic chess-playing Baron Egon Von Ruber, previously met. Exciting events follow fast. An elderly British agent, Ashenten (cf. Somerset Maugham) is killed and thrown out the window; there follows an interrogation by a German agent of the old school with a clubfoot from the wrong war (cf. Valentine Williams and Dr. Adolph Grundt, "Clubfoot"), after Von Ruber has shot a German agent Gisela Margenstein—and thrown her out the window. Parker gets some help from a dandified young man whose signature is a haloed stick figure (some sort of saint, comments Von Ruber); Parker is warned off in Paris by a plump Frenchman with waxed moustaches, Hercule Poiret (*sic*) of the French Sûreté; finally,

Parker meets Solar Pons who passes the microfilms of the intended 1939 German invasion of Poland to his own brother Bancroft Pons—whereupon Parker is flabbergasted to find Pons was Von Ruber all the time. This ironical story captures accurately the characters' actions and reactions as anticipated on encountering the real Pons.

Carlo Fruttero, Franco Lucentini, and Charles Dickens(!) were the authors of the 1993 novel *The D. Case; or, The Truth About the Mystery of Edwin Drood,* in which they bring a covey of fictional detectives, including Sherlock Holmes, Jules Maigret, Poirot, Archer, and Marlowe to Rome to solve the unfinished novel, with not inconsiderable literary elegance and acumen.

In *Poisoned Pen* (vol. 1, no. 1.) was a useful article by R. Jeff Banks, referring to, inter alia, *Slaughter Road—EDGE 22,* by George G. Gilman, published by Pinnacle in the States in 1977, and apparently parodying such various stories as *Paladin, Have Gun, Will Travel, The Maltese Falcon,* and *The Da Vinci Rose* by Archie O'Neil. This western does indeed parody several sleuths. It is the story of Edge, a western gunslinger, of ruthless and callous disposition, and the opening chapter in the Palace Hotel parodies *Have Gun, Will Travel* and *Paladin*. Edge is hired to protect a Da Vinci painting, worth a million dollars, on a train journey; he objects, incidentally, to the millionaire owner using other guards, and a duplicate package, to such an extent that Edge slashes the painting in brutal pique. There are three partners in a detective agency, who are soon shot—Phil Marlowe, Samuel Spade, and Lou Archer—with references to Hammer and Shayne, and plenty of wisecracks. Chinese pageboys are referred to as "the yellow pages"; Archer comments, "Not even to be a moving target" (Ross Macdonald's first Lew Archer book, in 1949, was *The Moving Target*). On the same page: "However I look, feller, it's got to be better than the big sleeper and the one with the ivory grin" (*The Big Sleep* was the first Marlowe book, in 1939, and *The Ivory Grin* a Lew Archer book in 1952). An interesting parody, although rough and brutal, involving western elements, wisecracks, ceaseless action, but not quite a "tecker."

Leonardo's Law by Warren B. Murphy was also mentioned in *Poisoned Pen* (vol. 5), as being a parody of other characters, including an Ellery Queen locked-room mystery, *A Room to Die In*.

Dr. C. Northcote Parkinson is world famous for his series of humorous yet sadly true books on his theory of Parkinson's Law, which basically states staff empires abhor a vacuum in an office and will easily fill it to overflowing. In complete contrast to a series of books on this topic came *Jeeves: A Gentleman's Gentleman,* published by MacDonald & Janes in 1979, in which chapter 6 is headed "The Detectives," and chapter 7, "The Villain Unmasked." In the former we meet three, the same three as does Sergeant Beef: Hercule Poirot is small with an egg-shaped head, large moustache, of military aspect, and with eagle eyes; Lord Peter Wimsey is of foppish appearance with straw-colored hair brushed back from his forehead, with an ugly nose and faintly foolish smile; while Father Brown is round-faced, unimpressive, pale, clumsy, innocent, and apparently simple. In the Panamericana Hotel in Monte Carlo the Montague Todd kidnapping is to realize £500,000 by Friday, June 21. In chapter 7, Lord Peter Wimsey is on holiday at Port Grimaud, in the Gulf of St. Tropez, and there are references to a stage character, man-about-town, the Whimsical Sleuth by Wallace Edgar. At the Convalescent Home of the Redemption, on a yacht moored in the harbor, and in the town the action proceeds. There is a Chestertonian quotation: "Where do you hide a pebble? On the beach. Where do you hide a leaf? In the forest. Where do you hide a holidaymaker? In a hotel. And in which hotel among many? In the hotel from which he is missing." Jeeves, the classic valet to Bertie Wooster, created by P. G. Wodehouse, in this book notes the use of Glisterall hair oil, Dazzle toothpaste, and Seduction aftershave in this fascinating, credible, and smooth story from the unexpected pen of a famous and humorous writer.

A Neil Simon-ish parody of a clutch of sleuths came from opera singer Helen Traubel (1903–1972), who wrote a short story to give as a Christmas present, and later, assisted by Harold Q. Masur, wrote *The Metropolitan Opera Murders.* At a 1949 production of *Die Walküre* with Brunhilde Wagner, the front row is occupied by Agatha Christie, John Dickson Carr, Rex Stout, Erle Stanley Gardner, Q. Patrick, Raymond Chandler, and Ellery Queen, inter alia. The parodic touches include "had I but known," Lucy's lovely throat, Anglers Island, and a crime writer doped to help Brunhilde write a thriller (*Murder at the Met*) with twelve murders, the murder of a real conductor, Lieutenant Sam Quentin and Detective Rollo, and Brunhilde's scream being so powerful as to be registered on the Fordham University seismograph.

This is a cross-section of English and American authors parodying two or more sleuths in a book or short story, and does not include the many Sherlock Holmes meetings, under his own name or anagrams, with friends or foes, ranging from Arsène Lupin, who met Holmlock Shears, to Ellery Queen's account of Holmes versus Jack the Ripper. An example, similar to Sexton Blake and Kit Carson, was in a Barry Perowne (Philip Atkey) pastiche of A. J. Raffles, to be considered later. "Raffles and an American Night's Entertainment" (*EQMM,* March 1983), involves Raffles, Holmes, Watson, and Mark Twain, whose speech starts the story which includes a musical at the Savoy Theatre, London, an East End actor-manager, with Holmes's influence reducing Raffles's usual amoral approach. It will be remembered that Doyle was not pleased with his sister's husband, E. W. Hornung (1866–1921) creating a character diametrically opposite to his own Holmes, although he did write an introduction to Hornung's posthumous 1923 book, *Old Offenders and a Few Old Scores*. Another Holmes variation had him opposing Dr. Fu Manchu, as Solar Pons was to fight the equally evil Dr. F.

There were even parodies of parodies. W. O. G. Lofts, the prolific and precise bibliographer of boys' fiction, and Jon L. Lellenburg of the Dispatch-Box Press of Virginia wrote *The Adventures of Sherlock Holmes: A History and Bibliography,* published in 1976 by that press, listing every story and "author" including that of "Sheeluck Holmes" and Ferrers Locke, a relation of Charles Hamilton's Dr. Locke the Headmaster, who was parodied as Terros Shocke. *Magnet, Gem,* and *Greyfriars Herald* were magazines famous in England before 1940 (as was *Holiday Annual*) for stories of English public or boarding schools, including Greyfriars (the famous Billy Bunter, a fat scrounging schoolboy), St. Jim's, St. Hilda's for the girls, etc. — all by one indefatigable author, under such noms de plume as Martin Clifford, Frank Richards, Owen Conquest and Charles Hamilton (his real name) — all written with erudition, style, humor, atmosphere, and accuracy, read by me and my mother and father till they ceased publication. Sequels to stories of famous detectives are in a separate section, as are films, etc., in which the sleuths face yet more friends and foes.

Writing Teams of Captains Only

In the 1930s England started the fashion of books written by teams of leading crime authors, each taking a chapter, solving whatever problems he or she might have found to date, and leaving fresh problems for the succeeding writers. There would be an editor who would contribute the foreword and/or the first chapter, plus perhaps an afterword (Dorothy L. Sayers being one example), and the book could be sponsored by, say, the Detection Club. There was one striking example in the United States, and recently another has been traced in Australia; examples from newspapers in the 1950s have also been found, as serials in the daily issues of an evening paper are ideal circulation boosters, as were serials in morning newspapers in Great Britain in the 1920s and 1930s, in the French nineteenth-century feuilletons, the American comic papers, or funnies, and magazines. In 1985 a new British color morning paper *Today,* from an independent publisher, started serializing an Ed McBain story almost from the first issue. That group efforts are not finished was proved to me in 1985 when Gwendoline Butler invited me to lunch with a group of professional writers, meeting monthly in Richmond, Surrey, on the Thames near London—a group including Tim Heald, crime writer, critic, and former chair of the CWA, and Gyles Brandreth, prolific author, television writer and personality, and later member of Parliament. This club worked on a group-effort book, numbering among its members as it does a wide range of litterateurs. In England Macmillan and Victor Gollancz have reissued several of these group efforts, and the American book was reissued there. In 1986 another English publisher contacted the CWA to suggest the writing of another joint effort, chapter by chapter, from the members.

The two latest examples can conveniently be dealt with first. *The Rigby File* was published by Hodder and Stoughton in 1989, written by Tim Heald and a dozen others, reminiscent of *The Floating Admiral* (1931), see below, and the *Sunday Times* 1960s advertisement "I Knew Daily Sinuten!" Dorothy Mayotte Rigby, born 1920, was expelled from exclusive Cheltenham Ladies College along with Camilla, a secret agent. The contributions from the other crime writers make confusion worse, as they all prove her to be involved in every espionage, with H. R. F. Keating on cricket replacing the spy, Peter Lovesey on interpreting for Hitler, Michael Gilbert on the Vichy sympathizer, James Leasor on the Commander "Buster" Crabbe fiasco, Duncan Kyle on cryptography, John Ehrlichman on Watergate, and Anthony Price and William Haggard, inter alia.

The 1988 group effort was *Caribbean Blues* written by Mary Higgins Clark, Molly Cochrane, Max Allan Collins, Gregory McDonald, Richard Meyers, Warren Murphy, and Robert J. Randisi—all prominent members of Mystery Writers of America, in a story of murder and other crimes on a cruise liner, with several PIs aboard. As a result the authors were invited to stage a murder mystery on the Cunard *Countess,* May 16 to 23, 1987, around the Caribbean islands, all profits to charity, each to write two chapters with his or her own sleuths. It is set on the *Countess* from Saturday, May 16, 1938. (Oddly enough, May 16, 1938, was a Monday.) Max Allan Collins's sleuth is Nate Heller; Warren Murphy, married to Molly Cochrane, wrote the Trace series; Gregory McDonald the Fletch and Flynn books; Randisi created a jewel thief, Dan Hisi. The Caribbean Blues are three perfect sapphires; the owner is the first of the three murder victims; there are wisecracks and puns; and being contemporarily written, there are various solutions—all wrong—separate crimes, confusions, the tough-PI approach. Murphy wrote seven chapters and the postscripts; Clark just the prologue and epilogue; and Collins, with Bill and Karen Palmer, owners of Bogie's Restaurant and Mystery Tours, the solution in chapter 18.

It will be easier to consider these books in alphabetical order of the titles rather than of the authors, who may be in their own specific sequences. We shall see that the mold is basically the same throughout, with only tactical alterations, and the occasional addendum in later issues. Edmund Crispin has a sardonic comment to make on clubs in his short story "The Quick Brown Fox," first published in the *Evening Standard,* and collected into *The Evening Standard Book* (1950). In a club argument that "detective stories *are* anti-social" in that criminals draw inspiration and ideas from them, Professor Gervase Fen contradicts with, "For all the use criminals make of them, the members of the Detection Club might as well be a chorus of voices crying in the wilderness." He then tells of a case he solved of a murderer trying too hard to confuse the investigators into an obvious line of deduction, through which he had seen.

Ask a Policeman was written by members of the Detection Club (founded in 1928) in 1933, and reissued exactly fifty years later, and running to 312 pages: part 1, "Death at Hursley Lodge," by John Rhode (Cecil John Charles Street [1884–1964], author and original of Colonel March, as we have seen); introduction and letters from Milward Kennedy (Milward Rodon Kennedy Burge [1884–1968]) to Rhode and back, amplifying the problems and answers of the modus operandi. Part 2, introduction and letter from Kennedy to Rhode; followed by "Mrs. Bradley's Dilemma," by Helen Simpson (1897–1940); Beatrice Bradley was the creation of Gladys Mitchell; and Helen Simpson's sleuth was actor John Saumaurez. "Sir John [Saumaurez] Takes His Cue" is by Gladys Mitchell.

Part 3, "Lord Peter's Privy Counsel" (a pun on the Privy Council, the main British government committee) is by Anthony Berkeley; Lord Peter is Dorothy L. Sayers's creation, and Berkeley wrote of Roger Sheringham. In this section Lord Peter is to call on an Archbishop suspected of murder; the prelate is referred to as the Archbish, with an apology, and significantly this is the term used by P. G. Wodehouse's Bertie Wooster—Wimsey and Wooster being alike in many ways, including being portrayed on British television by the same actor, Ian Carmichael. His man advises Wimsey to wear the "pale grey willow-pussy with the mauve pinstripe" with amethyst tie and socks as the most appropriate calling dress. Part 4, "The Conclusions of Mr. Roger Sheringham" is by Dorothy L. Sayers to complete the set. Part 3 starts with an introduction; a letter from Kennedy to Rhode; then "If You Want to Know," by Kennedy, and a final note from Kennedy to Sayers agreeing that Sheringham is not to show interest in the policemen, so overlooking a point Wimsey did not overlook.

There is a map at the front of the book, as was the custom in the 1930s. The title of the volume was suggested by publisher Arthur Barker according to the introduction to part 2, and there is a reference to the "muddles" in asking the authors for the views of detectives other than their own. The story is of Lord Comstock (is it coincidence that "comstockery," prudery, comes from Anthony Comstock [1844–1915], an American denunciator of the nude in art?), a newspaper publisher killed at Hursley Lodge (a "hurst" is a wood or grove), and his recent visitors, and therefore the suspects, include the government chief whip (the member of Parliament responsible for keeping government supporters in line in the

House of Commons), an archbishop, and an assistant commissioner at Scotland Yard. The contributors write in the style and psychology of the detective's author allotted to them, and each offers a different solution, with the passing policeman as a vital clue. The title comes from a popular Victorian music-hall song, "If You Want to Know the Time, Ask a Policeman," an allusion to a fraud inquiry alleging every police officer could afford and did possess a gold watch, lifted from a crook he caught—not the friendly song it seemed.

The next two are short, postwar serials published together in 1984 by Gollancz, *Crime on the Coast* and *No Flowers by Request*. The former was a serial in the now defunct daily newspaper *News Chronicle,* between August 3 and 17, 1954; the first chapter was by John Dickson Carr (from the play *Bet with Death*), and subsequent chapters were by Valerie White, Lawrence Meynell (who started his writing career of over sixty years in the 1920s, and had lost none of his lightness of touch at the time of his death), Joan Fleming, Michael Cronin, and Elizabeth Ferrars (of whom we have spoken already), each contributing two chapters. The action starts in a funfair at Breston (Brighton?) on the south coast.

No Flowers by Request was serialized in another vanished London paper, the *Daily Sketch,* in 1952, and the contributors were Dorothy L. Sayers, E. C. R. Lorac (also Carol Carnac [1894–1958]), Gladys Mitchell, Anthony Gilbert (Lucy Beatrice Malleson [1899–1973], creator in 1936 of the extrovert lawyer-sleuth Arthur Crook), and Christianna Brand, who wrote three chapters, the others contributing two chapters each. Written in the first-person feminine, it tells of the murder of Mrs. Carringford and a houseful of suspects, with a strong denouement.

Both stories were written with great smoothness, with absolutely no trace of any joining between the universal styles adopted successfully by the teams of very able writers.

Although *Double Death* is short, it was published by itself in 1939 by Gollancz, and reissued by that company on August 22, 1985, and described as "a tale of poisoning and detection first published in 1939." Neville Wood, a British collector and writer, wrote about this book in *Poisoned Pen* (vol. 1, no. 3). The prologue is by John Chancellor, and the chapters are by Dorothy L. Sayers, Freeman Wills Crofts, Valentine Williams, F. Tennyson

Jesse (1889–1958, playwright of *A Pin to See the Peepshow,* editor, author of fiction and nonfiction such as *Murder and Its Motives* [1924], creator of the French detective Solange Fontaine, and wife of H. M. Harwood), Anthony Armstrong (George Anthony Armstrong Willis, author, humorist, playwright, particularly of the classic *Ten Minute Alibi,* later filmed), and David Hume (a prolific mystery writer in the 1930s and 1940s, not to be confused with a writer of the same name in the 1980s). Every character in the book is a suspect, from benefitting from a wealthy lady's will. Every author adds an addendum to his or her chapter. In the 1985 reissue there is a preface by John Chancellor and an epilogue featuring one chapter, "Millie and Her Lover."

Responsibility for the title rested with James W. Drawbell, the editor of the *Sunday Chronicle.* The story is of the murder first of Nurse Ponting, who had her experience of poisoning in a former case, followed by the murder of the patient, wealthy Mrs. Farland. All authors add their notes; there is a map of the town; David Hume sends notes to his literary agent, with various theories; the finale is ingenious; and a wry note at the end of David Hume's letter on the last page says, "May Heaven preserve me from such a fate in the future!" James Wedgwood Drawbell was himself the author of several books, including *Good Time! Love and Forget, This Year, Next Year, The Innocents of Chicago,* and *Film Lady.* It was David Hume who suggested the publication of the authors' notes, which Victor Gollancz approved.

The Floating Admiral is perhaps the best known or most striking example, and not only because of its eye-catching title. First copyrighted in 1931 and 1932, it was next reissued as a paperback in the United States in 1980, and then in hardcover in England in 1983. The book tells of an admiral found floating dead in a boat in a river. The dozen writers taking part included Agatha Christie, Dorothy L. Sayers, G. K. Chesterton, Victor L. Whitechurch, Edgar Jepson (novelist father of crime writer Selwyn Jepson), Clemence Dane (Winifred Ashton [1888–1965], coauthor with Helen Simpson of the Sir John Saumaurez, actor-manager, detective stories), Anthony Berkeley, and Milward Kennedy. Sayers wrote the introduction and Chesterton the prologue, and not only did each author carry on the story, but added additional problems. There are the usual solutions, notes on mooring a boat, a detailed map, and counsel's opinion on the validity of the will mentioned in the story. Significantly, the American paperback listed Agatha Christie's name in much larger type than any others, showing how her international prestige had increased since the first edition in Great Britain.

Not all critics were enthusiastic about this example. Robert Barnard, already mentioned as an author of skillful detective stories and former professor, in a letter to the present author dated September 6, 1982, said that he thought the book a dreadful mistake, almost unreadable, but with praise to Agatha Christie for not bringing in still more complications. R. F. Stewart in . . . *And Always a Detective* (1980), in a note referred to "forward writing without having backward-plotted" in the multihanded experiments of this book and the later *Double Death,* considered above.

Canon Victor L. Whitechurch wrote *The Crime at Diana's Pool* in 1926 (or 1927 or 1928 according to various authorities), with a crime at a party on the lawn, solved by the police constable and the vicar, and in his introduction the author set out his own views on the detective story.

Against that, however, when I interviewed David Williams for *Poisoned Pen,* already mentioned, he stressed he did not himself know the identity of the murderer in his own Treasure stories until chapter 18, and that those who thought they had solved the plot before then were simply guessing. Stewart has another interesting comment in chapter 6; "When the thirties produced books like *The Floating Admiral* with a new author for each chapter, it was only elaborating on a suggestion by the *Atlantic Monthly* in 1898 that one writer should start a detective novel and another finish it" (*Detective Fiction,* April 1898).

A specific comment comes from the French critic and crime writer Thomas Narcejac, writing on his own this time, *Une Machine a Lire: Le Roman Policier,* published by Denoel/Gontheir in 1975. In chapter 16, "Roman Policier et Cybernetique," the last paragraph reads: "Utopie? Ce serait oublier que des auteurs anglais ont releve le défi, avec un roman qui est resté célèbre: *The Floating Admiral.* Le premier chapitre, qui raconte comment on découvre dans un canot le cadavre d'un amiral assassiné, est du chanoine Whitechurch; et les onze chapitres suivants sont chacun d'un auteur (célèbre) different. Mais ainsi que l'explique Dorothy Sayers dan l'introduction chaque collaborateur s'attaqua à l'énigme offerte à lui dans les chapitres précédents sans avoir la moindre idée de la solution et sans introduire de nouvelles complications."

We come now to the recently discovered unique Australian example, recounted by Philip T. Asdell, in an article, "*An Australian Murder Pie*," in *Poisoned Pen* (vol. 6, no. 3, Fall 1985). He found it was published by Angus & Robertson, Sydney, in 1936, after a British example, which he believed was the 1931 *The Floating Admiral,* but which could equally have been *Ask a Policeman,* which we have seen was published in 1933. Sixteen or seventeen Australian writers took part, including M. Barbara Eldershaw (who was Flora Eldershaw and Marjorie Barnard) and Ethel Turner (who wrote about the Seven Little Australians), but none of these professional writers was a crime writer whom Asdell knew. The sixteen chapters are based on the academic scene, the editors were J. L. Ranken and Jane Clunies Ross, who apparently wrote the first two chapters, and the introduction says each author picked up the plot from the previously finished chapter.

In the fall 1986 issue, Asdell, who lives in Maryland, wrote that he had now received further details of more of the *Murder Pie* authors, from a librarian at the University of Sydney, leaving only four so far untraced, and all this confirmed his belief that none of the Australian contributors had had previous crime writing experience, despite high academic output.

The next example is the outstanding American book, *The President's Mystery Story,* by Franklin D. Roosevelt, Rupert Hughes, Samuel Hopkins Adams, Anthony Abbott, Rita Weiman, S. S. Van Dine, and John Erskine. The British first edition in 1936 from the Bodley Head had a preface by Fulton Oursler. There was another edition in 1957 with a final chapter by Erle Stanley Gardner, and some final evidence for loose ends by Perry Mason in the 1967 reprint. The story was originally serialized in *Liberty* magazine from November 16, 1935. Oursler explained that the president told him he had had an idea for years of a wealthy young man seeking to disappear completely and starting a new and honorable life unknown and elsewhere without fear of being traced, and that the president gave Oursler the idea to process. The latter approached "six successful American authors," only one of whom knew of the president's connection, that one being of course Abbott, a pseudonym of Oursler himself, the writers being described elsewhere as being "S. S. Van Dine, Rupert Hughes, and other names of equal distinction." Strangely enough, my reference to six leading American writers in an article covering this book in *Poisoned Pen* caused an American reader to write complaining that I should not regard them all as being leading. The first American edition was in 1936, but the 1967 reissue was *The President's Mystery Plot*. The writers make a homogeneous tale, with the wealthy man flying off to a new life, after a dramatic recognition by a dog and the help of the state governor.

Anthony Abbott (Fulton Oursler, 1893–1952) created Thatcher Colt, the wealthy police commissioner, most of whose books start with "About"—e.g., *About the Murder of the Night Club Lady*—said to ensure that both author and title headed every alphabetical list, and have a first-person narrator, as with S. S. Van Dine. Three of the books were filmed, two with Adolphe Menjou and the third with Sydney Blackmer portraying Colt. Oursler was also a religious author. Abbott lived at 244 West 70th Street, New York, where Joseph P. Elwell, a bridge expert, was mysteriously murdered.

Rupert Hughes's detective is Dick Memling.

Samuel Hopkins Adams (1871–1958) created Average Jones (Adrian Van Reypen Egerton Jones), wealthy sleuth appearing in one volume in 1911; one short story, "Night Bus," achieved world fame as the 1934 film *It Happened One Night,* with Claudette Colbert and Clark Gable. His writing career started in 1905 with *The Mystery,* cowritten with Stewart Edward White, and with sixteen illustrations by Will Crawford.

Rita Weiman was a playwright who was once commissioned to cover a famous criminal trial.

S. S. Van Dine we have already considered as the creator of Philo Vance, the dilettante sleuth, many of whose cases were successfully filmed, and of the "Decalogue; or, Twenty Rules" for writing detective fiction.

John Erskine's name appears in very few reference books or bibliographies.

Erle Stanley Gardner (1889–1970), the lawyer, achieved equal fame as creator of lawyer Perry Mason in more than eighty books, DA Doug Selby, that strange partnership of massive Bertha Cool and ex-lawyer Donald Lam, originally written as A. A. Fair, and as founder of the Court of Last Resort, which has helped many Americans caught in the legal whirlpool. As *The President's Mys-*

tery Story, the book was filmed by Republic in 1936, starring Henry Wilcoxon and Betty Furness, directed by Phil Rosen.

This version of group effort is unique in the outside idea being presented, quite apart from its presidential stamp. In 1932 in England a simple idea of a plot (a man writing to a woman and later finding her the woman he has married—with echoes of musical comedy) was suggested by a publican at Oxford to a group of British writers, including G. K. Chesterton and Helen Simpson, and was edited by an American professor, but these were individual treatments, more like a competition, and in no way a collaboration.

The Scoop and *Behind the Screen* were published in book form by Gollancz in 1983. Ralph Spurrier, a specialist crime-book seller in Sussex, England, always writes amusing and informative notes to his regular catalogues—he is a member of the Crime Writers' Association—and he has described how he traced these two stories in the newspaper library. These were written on different plans. *The Scoop* was written by Dorothy L. Sayers, Agatha Christie, Clemence Dane, E. C. Bentley, Anthony Berkeley, and Freeman Wills Crofts, while *Behind the Screen* was the effort of Hugh Walpole (later Sir Hugh, eminent English novelist, whose crime writing included *Portrait of a Man with Red Hair,* filmed with Charles Laughton, and *Above the Dark Circus,* a gripping tale centered on Piccadilly Circus, in London's West End), Agatha Christie, Dorothy L. Sayers, Anthony Berkeley, E. C. Bentley, Father Ronald A. Knox, with an appendix by Milward Kennedy.

The Scoop tells of the *Morning Star* newspaper's efforts to trace a murderer in the lonely bungalow at the Jumbles (cf. the two famous murders at the Crumbles, the beaches near Pevensey and Eastbourne in Sussex), followed by reporter Johnson's murder in a telephone kiosk at Victoria Station, returning from Brighton, a Sussex holiday resort. After inquiries ranging from Broad Street in the City of London to Bond Street in the West End, over the purchase of daggerlike jeweled pins, and mistaken identities among the newspaper staff, the murderer commits a spectacular suicide, thereby creating a scoop for the rival *Courier* journal.

Behind the Screen recounts the discovery behind an ornamental draft-preventing screen of Paul Dudden, a lodger in a private family. It was a competition run by *The Listener,* a magazine containing the printed talks and features of the BBC radio (as opposed to *Radio Times,* which gave the details of radio program for Services 1 and 2, regional radio, etc.). Readers were asked such questions as whether Dudden's death was accident, suicide, or murder, and so on.

Both stories were serialized in *The Listener: Behind the Screen* in 1930, and *The Scoop* in 1931. This first report with the questions for readers to solve was in the issue of June 25, 1930, and the results and winners in the issue of July 30. In the issue of February 11, 1931, appeared an appendix with Dorothy L. Sayers's comments on the modus operandi of both books. *The Scoop* had a rough outline, then each contributor worked to a sketch outline, using his or her own style and method. Alternatively, *Behind the Screen* had the first three members—Hugh Walpole, Agatha Christie, Dorothy L. Sayers—plotting the framework, and the other three members using their wits in consultation to solve the problems. Mention was made of a book by members of the Detection Club on these lines "for publication this year," obviously *The Floating Admiral,* which was two years before *Ask a Policeman.*

Six Against the Yard was another Detection Club effort, published in 1937 in the States, written by Allingham, Berkeley, Crofts, Knox, Sayers, and Thorndike, plotting six separate murders to be solved and criticized by former Superintendent Cornish. Berkeley's case parodied James M. Cain.

The final example was written earlier and concerns Sexton Blake, second only to Sherlock Holmes, and of whom some two hundred authors have written more than four thousand stories—from the first, "The Missing Millionaire" in *Halfpenny Marvel* (no. 6, December 20, 1893), by Hal Meredith (Harry Blyth, 1852–1898). Blake's adventures have appeared in magazines, books, periodicals of the monthly Schoolboys' Own Library type, television series, and films, and during the years different authors have given him different office addresses, staffs, cars, and enemies. John G. Brandon (1878–1941), to be considered later in connection with theatre, wrote Blake stories, and introduced Ronald Sturges Vereker Purvale, known as RSVP, to appear later in books. Edwy Searles Brooks wrote seventy-six Blake stories, and as Berkeley Gray wrote of Norman Conquest, with scenes from the earlier Blake saga—for example, the antagonistic Waldo the

Wonder Man's activities and a process known as De-Blakenizing. The magazine *Union Jack* had six authors' separate stories leading to a common climax: Blake had been found unconscious from a blow on the head on top of a tram in the Wood End depot; next to a stout, elderly, clean-shaven man dead of heart failure. The prize for the successful reader was a bloodhound—if he wanted it. He did, so the magazine had to find one for him.

Just before the magazine metamorphosed into *Detective Weekly,* a serial appropriately named *The Next Move* was written by Robert Murray, R. M. Graydon, Anthony Skene, G. N. Phillips, G. H. Teed, George Heber Hamilton, Gwyn Evans, and Gwynfil Arthur. *A Case of Sexton Blake* ran in the very last issues of *Detective Weekly,* parallel with the radio serial. All the named writers were established Blake creators. Skene wrote 185, and created Zenith the Albino. G. H. Teed (1878–1939) created Dr. Huxton Rymer, a demented former Hanley Street surgeon, and Roxane Harfield, another favorite enemy, and with R. M. Graydon was also Murray Hamilton.

John Newton Chance, as John Drummond, prolific crime writer, also wrote twenty-five Blake novelettes. This is not the same John Drummond who wrote both novels and crime stories, and which was the nom de plume also of Earl Strange, "Earl" being his rank, not a Christian name, and who told me his ancestor was Shakespeare's employer, as in Lord Strange's Men, and would I like to see the accounts?

Barry Perowne wrote a parody in 1937: *Raffles vs. Sexton Blake.* Even Dorothy L. Sayers invented her Lord Peter Wimsey for a Sexton Blake story she never finished. With so many authors writing about Blake for the same publishing house, it was not surprising that this group effort flourished so early and so easily.

Books of this type are a feedback challenge—to the authors, to blend their own styles, or to assume the styles of others to make a homogeneous entity; and to the readers, not only to follow the plot as usual, but to try to identify the changes in literary styles and rhythms.

4. . . . Is Another Man's Pastiche

"It seems to be imitation time . . . Is this a trend? No, sorry to say, only coincidence. But it has brought us some fine bonbons . . . Vintage stuff. . . . But for the pure pastiche."

So wrote H. R. F. Keating in the *Times* of London on May 6, 1976, neatly encapsulating the distinction with a difference. We have already seen at the outset the dividing line, and how many authors found it strange or difficult to admit to parody or pastiche. Are there authors who do not know the difference, or are there even some who do not want their readers to work it out for themselves? Take Robert Leslie Bellem (1902–1968) as an example— writer of several hundred short stories, marked for the raciness of descriptions of guns, blows, glamorous women, and ingenious titles. (Could anything better Pronzini's quote in *Gun in Cheek* on *The Case of the Loaded Garter Holster,* where a woman killed by shooting fire extinguishers in each ear resulted in a verdict of accident?) Bellem wrote the novel *Blue Murder* in 1938 (not to be confused with the same title used by both Rutland and Watson). It was reissued in 1987 with an introduction by Pronzini, who asks, "Was Bellem's tongue firmly planted in his cheek when he chronicled the adventures of his various private skulks and other pulp heroes? Or was he a 'serious' writer who had little or no idea of the comic absurdity of his style?" before quoting an example of Bellem's zaniness of private life.

Agatha Christie? I have already indicated that her autobiography quoted *Partners in Crime* as her own admitted parody, but that *The Body in the Library* has definite parodic overtones. One of her biographers has suggested that her early *The Secret of Chimneys* (1925), with its overtones of *The Prisoner of Zenda* and P. G. Wodehouse and Blandings Castle, could be a subtle parody of the Bulldog Drummond stories.

One of the early descriptions of pastiche was as a muddle, farrago, from the Latin *pasta,* and the French, from the Italian, a barley porridge. A wry comment on pastiche is an Italian detective story *Quer Pasticciaccio Bruto de Via Merulana* by Carlo Emilio Gadda (1893–1973), translated by William Weaver, with the English title *That Awful Mess on Via Merulana,* analyzed by Jo Ann Cannon in her "The Reader as Detective: Notes on Gadda's Pasticciaccio," in *Modern Language Studies* 10 (Fall 1980). It is an account of the police in the fascist Italy of the 1920s, and an "awful mess." It is also discussed in Tani's *Doomed Detective.*

The first pure pastiche to consider is by the versatile Kingsley Amis, whose *Lucky Jim* achieved fame also as a film. *The Riverside Villas Murder* dated from 1973 and is a pastiche of life in England in 1933. Basically it tells of a schoolboy, seduced by a neighbor, involved in the murder of another resident, finding himself the instrument of retribution for the murderer, thus absolving his own pretentious, lonely, widower father. The whole experience proves cathartic, including his harmless friendship with a bachelor chief constable. The book is full of correct touches of the period: the Wallace and Rattenbury trials, the Band of Troise and His Mandoliers, Don Carlos and Geraldo the bandleaders, and the boy's school (Blackfriars Grammar) would appear to be the City of London School for Boys, then situated at Blackfriars in London. The journey home from London Embankment, Waterloo Bridge, Brixton, Norbury, and Thornton Heath Ponds implies his situation in Surrey.

Peter Furneaux and his father, an alleged RFC (or RAF) pilot, live at 19 Riverside Villas with Ada Trevelyan the somewhat oversexed killer next door at No. 21. It is the boy's preoccupation with gliders, a popular toy of the period, which leads to the denouement of the killer of Chris Inman. The dust jacket draws the attention of the puzzle-solving reader to various pages. One has reference to the funny colonel, the chief constable, and the effeminate Inman; another has a reference to *The Hollow Man,* which is in fact a 1935 Dr. Gideon Fell story by John Dickson Carr (American title, *The Three Coffins,* and to "doors, windows, or chimneys"; and another page refers to *Be Absolute For Death,* another Lambe mystery by Regina Thyme (possible esoteric allusions to Ellery Queen from 1929, and Nero Wolfe from 1934?), to telling the truth even if it seems not to be so, and a summary misleading on one crucial point: "After all, the whole raison d'être of a murder story is to trick the reader. Isn't it?"

Apart from these "clues" there are descriptions of the colonel's crime library, and detective stories, and the colonel's car: "It has all my magnifying-glasses and false beards and reference books about bicycle tyres and tattoo marks in it." The ACC's books include the classic "teckers" of the period, J. D. Carr (from 1932), John Rhode (from 1924), Anthony Berkeley (from 1925), *House of the Arrow* (A. E. W. Mason, from 1924), *The Nine Tailors* (Dorothy L. Sayers, 1934), *The Incredulity of Father Brown* (G. K. Chesterton, 1926), *The Mysterious Affair at Styles* (Agatha Christie [The first Poirot book], 1920), showing him as a " 'tec-yarn fan," whereas his sergeant reads "real authors." Apart from these minor irrelevances of dates, there is an accurate ambience, and the reasoning of a young schoolboy is clearly delineated in an excellent pastiche.

While considering Kingsley Amis we can perhaps appropriately look at another novel, *Colonel Sun,* written by him under the nom de plume of Robert Markham in 1968, to the memory of Ian Fleming. There have been parodies of Bond, including such items as *Loxfinger* and *Matzoball,* and other continuations of his adventures, to say nothing of the innumerable films. We survey some of the books on Bond, his life, wardrobe, and his occasionally inappropriate choices of food and wine (a lapse shared with the more aristocratic Lord Peter Wimsey). This present book starts with an attack on the house of M, Bond's chief, from Sunningdale Golf Course, killing his two dogs. Colonel Sun and one henchman get killed, one pro-Bond woman, Lisa, is also killed, the other woman, Ariadne Alexandrou (much of the action is in Greece), proves an agent of GRU. There have been many other continuations of the great detectives, including Sherlock Holmes, A. J. Raffles, Commander Gideon, and some of them will be surveyed in the next section of this chapter.

James Anderson is a member of the CWA living in Glamorgan, Wales. In 1975 he wrote a brilliantly clever pastiche, *The Affair of the Blood-Stained Egg Cosy,* which one can read with great amusement and admiration. It told of a stately home in the 1930s in England, Aderly, complete with the typical plan of the first floor, with the twelfth earl a gun collector, a US millionaire Hiram S. Peabody (also a gun collector), a mysterious ex-naval officer, a junior minister (brother to the earl but selected for his merit not his birth or convenience), and a monocled dude (in the original English sense) Algernon Fotheringhay. Add mysterious foreign envoys (the Balkans again in those days), blackmail, femme fatale Baroness Anilese de la Roche, two murders, the hidden panel obligatory to such mansions, and a murder by a cannon. A denouement meeting has false conclusions and solutions of each problem, including a mysterious diamond necklace and an exchange of valuable guns. Everybody has secrets. Finally come comments on the imminent possibility of war forecast by Winston Churchill—and even a mention of Poirot. *Murderess Ink,* the companion volume to *Murder Ink,* comments: "Pick up a copy of James Anderson's *The Affair of the Blood-Stained Egg Cosy.* Their perpetrators tweaked the prose of the Twenties. Unfortunately, what got lost in the process was the era's very real upper-class elegance." Then came a reference to the spoof films *Murder by Death* and *Death on the Nile.* When I rang Anderson on Monday, November 18, 1985, he said: "My first books were espionage, etc., and serious, so I chose something lighter. I read the 1930s Christies, Sayers, and knew what to incorporate—stately home, secret passages, an old butler, a country copper scoring over the London detective, and a touch of the P. G. Wodehouse." I told him of Renate Rasp's comment when I took her to see Patrick Cargill play Poirot in *Black Coffee* in Plymouth in 1981: that he played him, like me, like Bertie Wooster, a comparison already marked up for this period. He said he had been asked for a sequel (published in America but not in Great Britain, in paperback by Avon, of which he kindly sent me an autographed copy) involving many of the original characters—the earl, the countess, their daughter Geraldine, Chief Inspector Wilkins, Merryweather the butler, and the same clichés.

A propos Wodehouse, he had a delightful comment on detective stories in the short "Honeysuckle Cottage" in *Meet Mr. Mulliner* (1927) when his hero, detective story writer James Rodman, ponders: "A detective story, he maintained, should have no heroine. Heroines only held up the action and tried to flirt with the hero when he should have been busy looking for clues, and then went and let the villain kidnap them by some childishly simple trick." Somerset Maugham and Ogden Nash would approve. Wodehouse, described rightly as one of the very best of English writers, was shrewd. We have seen how Charles Dickens tended to write about people and evils after they had vanished, like Bow

Street Runners and workhouses. In a letter to his friend, Denis Mackail, the author, Wodehouse wrote: "D[ickens] was still writing gaily about stage coaches, etc., long after railways had come in."

That same evening Marian Babson, CWA secretary for ten years until 1986, said she had been asked by American tour organizers to find an egg cosy for a window display; an egg cosy is not a readily recognized object.

In his letter of November 21, 1985, enclosing the promised copy of *The Affair of the Mutilated Mink Coat,* Anderson stressed that these novels were more a tribute to the genre than mere pastiche, and that he included every stock item, undertook careful research, and involved an unusual murderer. This book came out in America in October 1981, by request, but not as part of a continuing series. The characters from the previous book are joined by a film director and star from Hollywood—perhaps a slightly aging star—among other strange visitors, and each of them proves to have a mystery surrounding him or her. There follow two deaths. The earl tells Chief Inspector Wilkins he had lunch at the club with Lord Peter Wimsey. "Said he hoped he'd run into you sometime; he'd enjoy swapping case stories with you." Colonel Melrose, Westshire chief constable, refers later to the "three Great A's at Scotland Yard—John Appleby, Roderick Alleyn, St. John Allgood." The last named makes his dramatic entry in a white Bentley driven by his man, ex-convict Chalky White, well-dressed, Old Etonian tie, mutual friends with the earl, sweeping, very confident, disparaging of Wilkins, and with various ingenious theories all scattered when Wilkins solves the case, despite the chief constable and the chief at Scotland Yard being old friends. Wilkins is called to his next case, at Meadowfield School, where the matron has been found hanging and wearing a Native American headdress, a gentle reminder of the 1930s school murder stories. In the further helpful letter, dated December 11, 1985, the author indicated additional subtle touches. The cliché that the man found holding the gun by the body did not do it is upturned, because he did. Geraldine offers to read to Paul certain books: *Death of a Debutante* by Ariadne Oliver, mentioned in Agatha Christie's *Mrs. McGinty's Dead* (1952); Annette de la Tour's *The Screaming Bone* comes in Edmund Crispin's *Buried for Pleasure* (1948); and Richard Eliot's *The Spider Bites Back* comes in *Stop*

Press by Michael Innes (1939)—all UK dates and titles—but nobody spotted the joke, and he commented that the dates when these were written did not matter. These tributes rather than pastiches (to quote the author) are accurate, witty, and again full of atmosphere. His delightful sense of humor is underlined by the titles of some of his other novels: *Assault and Matrimony* (1980) which was made into a television film, *The Murder of Sherlock Holmes* (1985), and *Hooray for Homicide* (1985).

On Monday, May 13, 1985, I went to dinner with Marian Babson at her flat in the center of London. Before the meal she offered me a 1930s cocktail, from a colorful, exotic range which she had bought specially to experiment with for her new novel, *Weekend for Murder*. She had a proof copy sent me. Pointedly clever, wickedly witty, it tells of a weekend party with a staged murder in an English country house situated near Salisbury—but with a real murder to bedevil matters. The murder plot (set in the 1930s) is itself complicated to please the mainly American guests, and all the names used are evocative of the classics in detective fiction: Chandler, Dixon, Carr, Marric, Wentworth, Roberts Rinehart, Roger Ackroyd the house cat, Bertha Stout, Van Dine, Colonel Heather, Colonel Primrose, Edwin Lupin, Sir Cedric Strangeways, Algie Moriarty, Lady Hermonie Marsh, Haila Bond (Haily from Kelly Roos)—those I recognized. But Lauren and Brigid?—of course, Bacall and O'Shaughnessy, for the twins. We shall consider murder weekends in depth in the special section later in this chapter, meanwhile contenting ourselves with the antecedents of the murder party as here seen. The author refers to the invention of murder by Elsa Maxwell some years earlier to open Lady Ribblesdale's house in St. James's Park (although artist Neysa McMein of the Algonquin Round Table lays prior claim), with the Duke of Marlborough as the guilty party. Ngaio Marsh's *A Man Lay Dead* (1934) and Agatha Christie's Hercule Poirot and Ariadne Oliver story *Dead Man's Folly* (1956) are quoted as literary predecessors. The Marsh story tells of Sir Hubert Handesley's country house party with seven guests, one of whom receives a plaque secretly from the butler leaving him to touch his "victim" between 5:30 and 11:00 P.M., switching off the lights, sounding the Assyrian gong two minutes later, then everybody takes part in the trial. An unpleasant guest is found stabbed with a historic and valuable Russian dagger given Handesley for having saved the life of a secret society member, killed the previous evening in Soho. Chief Detective Inspector Roderick Alleyn solves the case.

There are two other books of similar origin. In 1929 Frances Noyes Hart (1890–1943) wrote her second mystery novel, *Hide in the Dark,* in which the thirteen March Hares attend a murder house party and after a real murder solve a mystery of a decade earlier, in this account popularizing murder. John Newton Chance, already mentioned above, wrote *The Traditional Murders,* in which a detective's wealthy relative holds such a party in the 1930s with malice aforethought and relatives who do not know one another and of whom he has a very low opinion.

The Murder Game, written in 1991 by an author described in different catalogues as either Joan Davies or Joan Flanagan, has an eerie mountaintop hotel, isolated by the obligatory storm, with a murder game that ends up with real bodies.

Babson dedicated her novels to seven murder tour operators. *Weekend for Murder* was her twenty-fifth book, and her novels are always marked by originality of thought and venue, to say nothing of her titles.

Parodies and pastiches of Sherlock Holmes total, as we have seen, more than a thousand, but there are instances of other Holmesian characters appearing in books and short stories—Mycroft, Lestrade, Moriarty, Moran—and even the Baker Street Irregulars, renamed the Baker Street Boys in a book by Brian Ball, published by BBC/Knight in 1983, based on a BBC-TV series by Anthony Read. The "boys" number six—Arnold Wiggins, Sparrow, Beaver, Shiner, and two girls, Rosie and Queenie. This is not the only anomaly. The two stories are alternatively titled "The Case of the Captive Clairvoyant" and "The Case of the Disappearing Despatch Case"; it is not the clairvoyant who disappears; he is murdered, and his assistant vanished of her own free will with the "boys." The despatch case does not disappear; it is stolen and soon traced by the boys. It belongs to Sir Alfred Connynham, a member of the cabinet, and erroneously described as a nobleman and a peer of the realm. Holmes and Watson make brief appearances, but Lestrade is an inglorious figure in the stories, narrated by his more understanding Sergeant Hopkins. Some other details seem casual—a music-hall bill of only a few acts when at that time there would have been more than a dozen, the mesmerist's female assistant and stepdaughter apparently coming out of hypnosis without any difficulty, and a Russian anarchist ejaculates "Teufel" when attacked. However, the stories make interesting, good, light reading and presumably viewing.

George Baxt's *Topsy and Evil* was considered a parody, but two interesting pastiches, involving famous women, were his 1985 *The Dorothy Parker Murder Case,* with the famous humorist involved in both a murder case and a love affair, and his 1987 *The Tallulah Bankhead Murder Case,* with a guest on the radio show of that extroverted, talented actress being murdered, a suicide, and a threat to the star herself. Another novel was the 1986 *The Alfred Hitchcock Murder Case.*

Dorothea Bennett in 1979 wrote *The Maynard Hayes Affair,* in which Sir Maynard Hayes, Bart., and Bruce Moore murder Grainger at college, then years later to bind Moore more closely to Hayes, they murder the bridesmaid's brother Jeremy—a tale obviously based on the Leopold and Loeb case, as was Patrick Hamilton's 1929 play *Rope,* later filmed by Alfred Hitchcock.

Another pastiche involving real persons with fictional characters comes from American Andrew Bergman, and his private eye, nondescript, self-opinionated, Jewish Jack Le Vine, with his New York office at 1651 Broadway at 51st Street. Richard Nixon, Humphrey Bogart, and Thomas Dewey appear in titles like *Hollywood and Le Vine* (1975) and the earlier *The Big Kiss-Off of 1944* (1974). The latter is a convoluted story of Le Vine being engaged by a young actress to recover some blue films before her producer sees them. Then the producer engages him to recover them. Then the millionaire-banker father of the woman (after a couple of killings) engages him. Then the top forces commanders and the FBI seek to scare him away—so he ends up with Thomas Dewey, endeavoring to hold the balance of power in the 1944 presidential election. An unbelievable ending has him taking the millionaire to Radio City to broadcast on ethics, breaking through and shooting a cordon of police and heavies, adopting a disguise of radio singers to blackmail in turn the Democrats to recover those two films. The description of New York, with its elevated railway, is accurate, and Le Vine follows the usual formula of drink, women, aggressiveness, cockiness, and slick Marlowesque one-liners coupled with a James Bond facility of defeating numerically superior odds. In practice, the war effort at that time would indubitably have wiped out the story.

Anthony Berkeley (Iles/Cox), a versatile author, wrote the amusing *Jugged Journalism,* published by Herbert Jenkins in 1925, with thirty-two illustrations by George Morrow; the twenty chapters include "The Detective Story" and "The Mystery Story," and a pastiche "The Frozen Fang" by Edgar Rohmer and Sax Wallace.

We have already seen the parodies of Philip Marlowe, and T. J. Binyon's comments. Robert B. Parker's Boston private eye Spenser appears in *The Godwulf Manuscript* (1973), *God Save the Child* (1974), *Mortal Stakes,* (1975) etc., and is described as an affectionate imitation by Binyon, who draws an analogy with *The Fairie Queene,* Marlowe as Mallory, and the Round Table. Marlowe with Linda Loring and Spenser with Brenda Loring, Marlowe's visiting card having a tommy gun and Spenser's crossed daggers, Marlowe leaving the DA's office for insubordination and Spenser (like Marlowe, after the writer) from the police for the same reason—all bear comparison. The creation of Spenser by Parker, whose plots are marked by variety and violence, could be taken as a tribute to Marlowe.

Another Chandler pastiche appeared in 1974 when Derek Marlowe, English author of *A Dandy in Aspic,* wrote *Somebody's Sister,* a book of quality, not to be confused with Dan J. Marlowe, American author of *Flashpoint* and creator of New York detective Johnny Killain.

Lawrence Block's titles frequently have a subtle humor—for example, *The Burglar Who Liked to Quote Kipling* (1979), *The Burglar Who Studied Spinoza* (1980), and *The Burglar Who Painted Like Mondrian* (1983). In the last, his well-known comical burglar Bernie Rhodenbarr finds himself mixed up with a tale of blackmail, a dead body in a closet in his lavatory, a blonde with fantasies of rape, and five fake Mondrians. In a pastiche of classic whodunnits, the finale is Bernie's staging of a confrontation.

In June 1986 critic John Conquest pointed out a new publication of Lawrence Block, *Five Little Rich Girls,* as a pastiche of Nero Wolfe, and with many in-jokes for aficionados. This was followed (in 1975 in paperback in America, and again in 1983, and in British hardcover in 1984) by *The Topless Tulip Caper,* in which investigator Leo Haig, and his underage assistant Chip Harrison investigate the murder of 123 fish owned by Dr. Thelma J. Wolinski, also known as naked nightclub dancer Tulip Willing, followed by the murder of another dancer and a suspect. Haig is a parody or pastiche on Nero Wolfe: five feet tall, fat, black goatee, habit of saying "phooey," raising exotic fish, Chinese cook, the legwork by notebook-carrying Chip (christened Leigh Harvey, but his parents changed it in the fall of 1963). He feuds with the New York police, and the denouement has all the cast in rows of chairs facing his desk. The cover refers to the "same blend of wit, parody, pastiche and gripping readability" as the previous book, and to the "references and jokes" relating to Wolfe and "the whole pantheon of great private eyes." There are many comparisons to Wolfe, and some references to Holmes and Watson, but no other sleuths are mentioned by name; the two or three casual, rather odd love affairs of Chip are similar to those of other private eyes, allegedly included because Chip's publisher requires them, and Haig assumes them. The time is obviously contemporary; the Mafia chief is Leonard Danzig; Chip's car is a twenty-year-old Cadillac, the last stick-shift model they made; and he does not live in the two floors of Haig's house, but in rooms a couple of blocks away. Before he came into the money that established his career, Haig "read every mystery and detective story ever published" (for example Pronzini), and narrator Harrison starts chapter 15, "Haig made me read a lot of mysteries." He ends chapter 9, "At 8:37 I let myself into his apartment." Chapter 10 is one line: "At 8:51 I let myself out." Characters have strange names: Gus Leemy, Rita Cubbage, Jan Remo, and Buddy Lippa in the nightclub alone. Humorous lines abound, like "But first you have some places to go and some people to see," from the song.

Originally published in 1974 under the title of *Make Out with Murder,* by "Chip Harrison," Block's novel had Haig and Harrison referring to Ross Macdonald and his Lew Archer for Nero Wolfe–style elucidation of the murders of four out of five millionaire sisters: Robin, Jessica, Melanie, Caitlin, and Kim Trelawney. The 1986 title was *Five Little Rich Girls,* by Lawrence Block.

Ernest Bramah (Ernest Bramah Smith, 1868–1942) created two famous characters. The first was the blind detective Max Carrados who appeared in one novel and five volumes of short stories. The second was Kai Lung, the Chinese storyteller whose anecdotes postponed his sentencing for various crimes. Eight volumes of short stories included *The Wallet of Kai Lung* (1900) and *Kai Lung's Golden Hours* (1922), and the books had an apparently genuine Eastern atmosphere that William White was to prove was not based on actual visits. His style has been described as "delectably ironic mock Chinese idiom," grudgingly by Julian Symons in *Bloody Murder* as "mock-Chinese tales about Kai-Lung which had at one time an unaccountably large number of admirers," and by H. R. F. Keating in *Whodunnit?* as "Chinese pastiche stories."

Some of Simon Brett's books come under the heading of parody; others include one pastiche, *Murder in the Title* (1983), in which he adopts the form of a stage play. Act 1 starts with chapter 1, act 2 with chapter 6, and act 3 with chapter 12. The book opens with a description of the opening scenes of the play *The Message Is Murder,* at the Regent Theatre, Rugland Spa, Herefordshire, with the maid answering the telephone as in so many plays. The suicide in act 3 is solved in the last line. Brett's experience has included radio and television production, playwriting, and stage directing, and his detective is, as mentioned above, the failed actor Charles Paris.

Gwendoline Butler is one of the most versatile English writers of modern and Victorian detective novels, gothic novels, and romances, for which her awards include the CWA 1973 Silver Dagger and the 1981 Romantic Novelist Association Award. In my interview on February 8, 1984, for *Poisoned Pen* magazine, she named *A Coffin for Pandora (Sarsen Place* in the United States), her Silver Dagger award–winning book as her only pastiche. This story is set in Victorian Oxford, a city well known to her, as she took her degree in history at Lady Margaret Hall, and her late husband, Dr. Lionel Butler, was at one time a don there. This 1973 book antedates H. R. F. Keating's *Murder of the Maharajah* in its neat use of the last line to establish the character in the later modern detective stories. "London is the place for Jack Coffin." *The Brides of Friedberg* (1977) is a clever tale of Victorian European royalty and English women of good family caught up in a web of poisonings; for this she had recourse to famous contemporary aristocratic diaries. In the further interview, on November 7, 1985, she drew parallels between her work and that of Charlotte Yonge; pastiche existed in that Butler takes a corruptible heroine as governess into a family, like Jane Eyre—corruptible in that she certainly knew her way around, she knew about her father and the woman, and she was out for her own ends. Whether writing as Gwendoline Butler, her modern sleuth being Commander John

Coffin, or as Jennie Melville (whose detective is a woman, Chief Superintendent Charmian Daniels), her more than fifty-five books show a chilling sense of the macabre and evil, clever characterization, good dialogue, and limitless invention of locale, characters, and atmosphere. After taking her degree at Oxford, she was a professional historian, like her late husband, so her research is always precise and accurate. With her it has been my privilege to lecture and broadcast in England and America. As Jennie Melville, she is the inventor of the women's police procedural, on which I wrote a monograph in 1993.

Ragan Butler wrote two period detective stories, *Captain Nash and the Wroth Inheritance,* and in 1977, *Captain Nash and the Honour of England,* another book acquired from Marian Babson. Set in London in 1772, an "advert, in the *Daily Courant,* July 5th 1772... My original scientific approach to the art of detection ensures the success of my endeavours" brings references to Alsatia, the London retreat of the criminal classes, period cant and crime, the earl of Bute as prime minister, the watch from Bow Street Office, and Fielding the famous magistrate. A fake duel, a royal secret, government spies, secrecy at all costs, the duke of Richmond, Mrs. Colley, and a royal duke—historically correct and essential for atmosphere when an author is creating a pastiche, writing about a period, and peopling it with fictional characters acting perhaps atypically yet credibly. We shall see other writers have this gift, which must keep the book spinning along at today's pace and therefore not use too much of yesterday's language. What took Dickens two pages will take a modern author two paragraphs.

Michael Butterworth was another author of pastiche with unusual titles. His 1985 book, *A Virgin on the Rocks,* is a reference to a famous religious painting. Set in Paris in 1933, thefts of paintings bring to the Café des Deux Magots such celebrities as Gertrude Stein, Alice B. Toklas, Ernest Hemingway, Henry Miller, Pablo Picasso, and Jean Cocteau who chat together like characters in a Hollywood film, then finally all six sign a letter of recommendation to Bernard Fosdyke in connection with the thefts and inquiry. The sense of period recalls Elliott Paul's parodies of Paris already considered.

Peter Chambers was chair of the CWA in 1984/85. He has written some sixty books under five different names. (Peter Chambers was from 1947 the private eye in thirty novels by American Henry

Kane.) His chief character is private investigator Mark Preston in over thirty-five books, in pure pastiche and more. When Chambers was nine years of age he used to visit the cinema to see gangster movies. His hero is a freelance operative in Monkton City, an original, imaginary town, for which he creates his own town planning, not based on maps of Los Angeles or San Francisco. He does not refer to specific events or persons, thus his books are timeless and cannot become dated. Preston is aged around forty. He has made reference to the Organization. The atmosphere is that of the film noir of the 1930s and 1940s, and the books of Raymond Chandler and Damon Runyon. Again, Chambers considers his books to be tributes to the genre, not just pastiche. Originally he wrote as Peter Chester, choosing the name because so many crime writers were on the same alphabetical shelf—Christie, Charteris, Chase, Chesterton, Chandler. Like Marlowe, Preston has a strict code by which he operates, and there is a refreshing absence of amatory experience in his life and work.

Another way of linking truth with fiction, which lies near the fictional treatment of historical fact, is the method Max Allan Collins first adopted in his 1983 *True Detective*. A clever title, it sounds first like the "troodic" magazines, with articles on true murders and crimes; more than a dozen of them were published in America, England, and Hong Kong. The second meaning is of a true or uncorrupted detective who is the hero in this accurate tale which mixes contemporary, real-life gangsters and public figures with fictional characters, including private eye Nate Heller; Frank "The Enforcer" Nitti; Cermak (the Chicago mayor who was shot by Joe Zingara as he rode with Franklin D. Roosevelt); Eliot Ness, who flamboyantly led the Untouchables; George Raft, a Hollywood actor, ex-dancer, and former driver for Prohibition bootleggers; Al Capone in jail; and the mysterious blond killer of Jake Lingle, a corrupt newspaperman often portrayed in films of the period. The illustrations of these characters include two corrupt policemen who threaten the narrator. The period covered includes the World's Fair, Chicago's pride and joy. A similar approach applies later to Nicholas von Hoffman's *Organized Crimes*.

Basil Copper, chair in 1981/82 of the CWA, has written more than eighty books, from science fiction to private eye stories, and from books on the occult to gothic novels. One of his most noteworthy efforts was taking over writing the Solar Pons short stories. Solar Pons was created by American author, editor, and publisher August Derleth (1909–1971), one of the American fathers of the macabre. Pons is a re-creation of Holmes, with Dr. Watson now Dr. Lyndon Parker. They live in Praed Street in the 1920s and 1930s, have the Praed Street Irregulars and Scotland Yard is updated; and the stories are all linked to the original canon of Arthur Conan Doyle. Members of the very active August Derleth Society explained that Derleth wrote the stories without visiting London, using road maps and railway timetables. A typical gothic novel of pastiche is Copper's *Necropolis,* published by Derleth's Arkham House in 1980. The title refers to the huge English cemetery at Brookwood in Surrey, and the special midday trains that ran there daily with mourners and coffins, and with the indicator still visible on a tin roof alongside the railwayline, though the Necropolis Station at Waterloo Road was bombed to pieces in air raids around 1941. The London Necropolis Company is still listed in the London telephone directory. The hero is the strangely named Clyde Beatty. The real-life Clyde Beatty was a leading animal trainer and the author of an excellent book on this subject. There are references to Sherlock Holmes, to Holmes and Watson, and chapter 31 is centered on Inspector Lestrade. Copper's private eye is Mike Faraday, and in a conversation on October 29, 1985, he explained that Faraday is ageless, is a gentler version of Marlowe (certainly there is a refreshing absence of casual "amatory infatuations," as Bernard Shaw calls them), and his background is based on maps, etc., of Los Angeles, similar to Derleth and London, perhaps.

We have already looked at Cecil Day Lewis's creation of Nigel Strangeways. Day Lewis (1904–1972), the poet laureate, was detective fiction author Nicholas Blake. His second book, in 1936, was *Thou Shell of Death.* Julian Symons in *Bloody Murder* says, "A national hero based distantly on T. E. Lawrence is the murderer." Another description was as an irreverent treatment of this national hero "not unlike" the legendary colonel with three names. Many books have been written by and about Lawrence, including biographies and novels. One, *The Murder of Lawrence of Arabia,* by Matthew Eden in 1979, dealt with the last eleven weeks of his life, and claimed he was killed deliberately by government agents to prevent his peacemaking attempts in the Near and Middle East he knew so well (better, perchance, than most politicians). His splendid house at Clouds Hill in Dorset is a strange mixture of Noël Coward elegance and primitive lack of comforts.

Taking real-life personages and events and turning them into period tales of detection is a skilled task. Elizabeth Ferrars wrote about one such writer, Lillian de la Torre, described by Anthony Boucher as "magical eighteenth century pastiches . . . most attractive book of detective shorts ever published," whom Peter Lovesey had already praised in *Murder Ink* as "brilliant pastiches like Lillian de la Torre's [1902–1993] *Dr. Sam: Johnson, Detector.*" Past president of MWA, she had written four volumes of these carefully researched short stories, always couched in rhythms and vocabulary straight out of Boswell. The first, mentioned by Lovesey, was published 1946 (first copyright listed 1944), and *The Detections of Dr. Sam: Johnson* in 1960. The stories appear in *EQMM,* and in the Queen anthologies—e.g., "The Monboddo Ape Boy" in the 1972 *Crime Without Murder; A Pride of Felons* includes "The Banquo Trap" set at the Theatre Royal, Drury Lane in 1776, with Johnson's friend David Garrick. The title refers to the trapdoor in the stage used for Banquo's ghost in Shakespeare's *Macbeth*. Johnson was a great theatregoer, although he told Garrick he would stop coming backstage to the green room as the silk stockings and actresses' bosoms inflamed his amorous propensities. De la Torre adds the traditional "Advt., Notes, and Life" to the first volume; the lighthearted tales, with the excellent atmosphere and original dialogue, start with the "Great Seal," first of the six in *EQMM*. Boswell did include much actual dialogue in his *Life,* which can be included if appropriate to a journey or event, and gives the correct rhythm and emphasis to created dialogue. A playwright and author of books of true crime, de la Torre believes a good detective has much in common with the Great Lexicographer, whose Dr. Watson already existed in the gregarious and at times gullible James Boswell. The return of *Dr. Sam: Johnson, Detector* and *The Exploits of Dr. Sam: Johnson, Detector* followed in 1985.

Another book mixing real characters with fictional is *October Heat* by Gordon Demarco, published in San Francisco in 1979 and in the United Kingdom in 1984. It is set in San Francisco in 1934, with references to Colonel Lindbergh, the hero aviator whose child was brutally kidnapped; Lamm; detective Riley Kovachs; and the 1931 version of Dashiell Hammett's classic *The Maltese Falcon,* with Ricardo Cortez and Bebe Daniels (the first of three screen versions). Real characters involved are Tom Mooney in jail and Charlie Chaplin at the United Artists studios. The dust jacket refers somewhat grandiloquently to "the shrewdest private eye since Marlowe," which must mean since Marlowe was written, presumably. There is a vast amount of technical data about baseball, which might be too much for readers outside the United States.

We have already mentioned August Derleth's creation of the original Solar Pons pastiche, both in the Orient Express multi-sleuth parody and in the continuation by Basil Copper. Derleth started the series in 1929, and wrote the *Adventures, Chronicles, Memoirs, Reminiscences, Casebook,* and *Return.* Copper wrote *Dossier, Further Adventures, Secret Files, Uncollected Cases, Exploits, Recollections,* and *Further Uncollected Cases* from 1979 on. In Derleth's *Return* is "The Adventure of the Camberwell Beauty," with Wayland Peters and Dr. F., Chinese master crook, the ruler of Limehouse. In his *Casebook* is "The Adventure of the Haunted Library," with Mrs. Ashcroft's comment: "Mr. Carnacki says it is not, but I can hardly doubt the evidence of my own senses." Later she mentions his turning down the case (Carnacki is William Hope Hodgson's psychic detective in nine short stories). In the *Reminiscences,* Derleth refers again to Dr. F. in "The Adventure of the Praed Street Irregulars," as does Copper in the *Further Adventures* in "The Adventure of the Defeated Doctor." In "The Adventure of the Proper Comma" is the delightfully subtle: "When I returned from Thorndyke and Polton with an analysis of the capsules." "Polton" of course being Dr. Thorndyke's valuable assistant in R. Austin Freeman's novels.

In the first chapter we saw Derleth's careful discrimination between the uses of parody and pastiches, in Richard Lancelyn Green's Sherlock Holmes collection. Green's introduction comments on Ellery Queen's championing of Derleth's Solar Pons, as of the Robert L. Fish Schlock Homes parodies, Michael Harrison's Dupin pastiches, and Barry Perowne's continuations of the A. J. Raffles stories first created by E. W. Hornung, Doyle's brother-in-law. Green did not include a Solar Pons story in his *Further Adventures* collection of short stories by various authors.

Derleth (1909–1971), versatile author, editor, publisher, poet, and critic, founded Mycroft and Moran as separate publishers from his original Arkham House, wrote true crime books, stories of sleuth Judge Ephriam Peck, and as Tally Mason could be further considered in the section on do-it-yourself crime.

Lillian de la Torre has much in common with Margaret Doody and with the next author, Michael Dibdin. The reason? Their detective stories are all period—different periods—and they have made detectives out of such diverse real intellectuals as Dr. Samuel Johnson the lexicographer (1709–1784), Aristotle the philosopher (384–322 B.C.), and Robert Browning the poet (1812–1899). Dibdin's 1986 book, *A Rich Full Death,* set in mid-nineteenth-century Florence with its colony of expatriate English, has a complicated murder plot, with Browning as the leading sleuth. To use H. R. F. Keating's categorization, this book is acroidal. It consists of a series of remarkable, lengthy letters written from Italy in 1855 by the American Robert Booth to a correspondent in America, Prescott, describing a series of murders. Starting with a women friend of Booth, then a dandy, a gourmand, a fake medium, a trickster "parson," a swindling City merchant, and a common criminal—all are based on Dante's *Divine Comedy,* which both the narrator and Browning deduce from clues in Browning's works. Booth proves from his letters to be a prurient, cheap, lascivious sycophant to the poet, who did indeed live mainly in Italy after his marriage to Elizabeth Barrett in 1846, and whose books, poems, and plays were published throughout this period. It is difficult to imagine anyone writing letters totaling nearly two hundred pages, and with fully detailed conversations not taken from official records, but the ending is ingenious perhaps to those who have no idea of Browning's actual life. There are some anachronistic errors; no one at the time would inquire if you had time "for a coffee," a phrase becoming popular after the 1950's. The title is an echo presumably of "a rich full life." Dibdin's previous book, *The Last Sherlock Holmes Story,* was also a pastiche.

Dibdin's 1993 novel is a pastiche with a startling difference. *The Dying of the Light* starts like a typical 1930s detective novel, with spinster Rosemary Travis entering the living room of a country house, and studying the usual residents sitting there—a colonel, a clergyman, Lady Belinda, strangers like the wealthy American invalid, Jewish financier—but one is missing. The house is Eventide Lodge, a home for the elderly. Rosemary and Dorothy while away the time by using 1930s detective novels, like Agatha Christie's *The ABC Murders,* to imagine murders and sleuthings in the lodge itself. This makes life more bearable, especially as the home is run by a brutal lesbian and her sadistic brother. Real murder takes place. Clues abound, red herrings appear in shoals, and standbys of the 1930s (like confessions, drugged cocoa and drinks, and suspects versus dull policemen) make this pastiche almost a wholehearted tribute to the Golden Age—but not quite.

In 1976 Peter Dickenson wrote an interesting variation on pastiche in *King and Joker.* His theory postulated that if the duke of Clarence had not died but lived to marry his fiancée (later Queen Mary), a new dynasty would have ensued. King Victor I and II, a new royal family, illegitimacies, practical jokes by one royal bastard, then two murders and the killer's suicide contrast with the modern nonroyal attitude of one princess and a new family tree. These factors, with convincing details of palace life, references to Winston Churchill, a great English leader and prime minister, and so on, make up a conjectural pastiche of what might have been but was not. It perhaps shows the royals in an unpleasant light, especially one princess who lacks the family team spirit as she investigates the murders.

Karen Blixen (Isak Dinesen), under another pen name of Pierre Andrezel, wrote an interesting pastiche of French serials with "ladies in distress" in *The Angelic Avengers.* The nineteenth-century French feuilletons serialized detective stories to increase circulation, as did British newspapers like the *Daily Express* and *Daily Mail* in the 1920s and 1930s; surprisingly, in 1986 so did the new British color daily newspaper *Today,* with an Ed McBain story.

John H. Dircks wrote a short pastiche published by Aspen House in 1974, called *Dr. Thorndyke's Dilemma,* with an introduction by Norman Donaldson, who two years earlier had written an even shorter illustrated pastiche, *Goodbye, Dr. Thorndyke,* published by Culver City. Such books, like booklets or monographs, are popular collectors' curios and ephemera, usually selling widely. Sherlock Homes parodies and pastiches are extremely collectible, bearing in mind the many Sherlock Homes societies.

An author who can perhaps be slotted in here is the remarkable

E. L. Doctorow, with two examples. The most appropriate, published in September 1989, is his *Billy Bathgate,* in which the young eponymous hero meets Dutch Schultz, a leading impetuous American gangster, his sidekicks Bo Weinberg and Abbadabba Berman with accountancy skills, and various fictional characters. Schultz was murdered in a restaurant by the organized crime movement, later named the Mafia again or the Cosa Nostra, to avoid his stirring up too much trouble in the fight with that curious lawyer and politician Dewey. There are some factual errors in the book—for example, Schultz's conversion to Catholicism, and Berman being a physically large man. Billy is the "opposite side" of Edgar Allan Poe. It was filmed in 1991 by Warner, directed by Robert Benton, scripted by Tom Stoppard, featuring Dustin Hoffman, Nicole Kidman, and Loren Dean, and billed as Schultz's blazing a crime trail through New York's clubland, a normal target for the mob. Doctorow's earlier book was *Ragtime,* with white and black characters against the background of the Jazz Age, but with such real-life actors as Houdini (the great magician) and Evelyn Nesbit (the woman in the Thaw murder scandal and trial, when playboy Thaw killed the lascivious architect Stanford White over Nesbit, one of the women in the famous red velvet swing). She later went on to be a minor film star as have wives and girlfriends of the other victims or gangsters, including the widow of Big Jim Colosimo, one of the early gangland chiefs to be murdered, who promptly starred in a stage show.

Margaret Doody wrote in 1978 a mystery story based on real people—set in Athens in the year 322 B.C.—*Aristotle Detective.* The great philosopher and teacher is the lead; he aids one of his former students, Stephanos, to clear the young man's cousin Philemon of the murder of Boutades. Of course crime has existed from earliest times, and there are recorded crimes solved and wrongdoers punished, from the Bible, and the Arabian Nights, and other legends. It takes great skill as we have noted to delineate the speech, thought, ratiocination, level of scientific or forensic knowledge, law, and punishment of a real or imaginary crime set in an earlier era—and to get the characters, decor, and atmosphere correct, be it philosopher or slave who acts as the sleuth.

Barry Fantoni created his own investigator in the neatly named Mike Dime, in two books, *Mike Dime* (1980) and *Stickman* (1982). One reviewer described the first as the "world of Marlowe switched to Philadelphia." There are references to the corner of Eleventh and Chestnut Streets, to 1948 Philadelphia gangsters, glamorous women, missing money, and violence, with such national topics as Harry S Truman beating Dewey for the presidency, in this fast-moving story full of correct ambience. The second book refers to a drummer (stickman) in 1949 Philadelphia and the Princeton class of '26. To quote the description, "Here is Barry Fantoni's second excursion into Chandler territory, and he proves triumphantly that Mike Dime is no pale imitation." San Francisco, Los Angeles, "Bay City" are not the only areas for private eyes, and we have now seen New York, Philadelphia, Boston, even a "Reef City" adopted for the locale of stories.

Real life mixes with fictional characters and actions, and there will be more, but it is less usual to find a modern gothic novel in this section. *Hollywood Gothic,* a thriller written by Thomas Gifford in 1979, is a murder mystery, plus storms, sliding hills of Hollywood (a normal occurrence after heavy rainfall), actual persons and creations, plenty of atmosphere, with some very unpleasant people involved. It is the fifth novel of Harvard-educated Gifford, former editor, columnist, and public relations officer, whose five plots are markedly dissimilar each to each. More about this species in the chapter on films and plays like *The Cat and the Canary.*

Mildred and Gordon Gordon wrote fact and fiction, sometimes using his FBI experience, but two novels have a satirically humorous tone of pastiche or parody. *Undercover Cat* (1963) and *Undercover Cat Prowls Again* (1966) feature D. C. Randolph, a cat based on their own Pancho, bought for two dollars, a sum which, as agent X-14 solving crimes and mysteries, he must have reimbursed hundreds of times over. He slips into buildings unnoticed or ignored by watchful criminals. The first book was filmed by Walt Disney in 1965 under the title *That Darn Cat;* Robert Stevenson directed the story of the Siamese cat who reaches a hostage and brings her watch to its owner, who calls the FBI.

Richard Gordon is a doctor and author famous for his series of humorous "Doctor" novels, several of which were filmed. He also wrote three books combining biography with a novel and much period data. One was *The Private Life of Florence Nightingale;* another with more pastiche and a crime angle was *The Private Life of Jack the Ripper;* and the third in 1981 was described as a novel,

The Private Life of Dr. Crippen. This books starts in Buckingham Palace in 1936 with the death of King George V, with Sir Eliot Beckett, VC, as one of the royal doctors. The story goes back to 1909 when Beckett meets an American millionaire's daughter suffering from consumption in Switzerland, their romance, and his setting up a Peoples' Surgery in London. His acquaintance and friendship with Dr. and Mrs. Crippen and Ethel Le Neve leads up to his supplying a drug to Crippen for his execution. Lord Beckett dies in 1955, still attending Ethel Le Neve in her obscure suburban home, and his widow is described as living in Shiplake Castle, Kent, in 1981. There is certainly plenty of detailed description in the book—clothes, fashions, restaurants, theatres and music halls, drugs and medical equipment, prices, etc.—but the details have the air of being taken from catalogues, advertisements, and news reports with the resulting slight aura of unreality. Among the real personages brought into the plot are Dr. (later Sir) Bernard Spilsbury, a leading pathologist, and Kaiser Wilhelm. Music hall comes into the plot as Mrs. Crippen was a performer as Belle Elmore at the time of the stage strike. There is much medical data about consumption and Crippen's dismemberment of his wife, although Beckett is shown as not being entirely convinced of her death. The capture of the fugitives from the liner by the use of radio and Inspector Dew are of course covered. The pastiche aims presumably to reconstruct the crime with period data and a general plot.

The former actress Caroline Graham had written three novels paying tribute to the Golden Age before her 1990 title, *Murder at Madingley Grange.* The owners of this Victorian stately home wish to establish fashionable country-house murder holidays when a real murder seems to upset the farcical turn of events. ("Farce" is sometimes a very appropriate term to apply to murder stories. Did not the great Wodehouse write an essay on the art of writing detective stories?)

Richard Grayson has written several books featuring the fin-de-siècle Parisian Inspector Jean-Paul Gautier, with titles like *The Montmartre Murders* (1982) and the earlier *The Death of Abbé Didier.* His descriptions of the capital city include mentions of the people, events, and inventions (like electric light and automobiles) affecting even slightly his plot and characters.

Robert Lee Hall selected the American statesman, writer, scientist, and inventor (of the lightning conductor, inter alia) Benjamin Franklin (1706–1790) as his sleuth in such titles as *Benjamin Franklin and a Case of Christmas Murder,* in 1990, and *Murder at Drury Lane.*

Another nostalgic tribute was by American-born Timothy Harris (although the copyright was by Hyde Harris) in 1977, *Kyd for Hire.* Described as a Thomas Kyd thriller—"he's the one who picks up the cases that Sam Spade and Philip Marlowe didn't stick around to handle"—Kyd, who also appeared in *Goodnight and Good-bye* (1970) is a widower private eye, with a modest office in Hollywood many blocks east of the stars' names in the pavement, who is consulted by a millionaire whose wife has committed suicide and whose daughter has vanished. Three murders, the statutory fights, a self-seeking police chief, submystery of jewel thieves, and a desultory romance lead on to the main puzzle of the missing son. There are many modern touches of police procedure and brutality to add to the background of a vivid city and life-style. The *Guardian* review said, "A new talent has come through the door gun in hand," recalling of course Chandler's remedy for flagging action. Harris, born in Los Angeles and educated at Cambridge, has also been compared with Ross Macdonald. The 1979 novel was set in Hollywood, and since then Harris has been a screenwriter.

Michael Harrison is a prolific author on many subjects, and one of his more unusual books is *The Exploits of Chevalier Dupin,* published by Mycroft and Moran (of the August Derleth house) in 1968. The book consists of seven short stories of pure pastiche. There is a foreword by Ellery Queen, referring to the five Edgar Allan Poe stories: "Of course, realistically speaking, it is too much to hope that anyone can write an absolutely perfect pastiche of Poe, especially a completely faithful duplicate of Dupin—Mr. Harrison himself would, we are sure, be the first to admit this." The stories are faithful in tone, word, and atmosphere, and there is an essay by the author on the origins of the real Dupin. The endpapers are a map by Luther Leon Norris, showing the operative area of Paris, "The Mystery of the Fulton Documents," etc., and the third-floor little back library, or book closet, overlooking 33 rue Dunot, Faubourg St. Germain, near rue Jacob, where the prefect and distinguished visitors like Bolívar come for advice. Harrison suggests Dunot is a subtle joke for "D'you know?" The narrator-Watson is Carter Randolph of Richmond, Virginia, always suitably amazed at Dupin's ratiocination. The essay on tracing the real Dupin in various libraries and Queen's foreword make compulsory reading before the stories. There was a UK edition in 1972 of *Murders in the Rue Royale* which gave five more short stories.

John Buxton Hilton's (1921–1986) *The Quiet Stranger* (1985) was set in Derbyshire in the 1870s. Again, the book covers a period without fingerprints or modern police or forensic methods, but with a graphic sense of Buxton Spa and the county, so much so that I had various conversations and correspondence with the author. At the CWA conference at Norwich, near where he lived, on Thursday, October 10, 1985, he said he possessed a "period mind," initiated by his having been brought up in his grandfather's era through his parents and his family home in a form of osmosis, so he is writing about what has actually reared him. He used to sit for hours listening to his grandfather talking about his life, obviously to such an extent that Hilton was almost living it himself. On the telephone on Tuesday, October 29, he further explained that another contributory factor was that a man lived in their house who had actually worked on the Matlock railway (Matlock Spa is another historic and attractive town in Derbyshire, south of Buxton but north of Derby and Belper). In a letter on November 6, and on the telephone three days later, Hilton explained how the Fen Country formed another part of his family background, steeping him in the dialogue, mannerisms, and life. His 1976 book, *Rescue from the Rose,* is a same-period story of little Rose Miriam Bennett, a barmaid with airs and graces, being murdered. References to Buxton, Derby, Ambergate (a railway junction between the two), and the railway itself color a murder solved by the barrister Bailey who lived in Buxton. Hilton's maternal grandfather, a gamekeeper born in 1860, remembered having the day off from school when Buxton railway station was opened. As I myself lived with my mother in Belper for three years during World War II I came to know the area well for its history, dialect (almost a foreign language at times), and customs. I have myself ridden in a small railway actually built by the great engineer and inventor of the railway, George Stephenson (1741–1848). Hilton was a retired senior government education inspector, and he obviously had a great capacity for absorbing another period and reestablishing it authoritatively in his own books in an accurate picture. He wrote twenty-three books as Hilton, his sleuths being Thomas Brunt (1870s) and Superintendent Simon Kenworthy (contemporary), and six more as John Greenwood, all featuring Inspector Mosley.

In addition to the parody in his work explained by Edward D. Hoch, a most prolific short story writer, in his letter of November 7, 1983, he enclosed a copy of *The Most Dangerous Man,* from *EQMM* (February 1972), written as R. L. Stevens. It is an ingenious story of a professor planning a robbery in London aided by Moran, a colonel, but his plot is foiled by a "tall, sharp-featured" man, Holmes. The surprising tag line is—"He is the most dangerous man in London"—in this neat, precise pastiche.

Yves Jacquemard and Jean-Michel Senecal, known as Jacquemard-Senecal, actors and playwrights, wrote in 1979 *The Eleventh Little Nigger,* translated by Gordon Latta. There are performances at the Theatre Gerard of Agatha Christie's *Ten Little Niggers* (later with various titles as play and film). Nine of the actual cast are found murdered in their dressing rooms. There is a mysterious young man in Paul Samson; six of the cast are found to have been connected with actress Edith Terray; then come two more murders and blackmail. Superintendent Parescot appears. Two accuse each other. Could it be the narrator or the police officer? A mysterious adopted son and an actress's son appear, as do unlimited red herrings. The final puzzle concerns a murdered son, different-colored eyes, and an adoptive or a real father sending a note for a meeting before a formal denouement. It is an unusual way of taking a classic murder story then adapting it as the basis of a pastiche which is not a continuation or a re-creation. It is a building-up of a new mystery as a homogeneous entity in the same mold, and not just a series of murders during a performance or an event—a clever and unique book. Another book in 1976 about murder in Strasbourg was entitled *La Crime de la Maison Grun,* translated into English again by Gordon Latta, in 1980, and titled *The Body Vanishes.* The playwriting partnership of these schoolboy friends started in 1963 when they were aged twenty.

Rubout at the Onyx is the eye-catching title of one of H. Paul Jeffers's books, written in 1981. The famous Onyx stood at various addresses on West 52nd Street, New York: in February 1935 at No. 35; after the repeal of Prohibition at No. 72 on the south side; by July 23 at No. 62; and finally at No. 57. Jeffers uses real people and true incidents in the book. For example, he tells of the composing of the Farley and Riley hit song "The Music Goes Round and Around" and a legendary professional jam session, inter alia. Among the personalities taking part are Mayor La Guardia, who asked Police Commissioner Lewis J. Valentine (the same Valentine who later hosted radio's *Gangbusters* program—"coming on like Gangbusters") why detectives got fat when Dick Tracy did not; Owney Madden; Paul Whiteman; and George Gershwin, even if at times it sounds a little naive "to stop a minute to hear his latest composition." A small-time crook, Joey Seldes, is killed on December 31, 1934. His widow Gloria asks Harry McNeil to investigate the murder linked to the theft of three million dollars worth of diamonds. Jeffers lists the actual incidents and persons that are true. He also wrote *The Adventures of the Stalwart Companions,* a Sherlock Holmes thriller set in New York City in 1881; *Murder on Mike* in 1984, a Christmas radio murder story; and *Bloody Business,* a survey of Scotland Yard sensational crimes and solutions.

Stuart M. Kaminsky is a versatile American writer on various subjects and a professor on the media. Several of his books feature Tinseltown—Hollywood—from 1977 onward, with such titles as *High Midnight* and *Never Cross a Vampire.* We can consider several novels under pastiche. *He Done Her Wrong* (1983) features Kaminsky's hero, Toby Peters, a private eye in 1942. The Engineer's Thumbs, a Sherlock Holmes society, meets at the Natick Hotel in downtown Los Angeles, at First Street five blocks from his own office on Hoover and Ninth in the Farraday Building on the fourth (or top) floor: Toby Peters, Private Investigator. He gets a call from Mae West, has a meeting with producer Cecil B. De Mille, sees Chester Morris (an actor whose portrayals include Boston Blackie), and Richard Talbot, Academy Award winner and star of the revised silent film, *Destiny's Darling.* There are references to Robert Taylor, and films about Dr. Wassall and Sergeant York, two hits of that period. Peters frequently falls foul of his overbearing, sadistic brother, Lt. Peters, as he solves the mysteries.

The Howard Hughes Affair (1979) has the millionaire calling in Peters, who finds himself meeting Hughes's famous assistant Noah, then actor Basil Rathbone (perhaps the best screen Holmes), who helps in the detecting using Holmesian deductions. Peters interviews Bugsy Siegel (a notorious gangster, partner with Meyer Lansky in the mob, later the Mafia boss of Las Vegas, murdered on June 20, 1947, at Virginia Hill's home), and playwright Bertolt Brecht, who gives him some help on life in Germany. Set in 1941 in the Pearl Harbor era, there are references to radio shows and news, but although the blurb mentions the Marx Brothers, Judy Garland, and Ian Fleming, they do not appear in the book. "Norma Forney" does, though, at Warners in *The Male Animal,* by James Thurber presumably, and her own play. Peters see Hughes shooting a film as yet unnamed, and suggests to him *The Outlaw* as a possible title. Nigel Bruce, Rathbone's screen Dr. Watson, is with Rathbone at the NBC radio studio for live Sunday broadcasts. Rathbone's was the second radio Holmes series, after his Holmes films, starting with *The Hound of the Baskervilles* in 1939, proved so successful. Rathbone had been a leading English stage and film actor before going to America, where he played Philo Vance in 1930 in *The Bishop Murder Case.* Bugsy Siegel in this book makes the famous remark, "In my business, we only kill each other" — later the title of a factual crime volume.

The third book is *Murder on the Yellow Brick Road,* earlier in 1977, and features Judy Garland (who is threatened), Clark Gable, and Raymond Chandler ("I was walking the mean streets," echoing his famous statement of private investigators). After an attempt to kill Judy Garland, one of the Munchkins is murdered — these are the small people in Garland's famous film *The Wizard of Oz,* which also features the Yellow Brick Road.

Bullet for a Star (1981) featured Errol Flynn; *You Bet Your Life* (1979), the inimitable trio (formerly quartet) of the Marx Brothers; *The Fala Factor* (1984), Eleanor Roosevelt and the presidential Scottish terrier; *The Devil Met a Lady,* with its pun on a film title, obviously starred Bette Davis; and *The Melting Clock,* the artist Salvador Dali. *Buried Caesars* (1989) is about General Douglas MacArthur, with Dashiell Hammett as Toby Peters's assistant. Kaminsky writes with a sense of familiarity with the Hollywood scene, filmmaking, and the star system, and the famous names are usually deceased, but their comments and interviews help the action along as part of the murder stories and in a natural way in these credible, nostalgic pastiches.

H. R. F. Keating, chair of the CWA in 1970/71, won its Gold Dagger in 1964 for *The Perfect Murder,* and again in 1980 for *The*

Murder of the Maharajah, described as a "delicious pastiche," and published to mark the fifteenth anniversary of Collins Crime Club (there had been predecessors to the Crime Club, as we have already noted). Set in Bhopore, India, on April 1, 1930, it features the murder of the maharajah and the investigation by District Superintendent Howard, assisted by an unnamed Indian schoolmaster. There are references to Agatha Christie's *The Seven Dials Mystery* (1929): "What happens in those books? Or what happened in one of Mrs. Christie's that I've read?" M. Parrot (*sic*) is mentioned as the schoolmaster reads his cases: "If only Monsieur was here now, Schoolmaster Sahib," and again as "Hercule Parrot Sahib." Howard says he read only one Agatha Christie, when he was laid up with malaria. There is picturesque and vivid detail: a silver train like a NEF that runs round the maharajah's dinner table; a small boy who might be the unwitting instrument of the murder; a shooting party; a neat reconstruction of the actual dinner with several false clues pointing to both Indian and English guests, including the dancer fiancée. Finally the clue comes in just one word at that original party. One critic called it "pluperfect entertainment, loving pastiche." The very last line follows the idea we saw adopted earlier by Gwendoline Butler in which the schoolmaster links up with another, later Keating hero.

Faye Kellerman, crime writer and doctor of dental surgery, married to fellow crime writer, professor, and expert witness Dr. Jonathan Kellerman, has written somewhat gruesome police procedurals, but her 1988 title, *The Quality of Mercy* (taken from Portia's famous courtroom speech in *The Merchant of Venice*) tells of Rebecca Lopez, in 1593, daughter of Roderigo Lopez, Queen Elizabeth's favorite physician, but a year later to be hanged at Tyburn—accused of plotting to poison the queen. The Lopezes are guilty of smuggling *conversos* out of Spain. Simultaneously, William Shakespeare sets out to avenge the murder of his actor-friend, Harry Whitman. William and Rebecca meet and fall in love as they pursue their trails through the slums of London (and the slums and rookeries at that time were dreadful, although middle- and upper-class life was quite civilized). The writer suggests Lopez might have been the original for Shylock. Shakespeare did indeed take famous personalities as characters—the French ambassador as Malvolio, Raleigh as Don Armado, and the queen's minister as Polonius. Shakespeare may never have set eyes on a

Jew, as they were banished from England from 1290 till 1698 (save for some physicians), after the Italians took over their function of lending money (a non-Christian activity), their *banco* giving us the word "bank."

Another writer deserving mention who, like Hoch, links Holmes and Moriarty, with the greater action to the latter, is Michael Kurland, whose 1978 *The Infernal Device* won him an MWA award. The device is one of the first submarines, in 1885; Moriarty is engaged by the Russians to catch Trepoff the anarchist; his journalist assistant, bound to him for two years in a way that leaves his future somewhat unresolved, refers to Oscar Wilde and Bernard Shaw as writers he is meeting. Lestrade and Watson also appear, as Holmes and Moriarty combine to defeat Trepoff's attempt to blow up Queen Victoria's yacht, by engaging in a fight with rockets and fireworks from two balloons (based perhaps on a famous French duel so fought). The picture on the front cover of the English paperback edition of 1979 appears to be actor George Zucco, who played Moriarty in the film *The Adventures of Sherlock Holmes.*

Browsing in a bookshop in New York with Gwendoline Butler I came across an unusual paperback by Gaylord Larsen titled *Dorothy and Agatha,* dated February 1992, but copyrighted 1990. This work of fiction is set in 1937 and tells of Dorothy L. Sayers finding a dead man in her house at Witham, in Essex, and members of the Detection Club led by Agatha Christie solving the murder and another linked to it. Among those appearing to help are E. C. Bentley (1875–1956), A. A. Milne (1882–1956), and thirty-five-year-old "C. C. Breen, or Colin Breen," a newly inducted member. (There is no record of a member named Breen in the club's list of members; in 1937 Christopher Bush was inducted, at the probable age of forty-nine.) The story is ingenious and brings in various real people, like Sayers's husband and son, Anthony Berkeley, and Monsignor Ronald A. Knox, but the book is full of remarkable errors: Berkeley was never president of the Detection Club, only the secretary. One travels to Witham from Liverpool Street station not Victoria. The English do not eat crumb cake. The Sayers house did not have a drive. Mrs. Christie's Morris was not a big car. The Sayers play was *The Zeal of Thy House,* not *in.* It is the *Times,* not the *London Times,* and it does not have a Sunday crossword. English generals are not addressed as "General John

Dana Pike." Agatha Christie could hardly drive up to Crewe and Chester so quickly. The references to "dessert," "matron doing for us," "upperclassmen," the Archbishop of Canterbury being addressed as "Your Eminence" instead of "Your Grace," Val Gielgud's early appearance as radio producer—all tend to kill the atmosphere for British readers of an amusing murder story, which is not difficult to read or solve quite early in the reading. We cannot quite approve Sayers's apparently attributing the anonymous limerick answering R. A. Knox's famous attribution to the Tree in the Quad to herself.

In 1975 Norman Lewis wrote *The Sicilian Specialist,* an amalgam of truth and fiction. His character Spina would seem to be based on Lucky Luciano, who died in Italy, and there are references to Bonachea Leon, and to three actual murders: President Kennedy, a South American president, and Coppola.

Peter Lovesey's 1983 success, *Keystone,* tells of 1915 Hollywood, when English variety actor Warwick Easton is renamed Keystone, on interview with the great Mack Sennett. The book is written in the first-person singular, from Easton's viewpoint. As a Keystone Kop he also meets Mabel Normand, Kops Mack Swain, Slim Summerville, and Chester Conklin, the famous Roscoe "Fatty" Arbuckle (whose career was so cruelly cut short), and Mae Busch. In the filming, there are three murders: a cop named Sullivan, a cameraman, and the mother of a dreadful, posturing actress named Amber Honeybee. Keystone is kidnapped and suffers much before solving the murders by two killers. There is ample color and lively situations—indeed, Hollywood seems to give this intrinsic inner glow to pastiche detective story authors from the earliest days to today. One realizes, however, that it is very unlikely that the real persons named could prove to be the killers, despite their known misdemeanors, in the absence of a factual reconstruction on the evidence of a true crime.

In 1955 was published what is perhaps one of the most remarkable pastiches ever written, *Murder in Pastiche; or Nine Detectives All at Sea* by Marian Mainwaring, who had earlier written *Murder at Midyears.* Victor Gollancz of London reissued the pastiche. The author is an American intellectual who has since returned to the States, according to her publishers. Her witty idea is to have nine famous detectives. In the section devoted to such group activities—and in the film, stage, and television chapter—

Neil Simon follows the same idea. Mainwaring's nine sleuths are easily recognized from their name adaptations. Although we have considered name changing to have a parodic tinge, this book is clearly titled for pastiche, and what is perhaps even more relevant, each of the nine chapters is written in the style of the original sleuth concerned: Atlas Poireau, Sir Jon. Nappleby, Jerry Pason with his secretary Stella Deet, Broderick Tourneur, Trojan Beare with his assistant Ernie Woodbin, Miss Fan Sliver, Spike Bludgeon, Mallory King, and Lord Simon Quinsey with his man Punter. The ship is the RMS *Florabunda,* bound for New York from Liverpool, October 3 to 10, 195-. Paul Price, an unpleasant columnist, is found murdered, so each sleuth adds his or her interpretation of the mystery, written (as mentioned) in the correct literary style with the appropriate conclusions, even if incorrect— for example, King reads psychological symbolism into the clues and facts (just as Ellery Queen can find all the facts in a case having a meaning in the Bible, or chess, or sayings). Finally, comes a letter from the killer to form the denouement. A cruise liner, like a theatre or college campus, makes an ideal scene for murders, as it is as much a closed community as any manor house or log cabin isolated by heavy snowfalls. Such books from the 1930s lead on to television, films, and more books in the 1990s.

Derek Marlowe, born in London in 1938, is a crime writer, playwright, and television and film scriptwriter who has described himself as "Ford Madox Ford wanting to be Chandler or Woolrich, and vice versa." He has written pastiches, and one of quality was his 1974 *Somebody's Sister,* a pastiche of Chandler and Hammett, set in San Francisco. His middle-aged PI is Walter Brackett, who would love to be Sam Spade or Marlowe or any sleuth in *Dime Detective*.

In June 1986, John Conquest drew attention to a book by L. A. Morse (who also wrote *Sleaze* in 1985) titled *The Old Dick* (1981), which he described as a battle between seventy-eight-year-old Jake Spanner and a Mafia boss, fighting their old battles over again with their crutches, until even they began to wonder why they were bothering.

By coincidence, *Sleaze* was reviewed in *Poisoned Pen* (vol. 6, no. 4 [Fall 1986]). *Sleaze* was the name of a magazine whose editor was protected by Sam Hunter, a run-of-the-mill PI. On another page was reviewed *An Old Fashioned Mystery,* a 1984 title by "Runa Farleigh," identified by the editor as a Morse pseudonym. In this the writer led ten guests to Rosa Sill's Komondor Island for her twenty-fifth birthday and inheritance, and so on to a string of murders of all the cast. The survivor in the epilogue is a real clergyman thought to have been the basis of this novel. Perhaps this stresses the width of Larry Alan Morse's writing between 1979 and 1985, when he seems to have stopped. *An Old Fashioned Mystery* is a pastiche of a Golden Age tale, set out as a manuscript left by an elderly lady who disappeared, and written in the appropriate style. *Sleaze* and its "prequel," to use a theatrical term, *The Big Enchilada* (1982), were parodies marked for humor, plotting, and violence; his second book, *Who Did It?* written in 1980 with Carlos A. Yorio, consists of short stories, each in a differing genre of the mystery.

Barbara Paul is another writer to use actual personae as detectives. In 1984 she wrote *A Cadenza for Caruso,* in which Enrico, the great tenor, tries his hand at sleuthing, and gets criticized for his pains. Next year, *Prima Donna at Large* had Caruso cajoling another great operatic singer, Geraldine Farrar, to do the actual legwork in the mystery of a French baritone's vocal chords ruined by an ammonia throat spray. Two other books had similar backgrounds: *The Fourth Wall,* in 1979, as its name implies, had a theatrical setting (the "fourth" is the invisible wall through which the audience watches); another title, in 1985, *The Renewable Virgin,* had a backcloth of radio and television.

Ellis Peters is a writer of detective fiction, including several with a medieval background, and as Edith Pargeter of historical novels. Under the first name she won the CWA Silver Dagger in 1980 for *Monk's Hood,* the religious background for which, and for another dozen books, is the Benedictine abbey at Shrewsbury in A.D. 1141, featuring as sleuth a monk and former knight, Brother Cadfael. His deductions are based on simple facts and shrewd religious psychology. Her titles give an indication of the range: for example *The Pilgrim of Hate, Saint Peter's Affair,* and *The Devil's Novice.* In his introduction to a short story in one of his anthologies, Lord Harding called *A Light on the Road to Woodstock* "this enthralling introduction to Brother Cadfael." There is no element of parody in this series as in—say—Umberto Eco's already discussed *The Name of the Rose.* Again, a monastery is an ideal closed community for a murder plot. Peters's writing has also been honored by the MWA and by the CWA Diamond Dagger in 1993. Brother Cadfael is a herbalist and a Welshman in these twelfth-century stories.

Robert B. Player (1905–1978) was a professor of architecture as well as the author of several clever pastiches with intriguing titles like *Let's Talk of Graves, of Worms and Epitaphs* (1975) over a period of thirty years. Robert Furneaux Jordan was principal of the Architectural Association School in 1948. Symons has compared his work to *The Moonstone* and marks it as above the normal level of pastiche from his humor and unusual disguises. *The Ingenious Mr. Stone* (1945) tells of a murder case in 1930 and 1931, the various sections written as by the parties concerned—including a Scottish solicitor—in murder and a mystery at a select school. *Oh! Where Are Bloody Mary's Earrings?* (1972) recounts the vicissitudes of the royal jewels from the time of the Armada to Edward VII, and whether they finally prove to be the originals or whether the Russian czars have managed to capture them, with interesting sidelights on the British royal family. Player's books' air of such credibility makes them seem truth rather than fiction, bringing in real persons—such as (in the last book) Lord Ponsonby, a courtier at the Windsor of 1887.

In the 1960s I first met Roy Plomley, a playwright, author, and broadcaster, famous for his creation of the longest-running British radio feature, *Desert Island Discs,* in which for over forty years his weekly "castaway" was interviewed on his life and his eight favorite gramophone records. We were connected with a theatrical company whose board meetings were held in the upper room of a closed famous Covent Garden tavern on Sunday mornings. In September 1984, Barbara Miller and I were staying at the same hotel—the Cavendish in Eastbourne—met him and discussed parody and pastiche. A few days later he sent me a copy of his *French Dressing,* published in 1978, inscribed and signed "Pastiche or Parody?" Set in the week of September 8 to 16, 1913, at an unfashionable French resort, a European monarch stays incognito, and his double gets murdered. Commissaire Emile Bonpain, Inspector Leonard Hanoteau, opera singer Ernestine Thibault, French agent Chanteloup Picard, the king of Mittenstein-Hoffnung, and fake British crooks Serry and Anthony shoot in and out of the Grand Hotel of the Baths and of Serbia (a neat touch, this), a carnival, amorous intrigues, and the resort itself. Meanwhile the body vanishes in a trainload of frozen cod in a manner reminiscent of a Feydeau farce. Sadly, Plomley died in 1985, but his widow, Dinana, an actress, allowed the BBC to continue her husband's program. Plomley was not only an excellent writer, interviewer, and television personality with great inventiveness and knowledge, but a man of great charm, gentleness, wit, and kindness.

Cork of the Colonies was published as *Fatal Flourishes* in 1979, expanded in 1984, and consisted of thirteen stories by S. S. Rafferty, set in different American states and first appearing from August 1975, in *EQMM* and *Alfred Hitchcock Mystery Magazine*. It featured Captain Jeremy Cork, "the first American detective," and his "Watson" and bookkeeper, Wellman Oaks. *The Massachusetts Peep-O'Night* dealt with a confidence trickster, Sarah Wilson, posing as a felon, marchioness de Waldegrave. There are references to checking footprints, the murder of a twin, chronograms (inscriptions from which a date can be extracted by adding the values of such letters as Roman numerals), a postmortem, Holmesian deductions, and trigonometry to give authentic feeling of the years from 1736 to 1754.

Craig Rice (1908–1957) was a mystery herself. Georgiana Ann Randolph also wrote as Daphne Sanders, Ruth Malone, and Michael Venning; ghosted books for actor George Sanders and ecdysiast Gypsy Rose Lee; had a number of husbands, and was featured on the cover with a profile in *Time,* January 28, 1946. Her most famous sleuth was hard-drinking lawyer John J. Malone. She collaborated twice with Stuart Palmer and his sleuth Hildegarde Withers, and she worked on two film scripts for Michael Arlen's Falcon, once with Palmer. In 1944 she wrote *Home Sweet Homicide* (her titles frequently had a quirky humor) about a crime writer with three children, as she had. "I would like to dedicate it, with my deepest gratitude, to my children, Nancy, Iris, and David. ... And, finally, if they hadn't granted their permission, it could never have been published at all." Twentieth Century–Fox made it into a film two years later with Randolph Scott as the eligible Lieutenant Bill Smith, Lynn Bari as writer Marian Carstairs, and Peggy Ann Garner, Connie Marshall, and Dean Stockwell as children Dinah, April, and Archie Carstairs. Her big, tall, stout, round, red-faced, greasy, balding, skeptical-eyed Sergeant O'Hare was played by the neat, elegant, slim, dry actor James Gleason. The children are instrumental in solving a neighborhood murder, while their mother writes and the lieutenant is gently drawn in. She also wrote and edited *True Crime Stories.* Ed McBain completed her *The April Robin Murders* in 1959.

Clarissa Ross, who wrote *Fogbound* in 1967, published *Only Make Believe* (the title of a song) in 1980, and this novel was peopled with real Hollywood personalities and offered a possible solution to a famous murder. Set in the 1920s, heroine Anita O'Hare, renamed Nita Nolan, comes to Tinseltown, meets alcoholic two-reel comedian Billy Bowers, Lew Mayers of Master Films (Louis B. Mayer?), and Classic Films producer, monocled German Rudolph von Eltz (perhaps Erich von Stroheim). She has one husband, three affairs (one with bootlegger Rommy Gallagher), and then is wiped out in a drugs-and-murder scandal. Real personalities in the book include Rod La Roque, Vilma Banky, Buster Keaton, Chaplin, Arbuckle, Mary Pickford and Douglas Fairbanks, Jack Pickford, Charles Ray, Richard Dix and his wife, Barthelmess, Francis X. Bushman, Lowell Sherman, Clara Bow, and William Desmond Taylor, Mabel Normand, and Mary Miles Minter—three names in a famous scandal. The story of the heroine's career, problems, and faults is credible, and the solution to the murder practical and ingenious. An interesting comparison can be made with an early book by Dennis Wheatley (1898–1977), *Such Power Is Dangerous,* written in 1933, of a power cartel in Hollywood, in which the great comedian Piplin (obviously Chaplin) will have no part, and actor Prichard Tix (Richard Dix again, the screen Whistler, from the radio detective) makes a brief appearance at a party.

Hollywood Detective, Garrison was written in 1975 by Jeff Rovin (listed in one important bibliography as Ravin), and is set in the Hollywood of 1927. Roger Garrison, formerly of New York, college graduate, wealthy, well dressed, with a Melrose Avenue office and assistant Ruby Harlow, is called in to the murder of Lyle Nast, head of Monument Pictures Corporation. The book is peppered with killings, sadism, explicit, rather pornographic amatory encounters, and a slight surprise ending with most of the characters killed off in the fifteen or sixteen deaths. Various stars are mentioned and in an apparent attempt to create atmosphere, many motorcars are described in some detail.

George Sanders, the actor, started his career in the English theatre, and went to Hollywood to play both the Saint and the original Falcon, later taken over by his brother, Tom Conway. In 1974 *Stranger at Home* appeared by "George Sanders," a rather humorless tale, fast plot, not too much description or psychology, reading like a film scenario. Hollywood's Michael Vickers returns to the hostility of his glamorous wife Angie, his housekeeper, manager, and three friends with their two wives and one girlfriend. Vickers was attacked and shipped away for four years, and one friend was murdered on the night of his return. The book finishes on a brutal note. The book Craig Rice ghosted with Cleve Cartmell for Sanders was *Crime on My Hands* (1944), of murder in a film studio.

Walter Satterthwait has also used real personae in his crime novels. *Miss Lizzie Detective* obviously featured the famous Lizzie Borden, of murder, theft, and doggerel fame, and *Wilde West* (1991) had Oscar Wilde (whose son and daughter-in-law, I am happy to say, have been my friends for many years) on his tour of the Wild West. He meets Doc Holliday under surprising circumstances, and in Leadville, Baby Doe, also featured in the opera *The Ballad of Baby Doe*. A series of murders in each town on his lecture circuit seem to involve the strange members of Wilde's entourage, but he solves the case dramatically in a city of ice. It may not be realized that Wilde's sense of humor allowed him to parody himself in America to promote the tour of the Gilbert and Sullivan operetta *Patience; or Bunthorne's Bride,* which in turn parodies Whistler, Swinburne, and Wilde.

Francis Selwyn, a British crime novelist and historian, created Sergeant William Clarence Verity, who appears in five novels, from *Cracksman on Velvet* (1974) to *Sergeant Verity and the Swell Mob* (1980). In the former, he is described as born in Redruth, Cornwall, on November 8, 1832, and a somewhat stormy member of the "Private Clothes Detail" (not mentioned as such in Charles Dickens's articles on the police). In connection with the 1857 Great Train Robbery, there are references to a penny gaff in Monmouth Street, an area in Seven Dials in London's West End noted for old-clothes shops as delineated by Dickens; such an area would have "penny gaffs" (cheap theatres)—indeed, in 1963, when the present writer sought election to the local council for that area, he was told of a blue-movies house which he discreetly brought to the attention of the policeman on duty. The Grand Pavilion Hotel at Folkestone, 84 Langham Place in the West End, and the Stephens Hotel and Clarendon Hotel in Bond Street (neither listed in the 1879 *London Guide*), are other locales, and the characters include William Baptist Cazamian, Lieutenant Verney Dacre, and Ed Roper. The actual criminals in the ingenious 1857 South-Eastern Railway bullion robbery—with duplicate keys, gold exchanged for almost the exact weight of lead shot in the guard's van, and a well-timed schedule—were Pierce, a clerk in a betting office; Agar, a professional thief; Burgess, a bullion-train guard; and Tester, a clerk in the railway traffic department at London Bridge. When Agar was due for transportation for life for other crimes, Pierce stole the cash and proceeds entrusted to him to give to Kay, mother of Agar's child. She went to the police, and Agar turned informer, and disclosed the plot which would otherwise probably have remained undetected. Pierce got two-years' imprisonment, Burgess and Tester fourteen-years' transportation. There are faint echoes of Holmes in a mention of a leaf in a tree, body in a churchyard, and money in the bank, a Chestertonian quotation we have already met in Dr. C. Northcote Parkinson's mass parody *Jeeves: A Gentleman's Gentleman*.

Sergeant Verity and the Imperial Diamond was published in 1975, and an edition the next year referred to the earlier book as *Sergeant Verity and the Cracksman*. This book tells of the theft of a valuable diamond and the kidnapping of a British army officer's daughter by a rebel prince, with the sergeant loaned from the private-clothes detail of A Division to the provost-marshal in Calcutta to solve both crimes. The callous inefficiency of the English army officers, politicians, and even Verity's cretinous superior, Inspector Croaker, are well depicted. There is a savage irony, almost a parody, in Verity's accurate solution of the cases after careful, period investigation, being casually neglected and overthrown at a time (1858) when the London police were strongly mistrusted by the ignorant public. There is repeated quote in chapter 16, when Verity asks the colonel, "Where would you hide a leaf? In a tree. Where would you hide a native felon? Among the biggest gathering of other natives," what he calls the "policeman's litany." The similarity to Chesterton will be noted, plus the Northcote Parkinson quotation, and the likeness to Holmes's comment, both dealt with elsewhere in this book, and above concerning the previous novel.

George Sims wrote in 1978 *Rex Mundi,* described on the cover by Roy Fuller as a "baffling but I think little-known real-life mystery." Cathar treasure sought near Corfu (described by Colin Wilson as probably books saved from the siege), Rennes-le-Chateau in the nineteenth century, and a famous Poussin painting dating from around 1630, of which one copy went to the Chatsworth collection of the dukes of Devonshire, make up the plot.

The number of books covering all aspects of the lives of great literary sleuths, including Sherlock Holmes and Lord Peter Wimsey, together with serious articles and analyses in quality newspapers and learned journals, is legion. Commander James Bond, although not strictly a sleuth, has had the same treatment. One book is O. F. Snelling's *007 and James Bond: A Report* (1964). This book is relevant here because of a comment on John Buchan's Richard Hannay, Sapper's Bulldog Drummond, and Dornford Yates's Jonah Mansell: "The Terrible Trio were fictional characters, and yet they weren't all *that* fictional. Each was based on someone their authors knew and admired. Over the years, if these characters developed and took on more and more of the creators' own personalities as the times passed, well, so much the better." We have already considered this point above on the dangers of identifying heroes with their authors and their circle, but Michael Gilbert, in the course of an invaluable conversation, commented that Yates was most surely basing Jonathan Mansell on his own persona—an interesting observation on character building for fiction. One example is indeed Sherlock Holmes, based on the famous Dr. Bell, but becoming more and more like Arthur Conan Doyle, as one book about them stresses in the title. Gervase Fen is another, although Bulldog Drummond's characterization was more apocryphal, perhaps. It was Roger T. Bell, an authority on cryptograms, who pointed out that Ian Fleming during World War II, in intelligence, would have found Dr. John Dee, Elizabeth I's spy, signed himself 007, and Bond, based on a man retired to the Caribbean, also had some of Fleming's ideas and opinions.

Another analytic study was *The Book of Bond; or, Every Man His Own 007,* by Lieutenant Colonel William (Bill) Tanner, first published in 1965, and illustrated by line drawings, for the chapters on drink, food, women, culture, clothes, etc., based on the Fleming books and how to ape the mores. It will be remembered that *Snobbery with Violence* emphasized the Bond solecism of "peas and new potatoes . . . as it's May"—in the wrong season. The complete industry in books on every aspect of a sleuth's life includes those beautifully published by Paulette Green on Sherlock Holmes's library, etc., and *The Lord Peter Wimsey Cookbook,* already discussed.

Maureen Stephenson's 1982 book *Autumn of Deception* tells of Mary Dordan, a governess, returning to her father's mill at Golding Magna, on the river Bourne, near Shropshire. There are mysterious murders of Alice Tull and dairymaid Rose Boultbee, then a mill hand, with druidical ritual and a gothic finale before a happy ending. A mysterious druid statue and a reference to the date of October 31, 1815 (Halloween), prefacing November 1 as an important date in the druidical calendar, add to the atmosphere, although a reference to "lunch" rather than the appropriate "luncheon" jars somewhat.

Jean Stubbs is a former member of the CWA committee and originally a member of the Romantic Novelists' Association. She has written books in both genres. On the telephone on March 26, 1985, from her home in Cornwall, her first reaction was that pastiche had not struck her as relevant to her own books on her nineteenth-century detective Lintott. I sent her a copy of a review in *London Mystery* (vol. 2, no. 97 [June 1973]) of her just-published *Dear Laura.* It referred to her previous true-life crime stories and described this book as "scrupulously researched," a "painstaking recreation." Her ninth book, it tells of the Croziers of Wimbledon (where Stubbs formerly lived): Laura, whose morphine is found in dead husband Theodore; brother Titus; and Theodore's mistress. The dust jacket comments, "The publisher was tempted to issue it as though the case had been a real one that had by chance escaped the attention of experts." Set in 1890, it refers to such convincing details of daily life as pantomimes, Zebo (a popular grate cleaner and blackener), buses, and the "rookeries" (the criminals' labyrinths in London). In the course of correspondence, telephone conversations, and meetings in Truro in 1985, and at lunch in Helston in 1986, when we were staying with Colin Wilson, she explained that the book was published as she had wanted, that it was not based on any one case (like her Blandy and Ogilvie books) but on five or six cases of husbands poisoned by their wives who had lovers. It was not based on the Bravo case. Inspector Lintott gets less abrasive as he gets older in her later books; he was based on Inspector Field, Charles Dickens's Inspector Yield in his essays and Inspector Bucket of the Detective in *Bleak House.* She accepted that her books are pure pastiche, as a creation of a period, and agreed her characters stand out three-dimensionally against her backcloths—backcloths woven with vivid, somber, meticulous and, understanding threads. Homosexuality, child prostitution (against which Stead labored so well), clandestine romance, anonymous letters, illegitimacy, servants' hall gossip, and acute observation—all these make up a tapestry of Victorian days. Both sides of the coin of life, with Inspector Lintott's skilled understanding and contrivance combining to disguise and subdue scandal, murder, and passions, make this a remarkable and fascinating book. Lintott appears also in *The Painted Face* (1974).

The Golden Crucible (1976) is set in January 1906, by which time Lintott is a former inspector from Scotland Yard. The magician Salvador's assistant Alicia has been kidnapped; Lintott's daughter Lizzie takes her place, and the three sail to America and travel to San Francisco in time for the earthquake and the fire. Lintott solves the mystery with help from Scotty and his dog. Lizzie falls in love with Salvador. The scenes of the earthquake and the relief attempts in which they take part are graphically described, and a most realistic theatre poster starts the book. Stubbs said in 1986, while arranging to broadcast for BBC-Cornwall, that having moved from detective stories to romantic novels, including her excellent four-book Garth series, she was then working on a book set in the 1940s.

Julian Symons in 1975 wrote a book which was not quite pastiche, or any nearer parody, but although in the Holmes category, its unusual approach makes it worth a closer look. *A Three-Pipe Problem* gives the clue, but actor Sheridan Haynes (note the initials) has been playing Sherlock Holmes in a successful TV series, and ends up living the part in the Baker Street flat created by the producing company. (Incidentally, in *Back View* by Harold Morris [1960] is propounded how 21 Baker Street metamorphosed into the imaginary 221b.) The series is due for scrapping when Haynes sets himself, with attendant publicity, to solve the Karate Murders then baffling London. His Irregulars are the modern equivalents—traffic wardens, the English auxiliaries to the police. The television company and its executives become increasingly bitchy and hostile and his series is scrapped when he successfully and dangerously solves the murders. American lecture tours vindicate Haynes on the last page.

In 1981 Symons wrote an unusual pastiche, *The Great Detectives,* a large, glossy book with evocative and accurate illustrations by Tom Adams, who designed the covers for many of the Christie and Chandler books. The seven chapters have individual approaches and styles, copious notes from the original books, and a long bibliography. Sherlock Holmes was visited in his Sussex retirement home by a woman alleging to be a reporter, for whom he solves a case involving a false suitor, an empty house, and a 1913 bank raid case of hidden spoils. Miss Marple's chapter is as by the original vicar of St. Mary Mead and *Murder at the Vicarage,* writing of his remarkable parishioner. Nero Wolfe is the subject of an interview with Archie Goodwin at the original brownstone regarding Wolfe's mysterious call from the government to travel to Yugoslavia, a trip from which he has not returned and on which he may have been killed; he had made his will before setting off. Ellery Queen's is a research article about the author-sleuth, his father, the mysterious chronicler, and a theory that there were two Queens—two brothers—a theory which W. F. Dannay merely agrees with the author is ingenious; many of the dates, as with Holmes and Poirot, do not tally with the chronology. Maigret's account is of his wife, Simenon, his office, and a new case involving state papers, a tall thin villain, and a sick diplomat, to say nothing of what is obviously Poirot investigating the case on behalf of the Belgian government. Poirot's is the sixth chapter, based on the notes of Captain Hastings, investigating Poirot's age, various addresses, his staff, etc. Finally comes a chapter of Philip Marlowe in the form of Symons interviewing a private investigator alleged to be the original of Marlowe, and a case involving a murder and a gangster, the newpaper being dated October 4, 1935, in the illustration. An interesting book which, like all those seeking to analyze lives, characters, and locales of fictional sleuths can rely only on careful imagination when the facts in the original stories themselves have been extracted, analyzed, and placed in chronological order. It will be remembered that Symons is no stranger to academic and literary research—witness his nonfiction books.

Donald Thomas is a novelist, poet, biographer, and true-crime writer. In 1984 was published his first novel featuring Inspector Swain of the Scotland Yard of the 1870s, *Belladonna,* followed by *The Ripper's Apprentice* and *Jekyll, Alias Hyde* in the same

Victorian classic crime era of fact and fiction. Then in 1993 came *The Arrest of Scotland Yard,* set in 1877, when four prominent senior officers of the Detective Division—Palmer, Meiklejohn, Clarke, and Druscovitch—were jailed for perverting the course of justice, by getting involved in the swindles of the notorious confidence men Harry Benson and Billy Kurr. As well as the actual frauds perpetrated, and the problems confronting an honest man not knowing which of his colleagues to trust, the story includes the murder of an alleged illegitimate son of Lord Byron, his eerie household, a flamboyant mansion in Brighton, and some of the bastard son's criminal activities. Background details are precise, and the fictional elements are blended in, such as Swain catching Kurr outside the Cave of Harmony in the genuine Evan's Supper Rooms (famous for its calculating waiter and Sloman the Improvisatore) in Covent Garden, then the main flower and vegetable market in London. It was this actual prosecution which did so much to harm the image of the English police, founded in 1829, and still even then regarded with loathing by much of England, thus causing the fashion led by Doyle of having amateur or unpaid detectives. In the course of the book Swain asks, "Where would you hide a leaf, Mr. Allardyce?" "A leaf, Mr. Swain?" "Policeman's litany, Mr. Allardyce. Where would you hide a leaf? In a tree. Where would you hide a corpse? In a graveyard..." We have seen this quote in Francis Selwyn's *Cracksman on Velvet,* the 1857 Great Train Robbery novel, and in Dr. C. Northcote Parkinson's *Jeeves: A Gentleman's Gentleman,* above.

In 1985 a new author, M. J. Trow, wrote *The Adventures of Inspector Lestrade,* Holmes's hapless Scotland Yard friend. Like Caryl Brahms and S. J. Simon in their surrealistic humor of *Don't, Mr. Disraeli* and *No Bed for Bacon,* this book mixes fictional persons and facts with real, in an ironically convincing way, for a series of murders based on the Struwelpeter poems. There are references to McNaghten and Warren, the 1890s top policemen, with Holmes's Lestrade. There is a mention of Sergeant Dixon, featured in a long-running BBV-TV series starring Jack Warner, after a film, sited in Paddington, and titled *Dixon of Dock Green.* There is an interview with Lord Tennyson, the poet; ten pages later is the query "Fingerprints—what are they?" The chapter titled "A Death in the Morning" introduces Lord Rosebery, Gladstone's righthand man, and Constable (later Crippen-catching Inspector) Dew, while Doyle himself is mentioned several times. The cast goes on to include the former slave Atlanta Washington, Burne-Jones at Alma-Tadema's studio in St. John's Wood, Ferdy Rothschild, the prince of Wales, the duke of Clarence, General William Booth of the Salvation Army, Dr. Neill Cream, Bernard Spilsbury as a young lad (later a great pathologist, Sir Bernard), Oscar Wilde and Lord Alfred Douglas at the Cadogan Hotel, and a delightful reference to Miss Augusta, Mrs. Miller, and "My Little Agatha," obviously referring to the child later to be Christie. One scene is set at Wildboarclough, six miles from Macclesfield (a "clough" is a ravine), another in the Minories, the White Elephant on Portsoken Street in the City of London, while Carlton Hall beyond Dymchurch Level in Kent brings in Russell Thorndyke's smuggler-parson Dr. Syn and Frank Podmore and the cottage loaf. Lady Cardigan (widow of the seventh earl) and her house Quorn is near Swain's Lane, by Highgate Cemetery. Sleuths include Holmes and Watson, Inspector Athelney Jones, Superintendent Abberline, Gregson, and Bandicoot, who says his is a Somerset name, although a bandicoot is a large Indian rat. Reverend Wemyss and Mrs. Drum add further color to this witty pastiche. In 1986, Trow, who lives on the Isle of Wight, wrote *Brigade: Further Adventures of Inspector Lestrade,* quickly followed by *Lestrade in the House, and Others. Brigade* follows the zany theme of Lestrade investigating a series of murders of elderly ex-soldiers from the Crimean War, interviewing the officers and officers' widows, meeting en route Gilbert and Sullivan, Winston Churchill, the countess of Warwick, Florence Nightingale, the Crowley family, Henry Irving and Bram Stoker his manager (just starting his new novel about Transylvania), Holmes's Yard enemies, plus other surrealistic encounters. When Dr. Watson says Friese-Green has invented a system which would enable films to be made of Holmes, Lestrade sneeringly suggests a passing baby named Basil would be adequate, but South African mother Mrs. Rathbone objects. Witty, accurate, ingenious pastiche, the Brahms and Simon formula is continued. The esoteric blend does not detract from a fluent, well-told story with a puzzle element. There are now a dozen titles.

(A digression on the play of names. Agatha Christie would not have known of the American novel, akin to the plot of *Ten Little Niggers,* found by Bill Pronzini; she may have read of Hercules

Popeau, the retired French detective, who appeared, inter alia, in *The Lonely House* [1920] by Mrs. Belloc Lowndes [1868–1947], creator of *The Lodger;* but she would not have come across M. Poiret, or "old Pawrey," another retired French sleuth, in Frank Howel Evans's short stories in 1909 and 1910. It would be nice to think the great French couturier, Poiret, inspired them all.)

The last example of pastiche is Nicholas von Hoffman's 1985 *Organized Crimes*. Allan Archibald, young and self-willed, gets to mix with gangsters like Al Capone, the Jake Lingle killing, Machine-gun Jack McGurn and his wife, a waiter, Jake "Greasy Thumb" Guzik, and various true incidents, like Nails and the shot horse (for throwing a gangster), McGurn's wife murdered with the waiter, and the killing of Mayor Cermak as he rode with President FDR. (Was Cermak the intended victim?) A logical and compelling book, the actual events adding to the atmosphere and the inevitability, it is in the same mold as *True Detective,* by Max Allan Collins, already discussed.

Play Crime

One surprising facet of crime writing is when authors are expert in other literary fields. Colin Wilson, Gwendoline Butler, and Jean Stubbs are three obvious names; but imagine crime writers venturing into the juvenile market. A few examples can be given both of juvenile crime authors and crime authors who occasionally stray into the field for young readers. Perhaps the most striking name (or names) is Edward L. Stratemeyer (1862–1930), who as Carolyn Keene created Nancy Drew and as Franklin W. Dixon invented the Hardy Boys, and who wrote under more than forty other pen names, and whose daughter, Harriet S. Adams, continued the phenomenal output. One ingenious book, *The Alaskan Mystery* (1985) in the Be a Detective Mystery series, involved Nancy Drew and Frank and Joe Hardy in a story whose several threads could be joined together in a computerlike reading, a system used in some later books. The reader makes his or her choice of action on the evidence offered on certain pages, and according to the choice made, proceeds to a specified page, but all the book's pages are filled, nothing is extraneous or missed, and the endings (in different parts of the book) are all logical. For example on one page the reader may elect to send the sleuths to the Pribiloff Islands on the next or to Fairbanks further on; the primitive mask that forms an important clue can take on different interpretations in the differing actions.

In *Camp Fire Stories* Nancy Drew and Frank and Joe Hardy have six mysteries in which they help their friends in the Camp Fire Organization, which teaches the young community service and environmental protection. *Super Sleuths 2* has the three young sleuths in seven original, unique cases with clues of clever, trap-laying criminals.

Ellery Queen Junior wrote several books about a group of juvenile sleuths, set in outdoor locations—such as a lakeside holiday resort—in a convincingly simple style. As with Nancy Drew (the heroine of several films) and the Hardy Boys, the sleuths always operate within their own powers of thought and action.

Similar to the Scandinavian stories of sleuth Agaton Sax is the example in this genre of the 1947 *Young Robin Brand, Detective,* described as "A Junior Novel," written by Freeman Wills Crofts (1879–1957). Many stories of English schoolboy heroes went from magazines to annuals to paperback or hardbound books, and some had the boys as detectives, with or without the English or French police, like Frank Richards or Martin Clifford, and other pen names of Charles Hamilton, in his very well written school stories magazines.

One surprising example of a detective author writing completely and diametrically opposite books is Mickey Spillane—Frank Morrison Spillane—famous for his very hard-boiled 'tec Mike Hammer, also filmed for cinema and television. His 1982 *The Ship That Never Was* is a story of two boys' adventures in the Caribbean involving such exotic ingredients as a lost tribe, a submarine, and a missing galleon, perfectly preserved and still viable; a fast-moving, action-packed story that again does not make the boys out to be grown men pretending to act, think, and talk like boys. Another story in this series is *The Day the Sea Rolled Back.*

Yokohama-born American writer Phyllis A. Whitney has been writing mystery and gothic stories since 1943, but some of her books for younger readers have received MWA awards, starting with *The Mystery of the Haunted Pool* in 1960.

These are just a representative sampling. We can find books of

Sherlock Holmes as a boy (meeting a juvenile Watson), and one cannot ignore the funnies, where sleuths ranging from Dick Tracy to Mickey Mouse have successfully solved many crimes.

Mention has been made of *Wild West Weekly,* when Sexton Blake met rancher Kit Carson. In Britain in 1949 Amalgamated Press acquired *Sun* and *Comet* comic strips, at the time when American "supermen" were in vogue. *Sun* had *Billy the Kid—The Masked Avenger,* with quiet rancher Will Bonney dressing as Billy the Kid on his horse Black Satan to track down criminals. There was one Sexton Blake strip in Thriller Comics Library (No. 14), *Sexton Blake and the Secret of Monte Cristo,* drawn by Eric Parker, the Sexton Blake Library cover specialist artist—but Blake's name was changed, and the drawings retouched.

Continued in Our Next . . .

A specialized category in this chapter must be those continuations of books and stories about famous sleuths by authors who received permission from the original writers or their estates, or even actually completed a book in progress at the time of the author's death. A brief selection will show the various methods used.

Margery Allingham (1904–1966) was married to Philip Youngman Carter (1904–1970). He completed her *Cargo of Eagles* in 1968, then wrote two more Albert Campion books: *Mr. Campion's Farthing* (1969) and *Mr. Campion's Falcon* (1970).

Kingsley Amis has been considered already for his pastiche *The Riverside Villas Murder* and for his James Bond story, which is a continuation, *Colonel Sun,* published in 1968 as by Robert Markham. John Gardner has also written Bond books.

Elizabeth Daly (1878–1967) created bibliophile Henry Gamadge as her sleuth in a series of novels from 1940 to 1954, all marked by his knowledge of and interest in books. Who more appropriate than Daly's niece to continue to write about Gamadge's widow, Clara, pursuing his civilized course of esoteric crime solving, in a series including *Working Murder, Murder Observed, Murder Machree* (where mysterious twins lead her to Ireland), and *Pushing Murder.*

William Vivian Butler, author of the study *Durable Desperadoes,* wrote in 1986 a jubilee novel, the twenty-fifth Commander

George Gideon story, *Gideon's Raid,* Gideon having been created by J. J. Marric, one of John Creasey's many pseudonyms. In this book, a police raid is directed by Gideon's son-in-law, Assistant Commissioner Hobbs, to catch the three top crooks responsible for 80 percent of London's crimes. An informer in the Metropolitan Police leaks the details. Gideon has to salvage the operation, but his wife, Kate, is kidnapped and held at gunpoint. His raid now becomes a nightmare.

Thomas Chastain, president of Mystery Writers of America in 1989/90, had published in July 1989 *The Case of Too Many Murders,* based on Perry Mason and other characters created by Erle Stanley Gardner. The famous television series was resumed after many years with Raymond Burr as a judge resigning office to defend his secretary, played by Barbara Hale again, and with her own son playing Paul Drake's son running his father's detective agency. A range of new police and prosecuting attorneys included one woman who called Mason's courtroom dramatics (when he had a female impersonator seen as a woman run out of court) outdated—just before he won, as usual. Burr died in 1993.

Charlie Chan, the inscrutable Chinese detective, was created by Earl Derr Biggers (1884–1993) in 1925 for six books, later to be fantastically popular on the cinema screen. The *Charlie Chan Mystery Magazine* followed the Saint, Mike Shayne, et al., in wide appeal, and in 1974 Michael Collins (Dennis Lynds) wrote *Charlie Chan Returns,* a novelization of the screenplay by Ed Spielman and Howard Friedlander. In the blurb to the omnibus edition, it is stated that Chan, too, is based on a real detective, on Chung Apana.

In his valuable *Murder for Pleasure* Howard Haycraft asked if Gerard Fairley and Francis Gerard were one and the same person. After Fairley died I wrote to his widow, Jean, to ask this very question, and on a postcard dated March 17, 1984, she stated categorically her husband was not Gerard. Sapper had written the Bulldog Drummond books, translated very successfully to the screen. Then books were written as by "Sapper and Gerard Fairley," finally "by Gerard Fairley Following Sapper." Sapper was the appropriate pen name of Lieutenant Colonel Herman Cyril McNeile (1888-1937); his last Drummond book was the 1937 *Challenge.* Fairley continued the series until *The Return of the Black Gang* in 1954. When Fairley died, the newspapers revived the story that he had been the original for Sapper's famous creation, but his biographer, Ion Trewin, in a letter dated February 29, 1984, in which he kindly put me in touch with Mrs. Fairley, stated this rumor had come about after a BBC radio broadcast in the early 1930s (Drummond first appeared in *Bulldog Drummond* in 1920).

In *The Book of the Sleuths* (1972) former actress Janet Pate stated that Drummond was "generally supposed to be based on Gerard Fairley." Further proof of how such stories can originate has been offered by the comparisons of certain writers with their creations. One such writer is John Buchan, of whose Major Richard Hannay Brian Connell wrote in his *Knight Errant* (1955): "Buchan, better known to the British and American public as the author of *Greenmantle* and *The Thirty-nine Steps,* was much more closely identified with the central figures of these books than has ever been generally realised. For a period between the two wars he was nothing less than the head of Britain's Secret Service." Both these assertions are disputed. Fairley and "Sapper" had stressed their collaboration in creating Drummond on facets of the former, and Buchan was never head of MI5 or MI6, although he was head of wartime propaganda in World War I. His standard biography states categorically that Hannay was based on General Ironside, later the chief of the Imperial General Staff (for this information I am indebted to Michael Gilbert's kindness). Apart from the initials—G.F. and F.G.—another point of similarity is that Gerard continued the famous Edgar Wallace series of *Sanders of the River,* with Captain Hamilton and Lieutenant Bones, also made into an excellent film in the 1930s starring Leslie Banks. Interestingly, Wallace showed a slightly supernatural event, when Sanders transports his image on leave from a Thameside party to Africa, when his men face a native revolution—an event which has been proved possible by scientists, as mentioned in chapter 3. Gerard wrote a series of stories from the 1930s featuring his detective John Meredith, all with alliterative titles—*Concrete Castle, The Dictatorship of the Dove, Emerald Embassy, Fatal Friday, The Prince of Paradise, The Promise of the Phoenix, Red Rope, Secret Sceptre, Transparent Traitor*—most of which were read in paperback during World War II. Penelope Wallace, Edgar's daughter, sent the *Edgar Wallace Society Newsletter,* containing the biography of this clever crime writer who was born 1906 and died in Africa in the early 1960s. When I was the first editor of the Chivers/CWA Black Dagger series I reissued two titles—*Fatal Friday* and *The Mind of John Meredith*—cleverly plotted, and in the latter Gerard appears as a major in the Essex Regiment, as he was in reality.

When Craig Rice died in 1957 her *The April Robin Murders* was finished by Ed McBain, and published soon after, as mentioned above. Bingo Riggs and Handsome Kusik operate in Hollywood, where April Robin was a 1928 silent movie star. In 1961 Larry M. Harris wrote *The Pickled Poodles* about Rice's famous trio—John J. Malone and Jake and Helen Justus—a medley of drunken poodles, murder, blackmail of a TV commentator, with a farcical touch but a weak ending.

E. W. Hornung created A. J. Raffles, the cricket-playing gentleman crook, as the antithesis of his brother-in-law's Sherlock Holmes. Barry Perowne is the pen name of Philip Atkey, nephew and secretary of Bertram Atkey (1880-1952), creator of the aristocratic sleuth the Duke of Devizes and "almost a gentleman" crook Smiler Bunn. With the permission of the Hornung estate Perowne wrote a million words in modern form over the years about Raffles, then in 1950 adopted the style of the original. Some short stories appeared in *EQMM*, others (like "Raffles and the Point of Morality," around 1973) in *Ellery Queen's Masks of Mystery,* in 1979. An interesting example of the former, in the March 1983 issue, was "Raffles and an American Night's Entertainment," which starts with a speech by Mark Twain, and involves Sherlock Holmes, Watson, an American riverboat, a Savoy musical, and an East End actor-manager—almost a mass parody or pastiche—and later was on television.

When Raymond Chandler died, he left four chapters of an unfinished Marlowe crime story. Robert B. Parker was authorized to finish these twelve pages, and the result was *Poodle Springs,* published in 1989 (Poodle Springs is Palm Springs). We have seen how Parker's Spenser is an affectionate tribute to Marlowe, both named after poets. This story has the murder of a blackmailing woman and a nightclub owner, a millionaire with a crazy daughter, and a cheap crook bigamist. Although the ingredients are right, the wisecracks are fewer. Parker followed this up with his own *Perchance to Dream* (a Shakespeare quotation), as a sequel to Chandler's *The Big Sleep.* After General Sternwood's death, his daughter, Vivian, sends her psychotic sister to a sanatorium from which she vanishes, so Vivian asks clubowner Eddie Mars to help; Marlowe must find Carmen before Mars does. It is strange how so many sleuths seem to be less interesting after they marry—Wimsey, Campion, and now Marlowe. When *Raymond Chandler's Philip Marlowe: A Celebration* by Byron Preiss was published, the former, important, intellectual magazine *Encounter* (no. 417, July-August 1989) had a three-page column by "M." It told of Marlowe meeting Professor Willard Grockle of Cynara University ("I have been faithful to thee, Cynara! in my fashion") further on from Beverly Hills; he shoots the dean and his secretary, Rebecca, as the new professor with twenty look-alikes arrive in Marlowe's office for Grockle to tell him: "It was a colleague, Byron Preiss. He wanted to celebrate Raymond Chandler's centenary in 1988. So with the estate's permission he got 23 mystery writers to write pastiche Marlowe stories, adding a last one from Chandler himself!"

In films, thirteen actors have played famous sleuth Drummond, even more playing Holmes, many Ellery Queens, Lone Wolves, Chans, Saints, Poirots, Marples, but an unusual continuation was Michael Arlen's Falcon, in a short story first played on screen by George Sanders, who started his career in the chorus of a West End musical. In his fourth film as Gay Stanhope Falcon, *The Falcon's Brother* (RKO, 1942), Sanders is killed, and his real-life brother Tom Conway took over the role until 1946, after which John Calvert played the hero.

Innumerable writers have contributed stories, paperbacks, and books to the Sexton Blake series over the years. Jon L. Breen also has some interesting comments in his aforementioned *Hair of the Sleuthhound*. Bruce Graeme, founder-member of the CWA and its second chair, in 1957/58, created Blackshirt and Monsieur Blackshirt. His son, Roderick Jeffries (Roderick Graeme, Peter Alding, etc.), carried on both Blackshirt and Son of Blackshirt books very successfully. Blackshirt was Richard Verrall, a gentleman cracksman.

Do-It-Yourself Sleuthing

We have already seen that the classic format of detective-victim-crime can take various combinations, but in the puzzle stories readers, whether objectively or subjectively, have the chance to solve the case for themselves. Ellery Queen is a specific example; his books and short stories frequently pause at the point where the reader has all the clues to solve the mystery. Over the years there have been more than half a dozen ways actively to involve readers, and we can perhaps start with the most three-dimensional version, which surrounds them completely.

Murder Weekends. Marian Babson's *Weekend for Murder* (1985) was based on the popular 1930s game of murder. In England and America there are many versions—on land, on sea, or by rail—for enthusiastic sleuths to pit their wits against the professional organizers. The following selection is merely representative of an expanding group.

Murder weekends in England had been devised by Joy Swift at various hotels in popular seaside, lakeside, or country resorts as Harrogate (Yorkshire), Brighton on the south coast, Bowness-on-Windemere, Blackpool in Lancashire, Woodhall Spa, and Southport's Quality Royal Hotel for the Prince of Wales Hotel Group. Professional actors, hotel staff, and genuine St. John's Ambulance men mingle in different stories each time, such as a school reunion. Visitors are involved as soon as they arrive, and do not even know if it is a genuine manager who greets them. Crime films, clues on notice boards, clue sheets put under their bedroom doors, reports in American and British papers, submitting papers of conclusions, and a Sunday morning denouement make up the program, which may start with a "murder" at the first dinner. The Christmas 1986 program at the Prince of Wales Hotel, Southport, was Lord and Lady Haskayne's four-day house party at their country seat, with the usual concomitants of games, tea, pantomime visit, Mastermind contests, fancy-dress ball, and a murder.

In England, the Trust House – Forte hotel group promoted Murder by the Sea, weekends of mystery and suspense at their Grand Atlantic Hotel at Weston-super-Mare. By 1991 Joy Swift's company, The Original Murder Weekends Ltd., was organizing a "Calendar of Crimes" throughout the year, of murder weekends at a large number of hotels belonging to this group, from the five-star Imperial Hotel, Torquay (Agatha Christie's Majestic Hotel in *The Body in the Library,* 1942, and the scene for the 1932 *Peril at End House,* as the writer learned as one of the organizers of the Agatha Christie Centenary at Torquay in 1990), to Cheltenham,

Shrewsbury, Canterbury, and North Berwick, with special weekends at Easter and Christmas.

The *EQMM* in April 1984 carried advertisements for mystery weekend vacations at Phoenixville of "Murder at the Inn" and "Ghost Stories," presented by Gaslight Mystery Theatre.

The 1984 California Weekend Mystery Train between Los Angeles and San Francisco, on Amtrak's Coast Starlight four-hundred-mile run, had passengers attempting to solve Orient Express–type crimes.

Advertisements in America were of an unusual British holiday in "Murders and Mysteries Tour, West Country," escorted by Marcia Muller, starting in Somerset, with a country-house Christie murder, addressed by biographer Janet Morgan, Baskerville and Du Maurier, Haunted Castles, Stalk the Ripper, and lectures by Marian Babson and Robert Barnard, at a fee of $1,649.

The *August Derleth Society Newsletter* told of the mystery weekend, held on Saturday and Sunday, October 5 and 6, 1985, at the Devil's Head Lodge, Merrimac, Wisconsin, in honor of the August Derleth Society, at a cost of $60. Saturday at 3:30 P.M., the limo arrived with the mystery guest; 7 P.M., society president Bill Dyke outlined the program; from 8 P.M. to 12:30 A.M., "chaos, murder, police, lab report, suspects"; Sunday, 11 A.M., Bill conducted the questioning over a strawberry champagne brunch, before 1 P.M. checkout, with the mystery solved. The previous announcement commanded: "Don't Be Shocked. Several bodies will be found on the premises throughout the weekend. Don't forget your flashlight!" in *Newsletter* (vol. 8, no. 4 [1985]), while vol. 9, no. 1, recounted the drowned body of Kate in the pool, daughter of the lodge owner Helena Braun, who recovers then dies. There were seventy guests, lab reports, one suicide, and three murders in the script written by Kay Price and Shirley Morgan. It was solved by ADS member Ron Herring as a *Chicago Tribune* reporter.

An unusual version of a whodunnit weekend in 1986 was advertised for £110 at the Old Swan Hotel, in the spa town of Harrogate in Yorkshire, and fifty signed up. It was at this hotel that Agatha Christie stayed for eleven days exactly sixty years previously, in 1926, under a significant false name, while the entire country searched for her. The event was mentioned but briefly in her autobiography.

The *Aberdeen Press and Journal* advertised for November 21 to 23 1986, a "Murder Mystery and Suspense Weekend" at the local Holiday Inn. For a charge of £60 readers could attend the Hen and Stag party in the hotel nightclub on the Friday evening, the ceremony, and the reception dinner-dance on Saturday, and the usual denouement on Sunday, presented by newspaper and hotel.

A popular BBC-TV detective series for some years was *Bergerac,* with John Nettles as a police sergeant on the Channel Island of Jersey. By February 1987, the island was capitalizing on this series, and one hotel offered guests the chance to be the sergeant and solve the crime.

An organization called *Cat & Mouse* (Talent Entertainments) advertised evenings or weekends all over the world.

The Hotel Thayer in America advertised "Get Away with Murder at the US Military Academy" weekends from mid-January to mid-March.

An English cricketer from Lancashire, Graeme Fowler, arranged a "Murder on a Steam Train" in the Rossendale Valley on Friday, June 21, 1991, as a special event for his benefit.

Another American annual mystery weekend had crime writers taking part at the Mohonk Mountain House, in New Paltz, New York.

In Norfolk, in 1987, Wensum Lodge, in King Street, Norwich, advertised "Murder and Detection," from November 27 to 29 at an adult education center.

Initiative Unlimited in 1989 organized murder mysteries for dinner parties and business clients in the London area, in a format similar to the murder games also considered in this section.

There are several other companies, including some that advertise in the English theatre newspaper *Stage*.

One murder weekend was featured on British commercial television, as a wedding at a stately home, on the evenings of August 18, 19, and 20, 1989, with viewers invited into the studio.

A personal example is perhaps a simple way of explaining the process. In March 1993 the City of London and Westminister Rotary Club, regarded as the premier in Britain and worldwide outside America, wanted something unusual for the President's House Party to be held one weekend at the elegant St. Pierre Hotel and Country Club in Chepstow, South Wales. This is a club famous for its two tournament golf courses. I was asked to organize a murder weekend. The plot was to be three candidates, with their women friends, to attend as the finalists for Britain for the newly devised (and imaginary) position as a director of Rotary for the whole country. Three members and three wives adopted the roles of advertising executive and woman friend, banker and sister, publisher and sister-in-law. I was present as Ken Ferris (a family name), an English police lecturer attached to US police as invigilator, with crime writer Gwendoline Butler, who had helped me with the script, as Mrs. Ken Ferris. The ad man dies of poison (offstage) at Friday's dinner; comes back as his twin brother coincidentally in the neighborhood; clues were posted on a notice board; the six were cross-examined by us and by several lawyers and magistrates in the company (with prepared questions); searches were made; a quiz was held; then Sunday morning Butler summed up in a denouement, enlivened by additions to the script, with prizes of her signed books donated by the president to the winners.

If you do not want to be so cerebral, London offers you a "Bus Trip to Murder"—City, West End, Greenwich, Ripper territory, and Tower Hill; or "Jack the Ripper" tours; or three different "Sherlock Holmes" tours.

For convenience, the other sections in "Do-It-Yourself Sleuthing" will be subdivided as follows:

Books. These can be further split into those books containing a number of puzzles (whether the book consists of puzzles only or a series of puzzles among other material, such as poems, articles, stories, et al., as in the weekend-type book) and those containing a series of short detective stories, each with a deliberate opportunity for the reader to guess the solution, and full-length detective stories with the ending missing, for readers to elucidate. We shall find a certain confusion over titles.

Dossiers. At various times, dossiers of various editions containing all the clues, files, etc., in a police report, have been marketed; the solution is usually included.

Games. These include jigsaw puzzles, card games, electronic board games, and specially devised packages.

Film, Radio, Stage, and Television. Productions in these media leave the audience to guess the solution.

Sundry problems. These range from newspaper competitions to actual battles of wits for those attending functions or venues to book puzzles of all sorts and conditions.

We shall start with a dozen or so examples—a selection of puzzles scattered through the volume itself, either as examples in a book on the subject, or in the weekend type or annual. The alphabetical listing of author or publisher seems most appropriate.

But first, the children. *From the Files of Police Dog 99: The Mystery of the Missing Moggie,* by Keith Brumpton, has maps, clues, cartoons, jokes for seven- to nine-year-olds to help police dog Rusty solve the crime. *Cat and Dog Mysteries,* by Jeff O'Hare, has Clue Cat and Deductive Dog, partners in Petropolis Police Force in fourteen mini-mysteries with clues and a hidden-picture puzzle for the seven- to twelve-year-olds. Dav Pilkey's *Kat Kong* has the eponymous villain escape from Mousepolis, capture Rosie Rodent, to be pursued to the top of Romano Inn by Captain Charles Limburger. The same author's *Dogzilla* uses adjusted photographs, collages, etc., to show the mighty canine terrorizing the mouse population.

Kingsley Amis continued the James Bond series and wrote the pastiche that started this chapter. Now comes his "Crime of the Century," a series in the *Sunday Times,* from July 12 to September 28, 1987, six episodes, then the winning entry and his book. The story is of serial murders, the initials A, B, C, with a reference to Agatha Christie, one criminal, setting up an enquiry, a QC, a psychiatrist, MPs, a crime writer Christopher Dane, the commissioner of the Metropolitan Police, and a retired detective chief superintendent (as in the so-called Yorkshire Ripper case). Letters pinned to the bodies (S O U T H), an anagram, plot to kill the prime minister in the House of Commons, a man with maps, a woman with an admirer, a Westminster TV "Crime 10" program lead to a plethora of red herrings. The foreword refers to interests in psychiatry of suspects, and to "thorough grounding in detective stories" or the parallel of "real" and "fictitious" lines, and the expertness of police procedure other than with Agatha Christie and John Dickson Carr, who can write well "unqualified by diplomas in applied ballistics, nuclear physics, computer science and the rest."

Isaac Asimov (1920–1993) has been mentioned as author of five volumes in the Black Widowers series of short stories, parodied by Jon L. Breen as the White Divorcées. Asimov, with a Ph.D. from Columbia University, also numbered among his impressive total of books and stories a robot detective in his 1953 "The Caves of Steel" in *Galaxy Science Fiction. The Union Club Mysteries* (1985) is a series of thirty crime-puzzle short stories narrated by a member of a gentleman's club who awakes from a nap, tells the tale, dozes off, then astounds his circle of friends and readers with the answers to interesting and varied mysteries.

Nick Bantock's *The Egyptian Jukebox* is described as a ten-drawer cabinet of double-page color spreads of an eccentric millionaire's collection of worldwide artifacts, each with a description of his strange experiences and the connection between the contemporary and ancient worlds. Readers must find clues in stories and pictures to solve the riddle, "Where do my worlds join?"

Simon Brett's novel *The Christmas Crimes at Puzzel Manor* has line-art puzzles to test Jack Tarrant of Scotland Yard and his girlfriend (and the reader), snowed up for the festive season in a carefully restored eighteenth-century English country house.

Scotland Yard Photocrimes, from the Files of Inspector Black, "Producer Amy Carroll," was published by Dorling Kindersley Ltd. in 1983. It consists of twenty illustrated cases, with photographs, clues, suspects, and eventually solutions, the pictures being posed by the members of the Scotland Yard amateur dramatic society. Three cases in this large, slim book titled "Industrial Espionage," "Theft at a Séance," and "The Kidnapped Baby," are identical with three cases, with line drawings not photographs, in a 1936 book we shall consider, *The Master Book of Detection and Disguise*—but titled "Industrial Espionage," "Theft at a Séance" and "Kidnapped." The present picture book has an illustration showing 1930s stamps and a reference to pounds, shillings, and pence (decimalization of money came to England in 1971). The book awards marks for correct answers, equating results on Scotland Yard entrance exams for ranks from police constable up to commisioner.

August Derleth (1919–1971) has already been reviewed for his masterly pastiche of Sherlock Holmes, in his Solar Pons series, including the mass parody of sleuths in the Orient Express story and other tales that included famous fictional creations. In 1957 he wrote *Consider Your Verdict,* in which the reader is challenged to find flaws in the statements of witnesses at coroners' inquests.

An unusual volume was titled *The Canterbury Puzzles,* dated 1907, second edition, amended; it was by Henry Ernest Dudeney, published by Nelson, and contained various puzzles, as "The Adventures of the Puzzle Club." The detective tales included "The Cornish Cliff Mystery," "The Runaway Motor-Car," and a geometric problem, "The Mystery of Ravensdene Park," inter alia, with all the solutions, of course.

The Magnet Detective Book, vol. 3, by Wolfgang Ecke, illustrated by Rolf Rettich, translated by Stella and Vernon Humphries (1980), was preceded by volumes 1 and 2, in Germany, from 1971 onward, as *Die Neusten und Spannendsten Geschichten, Schach bei Vollmond & der Unsichtbare Zeuge:* seventeen problems with answers, in three grades of difficulty.

In 1968 K. Franken in Germany wrote *Krimiscule fuer Junge Privatdetektive,* published in the United States in 1969 and in the United Kingdom three years later as *Puzzlers for Young Detectives,* with a special foreword on thrillers, Edgar Allan Poe, and the rules of the game. There are twelve cases to solve, with the answers to check against the reader's deliberations.

A similar book from Singer Features in America in 1972 was *Solve-a-Crime* by A. C. Gordon, with forty-seven short mysteries to solve, with answers.

The Master Book of Detection and Disguise, by former detective inspector Alfred C. Grosse, published in 1936, was a paperback book available in return for coupons from packets of Quaker Oats, a breakfast cereal. Young readers found advice on disguises, a "seebackroscope" (a kind of periscope designed to allow the wearer to see behind him), and the like. Also included were nine four-minute mysteries, four photocrimes, and other puzzles, with answers. We have seen that three of the photocrimes, which here are marked as "By Courtesy of *Weekly Illustrated,*" appear in another book nearly fifty years later, with differing titles and the occasional name altered, but with the illustrations (line drawings against photographs) identical. The clues are, of course, more in the pictures than in the accompanying text. Quaker Oats issued three other books for young consumers and readers—on conjuring, football, and espionage—each by well-known writers, the last named being by Lieutenant Colonel Graham Seton, author of *The W Plan.*

I once interviewed Alfred Hitchcock on BBC radio and broadcast about a sixteen-minute color film he made for a Cine Club of which I had been president, so I read with great interest *Alfred Hitchcock's Solve Them Yourself Mysteries,* published by Random House in 1963, in Great Britain by Max Reinhardt in 1965, and by the New English Library, in paperback, in 1968. There were five stories, with typical Hitchcock interjections—one story, "The Mystery of the Man Who Evaporated," actually including a MWA meeting attended by Robert Bloch, Erle Stanley Gardner, the Ellery Queen duo, the Great Merlini, et al., over a French restaurant in New York City. Harkey Newcomb is a writer of locked-room mysteries, then living in Laketown (two-hour's drive away from New York), now resident in England. Another paperback version, by Armada, with a hyphenated title, came out in 1980, missing the line drawings and one story, of "The Seven Wrong Clocks."

Photocrimes, dating from 1936, was another example of Do-It-Yourself detection, this time by Mileson Horton and Thomas Pembroke.

Hutchinson's issued a thick paperback book, *A Century of Entertainment,* at a price of sixpence; there is no date of publication, but references in advertisements to Edgar Wallace's *Smoky Cell* and to two authors named Dawson Gretrex and Grierson Dickson seem to imply the 1930s. The book contains six problems of Detective Inspector Blacker, with the answers on the following pages; the problems are neat and straightforward and the clues fair.

The Adventures of the Black Hand Gang, by H. J. Preiss, narrated the four adventures of Frank, Angela, Ralph, and Keith, illustrated with clues, and answers at the end of the book.

In 1978 ITV/Arrow published *Whodunnit?* by Alan Radnor. It had an introduction by Jon Pertwee, a television and West End stage actor who was an early Dr. Who in the long-running BBC-TV series of that name, and the book was made up of ten puzzles, based on a television series, for readers to solve and compare with the official answers. In the introduction Pertwee stressed "detailed and logical detective work," as opposed to "consequence or motivation of the criminal."

Detectograms and Other Puzzles by H. A. Ripley and F. Gregory Hartswick was published in 1968 and 1983 by the Bell Publishing Company of New York, Ripley providing the twenty-six detectograms and Hartswick the puzzles with answers. The first detective mysteries involved a Professor Stabus Stiggins, and the puzzles included murders with one suspect, problems with various unknowns to analyze, and others set out in telegram form, always giving the reader the full clues.

Sleuth! by Sherlock Ransord, illustrated, a Mycroft Merfy (*sic*) Hippo Books, Scholastic Publications (1986): twenty problems, cartoon strips, two stories, ordinary detective tales, or with codes, references to symbols (not used), with answers.

Do-It-Yourself sleuthing with a difference is in a book shown to me by Colin Wilson when I was staying with him in Cornwall in June 1986. It was *The Do-It-Yourself Bestseller,* edited by Tom Silberkleit and Jerry Biederman, published in 1982 by Dolphin: twenty-one chapters, twenty by world famous writers, with a first page and a concluding paragraph, and blank pages for the reader to complete, plus a blank chapter for the reader to write in its entirety. Examples included Isaac Asimov, "Let Go, Darn It!"; Ken Follet, "Soft Class"; Georges Simenon, "And Yet This Was a Man"; and Colin Wilson, "The Vamp." Subtitled "A Workbook," it is a unique way for the would-be writer to receive help from the greatest literary names.

More Two-Minute Mysteries by Donald J. Sobol was published in the USA in 1971 by Scholastic Book Services and consisted of more than sixty two-page mysteries, with titles like "The Case of the Airport Killing" and "The Case of the Silk Mantle", involving sleuth Dr. Haldejian and his grateful friend Inspector Winters. The answers are upside-down at each chapter end, and the problems take place all over the States, with many ingenious crimes, verbal tests, and traps.

We have commented on Torquemada's introduction to Agatha Christie's *The Murder of Roger Ackroyd* in the first paragraphs of this book. In 1934 Victor Gollancz published *The Torquemada Puzzle Book,* by "Torquemada," which contained a mystery puzzle novel, in which the reader had to rearrange random pages before solving the murders. It was dedicated to Dorothy L. Sayers, and was a well-nigh impossible puzzle to solve.

Lawrence Treat, a past president of MWA, is a leading name in American crime writing—short stories, one of which received the MWA Edgar in 1964; novels with alphabetical titles like *Q as in Quicksand* (1947); other novels like *Trial and Terror* (1949); and picture puzzle stories, in which the reader has a large, clear line drawing of the scene of a crime and has to answer various questions based thereon, and thus solve the crime depicted. *Crime and Puzzlement,* published in England in 1982, had twenty-four such picture puzzles, compiled during the years from 1935 to 1981. A similar title was *Crime and Puzzlement on Martha's Vineyard,* containing twenty-four problems suitable for both young and mature adults.

Zebra Books was founded by Roberta Bender Grossman, who died on March 13, 1992, in New York City. The company published mysteries, including the Solve-It-Yourself Mystery series, from the late 1970s, the clues in the drawings interspersed in the text, with the solutions sealed (as in some jigsaw puzzles) to encourage the readers.

The last example selected for this section on books is of a somewhat complex nature. John Fisher, author of many books on music hall, conjuring, and Alice in Wonderland, member of the prestigious Magic Circle, and a former senior BBC television producer responsible for such successes as the "Paul Daniels Magic Show" and the Bob Monkhouse and Terry Wogan chat shows, sent me a book with the comment that it ought to be in my library more than his. We have been friends for many years, since I was first called in by the publishers to advise and help on his famous book on music-hall stand-up comedians. This volume was *The Mystery Puzzle Book* by Lassiter Wren and Randle McKay, undated, but obviously 1920s or 1930s, with the foreword by S. S. Van Dine, already mentioned earlier for his appropriate comments. The book has various true and fictional puzzles for the reader to solve—for example, the Rice Will Forgery of 1900, the Dreyfus Forgery, and the Edalji Case (in which Arthur Conan Doyle interested himself). Another version was *The Baffle Book,* dated 1929, for the Crime Club, by Lassiter Wren and Randle McKay, yet another edition dated a year later, both first American editions. To add to the mystery, when I was broadcasting radio crime book reviews, John Waite, the presenter—and cousin of the Archbishop of Canterbury's special international representative, Terry Waite—asked me to review a new paperback, *The Baffle Book,* edited by F. Tennyson Jesse (1889–1958), wife of playwright H. M. Harwood. She wrote famous crime books—fiction and nonfiction—including the excellent *Murder and Its Motives*

(1924), and edited some of the *Notable British Trials.* This particular edition was dated 1984, contained twenty-eight chapters like the other books, but the actual cases did not tally; the edition "transposed some of the cases," according to the introduction.

In contrast is a short story, "A Problem in White," by Nicholas Blake, in the *Strand Magazine* (February 1949, as "The Snow Line"); "A Study in White," in *Queen's Awards,* 4th series (1949), reprinted (1988) in the anthology *Crime at Christmas,* kindly drawn to my attention by Colin Wilson. Arthur J. Kilmington was murdered in a snowbound Scottish express train, with two main clues, and six minor ones. The answer was given at the end of the anthology, the mystery having been solved by Henry S. Syansfield.

This selection of more than a dozen books gives a microcosm of those available to amateur sleuths. We now come to a similar group of full-length volumes giving the reader more detail, more scope, and a greater need to analyze and think. Edgar Wallace (1875–1932) started the trend with his famous self-published *The Four Just Men* (1905), and the £500 prize for the successful answer caused a surge of sales—and a flood of correct solutions.

In 1983 came a flurry of advertisements for *Who Killed the Robins Family?* (a reference obviously to Cock Robin of the nursery rhyme), by Bill Adler and Thomas Chastain (author of the 1976 "911," the police call), published in November, and serialized in the British newspaper *Daily Express,* October 31 to November 8. There was a £10,000 prize, an April 1984 panel of judges, and a May announcement. The murders took place in exotic locations (such as the new Orient Express), the wealthy family members seemed ludicrously trusting, and the solution of a clutch of different killers, with only one member alive was somewhat confusing, to say the least. Judith Hodgson wrote in *Philadelphia* (April 1984) an article "How Will I Kill Thee? Let Me Count the Ways" that one author was marked as having "created," the other wrote, that thirty-six characters were disposed of (allowing 3 ¾ pages each), so that "each chapter is little more than a plot outline for a murder." In 1984 was published a Warner paperback *The Revenge of the Robins Family,* chapter eight thereof being the full solution to the first book.

The Famous Five is the name of two very well known groups in England. One consists of the five schoolboys at the English public school, Greyfriars, created by record-breaking, prolific author, Charles Hamilton, or Frank Richards, or Martin Clifford or ... The other is the group of children created by Enid Blyton, from whom a typical title in the Famous Five Adventure Books series, with kits to crack the code, is *The Haunted Railway Game*. Other self-explanatory titles in this range of good children's books are *The Wreckers Tower Game, The Whispering Island Game,* and *The Sinister Lake Game*.

In 1946 Miriam Allen de Ford (1888–1975) wrote "Farewell to the Faulkeners," admittedly a short story, in which the reader had all the facts to enable him to be the investigating detective.

Murder in Space: Whodunit? was a 1985 paperback tied in with a television program original. The screenplay was by Wesley Ferguson, the book author listed as F. X. Woolf. It appeared on the British commercial television screen on August 13, 1985, and was a coproduction with Zenith of Canada. The book was published minus its ending, and told of four murders of astronauts on an international spaceship, and had to be solved immediately to avoid the murderer escaping. The ending selected could thus be filmed after August 13 with the successful mystery solvers in the studio audience. Arthur Hill appeared in the film. On Sunday, September 15, it was reported that nine successful contributors were in the studio to watch the filming of the solution, which was seen in the USA, Australia, and the Middle East.

Francis Van Wyck Mason (1901–1978) had a distinguished military career, and another as crime and historical novelist. His pseudonyms included Frank W. Mason, Ward Weaver, and Geoffrey Coffin, who wrote *Murder in the Senate* in 1935; that same year he wrote *The Washington Legation Murders* under his own name. His writing started in 1928. The two books we now consider appeared in 1937 and 1957, the first being *The Castle Island Case,* a straightforward murder case with all the clues given the reader in clear photographs of the action, taken by Henry Clay Gipson. As with the Dennis Wheatley dossiers, some famous people posed as the book's characters, including the author himself as Inspector Boyd, Carveth Wells as himself, and, as Bernard Grafton, C. Daly King (1895–1963), author of, inter alia, *Obelists at Sea* and *Obelists Fly High*. Mason's sleuth in thirty books is Colonel Hugh North, and this case for him is illustrated not only by photographs of the corpse, scenes of action, and newspaper clippings, but even an infrared culminating shot. A few years later in Book Catalogue No. 9 of Ralph Spurrier, referring to a customer in New Zealand, it was reported that pages 128 and 129 had been cut out of copies, with two pages glued onto stubs of the missing four pages, so the pagination is incorrect. The offending picture was of a couple kissing, yet a photograph of a naked female "corpse" in the surf was left in the book. Presumably this was discreet censorship. The other book is *The Gracious Lily Affair,* set in Bermuda (where Van Wyck Mason lived) and Hong Kong, and this mentions Freebooters Hall and Susan Stanhope from the earlier story.

A remaindered paperback, dated 1985, by Matthew Prize and Otto Penzler, the coauthor of the famous *Encyclopedia of Mystery and Detection* and other valuable books, was *This Prize Is Dangerous,* and the copyright was by Whodunnit, Inc., originally from the USA. The story told of the murder of Freddi Sanchez, a museum, Quin Jefferson a homosexual, Silas Griffin a missing father, a former PI-professor called in by the daughter, a glamorous wife, a girlfriend, a gun-running son and his friends, a millionaire collector of icons, and a yacht where the body was found—but no ending. There were to be two prizewinners—one in the UK, one in Australia—and the result would be advertised. The British publishers, W. H. Allen, said there were two such winners, but they could not trace who they were or the answer, and suggested writing to the American publisher—who never answered my letter.

Two unusual books, in a style reminiscent of the children's detective puzzles—wherein the reader chooses a course of action, then turns to the relevant page—are *A Call for Murder* (1988) and *Murder in a Locked Room* (1989), both by Alan Robbins. The murders of, respectively, John Foster Dulles, a small-town magnate, and the Great Baldini at the Society of Conjurors and Magicians Annual Convention are solved by the reader "ringing" round some ninety rooms or telephones, the numbers printed at the top of the page, to solve the murders. A directory is at the front, all technical points are explained (including three famous illusions in the second book), and the plotting is ingenious.

Another, smaller aspect of deliberate do-it-yourself detecting books came in the dossiers, fewer in number, and intrinsically more expensive, depending on the nature of the evidence presented and packaged for the reader—for the dossier includes it all: cigarette ash, reports, buttons, mud, photographs, et al., safely in small cellophane or glassine envelopes.

Pride of place in this section, because the examples were so well done, must go to English author Dennis Wheatley (1897–1977), who created four such dossiers in the 1930s, each with full, beautifully packaged clues and photographs with well-known personalities gladly modeling for gangsters, corpses, police, and witnesses. The first in 1936 was *Murder off Miami* (the US title in the same year was *File on Bolitho Blane*); next year came *Who Killed Robert Prentice?* (US title, *File on Robert Prentice*); in 1938, *The Malinsay Massacre,* and in 1939 *Herewith the Clues.* The reader has all the information needed to solve the puzzles, even interoffice memos, and the deductions needed are straightforward. Among the celebrities in the photographs are the author himself; Peter Cheyney, a crime writer; Val Gielgud, a BBC executive and crime writer; and actors and actresses. The dossiers became collectors' curios in the 1970s and 1980s, and some of the dossiers were precisely reproduced and sold reasonably—then these new dossiers were being remaindered as curios.

The next two dossiers are less well known, but both made solitary appearances in specialist British crime book catalogues. The first was by Q. Patrick, the pseudonym of Patrick Quentin, a conglomerate of four authors at differing times. *File on Fenton and Farr* dates from 1938, and was described as rare. The other was by Helen Reilly (1891–1962), mother of mystery writers Ursula Curtiss and Mary McMullen. *The File on Rufus Ray,* dated 1937, also described as scarce, was praised as a police procedural, and published both in America and England as part of a "series."

Another collection in the late 1930s followed the same pattern of clues and statements under the trade name of Crimefile.

Obviously, from the above, it can be seen that the dossiers ceased because of the production costs, but the aforementioned 1984 *Philadelphia* article by Judith Hodgson reviewed three new dossiers. The first was the *Consulting Detective Game* (Sleuth Books, $25), consisting of a plastic binder containing a lecture by Sherlock Holmes, ten cases with clues, a map, etc. The second was the supplement, *The Mansion Murders* ($10 to $12), on which she commented there were errors, anachronisms, and no sense of period. Finally was *A Study in Scarlet* (Morrow, $17.95), described as accurate, with clues, newspaper clippings, Watson's diary, notes, photographs, and Sherlock Holmes's marginal notes. Another catalogue referred to the *Book of the Dossier of A Study in Scarlet* (1985), but the article referred to was published in 1984.

A variation in England in 1991/92 was a bimonthly publication at £2.75, *Murder Trial,* published by Brainwave Publishing. No. 2 deals with the death of George Newton, at Kingsland, in Shrewsbury, Shropshire, on Saturday, November 18, 1992. The magazine consists of reports from police and pathologist, witnesses' statements, elimination of fingerprints, maps, drawings, suspect profiles, et al., all authentically reproduced, with color photographs. The last pages give the solution of the preceding issues's crime, and of the current murder, found by rubbing a blank space on the page with a coin. The main clue was a deceptively simple one in a plethora of detail.

Not quite a dossier, but you can purchase maps of Sherlock Holmes's London and Raymond Chandler's Los Angeles to help you trace the literary landmarks.

If we take the dossiers as intellectual games, it is logical to proceed to those games qua games which are intrinsically murder mysteries. They take several forms, from card games to board games, jigsaws to murder parties.

A jigsaw puzzle (the name simply means a picture as cut by a jigsaw, or narrow reciprocating saw) can be either a puzzle in an envelope with the answer, as happened in the 1930s with the popular radio, then film and book, Detective Inspector Hornleigh— who will be considered further in the next chapter, devoted to the media—or a more elaborate version, as occurred in a catalogue issued by Camille Wolff, a London crime-book dealer, whose house is wall-to-wall books. *The Secret Tangles,* published in 1933 by Leonard R. Gribble, prolific author of fiction and nonfiction under half a dozen noms de plume and a founder-member of the CWA, consisted of a book, some tissue pages of motive, a 150-piece puzzle of the climax with a panel showing the criminal only to those who had read the book. The book alone of such a set has been seen on sale for just a few pence.

Another interesting jigsaw was *Murder of the Only Witness* by J. S. Fletcher (1863–1935), the author of ninety-three 'teckers, including the classic *The Middle Temple Murder.* This jigsaw was a

1934 reprint, by Harrap, with the complete set of 150 pieces in a box at the rear of the book, described as scarce.

The Jigsaw Puzzle Murder by Walter Eberhardt was published in two parts in 1933: the book and the actual jigsaw in a box showing the criminal.

Jigsaws have leapt into popularity in the 1990s. Proof comes in *Booknews* (November/December 1993), from Barbara G. Peters, who runs the Poisoned Pen bookshop in Scottsdale, Arizona.

1,000 pieces	*Burning Evidence,* story by John Lutz
	The Ghost of Winthrop, by Katherine Hall Page
	Last Chill and Testament
500 pieces	*Murder in the Wind,* by Susan Kenney
	A Spy for a Spy
	To Kill a Lawyer
1,000 pieces ("old-favorites")	*Classic Case of Murder*
	Double Cross
	Glenmore Haunting
	Sonata for a Spy
500 pieces	*The Cookie Tree* (with recipes)
	Catch as Cat Can
	Death by Diet
	Feline Frenzy
	Final Run
	Missing Links
250 pieces (for children)	*Captain Blackwell's Treasure*
	Case of the Computer Sleuths
	Heading for Trouble
	Legend Under the Boards
	Menace or Tennis

There is even a *Cluedo* jigsaw puzzle, based on the board game considered below.

I know of two classic card games. The first is what may be an imcomplete set of cards picked up at a jumble sale for almost nothing by an English actress. The back of the cards show the well-known Crime Club logo of the masked heads, and Collins thought they were produced by the famous Waddington Group, who in turn said they thought the cards could have been sold by a company called Alf Cook, which they took over in the 1960s. No further evidence has so far come to light. The colored picture cards show, for example, Love of Money Motive for Confidence Trick or Housebreaking; Police Constable; Wine, Women and Song Motive; The Dandy Confidence Trickster or Housebreaking Expert; Finger-Prints Master Clue; and so on. The style of the dress and surroundings would seem to be the 1930s.

The second card game was *Peter Cheyney's Crime Club Game,* but does not tally with the cards I possess. This set shows H. Poirot, Detective; Supt. Battle, Assistant; Carlotta and Jane Murch, Assistants; Mr. Evans and Mr. Woodspring, Crooks; police car; crooks' house; etc. Battle, of course, like Poirot, was an Agatha Christie sleuth, and they appear together in *Cards on the Table.* In the 1930s there were many amusing card games, usually involving procuring sets of similar or consecutive cards, from Railways to Bob's Your Uncle, Happy Families to Grandfather's Whiskers.

The aforementioned *Booknews* cites not only the card games of *Master Criminals, Framed* (a movies game), and *Vanished,* but mystery crosswords. What about *Murder at the Bridge Table*—with tuition—that is sold in New York?

Turning now to board games, we can first consider an interesting comment in Geoffrey O'Brien's 1981 *Hardboiled America,* a history of American paperbacks from the genesis of Pocket Books on June 19, 1939, a well-illustrated and comprehensive survey of the lurid volumes—both text and covers. In discussing the Dell covers, with their keyhole logo, he refers to the detailed maps, with explanatory numbers, which were on the back covers, just as in 1930s books from England. There would be a plan of the mansion and the grounds, with a cast list. These plans would help the reader visualize the scene. O'Brien says of Dell covers: "The artwork of the maps bore a strong resemblance to the board of the once-popular game Clue, with its neat little rectangular rooms, stocked with tables, lamps, sofas, desks, and dressers, but with never a person or indeed any trace or personality in its furnishings."

Perhaps the most famous board game is *Cluedo,* in various versions, such as the new 1986 *Super Cluedo Challenge, Travel Cluedo,* or the *Cluedo Video Game.* It was invented by Anthony Pratt (a former pianist, then of Bournemouth, but later moving to Birmingham, in England), originally called *Murder* after the popular game of the 1930s and 1940s. It is for two to six players, aged eight years and upward. The board shows the various rooms in which the murder can take place: library, drawing room, etc.; the various weapons: knife, gun, candlestick, etc.; and the original six suspects: Dr. Black, Rev. Green, Col. Mustard, Prof. Plum, Miss Scarlett, and Mrs. Peacock. The 1986 version was augmented by three suspects (Miss Peach, Captain Brown, and Mr. Slate-Grey), three new weapons (blunderbuss, axe, and poison), and four garden ornaments, so this version can be played by two to nine players, aged twelve and upward. This appears again under both video games and stage plays.

Gangbusters was a game originally launched in America by TSR, and no longer stocked in Great Britain. Based on the era from 1920 to 1930, the players act as agents against organized crime. *Top Secret* is a later game produced in America by TSR, who originated *Gangbusters,* in which the players act as government secret agents. Further examples are *Trivial Detective,* a board game for two to six players; *Jack the Ripper,* for two persons, a strategy board game; *Gumshoe,* hard-boiled 'tec, 1930s, one to six players; and *The Willing Dead* and *The Icicle Twist Dinner Party* games.

Technical games can be video, computer, or laser. Two video games are the aforementioned *Cluedo Video Game,* launched in 1986, with video tape, detective casebook, etc., for two or more players, aged twelve to adult, and *Streetlife,* invented by Arthur Wood, a TV reporter at a local station in Houston, Texas, in 1982. The player has to assume the role of a pimp, deciding on the cars he will use, and the fees and bribes he must pay to women, police, and others.

One electronic mail game is *It's a Crime,* with gang bosses and rackets, in America, and licensed in England.

The final technical category is exemplified by *Murder, Anyone?* and *Any Roads to Murder,* mysteries described as "disc-interactive laserdisc" games allowing you to plot the course of a murder by choosing one out of sixteen story lines.

(Ponder a story in the British newspaper *Daily Express* on Monday, May 9, 1986: the Cluedo hunt for a killer. In Bournemouth, a fashionable seaside resort on the south coast, in a five-mile square, there were five different places where jewelry and clothes were found belonging to the murdered Sandy Court, aged twenty-seven. Detective Sergeant Des Donahue said, "It is like a game of

Cluedo but it is in deadly earnest," while promising that every telephone call would be listened to.)

The last and most unusual American murder game came to me from John Fisher, the author and television producer who sent me the early *Baffle* book, with S. S. Van Dine's foreword. He wrote to say he had purchased it for possible use on the *Paul Daniels' Magic Television Show* he produced for the BBC, but as it would not fit, he presented me with *How to Host a Murder: The Grapes of Frath*. The impressive box contains a host's guide, eight invitations, eight name cards, eight player clue manuals, six secret clues (a report, letters, etc.), plan of the ship, and a tape recording from the detective Mistale Dicluse (try pronouncing the name out loud). The eight suspects are Bella Donna Maria Cossa, Miles F. Latout, Wellington C. Waterloo, Desirée Flambeau, Mlle. Lucinde S. Gucie; Jules T. Hieffe, Captain Malcolm D. Meirre RN (*mal de mer* is seasickness), and Countess Natalia Irina Forilska; the victim is Archibald Bemmington Frath, owner of the multinational corporation Grapes of Frath. The ship, designed by Johan D. Botmacher, DD, built in 1921 by Frath Shipbuilders, is the MV *Guilded Vessel,* out for a week's Mediterranean cruise starting Saturday, June 7, 1925. There are included a suggested dinner menu and wardrobes for the night of the murder party. Each booklet has details for distribution and for retention, and for differing rounds of the game. Some booklets have names that do not tally with the list—for example, there are six clue packets, not seven, as well as different names, on the manuals, too. The invitations give full information on the ship, program, and guests. The guests are not who they seem to be, and all have motives. It all seems to be great fun, an ingenious do-it-yourself exercise, created in 1985 by Anne L. and Robert R. Johnson, distributed in America by a corporation delightfully named Decipher, Inc. Three other games from the list are *The Watersdown Affair,* January 1936: Sir Roger Watersdown is the head of Watersdown Beverages, with a weekend party at Watersdown Mansion. *The Last Train from Paris,* July 1940: an anonymous letter offers you a place on the government train to the south of France. *The Hollywood Premiere of Powar and Greede,* 1936 (sent to me by the makers): all with murder amid.

Another series is Murder à la Carte in much the same format, with sleuth Dr. Jock McClew, including *A Deadly Design,* murder in a couture house; *A Taste of His Own Medicine,* a 1947 murder at Headline Hall; and *A Vintage Murder,* murder in a 1937 wine chateau.

We can complete this section with a couple of conjuring tricks. The first is *Murder Among Friends,* devised by Jack Yates and Ken de Courcy. A card has a circle with names around it; one is secretly selected as victim; a five-pointed star is placed thereon, and one of four possible names is selected as murderer, and the star removed; the magician returns, taps the names on the circle as a member of the audience mentally spells out the victim's name letter by letter—to establish the name of the victim. It makes an effective, simply prepared and well-made conjuring trick.

The other illusion was presented in John Fisher's production of the *Paul Daniels' Magic Television Show* on BBC-TV, Saturday, January 3, 1987. "Murder by Magic" started when a butler was given an apparently free choice of three bags containing three different weapons. He was then taken to a model of a nine-room house: bathroom, library, kitchen, conservatory, bedroom, hall, games room, dining room, sitting room. A tape recorder instructed him to walk from his chosen starting room to the others, in the order of seven, four, six, five, one, one, one, three moves, after each of which one outline room was removed on rails, finally leaving him in the library, with a stabbed dummy in the clock, and the knife in the bag. These tricks follow a well-known basic principle, as indeed do most illusions. The number of moves has been set up to achieve a predetermined final position. Sometimes this principle can be adapted for use effectively for promotion or advertisement. Two such puzzles appeared in the British newspaper *News of the World.* The first was in the color magazine *Sunday* for October 24, 1982, for Thriller Book Fortnight. H. R. F. Keating set up a competition with prizes. Stella Forcraft was murdered, and the clues offered to solve this picture crime were blackmail, setting up alibis, the music at a disco, going to the cinema, card-players, having a scatty woman round for drinks with the watch wrong, calling a minicab, meeting a woman, the playing cards, the actual telephone call from the Paradise Disco—all these made up, or didn't, the six alibis.

Sunday magazine, for October 30, 1983, had "Who Killed Henrietta?" to mark Thursday, November 3, the day *Cluedo Armchair Detective* came out. In 1935 the *Daily Express* newspaper serialized Agatha Christie's *The ABC Murders* with a special column for readers' guesses, and published various letters therein. Similarly, the *Sunday Times* of Johannesburg, on June 18, 1967, ran a competition with a prize of two hundred rand, based on the Sherlock Holmes tale "The Adventure of the Second Stain," and had ninety-five answers and two joint winners.

In the July 1959 issue of *Suspense* was a competition story, with clues in the pictures, "Here Lies . . ." by Manning Coles, the partnership of Cyril Henry Coles (1899–1965) and Adelaide Frances Oke Manning (1891–1959). Coles, a former spy, wrote just a few items after his partner died in 1959.

For some years I have served as an international life vice president of the American Federation of Police, one of whose most praiseworthy activities is the maintenance of the Police Hall of Fame in Florida. Visitors to this unique collection and memorial can take part in a murder problem, and they receive a certificate if they are right. Similarly, a 1993 exhibit at the Fort Worth Museum of Science and History in Texas, entitled *Whodunit? The Science of Solving Crime,* gave visitors instant tuition in forensic detecting skills to decide which of three suspects committed the murder and robbery in the alley behind the Memory Diner. The exhibit then traveled to half a dozen other American cities. The Tower of David Museum of the History of Jerusalem, in Israel, has a historical murder problem that foxes most visitors.

Great Britain issued a set of five Sherlock Holmes stamps, each twenty-four pence, of different mysteries containing a puzzle with generous prizes. (Holmes had earlier appeared on a series of Turks and Caicos Islands postage stamps.) First day covers, October 12, 1993, could be canceled at either Baker Street or Granada TV, Manchester.

On Monday, February 18, 1985, June Thomson, former member of the CWA committee, was given a press party by publishers Constable and Sphere for her two books, *A Dying Fall* and *Sound Evidence*. At the historic and beautiful Middle Temple Hall, one of the famous legal halls in London, they staged a murder mystery on a set with a body in the library, with clues for critics and guests to solve for a magnum of champagne.

We have already seen that some books have been published based on problems set on television or radio, but there have been several cases of deliberate problem setting in stage plays, radio series, on television, and even in films, and this short selection can serve as a useful introduction to the last chapter, which is on parody and pastiche in three-dimensional forms—many in number and varied in content.

It is perhaps appropriate to start with radio. In the 1930s, the BBC had a successful mixed program every Monday, called variously *Monday Night at Eight* and *Monday Night at Seven,* with items ranging from "Puzzle Corner with This Week's Deliberate Mistake" to a weekly sketch "Inspector Hornleigh Investigates," with the actor S. J. Warmington as the inspector. The sketch finished, part of it would be rebroadcast until a voice called "Stop" when the clue was reached. Written by Hans Priwin, one example was reproduced in the book *Radio Variety*. Several films were made in England with Gordon Harker as the inspector and Alastair Sim as his sergeant; at least one book, *Inspector Hornleigh Investigates,* by H. W. Priwin, came out in October 1939, reprinted March 1940, with no references to war, only to peacetime conditions (for example, January flights to Paris). Sergeant Bingham is Hornleigh's assistant; the inspector is married, and his in-laws include a crime reporter who falls in love with a self-willed woman, mixed up in a tale of murders and an attempt at world domination by ingenious radio and engineering devices. One clue is that Scriabin's "Prelude for the Left Hand" leaves the right hand free to fire a gun, and another factor also used elsewhere (in a Sidney Horler book, for sure) is that visiting Americans from the police or FBI should not always be trusted when master criminals are being hunted.

For six years BBC radio ran the series *Inspector Scott Investigates,* starring the well-known British actor Deryck Guyler, featured in many radio comedy series over several years; each story had a "whodunnit break" before the inspector's solution.

The BBC, as is invariably the case, proved the pioneer in this category. It started broadcasting in 1922, as the British Broadcasting Company, from Savoy Hill, "2LO." The first radio serial, in December 1925, was titled *The Mayfair Mystery* (Mayfair is an elegant area in London's West End), to which listeners could send in correct solutions to win the prize of one hundred pounds. Then in 1982, to match the Christmas television production of Agatha Christie's *Spider's Web, Radio Times* (the official BBC magazine) published a parodic short story, "Murder with Mistletoe," by "Agatha Woddis," with a prize of a ten-pounds book token to the first reader spotting the vital clue to the murder of Neville Drapes, the imaginary dramatic critic of *Sentinel* (the BBC's other excellent house journal was *Listener*). Roger Woddis (1917–1993) was a poet, playwright, and contributor to *Radio Times* on, inter alia, crime writers.

American radio had many detective series in which some of the greatest actors and actresses were featured; one such series, *Calling All Detectives,* awarded prizes to those listeners sending in correct answers solving the regular mysteries.

BBC television started a true-life series called *Crimewatch,* with two regular presenters, joined by two police, a male senior officer and a female constable, backed by other officers and a battery of telephones. Recent unsolved crimes would be reenacted by professional actors: robberies, missing persons, and pensioners robbed of their pension books were some examples. Viewers with possibly useful information were asked to ring the program or the police forces involved, and later that same evening a further fifteen-minute transmission would show the results. Other officers might ask for help in solving other crimes. Once a private motorboat was stolen; after the appeal, it was promptly traced and returned. In May 1987, presenters Nick Ross and Sue Cook published an illustrated book about the program and its work.

An interesting and amusing use of television was transmitted to British screens on June 16, 1984, in the *Tales of the Unexpected* series, edited by Tony Wilmot, directed by playwright Gerald Savory, featuring Patrick Mower and Jane Asher, titled "*The Last of the Midnight Gardeners.*" Publisher Walter Oates of the *Stanley Mystery Magazine* holds a £5,000 competition for the perfect murder. As his wife's entry is bad, he retires so he can submit his entry, which is good. He dies; the wife's entry is found as though from him. Oates had been having an affair with his secretary. His doctor, who is a judge, proves to have been and still is the wife's lover—and indeed, it is Oates's winning idea which killed him off for their benefit. The CWA provided a display for this production.

October 20, 1982, in a Bookshop Week on BBC television, *Whodunnit?* featured a murder mystery on the new Orient Express. A team of actors carried out the plot; the real conductor, Alan Pegler (a professional actor, famous in steam railway circles), was able to play himself. In the studio, presenter James Burke chaired a panel of crime writers, including Dick Francis, trying to solve the crime. Afterward the relevant clues, etc., were reshown. The plot was devised by H. R. F. Keating, who wrote an article thereon in *Radio Times,* and whose book *Whodunnit?* came out that same week. The Orient Express had restarted only that May, and the program certainly confirmed the fantastic excellence and ambience, gratefully noted by all passengers, including my mother, Barbara Miller, and myself a few months earlier.

On the large screen came two films. *Ten Little Indians,* one of the several versions of Agatha Christie's *Ten Little Niggers,* was released in 1966, starring Hugh O'Brien, Wilfred Hyde-White, and others, shot in England but set in the Austrian Alps. It had a whodunnit break before the denouement, as did some 1930s films, and William Castle with his "Fright Break."

In 1986 came the film *Clue,* written and directed by Jonathan Lynn, produced by Debra Hill for Paramount, and based on the game of *Cluedo,* with six characters, six weapons, and nine rooms, first shown on British television by the BBC on Tuesday, June 20, 1989. Six strange characters arrive at an isolated Victorian mansion to be given pseudonyms by an outrageous butler, Wadsworth, played by Tim Curry. Among the top Hollywood comedians featured are Eileen Brennan (Mrs. Peacock), Madeline Kahn (Mrs. White), Christopher Lloyd (Professor Plum), Michael McKean (Mr. Green), Martin Mull (Colonel Mustard), and Lesley Ann Warren (Miss Scarlett)—and three alternate endings.

Some plays have been presented where the verdict from the audience, or a jury from the audience, can give alternate endings. An ingenious example of this was the American success, *The Mystery of Edwin Drood,* at the beginning of 1986, with George Rose as chairman of a music hall presenting this story, played fairly straight, with singer Cleo Laine as a madam; the audience voted for which of the six they thought the killer, then by applause who would marry whom. The musical was directed by Wilfred Leach, and there was a London production later, with Ernie Wise.

On August 1, 1986, Barbara Miller, Gwendoline Butler, and I visited the Theatre Royal, Windsor, near the royal castle, to see the new play *Cluedo,* at the start of its twelve-weeks tour of Britain. The cast was headed by Christopher Biggins, the play written by Robert Duncan. Six weapons, six characters, six motives, six locations; who killed Dr. Black at the 1935 mansion Tudor Close: Mrs. White, Miss Scarlet, Mrs. Peacock, Rev. Green, Professor Plum, or Colonel Mustard? Two policemen complete the cast, the others each being dressed in the color of his or her name. The inspector produces a game board as a plan of the house; the audience is given voting papers (collected in the intermission), then black cards are distributed on stage to the cast, the inspector is given a message "found in the hall," and his cue words alert the cast to that evening's killer and solution script. At first, audiences carefully chose the star, believing this to be expected and appropriate. A raffle each night gave a game of *Cluedo* to the winner from among the voters for the murderer. The set was elegant and outstanding.

This little selection of do-it-yourself sleuthing leads on to the last chapter, on three-dimensional parodies and pastiches, on stage and screen, radio and television.

5. P & P . . . in 3-D

Parody and pastiche have occurred in films, television, revues, on stage, and occasionally on radio. Some are adaptations of another—for example, a play or musical becomes a film, others are adapted from books, films are made for television, and cinema films are shown on television more than once. Therefore, it will be easier to show the trend if we take the whole series in alphabetical order by title, rather than author (or adapter, or screenwriter, or even composer).

The titles selected are obviously not the entire list; some may not be wholly incorporated into parody or pastiche despite their transmogrification into another medium. Some have already been mentioned in the earlier chapters, either as examples, like the duo of women detectives in *Fifty-Fifty,* or en passant. The items in this chapter are sufficient to show how the dramatic trend developed.

Two two-dimensional variations from the norm may highlight the three-dimensional list. Mention has already been made of the American television series *Wonder Woman,* a glamorous counterpart to Superman, etc., and designed as wartime encouragement. In 1993 was published *The Further Adventures of Wonder Woman,* edited by Martin H. Greenberg, one of the contributors being American advertising executive and crime writer Henry Slesar with *Behind the Screen,* not to be confused with the English group effort of that name. The other variation took place on Wednesday, November 24, 1993, when the Redfern Gallery in the West End of London previewed their exhibition of watercolors and designs by Martin Bradley, an international artist. One of the 1993 signed, titled, and dated watercolors, was No. 19, 76 x 57cm, *An Agatha Christie Novel for Christmas,* at £2,500. A beach tent on the sands, recalling *Evil Under the Sun,* and a broken scarab were among the clues in this reference to the issue of a novel every Christmas.

On March 5, 1935, Dorothy L. Sayers delivered a lecture at Oxford titled "Aristotle on Detective Fiction," which was later printed in her 1946 book of essays, *Unpopular Opinions*. Aristotle (384–322 B.C.) was a Greek philosopher, a pupil of Plato, and it is his *Poetics* from which Sayers drew her observations that his comments apply neatly to a study of detective fiction. Toward the end of this ingenious essay, she remarks, "For elsewhere, Aristotle takes the modern, realistic view, as when he says, for instance, that the plot ought not to turn on the detection and punishment of a hopelessly bad man who is villainous in all directions at once — forger, murderer, adulterer, thief — like the bad baron in an Adelphi melodrama." The Adelphi Theatre in London's West End, like the Lyceum Theatre, specialized for years in such melodrama, often further burlesqued in nearby musical theatres like the Gaiety. A similar analogy is the traditional western film, with the black hats (villains), white hats (heroes), and gray hats (those men who change their characters halfway for better or for worse).

Silly-assery from Wimsey and Blakeney to Ralph Lynn and George Grossmith has already been considered. What may not be realized is that considerable research was made therein by Norman Murphy in his book *In Search of Blandings,* later the subject of a television documentary. He certainly discovered conclusively the origins of the castle, grounds, Drones Club, Wooster, Jeeves, and many other factors in the Wodehouse canon. In October 1993, Gwendoline Butler and I gave the Christopher Marlowe Quatercentenary and the Sayers Centenary lectures at the Canterbury Festival in Kent. Reference has already been made to Sayers's reading the Greyfriars and St. Jim's school stories by Charles Hamilton under various pen names, and Wimsey's likeness to the Honorable Arthur Augustus D'Arcy of St. Jim's. I discovered that Hamilton based this character on C. Maurice Bland, editor of both *Gem* and *Magnet*, two boys' magazines, so Bland must take precedence over Whelpton, Cournos, and Ridley — the later candidates for the original Wimsey.

From the nineteenth century, the media — newspapers, radio, films, television, et cetera — have influenced detective fiction by popularizing it. The French feuilletons, followed by English newspaper serials, were but the start. Georges Simenon wrote of the changes made. After commenting on the Broadway, London, and Paris stages with their "countless adaptations of novels," he remarked that authors' contracts now cover commercially "magazine serialization to the theatre, cinema, radio, and television," which, with the paperbacks, have brought the novel away from "scholars, snobs, or the idle. It has forced its way into everyday life." He then draws attention to the phenomenon, already mentioned in connection with Dickens above, that the many heavy, long, descriptive passages in Balzac, Tolstoy, or Stevenson are invariably skimmed by readers who no longer need them now they are familiar with the settings from "photography . . . illustrated magazines and periodicals, movies . . . television." Similarly, we shall see not only how, say, *Guys and Dolls,* the musical comedy and film, has introduced Damon Runyon's real-life Broadway characters to millions, but how such films as Bob Hope's *The Cat and the Canary* and *The Ghost Breakers* have changed the whole format of the 'tecker.

Before we analyze the three-dimensional parodies and pastiches, we can consider an unusual theatrical crime novel that acts perhaps as a mirror image to the genre. Beverley Nichols (1898–1983) was a novelist, poet, composer, editor, playwright for stage, radio, and film, and a dramatic critic. He wrote approximately sixty books, including five detective stories featuring his retired and retiring private investigator Horatio Green, author of *First Principles in Detection. Death to Slow Music* was first published in 1956, reprinted in 1975, dedicated to W. Somerset Maugham, and takes place in an English south coast holiday resort, "Seabourne," which reads very like Brighton, for which town the author wrote the official handbook in 1933. In his foreword, Nichols comments on the "strangest phenomena in literature," which is that "the most extraordinary thing about the great detectives of fiction, who are real to us as our own uncles, is that they are entirely mythical creatures; nobody like them ever existed . . . resembling Sherlock Holmes, Hercule Poirot, Father Brown or . . . my own Mr. Green." In this useful essay on how he writes his detective stories, he comments that the genre springs not from character, but from situation. *Death to Slow Music* starts with a murdered woman during rehearsals for a new musical play by Nigel Fleet, playwright, actor, composer, director, entertainer, famous for his wicked wit, clipped tones, and a lifetime devoted to the theatre. The suspected accompanist is the next spectacular victim. The finale is dramatic, and the denouncement to the assembled cast impressive. On the 1975 book jacket, Nichols explains how he sent the manuscript to Noël Coward, to whom some might liken Fleet. The Master replied that he approved, wished him well, liked the character, considered it inevitable readers would compare—"But I don't give a damn." (A reference to Fleet's Grand Fete on Saturday, September 17, could date the novel as 1955, when he is described as aged forty and of "a younger generation than either Noël Coward or Ivor Novello." Coward was fifty-six in 1955). Nichols's last detective novel, *Murder by Request* (1960), pokes gentle fun at the genre, the first victim being a keen reader thereof.

Ace Crawford, Private Eye was an American television series, shown also on British screens, cowritten by and starring Tim Conway, with the accent on comedy. It was a parody of the Bogart type, with the girlfriend, plenty of wisecracks, nothing going right, fake lead-in and lead-out in the classic style, but with extra eccentric touches (for example, the bar is run by a dwarf).

Alphaville was a film written and directed by Jean-Luc Godard in 1965, with Eddie Constantine as Lemmy Caution (one of the creations of Peter Cheyney, 1896–1951), Anna Karina, and Akim Tamiroff. A futuristic story filmed in modern Paris, it concerns an investigator from Lands Without coming to this communistic country to track down Professor Von Braun (Leonard Nosferatu, cf. Dracula). There is an aura of unreality about the action and characters, despite the clinical, dispassionate air. It can be compared with Godard's 1985 film *Detective*, in which the sleuth is trying to solve a case of murder from ten years ago that had cost him his job. A somewhat tortuous, almost sociological story starring Johnny Hallyday, for many years with Richard Anthony a leading French pop star, and Alain Cuny. The French can parody and pastiche the genre with ease—for example, the 1970 film *Borsalino* (the white hat of a gangster) set in 1930s Marseilles and starring Jean-Louise Trintignant, with fast action, humor, strong characters, and at times a deliberate overstressing to reach the laughter of caricature of such films (for example, in the fight in the billiard room).

What happens when an author or his character confuses himself with his own sleuth? A slight case of this was Jeremy Lloyd's book, above. The film *American Dream* portrays Cathy Palmer (played by JoBeth Williams), a housewife who wins a prize for writing chapters for a female Bond character, Rebecca Ryan.

When her bag is snatched and she is run down by the Spanish ambassador's car, she ends up in the hospital thinking she is the real Rebecca Ryan. She teams up with the real author's son Alan McMann—a neat name, this Scottish for "Son of Man"—played by Tom Conti, lightheartedly, until she meets the Spanish ambassador, who attempts suicide and is saved by Alan; meanwhile someone shoots at Rebecca... The idea has been used elsewhere. Lloyd's book: a romantic television play with the lovers interrupting the author's book: a romantic television play with the lovers interrupting the author's work on her word processor, a *Magnum* episode below. In addition, there are Mark Schorr's Red Diamond books, *Red Diamond, Private Eye* 1983), *Ace of Diamonds* (1984), and *Diamond Rock* (1985). Simon Jaffe, New York cabdriver is a Diamond fan who is tricked and comes to imagine himself the sleuth. Sometimes he goes back to being Jaffe with his real-life problems, almost like a time-warp fantasy. In the Broadway and London hit musical *City of Angels,* also considered below, we shall see the writer's characters reflecting those around him, and played by the same actors and actresses. The exceptions are the author himself and his private eye, a Marlowe-ish creation, who argue together and score off each other.

Arsenic and Old Lace was a long-running Broadway success, then an equally successful West End hit in London; the film starred the inimitable Cary Grant in this tale of an eccentric family. Eccentric? Two elderly ladies gently poisoning lonely elderly gentlemen with elderberry wine, a brother in the cellar involved in the Spanish-American war, a man who looks like Boris Karloff. It was written by "Josef Kesselring," in reality the top writing team of Howard Lindsey and Russell Crouse. When it was reviewed in Glasgow, Scotland, at the Citizens Theatre, in October 1985, one critic wrote: "Potential for parody, both of the thriller in general and of the play itself." Mortimer Brewster, a critic who loathes espionage thrillers, relives the ludicrous plot of the play, ending up gagged and bound to have it retold him by an equally ridiculous playwright. Take this comedy as parody, and it can be seen as the beginning of a new trend of the "ridiculous," as had happened with *The Cat and the Canary* twice, below. The play is intrinsically very funny and an innovation.

The Avengers was a very popular television series for many seasons in two different forms, both in Britain and America, with the hero as a typical English gentleman, in a bowler hat (or derby) that doubled as a weapon. The stories were usually ingenious, sets unusual, with strong casts, including various leading ladies to partner the hero, John Steed. One parody was *Legacy of Death*, in 1968 and repeated in 1984, featured in the book *The Avengers,* by Dave Rogers, in 1983. Written by Terry Nation, directed by Don Chaffey, produced by Albert Fennell and Brian Clemens, in the sixth season it featured a dagger with a falcon's head, and the legacy of a black pearl that finally dissolves in a glass of wine. The characters were Sidney Street (cf. Sidney Greenstreet), played by Stratford Johns, Humbert Green (the Peter Lorre character), played by Ronald Lacey, Oppenheimer, Slattery, Zoltan, Gorky, Winkler, Dr. Winter, Dickens the Solicitor, Ho Lung, Farrer, and Von Orlok, most of whom get killed off. Having known Stratford Johns, an actor famous for many police roles on television and the original Daddy Warbucks in the London cast of the musical *Annie,* for some twenty years, I wrote him about this parody. In his reply, dated May 26, 1984, he explained the black pearl was a black tennis ball. "I had the idea, not in the script, of seeing the funny thing, and with a look at Steed, and a shrug of the shoulders, drop the poor thing back in the wine." He also said his white suit (as affected by Sidney Greenstreet) was originally Orson Welles's, and was much padded for him. Both Stratford and the show got excellent American reviews.

It is important to clarify the importance of *The Maltese Falcon*. Author Dashiell Hammett's cynical comment on his own parody of the genre has already been quoted. There had been three famous film versions: *The Maltese Falcon* (1931), with Ricardo Cortez and Bebe Daniels; *Satan Met A Lady* (1936), with Warren William (Sam Spade, but named Ted Shayne), Bette Davis, and Alison Skipworth playing the fat man (Gutman); and *The Maltese Falcon* (1941), with Humphrey Bogart as Spade, Mary Astor, Sidney Greenstreet, and Peter Lorre. One rather unlikely derivation of the villainous Gutman has been noted. The falcon in the story is empty of the supposed fortune. In 1530 the Order of Knights of St. John were persuaded by the French and Spanish kings to take over Malta as their new home, their original having been lost to the Turks, for a rental of one falcon a year payable to Sicily.

There have been other parodies in the *Avengers* series. "The Curious Case of the Countless Clues," repeated on April 28, 1984, by Phil Levene, had a ministry investigator in a deerstalker, by the name of Sir Arthur Doyle, played by Peter Jones, with a woman Watson. Various wealthy men apparently "kill" others: Sir William Burgess, a cabinet minister "kills" Dawson, Bobby Flanders "kills" Scott; there are plenty of clues (handkerchiefs, buttons, cigars), then they are cleared by two crooks in exchange for their valuable paintings. Steed, one of whose partners was Emma Peel (from the phrase "M Appeal," i.e., Man Appeal, as used by a famous meat extract advertisement), had a boss named Mother, played by the plump actor Patrick Newall sitting by a swimming pool, rather like the boss in the famous American *Charlie's Angels* in 1969, with various glamorous leading actresses doing all the legwork.

"Fog," repeated on May 19, 1984 had Nigel Green as president of the Victoria Club, and Guy Rolfe, in a story of murders in gaslight, ghoul style, in the manner of Jack the Ripper. There could also be a faint echo of another classic, from Robert Louis Stevenson (1850–1894). In 1882 he wrote *New Arabian Nights,* which includes several famous short stories, perhaps the best known being "The Suicide Club." In this, Prince Florizel of Bohemia, a pleasure-loving, globe-trotting royal, meets in a Leicester Square restaurant the Young Man with the Cream Tarts, who leads him to the Suicide Club, whereby at each meeting a would-be suicide is selected by drawing a card, to be skillfully murdered without trace by a fellow member. It was filmed in 1936 by MGM as *Trouble for Two,* with Robert Mongomery (who played Lord Peter Wimsey in a 1940 film, also MGM, *The Haunted Honeymoon* (British title, *Busman's Honeymoon,* from the book of that name), Rosalind Russell, and Louis Hayward. Prince Florizel, who ends up running a cigar kiosk through neglecting his kingdom, was based on the English King Edward VII, the hedonistic son of Queen Victoria.

The "Band Wagon" has been a colloquial term for many years, in the sense of "jumping on the bandwagon." It was originally a wagon or cart used in New Orleans Carnival parades, just as floats are used today in British and European carnivals. The musicians would play during the procession, and the trombonist, because of the length of the instrument's slide, had to play over the end of the cart, the "tailgate." In the 1930s a top BBC radio program every Wednesday evening was *Band Wagon,* featuring comedians "Big

Hearted" Arthur Askey and Richard "Stinker" Murdoch, and "Mr. Walker Wants to Know," in which a traveling rag-and-bone man presented a problem for listeners to solve, answered the following week. *Band Waggon* (note spelling) was the 1940 British film with the two comedians and Jack Hylton and his band, in which Nazi spies in Doom Castle in Sussex and a private TV station attack on the BBC resulted in the show's adaption for radio; various BBC personalities took part. (Broadcasting House was the scene for the book *Death at Broadcasting House* [1934] by Val Gielgud, himself for thirty-five years head of drama for radio—later a British film.)

The Band Wagon was an MGM film in 1953, featuring Fred Astaire, Jack Buchanan, and Cyd Charisse, with Oscar Levant, directed by Vincente Minnelli, book by Betty Comden and Adolph Green and songs by Howard Dietz and Arthur Schwartz, some of the fantastic numbers including, "That's Entertainment," "Dancing in the Dark," and "By Myself"—the music, comedy, choreography, and dancing making this film a Hollywood success. The Astaire number "Girl Hunt Ballet" starts with a lurid-colored book cover that has been deemed a parody of the Spillane covers by Signet Books. Buchanan plays an intellectual actor-director who intends to present a new play about a crime writer–investigator as the Faust legend with Astaire, a top film song-and-dance man, partnering classical ballerina Charisse. When it fails at the out-of-town tryout, Astaire and the others turn it into a hit musical, featuring the PI Rip Ryder solving the case in a glittering and technically perfect dance ensemble. There are several subtle touches, parodic and witty. Astaire portrays himself. Jack Buchanan's director is an amalgam of Orson Welles, Norman Bel Geddes, and José Ferrer. The music comes from Broadway shows between 1923 and 1937, including the original *Band Wagon* of 1931, at the New Amsterdam Theatre, with Fred and Adele Astaire, just before she married and retired. The "Girl Hunt Ballet" certainly parodies Spillane, of whom Minnelli commented, "The writing contained the seeds of its own parody." Note the poetic reference to "a rag and a bone and a hank of hair"; the allusions to the 1897 *The Vampire* (Bram Stoker [1847–1912], secretary to actor-manager Sir Henry Irving, wrote *Dracula* in 1897, the Transylvanian vampire, based on Vlad the Impaler, who threw his victims from the castle walls onto pointed stakes—sideways, feet first, or head first, according to his idea of punishment); and the fact that the song "I Love Louisa" was the Bavarian merry-go-round number in the 1931 *Band Wagon*. Other detective stories have actually been turned into musical comedies.

Baxter's Last Case; or, X Equals Murder was a play by Dave Fox presented at the Gate Theatre, London, in November 1983, and featured a writer of crime novels, Edith Styles, and a poisoned cup of tea. The title is an obvious parody of *Trent's Last Case;* there have been several such plays presented in smaller or provincial theatres in England with an element of parody. One example in the West End with a very small such element was *Who Killed Agatha Christie?* a play about the murder of a homosexual dramatic critic named Christie, nicknamed Agatha, and with some involved scripting.

The Black Bird was a 1975 color film, ninety-eight minutes, directed by David Giler. It featured George Segal as the son of Sam Spade, Stephane Audran, Lionel Stander, Lee Patrick playing her original role of the secretary in the 1941 version, Elisha Cook, Jr., who was the gunsel in the 1941 film, and Signe Hasso. The search is on again for the Maltese Falcon. As Segal walks down the "mean streets," the blacks comment, "There goes a Spade!"

Boston Quackie, was a classic cartoon parody on Boston Blackie, created by Jack Boyle in 1919, played in the films by Chester Morris, following Bert Lytell, Lionel Barrymore, and several more predecessors. With Daffy Duck and Porky Pig it is a cloak-and-dagger spy spoof, televised by Chuck Jones, who served his apprentice years at Warner Bros., and has three classics: *My Favorite Duck, Tom Turk and Daffy,* and *The Scarlet Pumpernickel.* He also originated Little Orphan Airedale, so his talents for parody are everywhere apparent.

Bugsy Malone is a West End play with music, a popular film, and book written in 1976 by Alan Parker; it was staged in London in May 1983, at Her Majesty's Theatre. In New York in 1929 Bugsy is needed to help Fat Sam Stacetto in his fight with Dandy Dan. Bugsy meets Blousey Brown (later to become the star of Fat Sam's speakeasy), Tallulah, and the other girls there. Other characters are Looney Bergonzi, the janitor who wants to be a star, police Smolsky and O'Dreary, and so on—but the entire cast is children. They wipe each other out with splurge guns firing whipped cream and with custard pies; the sedan cars are pedal cars, in a

Mack Sennett–style chase. The ending is not quite clear as most of the cast is officially wiped out by then. The chapter headings are delightful: "Mugsy (At Last)"; "Mr. Big"; "Splurge Inc."; "You're Aces, Bugsy"; "The Pay-Off." The romance is a subplot, as is the discovery of boxing prodigy Leroy, all played with the rhythm and action of 1920s crime movies. The play is frequently staged.

When I was broadcasting on *Movie-Go-Round* for the BBC in 1966 and 1967, I gave a talk, "Are Thirteen Bulldogs Unlucky?" when the Richard Johnson Bulldog Drummond film was released. The title was a paraphrase of a Jack Hulbert musical, when Cecily Courtneidge asks him (as her fiancé), "Are thirteen toast racks unlucky?" Thirteen actors had played the British hero to date. *Bulldog Jack* was a British film of 1934 with light comedy actor-comedian-dancer Jack Hulbert as a playboy who impersonated Drummond. Also in the film were his brother Claude Hulbert and Ralph Richardson as the villain, at the same time Richardson was playing Drummond in *The Return of Bulldog Drummond*. Directed by Walter Forde, Jack Hulbert is involved in a car crash with the real Drummond, played by Athol Fleming, and so has to impersonate him. Hulbert's brother, light comedian Claude, played Algy Longworth, and others in the cast were Fay Wray, Cyril Smith, and Paul Graez. One sequence had the Hulbert brothers in adjacent kiosks telephoning all the hospitals to trace the number of the ambulance that had kidnapped the heroine. When Jack peers round, he sees Claude asleep, so he politely says "Goodbye" and hangs up his telephone.

Bullshot Crummond was the title of what the English organization calling itself Low Moan Spectacular presented as a "satiric reminder" on Broadway in October 1974, by Alan Shearman, the hero being Captain Hugh Bullshot Crummond. In October 1983 came a ninety-minute film, *Bullshot,* a parody based very casually on the books. The plot involved the daughter of a scientist kidnapped for his formula, a poisonous spider, and even an octopus. Diz White played the daughter, Michael Aldridge her father, Ron House and Francis Tomelty the villains, and Mel Smith was a reformed crook. Outwitting poison gasses and plots, winning the London-to-Brighton Road Race, airplanes, and witty spoof dialogue lead on to the villain in the last shot.

A very successful series of films from 1958 to 1978 was the

Carry On series, a very broad comedy bordering on what has been described in music-hall as "honest vulgarity." A television series was promoted by British commercial TV in 1975, and one episode on November 23 in *Carry on Laughing* parodied rather lamely Lord Peter Wimsey and Bunter, with Jack Douglas as Lord Peter Flimsy and Kenneth Connor as Punter. Joan Sims and Peter Butterworth were other members of the film series in the cast, the writer was Lew Schwartz, the director was Alan Tarrant, in a piece that one critic said was "suffocated as much by the Dorothy Sayers format as by the inclement conditions," with "an enviable cast is wasted."

A Case for Mickey Slain was a parodic musical first staged at La Bonne Crepe, a fringe theatre in Battersea, London, in 1987, at the Edinburgh Fringe Festival in 1988, then revived again at Battersea in May 1994, following the success of the musical *City of Angels*. The Battersea musical was written by Paul Prescott, music and additional lyrics by Simon Gillman, lyrics and direction by Prescott. The small cast was led by Jonathan Avery, who was in *City of Angels*, as Slain, a 1950's London private investigator. Joanna Monro played the triplet sisters he meets, and four others play all the other roles in a spoof whose script was singled out for its speed and ingenuity.

It will be remembered that Anthony Shaffer, one of a pair of brilliant literary twins, wrote a play premiered in Guildford in October 1977, the intriguing (to use the word in one of several of its correct senses) *The Case of the Oily Levantine,* a reference to the obligatory foreigners in 'teckers, and to British insularity, even expressed to Poirot himself, as he amusingly noted. This parody in a country house had seven suspects—debutantes, butler, admiral, lawyer, and so on—but an unusual trick of casting had George Cole as the murdered blackmailer from Smyrna in act 1, and the tweed-clad Sussex detective in act 2. All the suspects had good reason to kill the blackmailer, as each is proved to be somewhat shady, but, as with Agatha Christie, comedy can mix successfully with crime, as we shall see again when we consider Bob Hope.

James Bond has been parodied in books; there have been continuation adventures, and a string of spectacular films with Roger Moore (television's the Saint) and other actors, some being remakes of earlier films. There was one parodic film in 1966 very loosely based on Ian Fleming's *Casino Royale*, 1953. The illustrious directors included John Huston and Robert Parrish, and the actors taking part in this comedy included Jean-Paul Belmondo, Charles Boyer, David Niven, George Raft, Deborah Kerr, Woody Allen, Peter Sellers, and Orson Welles. Among the usual effects and odd weapons inevitable in every Bond film are a two-way wrist TV-watch with six channels from Harrods, an "American idea—from one of their comic strips," an obvious allusion to Dick Tracy, who was always shown in the 1930's with his two-way wrist radio long before these became common. The aim of this film, *Casino Royale,* which was not one of the regular series of Bond extravaganzas, appeared to be to show the different facets and modi operandi of varying Bonds in farfetched circumstances, as indeed they were in the other films.

The Cat and the Canary is another play that was to change the course of mystery plays and films. Written by John A. Willard (1885–1942), from an idea he got on bombing raids in France, it was premiered on February 7, 1922, at the National Theatre, with Florence Eldridge and Henry Hull, the author playing Harry Blythe. It has no connection with a short novel in 1908 of the same name by Margaret Cameron. It was described as "A Melodrama in Three Acts," and was later published in book form.

It proved a great success as a film, several times. Paul Leni directed the first in 1927 for Universal, silent, with Laura La Plante; the doctor was disguised as Dr. Caligari; the film had shivering subtitles for atmosphere as the characters screamed; the dead recluse and the bottles melting into the castle on the Hudson in the Carl Laemmle film. *The Cat Creeps* was the 1930 title of the Universal version, starring Helen Twelvetrees, Jean Hersholt, and others, directed by Rupert Julian. The third hilarious version of the heiress being frightened into insanity on the reading of the will in a mysterious, sliding-paneled mansion was *The Cat and the Canary* (Paramount, 1939), with Bob Hope, Paulette Goddard, and Douglas Montgomery, directed by Elliott Nugent—a splendid amalgam of thrills and laughter, which here leads to an interesting quotation with far-reaching results. Richard Mealand, in an article, "Hollywoodunit," in Howard Haycraft's *Art of the Mystery Story,* wrote, "When Bob Hope appeared in *The Cat and the Canary* and *The Ghost Breakers* he knocked the old fashioned horror story into a cocked hat; the result was bound to be such japery as *Arsenic and Old Lace.*" We have already seen that this last play and film in turn led to yet more parody, but *The Ghost Breakers?* This was originally a play, *The Ghost Breaker*, by Paul Dickey and Charles W. Goddard, filmed in 1915 with H. B. Warner, in 1922 with Wallace Reid, and a third time (in 1940) with Bob Hope and Paulette Goddard. Hope is a radio columnist, on the run from gangsters, who meets a woman inheriting a mysterious mansion beset with a strange lawyer, a ghost, a zombie, murderer, and secret panels, in a similar mold to the *Cat*. Indeed, it has been described as a sequel to the *Cat,* and one of the Bob Hope biographies called it a "spoof of the horror melodramas of the day, complete with an old dark house." (We noted above Donald Westlake's description, "A Gothic is a story about a girl who gets a house.")

Another version of the play was filmed in 1953 with the comedy team of Dean Martin and Jerry Lewis, Lizabeth Scott, and Carmen Miranda—the heiress's castle being on an island.

There was yet another, rather strange and lesser-known, film titled *The Cat and the Canary,* made in Britain around 1967, turned into a book in 1977 by Gerry Kingsley, based on the screenplay by director Radley Metzger. Set in isolated Glencliffe Manor, Yorkshire, the components this time include a woman lawyer, two lesbians, a torrid affair between the juvenile leads, a millionaire seen on film reels preserved for twenty years until September 1954, with ambiguous references to millionaire Cyril West, two sadistic deaths, a necklace in the film refrigerator, changes in careers, and a romance between the decertified doctor and one of the lesbians. The distinguished cast included Honor Blackman, Wilfred Hyde-White, Beatrix Lehmann, Wendy Hiller, and Daniel Massey—talents out of all proportion to this version of a classic.

Indeed, Bob Hope's films were followed by others in a similar vein; for example, *Murder, He Says,* or *Spooks Run Wild* with the East Side Kids (a gang of New York boys, when the East Side was the poorer side), Bela Lugosi, the young Ava Gardner, in a 1941 film of magic, mystery, comedy, and a misleading description of the Nazis.

It is interesting to trace the two links from 1940 of the comedy-horror story, which is paralleled by the comedy-thriller and comedy-'tecker, *The Ghost Train,* by actor-playwright Arnold Ridley dating from the 1920s. This is constantly being staged around the world and has been filmed twice in England, the first time in the

1930s with husband-and wife team Jack Hulbert and Cecily Courtneidge, and second in the 1940s with Arthur Askey and Richard Murdoch, all of whom have been mentioned above, and Linden Travers as the heroine, who was also the misused heroine in the 1951 British film *No Orchids for Miss Blandish,* from the James Hadley Chase book. A 1971 version was titled *The Grissom Gang.* *The Ghost Train* also became a novel. It tells of a train stopped unexpectedly and "accidentally" by Teddy Deakin in a small deserted station in Cornwall, a group of passengers thus stranded in the waiting room. The station master tells of a ghost train that rushes through every night, intoning, "Where do it come from? Where do it go?" Swinging his lantern he sings the hymn "Rock of Ages," then is found dead. Mysterious visitors, including a doctor and a frightened heroine, suddenly arrive, the train rushes through, then the silly ass Teddy is revealed as a detective trailing smugglers, the train falls off a bridge, and a lady with a parrot (played both by Cecily Courtneidge and Barbara Miller, on film and on stage) wakes up in time to travel on.

Charlie Chan and the Curse of the Dragon Queen—no, not one of the long-running American series with Warner Oland, Sidney Toler, or another, but a 1980 parody, featuring Peter Ustinov as the inscrutable Chan—parody indeed. One murder was by flooding an elevator shaft, another by electrocuting a saxophonist with beer in a disco. There was a chase with undertakers, the action moved to the Eltings Theatre where a season of Chan films was being shown, so Chan would take his bow in the chase—all very much in a comedy-spectacular format. Ustinov is a talented West End stage and film actor and playwright who has also portrayed Poirot on film.

The Lady Vanishes (Gainsborough, 1938) became a classic for Alfred Hitchcock, Essex-born film director whose name appeared above the title as greater than the many stars he used. Based on the book *The Wheel Spins* by Ethel Lina White (1936), it told of a train, like the Orient Express, crossing Europe while an English girl cannot get anyone to listen to her story of the vanished English woman, until almost too late. Margaret Lockwood as the heroine, May Whitty as the vanished English spy, Michael Redgrave, Paul Lukas as the kidnapping doctor-spy, and Basil Radford and Naunton Wayne as Caldicott and Charters expanded as the cricket-loving Englishmen. Radford made various films, such as *Whisky Galore!* and Wayne was a stage actor and radio comedian. As aristocratic cricket enthusiasts, they were to appear in more films, like *Crooks Tour,* chasing a gramophone record with a secret message; *Night Train to Munich*; the wartime *Millions Like Us*; *The Facts of Life*, part of the 1948 Somerset Maugham film *Quartet*; a short horror golf story; and various BBC radio serials immediately after World War II (including one in which they leave a corpse on the London underground railway—but on the Inner Circle, so it returns to them). They always solved the mysteries, however, in a debonair manner, not always so brightly. When *The Wheel Spins* was filmed a second time, the roles were taken by Arthur Lowe and Ian Carmichael, the latter famous for portraying that monocled pair, P. G. Wodehouse's Bertie Wooster and Dorothy L. Sayers's Lord Peter Wimsey. In January 1985, BBC-TV Channel 1 presented a six-part serial *Charters and Caldicott,* featuring, respectively, Robin Bailey and Michael Aldridge, in a similar story of murders, mystery, and a denouement at Lords Cricket Ground; they were portrayed as older men, but still with elegant, distrait, vague enthusiasm and luck. The 1985 paperback published by the BBC was novelized by Stella Bingham keeping close to Keith Waterhouse's original script of two wills, disguised women, three murders near the two heros, a takeover of a lemonade company, treasure in a sunken Nazi submarine, an interfering clubman from the Treasury, and an ambiguous ending. Aldridge as Caldicott was the brainier partner.

The year 1978 saw one of the most remarkable screen parodies in *The Cheap Detective* (Columbia-EMI-Warner, American, ninety-two minutes, in color), written by Neil Simon, famous for a string of Broadway and film successes (*Come Blow Your Horn, Plaza Suite,* and many others), to say nothing of some of the original scripts for the delightful *Sergeant Bilko* TV series, featuring Phil Silvers, of which more anon. It was directed by Robert Moore, produced by Ray Starke, with a cast of very well known actors, headed by Peter Falk and Nicol Williamson, six women led by Ann-Margret and Eileen Brennan, and such long-shining stars as Sid Caesar, James Coco, and Fernando Lamas. In 1940 San Francisco private detective Lou Peckinpaugh is accused of murder; he meets various women including his old love Marlene Duchard who is urging the pianist in Nix Place (cf. Rick's in *Casablanca*) to play a certain song; she is married to a war hero being chased by the Nazi Colonel Schlisser ("Colonel Prince

Count Baron von Schlisseldorf, German military attaché to Cincinnati"), so Lou and the French Underground outwit the Germans to get the hero to Oakland. Lou then meets the gargantuan Jasper Blubber and his assistant Boy, who are seeking treasure, then the wealthy, crippled art collector Ezra Desire, who has a glamorous wife Jezebel—murder, discovery of the treasure, solutions of mysteries—and happy memories of *Casablanca, The Maltese Falcon,* and Raymond Chandler's books parodied almost to caricature, bringing the esoteric to the exoteric, very tastefully and very funnily. Falk with a lisp takes the Bogart character, Dom DeLuise the Peter Lorre part, and John Houseman the Sydney Greenstreet role. Falk is endeavoring to solve the murder of his partner, and the zany touches include finding the husband in the toilet bowl. It was novelized by Robert Grossback. Another similar multiparody Simon film is considered below. *Casablanca* was also parodied in the Marx Brothers film *A Night in Casablanca,* with yet more typically surrealistic comedy routines.

In May 1993 was revived at the small King's Head Theatre in London *Cracks,* by Martin Sherman. Originally premiered in Connecticut with Meryl Streep and Christopher Lloyd, it was to fail on Broadway. It dates from 1975, and answers "Whodunnit?" by naming the playwright. Nine partygoers are consecutively shot, starting with a bisexual California commune host. The other characters are a drunken guitarist, a seventeen-year-old nymphomaniac, a blue-movie maker, a housewife whose nerves are collapsing, a wealthy middle-aged "glamour girl," a drug-addict controlled by her dead analyst, a transvestite docker, and a Jewish homosexual who wants to be a Benedictine monk. (Irresistibly, it recalls to my mind the play *The Metal Flower Blossom* by Colin Wilson, which I directed in December 1960—the characters were an artist, two rather nymphomaniacal women, two necrophiliacs, an Eastern levitater, a homosexual, a ballet dancer, an American millionaire, a prostitute, a Negro, and a virginal young secretary. Wilson turned it into a book, *Adrift in Soho.*)

A remarkable film that was to start a new trend in television advertisements was the 1981 *Dead Men Don't Wear Plaid,* of the Aspen Film Society. It was directed by Carl Reiner, who wrote the script with leading actor Steve Martin and George Gyp, and appeared in it himself as the Nazi general; he also appeared in such films as *Oh God!* with George Burns, was the head writer for *The*

Dick Van Dyke Show, and straight man to Sid Caesar. Rigby Reardon, a private investigator, is hired by Juliet Forrest (Rachel Ward) and solves the mystery of her father's disappearance successfully, till the final confrontation with Von Kluck who aims to make the United States disappear with cheese [sic], and even blows up a town in Oregon. The uniqueness of the film was in the editing and cutting—as the hero carries on his investigating he meets the stars of some of the greatest films and their answers match his questions; even the telephone conversations, arguments, and fights all mesh due to very clever cutting. A knock on his office door, and Alan Ladd is outside. He calls at a flat, and Ray Milland (from *The Lost Weekend*) answers his query. Burt Lancaster, Cary Grant, Veronica Lake, Barbara Stanwyck (in *Sorry, Wrong Number*), Lana Turner, Bette Davis, Charles Laughton, Ava Gardner, and many others appear in clips from *Double Indemnity* (1944), *The Big Sleep* (1946), *The Killers* (1946), *This Gun for Hire* (1942), and many, many more. The story gets a little obscure at times. Bogart as Marlowe, helps him. The Hotel in Peru is the Hotel Guano—plus music by Niklos Rosza, and costumes by Edith Head, the last film on which this great Hollywood designer worked. Using period songs in a television play is not unusual, and film clips are frequently used, but after this film came some television advertisements in England for a famous lager in which British comedian Griff Rhys Jones was apparently talking or fighting (with clever cutting again) with Humphrey Bogart or Gary Cooper or Barbara Stanwyck. The film was interesting, not just as an experiment, but because of the pleasure of recognizing the clips, all duly listed at the end in acknowledgments, in this amusing, farfetched, but clever film idea.

Dead Reckoning, a 1946/47 Columbia black-and-white film, is a takeoff on both *The Maltese Falcon* and *The Big Sleep* (Warner Bros., 1946, Philip Marlowe story), in both of which Bogart starred. In this film Bogart is investigating the death of a paratrooper friend.

What sort of musical would *Death Beat* have turned out to be? This 1960s projected version of Agatha Christie's *Hickory Dickory Dock* (1955) had John Dankworth as orchestrator, Sean Kenny as designer, John Wells as scriptwriter, Alex Weissenberg as composer, possible top producers, and either Peter Sellers or Martin Gabel as possible Poirots—Gabel had played him on American television in 1962 in *The Disappearance of Mr. Davenheim.* It was not produced.

Dick Tracy has been a famous long-running cartoon strip for years and was featured in several films. In 1970 came a musical *Dick Tracy,* costing half a million dollars, adapted by Tony Piano, music and lyrics by Michael Colicchio, but it never reached Broadway. Ten years earlier *The Dick Tracy Show* was a series of five-minute color cartoons, with the voice of Everett Sloane as Tracy fighting juvenile equivalents of Splitface and Cueball, Pruneface and Flattop, with assistants Hemlock Holmes and the "Retouchables" (cf. the Untouchables).

Ding Dong Dead by Robert Thomas, adapted by Mawby Green and Ed Dielbert, was premiered at Farnham in December 1991, as a spoof set in a lonely house in the Chevreuse Valley in France with a wealthy wife seeking divorce, a husband seeking to kill her and impersonating his own brother, comic detective and police, bodies coming back to life, a maid gangling rather than glamorous, crinkled curtains for the obligatory first scene in darkness—all played for laughs.

Disorder in Court was a fifteen-minute 1936 Three Stooges film comedy, also featuring Susan Karan, Dan Brady, Tiny Jones, and Bill O'Brien. This chaotic story involved a witness in court for the murder of a dancer, with three musicians, the woman dancing, the clerks lost, and a talkative parrot with a letter attached to its leg naming Kirk Robin (cf. Cock Robin) as the killer. (There had been a 1930s film, *Counsel for the Defence,* with Otto Kruger, in which he proved a shot could not be heard over a band playing.)

Dragnet was a 1991 film with Dan Ackroyd as Joe Friday and Tom Hanks as his sidekick, in a spoof on the popular TV series, from which at least one book was derived by Jack Webb, the original Friday: "Just the facts, ma'am."

Drat! the Cat was a 1965 stage musical, with music by Milton Schafer, written by Ira (*Rosemary's Baby*) Levin. It was a spoof of cops and robbers about a thief and a playwright, with Lesley Ann Warren, but had only a few performances. After such plays as *Veronica's Room* came the great success of the author's *Deathtrap.*

This last play is a cleverly written amalgam of plots and counterplots, with playwright Sidney Bruhl slipping from the heights of his career, his wife Myra suffering from heart trouble, and a former pupil Clifford Anderson, who brings the author his own new play, *Deathtrap,* which the Bruhls realize could restore his career—if it were in Bruhl's name—but who is collaborating with whom to murder the third angle of the triangle? Will they succeed? Or is there another pair of plotters? It was filmed in 1982 by Warner with Michael Caine.

The Dream Sequence Always Rings Twice (echoes of James M. Cain's title) was a television spoof on the 1940s PI, nightclubs, trench coats, and trilbies, with an introduction by Orson Welles, and shown on BBC television on August 21, 1986. First came a discussion of an unsolved murder involving a sultry singer and a trumpeter, then strange dreams in black and white. The story editors Carl Sauter (1959–1993) and Debra Frank were nominated for both Emmy and Edgar awards for this episode. *The Postman Always Rings Twice* is referred to in the *Moonlighting* series, and previously there had been various Hollywood films with dream sequences, such as *The Chase* (1946) with Robert Cummings, Michele Morgan, Steve Cochran, and Peter Lorre, when Cummings on the run with Cochran's gangster wife, Morgan, finds his own killing a dream from which the telephone awakens him.

Another such film was Fritz Lang's *The Woman in the Window* (Paramount, 1944), based on James Harold Wallis's (1885–1958) 1942 novel, *Once Off Guard.* Edward G. Robinson, as Professor Wanley, meets Alice Reed (Joan Bennett), commits the murder of her protector; she is blackmailed by Heidt the bodyguard (Dan Duryea), whom they try in vain to kill—so he commits suicide—and wakes from the dreadful dream. The screenplay was by Nunnally Johnson, and the three stars, who a year later appeared in Lang's *Scarlet Street* (based on *La Chienne* by Georges de la Fouchardière and André Mouezy-Eon), were supported by Raymond Massey as the investigating attorney.

Far East was a 1980 parody film with Secret Service agent Charles Bind, Number One, surviving nonchalantly in an elegant dinner jacket.

The Farndale Avenue Housing Estate Townswomen's Guild Dramatic Society Murder Mystery "Murder at Checkmate Manor" is the title of a play by Walter Zerlin Jr., and David McGillivray, presented at the Redgrave Theatre, Farnham, Surrey, on July 30, 1985. It should be explained that there was a slight vogue in England for abnormally lengthy titles, and for plays that made fun of amateur theatre and detective stories, and that Townswomen's Guilds (area groups of energetic and powerful women residents) usually formed their own drama groups for presenting plays, often in area competitions. This is one of the two parodies of crime fiction, see below.

Fatal Attraction was a play by Bernard Slade, author of *Same Time, Next Year,* at the Theatre Royal, Haymarket, London, in November 1985. A six-hander mystery play, set in a Nantucket beach house, with Susannah York as a Hollywood star and Denis Quilley as an author and perhaps a detective, it had a shadowy stranger midstage, dark corners, bon mots, rape, homosexuality, and a Jacuzzi as modern additions to an unbelievably complicated story, even regarding who was who, a program note saying the author cannot describe it without revealing the very plot. It perhaps raises echoes of *The Cat and the Canary,* but that had a clear-cut plot amid all the mysteries, gloom, and tension.

In a different vein, *Fathom* was a 1967 Fox film from a novel by Larry Forrester, *A Girl Named Fathom.* Raquel Welch played Fathom Harvill, named after the initials of six uncles, Richard Briers and Ronald Fraser were the British agents of HADES, turning out to be crooks, Clive Revill was the mysterious black-monocled millionaire womanizer Steapkin—all in a complicated plot involving chasing after a nuclear device that was really a jewel-encrusted statuette finally dropped from an airplane into a birthday cake (shades of 1930s comedies). Fathom was a California dental assistant and amateur skydiving champion, which did at least give some spectacular shots.

The Fiendish Plot of Dr. Fu Manchu, a 1980 film, was the last film made by Peter Sellers, a madcap parody that unfortunately did not succeed.

Four Plays for Coarse Actors was the title of a book of short plays, in acting edition, by Michael Green, published by Samuel French, Ltd., in 1978. Green has written several humorous books on various subjects, from rugby football to other sports and pastimes, and this book included the play *Streuth,* first performed at the Questor's Theatre, Ealing (mainly used by nonprofessional groups), in November 1972, and at the Edinburgh Festival. The scene is the drawing room of D'Arcy Manor, and the stock cast includes Mr. and Mrs. Oliver D'Arcy, Hubert with many cigarette cases, the major, the vicar (Rupert), the inspector, James the butler, cook, a nonappearing sergeant, and the prompter. It proves to be a circular script at the end through wrongly repeated cues. Again, a parody of amateur groups, and 'teckers, and a play on the title *Sleuth*.

The Gay Desperado was a 1936 film from Rouben Mamoulian, from a story by Leo Birinski, scripted by Wallace Smith. Leo Carillo is a Mexican bandit chief (copying carefully James Cagney, Edward G. Robinson, and George Raft), with Harold Huber and Mischa Auer as his henchmen, aiming to kidnap a singing caballero (Nino Martini) and a spoiled heiress (Ida Lupino). It starts off with slaughter in Chicago, but on film, and the songs include "The World Is Mine Tonight" by Holt Marvell (Eric Maschwitz) and George Posford, famous names in the world of musical comedy.

Get Smart was a cleverly titled series on NBC-TV from 1965 to 1969, repeated on British television, and published in book form under such titles as *Get Smart! Sorry, Chief . . ., Get Smart Once Again!, Max Smart and the Perilous Pellets, Max Smart—The Spy Who Went Out to the Cold,* and *Missed It by That Much!*, which give a very good idea of the humorous mishaps of Maxwell Smart, Agent 86 for Control, played on television by Don Adams. This spoof on spy yarns relied on situation, reactions, and comedy business to a highly successful level. Spy City was a venue; Guro Optimo, Lucky Bucky Buckley, and KAOS agent V.T. Brattleboro were typical names; and the actual chuckleheaded activities and misunderstandings in, say, a gothic castle resembled the films of Abbott and Costello—like finding a way out through a dude ranch swimming pool, or a submarine near New York. Copyrighted by Talent Associates–Paramount, this was an Emmy Award–winning series, reprinted to 1969. Book No. 8, As an example of the series, *Max Smart Loses Control,* by William Johnston, has computers named Fred and Hymie, one with a "dog named Fang." One installment in this series, created by Mel Brooks, had wage-cut Smart set up as a PI—"It's Smart to Hire Smart"—with fellow Agent 99. The first client is an alcoholic, nymphomaniacal wife, Mrs. Weatherley, who goes out the window, followed by a large white-clad man, Mr. Peter (played by Berry Krofour), and small bug-eyed lisping Mr. Sydney (Paul Roth)—cf. vide Lorre and Greenstreet; the former gets shot, the latter also exits via the window. "Missed it by that much," Smart comments in his Bogart lisp.

The Gracie Allen Murder Case was a 1938/39 film by S. S. Van Dine (1888–1939) from Paramount, with Warren William repeating his performance as Philo Vance. Apart from Van Dine's short films, each of his main features involving Vance had a six-letter title—Bishop, Garden, Benson, Canary, etc.—as we have seen. This particular story was made for his friend Gracie Allen, the comedienne, who helps Vance solve the murder of a convict at a picnic for perfume factory workers. Ellen Drew and Kent Taylor were also in the cast. Gracie Allen was married to that outstanding American comedian George Burns, and their double act was famous on the variety stage and in many leading American films. Burns continued in films and television after his wife's death, and also wrote several books. Thanks to BBC-TV producer John Fisher, we were in the audience for Burns's famous BBC interview by Michael Parkinson at London's University Theatre. I wrote to him to see if he had any comment on this film, but I did not get a reply to my letters.

"Grange Hill Street Blues" links two leading television series: the English *Grange Hill* school and the American *Hill Street Blues* police. Two British comedians, Griff Rhys Jones and Mel Smith, presented a BBC television series, *Alas Smith and Jones* (note the spelling), and on October 31, 1985, the program contained a sketch under this title, satirizing both of the named series. Mel Smith was Sergeant Jablonski, holding the morning parade, and Jones was the grubby, hairy plainclothes detective, as Smith gave the 8:45 A.M. roll call for his teachers based on the police system—ending with Smith taking a rifle out of the cupboard and saying, "Let's get them before they get us!" This is a reference to the *Hill Street Blues* program seen in Britain earlier that year in which the American Jablonski did indeed say that. The American Federation of Police immediately lodged a complaint, the studio apologized, but the AFP demanded rectification; a later program had Jablonski explaining he merely meant an old police warning of preparedness. I wrote an article about such mistakes in television crime programs in *City '85,* the monthly magazine of the City of London Police. Some are technical errors; others give a very messy impression of police work.

Gymslip Vicar was a play written and adapted by four members of the Cliff Hanger Company in May 1984 in England. One reviewer called it an overdone parody of police thrillers, television drama, and tabloid press stories. A "gym slip" is a tunic or belted pinafore dress worn by schoolgirls.

Hammett was a 1982 film produced by Frances Ford Coppola, directed by Wim Wenders, with Frederick Forrest playing Hammett in the 1920s, in one of his own plots involving pornography, murder, blackmail, Pinkerton men (Hammett had been a Pinkerton operative), and a lost manuscript. Elisha Cook, Jr., an actor famed for some very chilling film roles, appeared as a taxi driver. This is another example of writers apparently getting involved in their own books or plots, some having already been considered in the books reviewed, and one yet to come in a play similarly linking Raymond Chandler to his creations.

The book *Hammett* was first written by Joe Gores in 1975, on the premise of Hammett acting as a sleuth in a mystery typical of his own writing, and is based on scandals of San Francisco in the 1920s and 1930s, with sundry real characters in fictional guises. Based on Gores' own researches, it has notes on various aspects of Hammett and the city, including references to the real district attorney, Brady, appearing as Bryan in Hammett's *The Maltese Falcon,* and to Peggy O'Toole, the original of Brigid O'Shaughnessy, in that same book. Gores verifies Hammett's 1928 address of 891 Post Street, where he had Sam Spade living in *The Maltese Falcon.*

The Haunted Through Lounge and Recessed Dining Nook at Farndale Castle—if the title of this play sounds vaguely familiar, then the author's names will cause no surprise—David McGillivray and Walter Zerlin, Jr.—as we considered another of their plays above. This production was at the Donmar Warehouse, in London, in February 1984, and was likened to an amalgam of *The Cat and the Canary* and *The Rocky Horror Picture Show* as performed by Farndale Avenue Housing Estate Townswomen's Guild Dramatic Society. With the same aims of parody, the stock characters include such ominous names as Crematia, Lady Madge Greave, and Mr. Tombs. Plays like this are perhaps novelties, if not too frequently performed.

Haven't a Clue; or, Murder at Withering Heights was a play that toured in 1987 in Britain by a theatre company called Bristol

Express Theatre, following on a previous successful comedy tour. A spoof of the Agatha Christie country-house murder, it started with the advertisements and trailers beloved of the cinema, before the guests are seen assembled at Withering Heights, home of Lady Withering. The party included Teddy Withering in love with the attractive Angela Cholmonedeley-Plodmondeley, his enigmatic brother Jack, a mysterious bishop and the actress who said to him (the Saint's favorite aside, "as the actress said to the bishop"), the Hon. Algernon Ponsonby-Fortescue, and the escaped psychopath Cecil, plus various deaths and the sleuth Maigret Ridderford (a pun on actress Margaret Rutherford, who played a somewhat unlikely Miss Marple in several films).

How to Destroy the Reputation of the Greatest Secret Agent— English playwrights and song composers are not alone in finding abnormally long titles, for American playwrights have tried, and so have French filmmakers. This 1973 film was directed by Philippe de Broca, with Jean-Paul Belmondo doubling as François Merlin, a pulp writer and Bob Saint-Clair, and Jacqueline Bisset as Christine and as Tatiana, the parts of Charron and Karpof played by Vittorio Caprioli. This is another example of actors playing two different roles together in a film that perhaps bears resemblance to *That Man From Rio,* also seen on British television.

Alan Ayckbourn is an English playwright known for his ingenuity in titles, plotting, and strategy; for example, he wrote three plays with the same six characters, so that, but for just one line, all three plays could have been acted simultaneously on three visible, linked stages. *It Could Be Any One of Us* premiered like many of his plays at the Theatre in Scarborough, a historic seaside resort in Yorkshire, in October 1983. It has a manor, a storm, various motives, a composer who plans to disinherit his dependents in favor of a former pupil (now a homely, boring petshop owner) in this parody of detective plays.

Just Ask for Diamond was a British film, premiered in December 1988, made by Stephen Bayly, photographed by Billy Williams, scripted by Anthony Horowitz. A parody of *The Maltese Falcon* and Chandler's *Farewell, My Lovely,* it featured Colin Dale as the thirteen-year-old Nick Diamond (cf. Sam Spade), as two teenager PIs run a detective agency in Camden Town in North London.

Another television program in which the cast members play two parts each and again real life is confused with fiction, until the latter proves the answer to the crime in the former, *Magnum* is a popular series with Tom Selleck playing an investigator ordered about by an English butler of an unseen employer. "Kiss of the Sabre" was shown on British television on May 20, 1986. Selleck's role was Sebastian Sabre, Cassie Yates played Betty Windon and Colette, John Hillerman the butler Higgins and Boris. Magnum is investigating a hit-and-run attack on Rossell Smythe, who died during the inquiry. Betty Windon keeps interfering, and as a writer transposes the story into one of a white-clad sleuth, with luxury cars and airplanes, Boris his butler, Dobermans—everybody thus in two roles as the story transmogrifies into a fraud with solicitor, insurance agent, doctor, and "victim." The story having come right, the writer, who operates under a male pseudonym, leaves in the dramatic way of her own self-played heroine.

The Last of Sheila was a film directed by Herbert Ross in 1973, with screenplay by Anthony Perkins and Stephen Sondheim. James Coburn played Clinton Green, a Hollywood producer whose wife, Sheila, had been killed. Six suspects led by James Mason and Raquel Welch, with Dyan Cannon and Richard Benjamin, are on his yacht *Sheila* on a Mediterranean cruise. Shot in Nice, the movie has the group forced to solve the mystery as in a game to find the killer. A further murder, with everybody still suspected, leads to a rather satirical denouement. The film is reminiscent of the yacht party murder game mentioned in the Do-It-Yourself section earlier—ingenious and homogeneous.

The Late Show was a ninety-minute US TV film, shown on BBC-TV Channel 2 on November 6, 1984, repeated May 30, 1988, and is a satire on the link between a partner's death and a missing cat, with a very trying, nonviolent heroine. Art Carney plays Ira Wells, a retired PI; Howard Duff is the ex-partner killed in the first scene; Eugene Roche is Birdwell the fence. There are two main crooks—and eight murders—with the last two in a shoot-out. Lily Tomlin, the nonviolent heroine, comes to enjoy the violence and links up with the detective at the end. Shot in Hollywood in 1977, it was written and directed by Robert Benton.

Laurel and Hardy had a great and lasting influence throughout the dramatic arts. Their films are rerun daily throughout the world; their fan clubs are strong; their influence has been admitted by comedians like the British team of Morecambe and Wise, and straight actors like the English Alec Guinness, in a television interview for BBC. It is right therefore to examine the influence they have had on even crime films and stories, with *The Laurel and Hardy Murder Case,* a 1930 film produced by Hal Roach. For much of the technical data on this film I am indebted to author Basil Copper (past CWA chair and, as seen above, the continuing writer of August Derleth's Solar Pons chronicles) and stage and TV actor Jeffrey Holland, both keen and active Laurel and Hardy fans. Three reels, sound, made September 6, 1930, released by MGM, directed by James Parrott (formerly the comic Paul Parrott), dialogue by H. M. Walker, the title is derived from the Philo Vance stories. Others in the cast included Fred Kelsey as the police chief, Frank Austin as the butler, Stanley Bysten as the detective, Lon Poff and Rosa Core as the elderly couple, and doubles played by Ham Kinsey and Cy Slocum. It was originally titled *The Rap*, and also had German, French, and Spanish versions with a sleeper-train sequence. The story was ingenious. Laurel and Hardy are sitting by the dock when they read in the newspaper that heirs are sought for a fortune; as they qualify, they proceed in a rainstorm to an eerie mansion, Laurel Manor, complete with butler, five other claimants, a crook disguised as housekeeper, and everything happens in the best gothic cat-and-the-canary format—a chair tilts unwary occupants backwards into the cellar, there is a cat and a bat (cf. the Bat), and so on. At the final fall, they wake up just as they are tumbling off the dock into the harbor—another classic dream sequence.

Another Laurel and Hardy crime film was *The Big Noise* (1944), in which they play PIs set to protect wartime inventor Arthur Space, complete with Veda Ann Borg, a gang next door, a cheeky small boy, and neat use of theme tunes—"Dream Walking" with the sleepwalking widow, "Flying Trapeze" with a parachute jump, and the then-popular nonsense song "Mairzy Doats" ("Mairzy Doats, Dozy Doats and Little Lamsy Divy," i.e., mares eat oats, does eat oats, and little lambs eat ivy).

A slightly different effect came in the book *If Laurel Shot Hardy the World Would End,* written in 1970 by Stanton Forbes, an author who also wrote as Tobias Wells, Dee Forbes, and Forbes Rydell (jointly with Helen Rydell), whose real name is DeLoris Stanton Forbes.

The year 1993 was, as mentioned, the centenary of the birth of Dorothy L. Sayers, and for their 1993/94 Christmas holiday attraction, the English theatrical touring company Eastern Angles presented *Lord Peter Wimsey and the Bergholt Bells,* written and directed by and featuring Ivan Cutting in a cast of five at Ipswich, Suffolk, in East Anglia. Set in East Bergholt, a village made famous by painter John Constable (1776–1837), where the rector is found dead under the tenor bell in the church's famous bell cage, Harriet Vane is a suspect until Lord Peter arrives in his Daimler car named Mrs. Murdle. Bell sounds and a bell song play an active part in this spoof, with the cast members playing a stream of parts.

The McGuffin was a BBC-TV Channel 2 play on January 12, 1986, written by Michael Thomas, from the 1984 novel by John Bowen—his first in twenty years. The play and novel, tributes to Alfred Hitchcock, tell the story of a film critic getting himself mixed up in a murder plot. To emphasize this, the television play had in the cast Ann Todd (from *The Paradine Case*), Anna Massey (from *Frenzy*), Bill Shine from *Under Capricorn,* and the director Colin Bucksey made a Hitchcock-type appearance. Hitchcock called the object on which the story turned (such as Desdemona's handkerchief), the McGuffin; here it is a roll of scandalous film. One character was called Mickey Rooney; the Man in the Brown Suit (cf. Christie) was an unnamed policeman or agent; the Young Man with Silver Hair was one of the original villains. The book itself carries the tribute further: written in the first person by critic Paul Hatcher, Hitchcock's influence is expressed by the chapter headings: "Rear Window," "Vertigo," "Man Who Knew Too Much," "Blackmail," "Rich and Strange," "Easy Virtue," "The Lady Vanishes," and so on. When the hero is inveigled to a pornographic film festival in Liechtenstein, Hitchcock himself makes a brief appearance on the street outside the cinema. Several deaths, a roll of film showing four famous men in criminal circumstances, a dog Bonzo, and ruthless actions by secret agents including English and American add up to a strange tale of one man fighting the system in vain. The one-page sequel, in the third person, leaves various matters unsolved, as whether Hatcher has finally been liquidated deliberately and how the four miscreants have been punished, but author and playwright wrote fast, so the emphasis was on action as in a filmscript. Recent events in England have shown it is not difficult to leak such stories now in various lands.

Masquerade is a popular title for films, because of its intrinsic meaning, and one film of that name was the 1965 British one with Jack Hawkins, perfect delineator of the English officer and gentleman, and Cliff Robertson, a film described as very much a spoof from Victor Canning's novel *Castle Minerva* but that could nevertheless stand on its own, like Sandy Wilson's famous pastiche musical, *The Boy Friend.*

A Masterpiece of Murder was a TV film first shown in Britain on January 27, 1986. It featured Bob Hope as down-at-heel PI Dan Dolan, who meets Frank Aherne, played by the elegant Don Ameche, at a party. Thirty years earlier Hope had arrested Ameche for burglary; now the latter is wealthy. The host is murdered; there is a mystery of a painting in a private gallery, and, needless to say, many gags in Hope's first TV movie. Also in the distinctly stellar cast were Stella Stevens, Jayne Meadows, Frank Gorshin, Anne Francis, Anita Morris, Yvonne de Carlo, and Jamie Farr (playing himself).

At Christmas 1985 and again in 1986, Thames Television, one of the commercial British networks, presented *Minder on the Orient Express,* written by Andrew Payne. *Minder* had been a successful series for several years, featuring George Cole as Arthur Daley, a small-time London businessman with not too honest a viewpoint, and Dennis Waterman as his minder, an ex-convict, and ex-boxer. There had been a romantic film previously based on the famous train, and a set had been built in Leeds, Yorkshire, which this crime film used. On a trip to Venice, eleven crooks and two contract killers (the number compares with Agatha Christie's team of twelve out of thirteen vengeful assorteds) are seeking the clue to a safe-deposit box in which a deceased gang leader had stashed away his considerable share of loot from a bullion raid. The code can be broken by analyzing a photograph of a famous football team. Finally, the gangleader's daughter has her handbag stolen by young thugs in Switzerland, so no one can retrieve the cash, which compares with the ending of *The Maltese Falcon.* There is another play with a very similar plot: *Underground. Minder* has many complications and a cross-section of criminal characters, played by such actors as Honor Blackman (Pussie Galore in *Goldfinger*), English and European—with one fat man—plus English and French policemen, getting in their own and everybody else's way. An unpleasant English policeman finds his expense allowance too low for Orient Express prices, so is reduced to scrounging cocktail nuts and the like.

Mickey Spillane's *Mike Hammer: More than Murder* was a spoof film featuring Stacy Keach, shown on British television on February 7, 1984, intended to be followed by a series and described as "a glorious and good-natured send-up of the whole Chandleresque tradition."

Mulligan's Last Case, by Ian Blair, in July 1978, was a play based on the theme of a Lancashire author, Harry Bird, getting mixed up with his own creations, mainly Brad Mulligan. His attractive young cleaner proves another, and also involved are his parents, Mulligan's sidekick Charley Boy, Lulu, and three thugs—one of whom is a woman in man's clothes.

Murder at Garsington Manor was a play performed at Warwick, England, in July 1983, showing Ottoline Morrell's time with poet T. S. Eliot, Frieda Lawrence's Bauhaus lecture, various accounts of the events, with the butler as the detective—a unique innovation.

Neil Simon's brilliant 1978 parody film was *The Cheap Detective*. His earlier and even more ingenious parody film was *Murder by Death* (1976), Columbia-Warner, American, ninety-five minutes, color, and with the same director and producer as the later film, Some of the cast were the same—Peter Falk, James Coco, and Eileen Brennan—but the other distinguished names included Truman Capote (*In Cold Blood*) as the owner of the mysterious mansion, Alec Guinness, Elsa Lanchester, Maggie Smith, Estelle Winwood, David Niven, and Peter Sellers. Lionel Twain, an eccentric millionaire, has a blind butler and a deaf-mute cook at his gloomy gothic mansion, to which he invites five famous detectives of fiction, challenging them to solve before dawn a mystery which will include the disappearance of the butler's body and of the dining room itself before five beautifully logical, contrasting, and incorrect solutions are presented by the five: England's Miss Marbles with her wheelchair-bound companion, the elegant Dick and Dora Charleston with their dog Myron, Europe's Milo Perrier with his chauffeur, Sam Diamond and his secretary, and the Chinese Sidney Wang with his adopted Japanese son—parodies of famous originals. (Incidentally, how many realize the Thin Man was not the elegant William Powell as Nick Charles but a man in the first of their films?) The cast was listed "in diabolical order," and the film was full of witty remarks. Gerald Mast called the 1970s the genre genre, and *A Short History of the Movies* said in 1981 that this film and *The Cheap Detective* "parodied the plot structures, stylistic conventions, and movie stars of Hollywood Past, usually by compiling a catalogue of Studio Era clichés." It was also said that Dick Richards's *Farewell, My Lovely* (1975), with Robert Mitchum as a 1940s Marlowe, was an escape from American life's problems. Neil Simon wrote the screenplay of *Murder by Death,* and H. R. F. Keating turned it into an equally witty book. An intriguing aspect of the script was that each sleuth had cause to dislike the mysterious millionaire. Elsa Lanchester's Miss Jessica Marbles had been jilted by him. Peter Sellers's Sidney Wang had a resentful son. Peter Falk's Sam Diamond had been picked up in a homosexual bar. James Coco's Milo Perrier had been deprived of his pet poodle, and David Niven's and Maggie Smith's Dick and Dora Charleston were much in debt. *The Affair of the Blood-Stained Egg Cosy* could be compared with this film.

Murder by Misadventure was premiered at Theatre Clwyd, in Wales, in February 1992 before its West End run and was written by Edward Taylor, a former BBC radio producer and scriptwriter with many comedy shows to his credit. It featured the elegant Gerald Harper as Harold Kent and William Gaunt as the shabby alcoholic Paul Riggs, partners in writing crime stories; Deborah Watling as Emma Kent; and Rowland Davies as Inspector Egan; it was directed by Val May. When the partnership seems to be floundering, and they plot the perfect murder, could it be applied to real life, and, if so, to whom? Locked rooms, bloodstained clothes, vanishing bodies—are the Kents planning to murder Riggs, or is it the other way round? This familiar theme of plot and counterplot has been popular in British thrillers since the 1930s.

Murder by the Book was a TV film in 1972, with Robert Hays, Hank Mercer, Victor Grevill played by Fred Gwynne, Marise Winfield by Catherine Maria Stewart, and Celeste Holm playing Claire Mercier. It was written by Michael Morell and directed by Mel Damski. The hero created Biff Deegan, a tough 'tec in seven books, then tried writing the intellectual 'tec Amos Frisbee. In a story of a valuable but fake statue of an Etruscan dancer, Biff Deegan advises the author how he would act with various murders going on. The author goes back to his Deegan books, and sees a woman being snatched.

Murder by the Book is not to be confused with Rex Stout's 1951 Nero Wolfe novel, or with Frances and Richard Lockridge's 1963 Mr. and Mrs. North novel. *Murder by the Book*, again, was a British sixty-minute television play in 1986, written and produced by Nick Evans, and starring Ian Holm as Poirot and Peggy Ashcroft as Agatha Christie setting out to kill off her character about whom both personally and as Ariadne Oliver she had had misgivings. Richard Wilson played Max Mallowan and Michael Aldridge her agent Edmund Cork. In an interview Holm said that he had found an image of Poirot that all other actors playing him (at least ten in England and America) had missed—a drawing in the *Sketch* in 1923—but this drawing by W. Smithson Broadhead in the *Weekly Sketch* was reproduced as far back as 1971 in *The Murder Book* by Tage La Cour and Harald Mogensen, from the Danish two years earlier. Another actor to play Poirot—David Suchet in 1989—once commented that he had traced Poirot's telephone number as Trafalgar 8137. This point is dealt with somewhat cursorily in Anne Hart's small book, *The Life and Times of Hercule Poirot* (1990), in that this number must have been unique in the 1930s as it was Whitehall exchange names that covered an area in London's West End. Poirot's flat, 203 Whitehaven Mansions, is vaguely in Mayfair or W. 1.—for Suchet's television series a block of flats in Charterhouse Square was selected. British Telecom confirmed to me that Trafalgar came into being as part of the former Whitehall exchange on March 30, 1949, later to vanish into 839 when the historic exchange had to go to facilitate intercontinental dialing.

The Murder Game, a play by Constance Cox, was produced at the Byre Theatre, St. Andrews, Scotland, in August 1986, directed by Marilyn Gray. In 1936 Brian Hamilton, a former racing driver getting a divorce from his rich wife, has a mistress; a sinister, smiling stranger appears, with ideas for party games and strangulation. Reviews indicated a lack of psychological motivation in the solving of marital problems by the stranger, but complimented the set apparently made of chrome and Bakelite, one of the earliest 1930s forms of plastic and, like chrome, used for domestic furnishings at that time.

Murder in the Fifth Position was a ballet created in 1983 by choreographer Stuart Hoppe, formerly with New York Metropolitan, and in the East End theatre, for Extemporary Dance Theatre. The dancers portrayed guests, victim, murderer, and butler in a manner described as à la Agatha Christie. This ballet is not to be confused with the detective story *Death in the Fifth Position,* a 1952 Peter Cutler Sergeant II book by Edgar Box, the 'tecker pseudonym of Gore Vidal.

Murder in the Mist was a thirty-minute film of a sleuth, Meg Hammer, tracking drug peddlers in seedy surroundings. Made in 1980, screenplay/director Lisa Gottleib, with Joyce Hazzard as Meg Hammer and Ron Dean as the Boss, the film was a success at the Edinburgh Film Festival that same year and the London Film Festival a year later.

The Murder League has already been considered in Chapter 2, on parodying detective writer clubs. On February 20, 1989, it was premiered at London's Savoy Theatre as *Over My Dead Body* (the title also of Rex Stout's 1940 Nero Wolfe book). Donald Sinden played Trevor Foyle, June Whitfield Dora Winslow, and Frank Middlemass Bartie Cruikshank, the founder-members of the Murder League in the elegant Pall Mall. It was directed by Brian Murray, and had an excellent set. Donald Sinden told Barbara Miller and me he based his beard on Compton Mackenzie's, and in a letter dated March 31, 1989, wrote, "I think the two Americans have made quite a good job of adaptation." They were Michael Sutton and Anthony Fingleton. The program was gotten up to look like a notebook and gave details of the leading crime writers' organizations. Parody murder—with gun, knife, and hanging in a locked room, ingenious twists, the real murder switched twice, and a great tag line. It would not have been possible to stage the book as it stood, with ten murders and the crafty lawyer.

Murder on the Metropolitan Line, by Chris Woods was a satire on Christie's *Murder on the Orient Express,* staged at the London Fringe theatre, the Catacomb, on March 3rd, 1975. The metropolitan line is one of the sections of the London Underground system.

Murderer was a 1975 play by Anthony Shaffer, author of the successful play and film, *Sleuth,* at London's Garrick Theatre. Norman Cresswell Bartholomew, failed painter and murder aficionado, is playing at murder, then believing he has murdered his wife; but he hasn't. The play had again tricks and fantasies, but did not achieve the success of *Sleuth.* Robert Stephens headed the four-strong cast.

The Musical Comedy Murders of 1940 by John Bishop was premiered on March 23, 1988, at the Greenwich Theatre, from the Broadway Bill Weldon Circle Repertory Company of New York City. Set in December 1940, in a mansion in Hastings-on-Hudson, it parodied both the Bob Hope classics and *The Old Dark House.* Simon Cadell was Eddie McCuen the Hope character, Maria Friedman was Nikki Grandall the Navy spy, Margaret Courtney Elsa von Grossenkneuten ("Big Breasts"), with Tom Baker, Ken del la Maine the killer producer and Simon(e) Butteriss as Helma Wenzel the transvestite maid, killed in the first minutes.

MUSICALS

Books have been adapted into musicals, either plays with music or musical comedies, but a few more examples to those above may clarify the operation.

Perhaps the first name to be considered has already been referred to, in the inimitable Damon Runyon (1880–1946). He wrote superb short stories, in the historic present, with titles like "More than Somewhat," "Furthermore," "The Turps," "My Wife Ethel," many concerned with Broadway and its colorful, slightly less honest characters. (It was his books that sent us to eat at Lindy's just as the ballet sent us to look at Tenth Avenue.)

Guys and Dolls, opening in New York on November 24, 1950, starred Robert Alda, Vivian Blaine, Sam Levene, and Stubby Kaye. The London 1953 production had Vivian Blaine, Sam Levene, and Stubby Kaye; and the film had Vivian Blaine, Frank Sinatra, Jean Simmons, Marlon Brando, and Stubby Kaye. In Runyon's books Capone is Big Black Marrio, Dave the Dude was Frank Costello, Missouri Martin was Texas Guinan, Waldo Winchester Walter Winchell, Regret was Abba Dabba Berman, and so on. Three films can be mentioned—*The Big Street* (1942) Lucille Ball and Henry Fonda, *Tight Shoes,* with John Howard, and *Little Miss Marker* (1934), with Shirley Temple remade in 1969 with Bob Hope as Sorrowful Jones (not forgetting *The Lemon Drop Kid,* dealt with elsewhere)—but his play from 1935, *A Slight Case of Murder,* written with Howard Lindsay, of the retired bootlegger, Marko, at the races, chased by loan sharks, and with four corpses in the spare bedroom, was not given an English premier until June 1991, at Nottingham. It had however been filmed twice before 1991, by Warners, the first time in 1938 as *A Slight Case of Murder,* with Edward G. Robinson, Jane Bryan, Willard Parker, Ruth Donelly, and Harold Huber (later to be one of the actors to play Poirot). In 1963 the title was *Stop You're Killing Me* (not to be confused with *Don't Stop, You're Killing Me* discussed below) with Broderick Crawford, Claire Trevor, Virginia Gibson, Sheldon Leonard, and Margaret Dumont, that stalwart lady stooge from the Marx Brothers films. Of the former film, critics as diverse as *Variety* and Graham Greene were unanimous in praise of its crazy humor and skilful treatment.

The Case of the Dead Flamingo Dancer (sic) by Ben Butler and Donald Oliver, which premiered in August 1991, had a tap-dancing 'tec, a dancing woman photographer, a butler, a character named Courtley DeManor, and a Spanish dancer, inter alia.

In 1993 Gwendoline Butler drew my attention to the American musical which had opened on Tuesday, March 30, in London's West End Prince of Wales Theatre, *City of Angels,* which had won a plethora of awards in New York and had played all over the States. We went to see it together. It was a brilliantly witty parody of 1940s 'teckers and the Hollywood of that era. The author was Larry Gelbart (of *A Funny Thing Happened on the Way to the Forum* fame), and the composer Cy Coleman, who wrote such successes as *Wildcat, Little Me,* and *Sweet Charity*. It was advertised as "The Hollywood Musical," with press reviews like "the wittiest musical ever written" and "one of the most clever and exciting musicals for many years." It tells of writer Stone and his creation, former cop private eye Stine (cf. Stein), as he adapts his book for Master Pictures of Hollywood. All the other characters portray living types and Stone's creations. The PI's secretary is the producer's secretary; the leading lady is the femme fatale killer married to the millionaire in the iron lung in the hothouse—shades of Marlowe—the millionaire's daughter is a nympho actress playing her role, Stone's wife is Stine's first girlfriend, and so on. Ingenious decor and sets, crisp one-liners, and parodic touches like whiskey in the bottom desk drawer and a huge gangster as Moose in Chandler's novel are added to numbers like the Stone-Stine duet "You're Nothing Without Me," reprised in the studio finale. I found the action, pace, and parody dramatically superb, but Butler thought it lacked heart.

In 1941 at what was then the west end of London's beautiful Hippodrome Theatre, later a popular cabaret restaurant, I was taken as a schoolboy by my father to a musical fascinating from its sheer ingenuity. *Get a Load of This* is also the title of a 1942 James Hadley Chase short story collection; the lead story was the musical presented by George Black, produced by Robert Nesbitt, the cast including Vic Oliver (an Austrian-born American comedian and musician, son-in-law of Winston Churchill, BBC comedian with Ben Lyon and Bebe Daniels during World War II, former deputy head of the Opera House, Graz, former tennis international, later conductor of the British Concert Orchestra). Others in the cast were Valerie White as Fanquist, and Hal Bryan, plus many beautiful showgirls and dancers, as Oliver played Vic Vandyke, owner of a prosperous nightclub, the other two his secretary and bandleader. Jack and Daphne Barker, a popular piano and song duo, played two entertainers, and Halama and Konarski the specialty dancers. The stage showed the floor of the nightclub, with diners' tables arranged in the front stalls, and the wall by the entrance stairs dissolved to show Vandyke's private office, where he had to cope with the gangsters moving in on him. The ballet was called "Lady—Here's Your Wreath," the title of another Chase detective story. In 1960 the musical had another excellent summer season, following a 1957 success at the Winter Garden Theatre in London, under the title *Don't Stop, You're Killing Me,* starring the elegant, quick-witted ad-libbing comedian and actor Bob Monkhouse, who was kind enough to give me the details in his letter dated January 5, 1988. He had helped overhaul the script, and played himself as the nightclub's host and comedian. The boss was Jerry Desmonde, Hector Ross the gangster who killed him, the bandleader was played by Bert Waller, the musical attraction was the Peters Sisters, the specialty dancers Kazbek and Zara with their whip act. The ballet was "Slaughter on Tenth Avenue" (mentioned elsewhere), and Joe Davis directed, in a six-month run, closing with three excellent weeks' business in Blackpool. He commented, "I recall it took our audiences 30 minutes or so to grasp the concept of a gangster thriller within a comedy and music show."

The Life and Times of Al Capone was a satirical musical premiered in England in March 1979.

Murder at the Vanities was a musical by Rufus King (1893–1966), creator of Lieutenant Valcour and the famous producer

Earl Carroll. This "musical mystery play" had Bela Lugosi in the 1933 Broadway run, and a year later came the Paramount film with Carl Brisson and Kitty Carlisle as two show stars (the vicious leading lady gets murdered), Jack Oakie as the former press director, Victor McLaglen as the detective, and Duke Ellington and his orchestra on stage. The spectacular finale was "Cocktails for Two," there were two murders, Brisson's mother was the wardrobe mistress, formerly a Viennese opera singer charged with manslaughter. The mystery is solved during the first night while Earl Carroll is away ill.

Sherlock Holmes has starred in musicals, too. In 1966 an American actor friend, Delos V. Smith, Jr., gave me the LP disc of *Baker Street,* a Broadway musical with Fritz Weaver as Holmes, Martin Gabel as Moriarty, and Inga Swenson singing delightfully as Irene Adler. The action was swift, the score and lyrics clever, and much atmosphere and character retained—for example, in Holmes's soliloquy in the carriage as he ponders Adler's role, and Holmes's analysis of the mud from the street outside the post office, now no longer in existence. Another musical was *The Diamond and the Goose,* by composer-musician John Dankworth, written by Benny Green, at the Barbican, in the City of London, in December 1986. In 1978 came to the West End *Something's Afoot,* a musical spoof thriller owing much to Holmes, Miss Marple, and to Lundy Island, an island off the west coast of England, the alleged original of Agatha Christie's venue for *Ten Little Niggers* (1939), itself frequently filmed under various titles. The music and lyrics for this pastiche were by Americans James McDonald, David Vos, and Robert Gerbach; the plot concerned the murder of the rancorous owner of Rancour's Retreat; and the detective was Miss Tweed. "The game's afoot" comes from Shakespeare's *Henry V.* (It is now believed from later research that Burgh Island, off Devon, near Plymouth is the scene for *Ten Little Niggers* and *Evil Under the Sun,* and there is a hotel there, once owned by Archibald Nettlefold, a leading name in British film.)

A very short lived American musical proved sadly to be *The Thin Man* in 1991 by Arthur Laurents, a very talented writer, with Barry Bostwick and Jo Anna Gleason.

In various contexts the contribution of the English-born American comedian Bob Hope has been stressed—for example, with *The Cat and the Canary* and *The Ghost Breakers.* He made countless film comedies and musicals, often with a strong element of spoof. Titles like *They Got Me Covered, My Favorite Blonde,* and *My Favorite Brunette* give an indication, and his costar Bing Crosby from the *Road* series films would usually make an unlisted, brief appearance. Of *My Favorite Brunette* (1947) William Luhr in his book *Raymond Chandler and Film* (1982) makes the interesting comment that it "indicates that the *noir* style associated with Chandler had become sufficiently pervasive to be parodied." He draws attention to Hope as a child photographer becoming a private detective, as shown in a brief appearance by Alan Ladd (who had been in Chandler's film *The Blue Dahlia* the previous year), and by adopting the direct narration of such films noir as Chandler's own *The Brasher Doubloon* that same year from Twentieth Century–Fox. Alan Ladd is the PI, Bing Crosby makes a cameo appearance as an executioner, Peter Lorre and Lon Chaney are the villains, and Dorothy Lamour, the glamorous heroine of the Hope-Crosby *Road* films, is the niece of a uranium-mine owner, captured by the gang. Hope is accused of murdering a geologist; he tries to be a PI in Ladd's absence in this very funny parody complete with its Marlowe-type narration, references to Bogart and Ladd as PIs, and whiskey in the desk drawer.

The Brasher Doubloon, like the Mike Shayne *Time to Kill,* was based on Chandler's *The High Window.* This Hope film is a spoof on Chandler's *Farewell My Lovely.*

The Thirteenth Guest was filmed in 1932 with Ginger Rogers and Lyle Talbot, and remade in 1943 by Monogram as *The Mystery of the Thirteenth Guest,* with a script by Tim Ryan and Frank Faylen, starring Dick Purcell as a wisecracking PI, Helen Parrish as the heroine, and Tim Ryan as the policeman. This film, like *The Cat and the Canary,* had all the ingredients: a masked murderer, hidden passages, a deserted mansion, an electric killer telephone, suspects, three detectives (two police and one private), as the heroine returns to the deserted mansion on her twenty-first birthday. An imposter with plastic surgery is killed off, followed by more murders, the bodies being placed in chairs as at the original dinner party.

"Next Stop Murder" was the title of an episode, shown on BBC-TV Channel 2 on June 19, 1986, of the series *Moonlighting.* This is based on a wealthy young woman finding all she has left of her estate is a small detective agency, run by a brash young man. She keeps the agency, taking part in its running, continually sparring with the manager, in a manner vaguely reminiscent of the more sophisticated and better-drawn Nick and Nora Charles of Dashiell Hammett. Cybill Shepherd played Maddie Hayes the owner, Allyce Beasley Ms. Dipesto, and Rock Jason was J. B. Harland in this story by Ali Marie Matheson and Kerry Matheson. Dipesto wins a weekend trip on novelist Harland's Murder Train, a luxury train with a hostess (it will be remembered that among the examples already dealt with in this category is the train between San Francisco and Los Angeles). A real murder takes place on the train, so the two sleuths investigate. Another episode was described as a Chandler tribute.

Night Train to Murder owes its title to such films as *Night Train to Munich* with Charters and Caldicott, *Night Train to Paris,* and the Charters and Caldicott BBC radio comedy-thriller serial *Night Train to Surbiton* (the wealthy town in Surrey). This TV spoof-thriller was written by comedians Morecambe and Wise and producer-director for Thames Television Joe McGrath in 1983. The two comics played themselves as in a 1940s murder mystery, with Fulton McKay and Kenneth Haigh, and it was transmitted on January 4, 1985. They are traveling on the night train to Scotland, reading lurid thrillers, which gradually come to fruition, step by step. Three members of the Austin family are murdered, then the solicitor, then Big Jim a servant, by a man in an opera phantom mask. There is a twin of the Scottish cousin and a Scotland Yard officer is the butler outwitted by the crook, in a short story not marked by strong parody. Several questions are left unanswered about the villain, a young man in love with the heiress, the link of the solicitor with the killer, Morecambe's link with the other cousin, and various tricks, such as the suit of armor (cf. a Berkeley Gray story), a lowering ceiling (cf. Poe), the mask (Phantom of the Opera), and reading the will at midnight, once they have all arrived in Scotland.

O'Malley, from American TV, is a PI, the antithesis of Marlowe and Spade. He is ex-NYPD, cigar smoking, clarinet playing, impecunious, feckless, back in New York from California to help with the estate of a friend, scrounging an office in the friend's son's art gallery. He gets involved in a case of forged Krugerrands, has his car towed away, gets arrested while pursuing a suspect in the lavatory at a bingo hall—but the mayor releases him, before the case is solved. Mickey Rooney was O'Malley.

Edgar Wallace has already been considered. After a visit to Chicago, he wrote a highly successful play, *On the Spot,* first staged in London in 1930, on Broadway a year later, and filmed in 1938 with the title *Dangerous to Know*. Pirelli is a gang leader, based on Al Capone of Cicero and Chicago, who is framed by his mistress, a Chinese woman he had betrayed, for a murder he did not commit—always a dramatic irony. Pirelli is a complex man, given to playing the organ. Charles Laughton made a great hit in the part.

On Your Toes was an outstanding musical first staged in 1936, revived in London in 1984, written by Richard Rodgers and Lorenz Hart, with further creative contributions from George Abbott and George Balanchine. It is a send-up of 1930s film musicals, gangsters, and backstage glamour. Rodgers wrote two ballet scores: "The Princess Zenobia Pastiche," into the comedy, and the famous "Slaughter on 10th Avenue," a literary landmark not to be missed. There is a delicious moment when one dancer in the show has to keep dancing to avoid being shot by gunmen in the stage boxes.

In Belgium in the early 1960s were first seen the films of OSS 117, the hero of many books by Jean Bruce. Later some titles like *Les Anges de Los Angeles* were written by Josette Bruce. OSS 117 is a master spy and counterespionage agent sent round the world, always successful, and with a panache and skill that leave James Bond far behind. One film was *Furia in Bahie pour OSS 117* (1965) with Frederick Stafford, Mylene Dymengeot, and Raymond Pellegrin. As already stated, in one scene OSS 117 enters an operating room on the top floor of a skyscraper, leaps on the arc light over the operating table, then like Berkeley Gray's Norman Conquest, swings forward so his feet send one crook through the windows to the ground, later using the table itself as a battering ram to rout the foe. There are more than a hundred books in this series in French in various paperback editions; like San Antonio and Fantomas, he is hero and legend to the French. Frederick Stafford played the lead in Alfred Hitchcock's 1969 Universal film, *Topaz,* with Dany Robin, based on Leon Uris's 1967 novel.

Paramount on Parade in 1930 was one of the earliest star-studded films made by the Hollywood studios. "The Star Spangled Manner" was another example for excellent wartime entertainment and morale boosting. In the prewar 1930 film Clive Brook (an aristocratic English actor playing Holmes as he had done the previous year in the Paramount *The Return of Sherlock Holmes,* directed by Basil Dean) and William Powell as Philo Vance (which he had also played in 1929 in Paramount's *The Canary Murder Case*) were shot by Warner Oland as Dr. Fu Manchu (whom he had portrayed in 1929 for Paramount in *The Mysterious Dr. Fu Manchu* and in 1930 in *The Return of Dr. Fu Manchu*; he was to play Charlie Chan for Fox from 1931 till his death in 1938). Eugene Pallette played Inspector Queen, Ellery's father. This film was, of course, a spoof on the characters and the genre.

Partners in Crime has been dealt with as Agatha Christie's admitted (and main) parody, including the rather limp 1983 London Weekend Television series. The likable young couple of Tuppence and Tommy Beresford had made earlier appearances, starting with a 1929 German film *Abenteuer, Gmbh* with Carlo Aldini and Eve Gray. An American television program on December 7, 1950, based on the case of the missing lady, starred Lee Bowman and the glamorous Barbara Bel Geddes, then BBC radio had a thirteen-part weekly series, from April 13 to July 13, 1953, starring husband-and-wife team Richard Attenborough and Sheila Sim, who were to be in the opening cast of the world's longest running play, Christie's *The Mousetrap.* Joan Jefferson Farjeon, a designer from a famous family, told me she had been asked to design this play; she refused, but the producer thought it would not run long anyway.

The number of sleuths parodied by Christie is impressive—more than she listed. Douglas Valentine, A. E. W. Mason, G. K. Chesterton, H. C. Bailey, Anthony Berkeley Cox, Edgar Wallace, R. Austin Freeman, Isobel Ostrander, Freeman Wills Croft (and Christie herself) show the depth of her own reading of detective fiction.

Police Squad was a hilarious American parody of police procedural series, shown on BBC-TV in 1989, and later a big-screen film as *The Naked Gun.* Leslie Nielson played Detective (later Lieutenant) Frank Drebin, and every cliché was neatly hit: Drive back to the office—so the car is driven backward; just one stop—a crash. Detectives are guarding a threatened dance teacher—so the fat coppers are rehearsing in leotards. Titles never agree with captions. The cast lists never tally (e.g., Abraham Lincoln and

William Shatner). The canteen and car wash are actually in the police office. Drebin disguises himself as a locksmith in a protection racket; the "L" is blown off his window, so a farmer arrives with his ox. The freeze-frames so beloved by series like *Murder, She Wrote* are used—but the coffee keeps flowing. A fight starts with a gun, then a knife, then a club, then a Picasso. If a name rings a bell, it rings. A convict has his name on his shirt. An attorney is blown up into a tree. The coats and clothes in a charity box question a woman—and so on. On the BBC-TV *Wogan Show,* Nielsen said it was a series you had to watch all the time to avoid missing points. The film *The Naked Gun* had Drebin having to foil a plot to blow up the queen on her visit to Los Angeles; Victor Ludwig was the villain, his assistant Victoria (Priscilla Presley) tracking Drebin.

Private Dick, a play by Richard Maher and Roger Mitchell, opened at the Whitehall Theatre, London, on June 26, 1982. Robert Powell was Philip Marlowe, Lee Montague was Raymond Chandler and three other characters, another actor played four parts, and an actress played Miss Wonderly. Music was provided by a pianist and drummer, and was of the period. There was an ingenious set of offices, fire escapes, and distant skyscrapers; the actual program was in the form of a notebook. The throwaway said, "Philip Marlow [sic], private dick, grabbed the phone. The man said he was in trouble and that the name was Raymond Chandler." Chandler does seek Marlowe's advice and help, and is therefore involved in one of his own mysteries, with the intriguing Miss Wonderly (the pseudonym of the heroine of *The Maltese Falcon*). Interesting, a trifle confusing, unusual, fast moving with four players taking ten roles, but it was a play of atmosphere.

Playwright Tom Stoppard wrote a parodic play, *The Real Inspector Hound,* with characters like Mrs. Drudge and Simon Gascoyne, at Muldoon Manor, with nearby cliffs, high water, and swamps. When it was presented at London's Olivier Theatre, one critic called it "a country-house mystery in the manner of Dorothy L. Sayers," another that it was "verbally over-wrought parody of an Agatha Christie," and third was "reviewing a conventional country-house murder mystery." It had many of the Golden Age touches, from telephoning parlor-maids to stolid police.

In the article by Regis Messac, "Les Parodies de Roman Policiers," in *813* (no. 14, December 1985), appears a play, *Roi* granddaughter and André's ex-wife. She is not helped by being kidnapped, seeing one kidnapper shot, and finding a valuable Stradivarius violin in Rome Station—with a microfilm in the bow. Was her husband a Swiss terrorist or a CIA member recruited at Oxford University to combat communism (as opposed to Cambridge men recruited for the Soviet Union, like Burgess, MacLean, et al.)? She finds André was not blown up in the airplane explosion, he reappears to help then flies off to another life in Singapore, where it seems Colette will one day join him happily and secretly, now she knows he was an honorable spy. There are some exciting car chases, delightful scenery, good characterizations, humor, and tension in this screenplay by Daniele Thompson. There are some similarities with the film *Charade* (1963), directed by Stanley Donen, with Cary Grant, Audrey Hepburn, Walter Matthau, and James Coburn, where Hepburn returns to her Paris flat to find all her furniture already gone, and she does not know which man to trust. Part of *Charade* seems to have been shot in the charming, comfortable Ste. Anne Hotel, in rue Ste. Anne, in the First Arrondissement.

In May 1970, the well-known stage designer Sidney Jarvis invited my mother and me to see a play at Leatherhead, Surrey, for which he had designed the set—a play which had not been performed since 1922. *The Silent House* was written by John G. Brandon and a coauthor about whom little is known, George Pickett. The play was a comedy-thriller with lashings of bravura. Two former members of the Royal Flying Corps (predecessor to the Royal Air Force in World War I) take a country mansion. A mysterious Portuguese appears from a secret passage, only to be murdered. A menacing Chinese doctor and his beautiful English ward live at the Red House on Barnes Common, with a room capable of being flooded with poison gas for unwelcome visitors. Ex-convict Bruiser Badger Hawkins appears as an unlikely "butler." There is a fortune in missing bonds which must be discovered by a certain date not too far off, but the hiding place is guarded by a cobra which kills the villain after the hero has saved the heroine. This production was directed with a distinct leaning to parody, but Ivan Butler, actor-producer and author of such books as *Murderer's London,* wrote on July 9, 1983, that the 1922 production was definitely not a parody. No copies of the script had been traced for years, said the theatre program. John Gordon Brandon (1879–

(1908), by Flers, Caillavet, and Arène. Act 1, scene 7 refers
"parodies du genre les plus spirituelles," with Commissaire S
cial Blond "Disciple de Sherlock Holmes" analyzing the trou
knees of the rich Deputy Bourdier, asking why he is sitting in
own study, in a coat three years old, with ink on his finger
strange expression, etc.:

> *Blond:* Vous êtes le secrétaire de M. Bourdier.
> *Bourdier:* Mais, Monsieur, vous m'embêtez. Je suis M.
> Bourdier!
> *Blond:* Vous êtes . . .
> *Bourdier:* Je suis M. Bourdier lui-même!
> *Blond:* En bien, Monsieur, vous avez tort!

We have seen other examples in this and earlier chapters
only apparent correct diagnosis being completely wrong.
   Roxie Hart certainly made a hilarious, irreverent mocl
the law and parody of the genre. It first appeared as t!
Chicago, in America in 1928, from Warner Bros., with
Haver, Victor Varconi, and Robert Edeson. In 1942 the n
sion was *Roxie Hart,* with Ginger Rogers as the heroine,
Menjou as the lawyer, script and production by Nunnally J
direction by William Wellman, music by Alfred Newm
Lynne Overman and George Montgomery in the cast. T!
is of a showgirl whose lawyer tells her to stand trial for
of which she is definitely innocent—for the publicity
gets her off. The stage musical was titled *Chicago* agair
two West End runs. The story is based on an actual eve
is alleged that one of the women featured was living in
and would not agree to a production while she was stil!
   The Secret Drawer (Le Tiroir Secret) was designed 1
part series on French television; it was shown on BBC
parts, with English subtitles, on January 1 and 2, 1987,
famous Michele Morgan, and other well-known act
Gelin, Jeanne Moreau, and Rossano Brazzi). After he
band André's death, the elegant Parisienne Colette f!
taking all her furniture for an unknown debt; in a secr
a desk is a wallet, with a photograph, luggage ticket, e
to solve the mystery of his double life, helped by her
band, an inspector of police, and her family, main!

1941) was a prolific author. He invented Ronald Sturges Vereker Purvale—RSVP—for the Sexton Blake series. His books included *The Big Heart* (1924), *Young Love,* and many others. *The Silent House,* "the book of the famous play by John G. Brandon and George Pickett," was published by Cassell in 1928, copyright by John G. Brandon. The story starts with a voyage to England, then the young Chinese nobleman in Oxford, visiting the East End, meeting Badger Hawkins, then developing on much the same lines as the drama on stage. Adaptations from books can take many and varied directions; for example, the long-running West End stage play *Murder at the Vicarage* and the later BBC-TV version had marked differences from Agatha Christie's 1930 book.

The Singing Detective was a BBC-TV serial by Dennis Potter in November 1986, and was the subject of much comment over indecency and obscurity of plot, which had also been leveled at his previous work. The serial had a very confused story with various anomalies. Philip Marlowe, writer of cheap detective stories, in the hospital with skin diseases, is foul mouthed, bad tempered, ungrateful, and rude. The time is the present; he appears to be in his fifties, or nearly. He says his parents christened him Philip deliberately, but the first Marlowe book was not published until 1939. His books are shown with gaudy, colored covers, but not the normal paperback size or like the former Sexton Blake Library, rather a little like the 1930s abridged series mentioned earlier, apparently already out of print. Potter's gimmick in this and other serials is to transmogrify the characters into song-and-dance men and women, singing a number of the 1930s, 1940s, or 1950s, miming to the actual voices of Bing Crosby or Connie Boswell or the Ink Spots, whichever fits best. Similarly the people around the antihero take roles in his earlier life or his fantasies—the nurse as a nightclub hostess, for example. The series added nothing to the genre, which Potter said he admired. The serial is not to be confused with the earlier book, *The Dancing Detective*.

Sleuth was a successful play and film by Antony Shaffer, with a clever stunt over the "actors" in each scene. Julian Symons, in *Bloody Murder,* referred to the author "whose affectionate send-up of Golden Age stories in his play *Sleuth* was much acclaimed." Antony is the barrister half of the twins who write together as "Peter Antony." Even the programs add to the plot's complexities.

More films come into this chapter. Garson Kanin wrote the 1956 *The Girl Can't Help It*; E. C. Bentley's *Trent's Last Case*; and the others already mentioned. A famous comedy was the 1959 *Some Like It Hot,* United Artists, directed by Billy Wilder and written, as a book, by Wilder and I. A. L. Diamond, featuring Jack Lemmon and Tony Curtis masquerading as members of a ladies orchestra. The film reproduced the St. Valentine's Day Massacre, 1929, at Bugs Moran's headquarters—2122 North Clark Street, Chicago—and also starred George Raft. This is not to be confused with the film of the same name in 1938, later retitled *Rhythm Romance,* with Bob Hope and Shirley Ross, Hope's least favorite picture, but which had the excellent song "The Lady's in Love with You." Interesting though that one of the men killed in the garage (of which the bricks were later sold for $250 each) was not a gangster but a professional man who liked mixing with them. The Hope film, which also starred the great drummer-bandleader Gene Krupa, had previously been filmed in 1934, as *Shoot the Works,* and they were based on the famous play *The Great Magoo* by Wilkie C. Mahoney, Ben Hecht, and Gene Fowler.

Agatha Christie has indulged lightly in parody and pastiche, and one of her plays had this touch—*Spider's Web,* at London's famous Savoy Theatre, starting a long run in 1954. The effervescent wife of a Foreign Office man, Clarisa, played by Margaret Lockwood, says, "Suppose I were to find a dead body in the drawing-room? What am I to do?" The rented house has a sliding panel, which makes her teenage daughter Pippa think, "It would be very convenient for holding a dead body, wouldn't it?" So much happens in a few hours—murder, stolen goods, blackmail, secret panel, and whatever, all in a lighthearted way with little consideration for the bemused police—that her staid husband puts it all down to her romanticizing. In *Theatre* (1954/55), Ivor Brown, a distinguished theatre critic, pointed out in his review that *copia* ("plenty") was once the greatest asset. Sophocles wrote 100 plays, Euripides 92, Lope Da Vega 2,000, and Goldoni 300. Compare at this juncture the number of symphonies—how they have dwindled since Haydn, or remember there were 25,000 operas written before A.D. 1700—how many since? He then approvingly noted Christie always has humor in her murder plots: "Has any writer had a greater corpus of corpse-ridden books and plays? . . . For her the library or the lounge-hall immediately becomes a mortuary:

the routine is as regular as clockwork: instruments, blunt and sharp, have been employed: the staff are easily suspect—they still have resident domestics in Christie's household—and the kith, kin, and local gentry contain the right ration of shifty characters." He pointed out this comedy-drama was just right for Margaret Lockwood's return to the stage, coupled with her Eliza in Shaw's *Pygmalion*. He asked how many realize the title comes from the "tangled web we weave / When first we practice to deceive"— Who wrote that? Walter Scott, in stanza 6 of "Marmion."

A British film which can claim to have helped the cause of parody was *Summer Lightning,* starring Ralph Lynn, who, with actor George Grossmith, helped evolve the character of Wodehouse's Bertie Wooster. It was, of course, based on Wodehouse's 1929 novel. Although I never met Wodehouse, I did have a letter from Guy Bolton, asking if I would be interested in revising with him the book of the musical *If I Were You.*

Super-Sleuth was a 1937 film, written by Gertrude Purcell and Ernest Pagana, directed by Ben Stoloff. Jack Oakie was Willard Martin, a top movie 'tec, living in a mansion, Ann Sothern was his girlfriend Mary Strand, Edgar Kennedy was Lieutenant Garrison, and Eduardo Cianelli was the mysterious Professor Herman. Martin, always criticizing the police, receives two threatening letters, so he brings in police as actors, but the leading man is shot by mistake, a jilted extra is charged, a lineup of men for witnesses to identify fails to pinpoint the professor, but picks Martin. His girlfriend has him arrested for safety, as she is worried by his attempting real-life detection, but the professor bails him out. This professor owns the "Crime Does Not Pay Exhibition" with some fascinating items, like guillotines, and his final fight with Martin brings most of them into action, together with the professor's black butler, with a sound-effects van to complicate the issue. Martin, wielding a Sherlock Holmes pipe, is victorious, and as always with this comic actor, incorrigible.

The theme of a nonbrave hero forced into heroics has been popular since the Broadway play by Edward Childs Carpenter which first produced the film *Whistling in the Dark* (1932) with Ernest Truex (the voice of President Truman on films), Una Merkel, and Edward Arnold (who also played Nero Wolfe on screen) as the villain. The 1940s film had Lionel Atwill as the villain, with Walley Brown and Alan Carney as the sleuths. There were three Red

Skelton films. First was *Whistling in Dixie,* with Ann Rutherford, Rags Ragland, and George Bancroft in 1942, *Whistling in the Dark* a year later, then *Whistling in Brooklyn,* with Ann Rutherford and Rags Ragland again, Henry O'Neill, Sam Levene, William Frawley, and Steve Geray. A similar film was *The Fox,* also in 1943.

BBC-TV showed a spoof-thriller on December 19, 1983, *Talent for Murder,* with Angela Lansbury (who had played Miss Marple) as a wheelchair-bound crime novelist, Laurence Olivier as her doctor, and Hildegarde Neil as her daughter-in-law. Perhaps from this came the long-running Universal Television series *Murder, She Wrote*; this is not to be confused with *Murder, He Says,* which in turn came from a line in a ballad: "He says Murder, he says, as he holds me in his arms." This series started in England on Sunday, May 19, 1985, with Angela Lansbury as Jessica Fletcher, starting a career as a crime novelist and Marple-type sleuth in New England. "Who Killed Sherlock Holmes?" was a murder at a fancy dress party in a publisher's country house, with Arthur Hill as guest artiste. Cyd Charisse, who appeared in one story, said in an interview she had played a "red-herring" in the series; Milton Berle, Vivian Blaine, Robert Stack, and Van Johnson have also appeared. Later stories were slightly shorter, as is usual. *The Murder of Sherlock Holmes* by James Anderson was published in paperback, then came two more: *Murder, She Wrote,* based on *Deadly Lady* by Peter S. Fischer, and *Hooray for Homicide,* based on a story so titled by Robert Van Scoyk. One has a producer murdered before he can turn a Fletcher book into a sex horror movie; the other has four daughters who might push their millionaire father overboard in a hurricane, when he is safe in Fletcher's front yard.

"The Teddy Bear Who Knew Too Much" was a delightful title of a lengthy playlet in a top-running BBC-TV comedy series, *The Two Ronnies,* with comedians Ronnie Corbett and Ronnie Barker (who is also a brilliant actor). Corbett was Miss Marple, Barker was Poirot, Jenny Agutter and Ian Ogilvy were the family of a colonel found murdered in his stately home, and Barbara Miller (who had appeared in the international BBC-TV series *Blackadder*) was the shortsighted housekeeper, Mrs. Tremble, who mistakes a hatstand for Poirot, and, challenged to fire a gun, smashes ornaments and even a suit of armor in all directions. Miss Marple proves Poirot did the murder, after hiding under the bed, so the bullet went through the colonel's teddy bear. Not only was this excruciatingly funny, but the script was so correct, and the stately home hired by the BBC was a magnificent mansion owned by a famous family near Windsor.

That Man From Rio was a French film mocking spies and sleuths, directed by Philippe de Broca, and with Jean-Paul Belmondo, Françoise Dorleac, Jean Servais, and Adolfo Celi, made in 1964.

Theatre of Film Noir was a play by George F. Walker, staged at the Institute of Contemporary Arts, London, in June 1983, a "parody of [the] French idea of Forties American gangster movies," dating from Paris in 1944.

Time to Kill was a strange hybrid 20th Century–Fox film of 1942, based on Chandler's *The High Window*. Lloyd Nolan, as Mike Shayne, takes this case from Marlowe; also playing were Heather Angel, Ethel Griffies, Ralph Byrd, directed by Herbert Leeds. Chandler's *Farewell, My Lovely* became a Falcon film in 1942: *The Falcon Takes Over* from RKO, with George Sanders. It was the last time they each played their respective series sleuth.

A Tomb with a View was a new play at the Palace Avenue Theatre, Paignton, South Devon, in August 1986, written, promoted, and featuring Norman Robbins. Ingredients include the reading of Tomb's will, Marcus Tomb thinking he is Julius Caesar, sister Dora giving arsenic and hemlock in homemade wine, and Emile in man's attire. Monica a man-eater, Lucian a megalomaniac, elder brother Oliver in the cellar, the ugly maid Agatha, solicitor, house cut off, three visitors including a strange nurse—this seems to be parodying Agatha Christie and *Arsenic and Old Lace,* and one critic said it had too many red herrings.

Too Many Crooks was a pastiche musical presented by an amateur group, the Inter Varsity Club at St. Mary Abbot's Hall, London, on May 15, 1975. The book was by Joan Meier, lyrics by Clive Chester, and ingenious music by Peter Gladstone Smith, all club members. It told a rather Father-Brownish Anglican canon solving jewel thefts in Paris and on the Riviera, with an American duchess, an ambassador, tourists, criminals, and a disguised policeman in a large cast.

Underground was a play by Michael Sloan, which first starred Peter Byrne, Leon Greene, and Dave King. A beautiful set of an underground train was the best part of the play. The train ends up in a siding; there is a murder and an attempted murder, all passengers in the coach prove to have a grievance against the Swiss Embassy official traveling with an official bag, but who was a Nazi; the dead and wounded were not, so they all ask the ex-Nazi to commit suicide—and off goes the train. Shades of *Murder* and *Minder*—on what Express? It was revived in July 1983, with Raymond Burr (Perry Mason and Ironside), but one critic referred to the "incredulity of it all."

Vivement Dimanche was a 1983 François Truffaut film with Fanny Ardant, and Jean-Louis Trintignant, as a homage to the 1960s hard-boiled Charles Williams thrillers, with dead blondes, shady lawyers, suspicious maids, and atmosphere. One critic said, "It never stretches itself beyond the limits of pastiche. . . . It's dangerously near to self-parody" (which cannot be easy). Another referred to "rather dubious delight in counterfeiting the jigsaw construction and wised-up tone of a better-than-average B movie."

Where There's A Will was the title of a Will Hay film comedy in the 1930s about a lawyer whose office is used by American gangsters to rob the bank beneath, and later of a detective story, but the title was used yet again in program no. 45, November 27, 1956, no. 3545, in the *Sergeant Bilko* television comedy series. Written by Nat Hiken, Leonard Stern, Tony Webster, and Billy Friedburg, this story had Gregg Chickering, cut off by his late uncle with just one dollar and a one-eyed parrot named Cyclops. Bilko tells the mean cousins the parrot holds the clue to a treasure map, to induce them to buy the parrot, but Chickering believes him and will not sell it. This is an obvious parody of *The Maltese Falcon*. The show depicted the original movie protagonists—Bogart, Lorre, Greenstreet, Cook—with Bilko as a stripe-suited, winking criminal, the Weasel, with a farrago of improbable plots involving a range of fictional, extravagant criminals. Chickering's four scheming relations, who had inherited the entire estate, prove as gullible as the ex-soldier to the extent of combining to trace a mythical $30 million diamond cache on an imaginary island. Silvers's soldiers impersonate *The Maltese Falcon* cast.

Who Done It? was a 1942 Universal comedy-thriller featuring comedians Bud Abbot and Lou Costello as soda-jerks at a New York radio station where murder occurs. It was written by Stanley Roberts, Edmund Joseph, and John Grant, and features also William Gargan, Louise Allbritton, Patric Knowles, and William Benddix, directed by Erle C. Kenton.

Whodunnit? was a play by Anthony Shaffer, originally titled in 1979 *The case of the Oily Levantine*; in 1982 in New York it was Whodunnit? and touring in Great Britain in 1986 and 1987 under the latter title. With *Murderer*, they were both sequels to *Sleuth*. Shaffer wrote screenplays for Christie's *Death on the Nile, Evil Under the Sun*, and *Death Comes as the End*. The description reads: "The play is meant to be a pastiche of the classic 'thirties' detective stories when everyone not English is a yid, a dago or a wop." Acts 1 and 2 are set in the Chapel of Orcas Champflower Manor; the cast included Lynda Baron, Michael Knowles, and Jack Douglas playing such characters as the butler, Andreas Capidistriou (the oily Levantine), the respectable family lawyer, the eccentric archaeologist, Lady Tremurrain the dotty aristocrat ("murrain" is a pestilence), Dame Edith Runcible (echoes of Edward Lear), a ne'er-do-well, etc. Times: early and later evening. The throwaway calls it "the fatally funny murder mystery" and asks, "Who's who in the Gothic Mansion? Whose is the mystery voice? going on to refer to two chilly murders. One review commented, "despite its air of satire," and a letter to *the Stage* criticized its being called a new comedy-thriller, and said one needed to magnifying glass to read the program notes.

A Woman's Vengeance (Universal International, 1948) is worthy of note because the script was by Aldous Huxley (1894-1963) in Hollywood, was based on his own 1922 story, *A Giaconda Smile*, which we have seen was in turn based on the actual Greenwood murder case. Zoltan Korda was director and producer, Charles Boyer played Henry Maurier, Jessica Tandy Janet Spence, and Cedric Hardwicke the Doctor.

Bibliography

Adams, Tom. *Agatha Christie: The Art of Her Crimes* London: Everest House. 1981.

Barbour, Alan G. *A Thousand and One Delights* New York: Collier. 1971.

Barnard, Robert. *A Talent to Deceive* London: Collins. 1980.

Boileau-Narcejac. *Le Roman Policier* Paris: Universitaires de France. 1975.

Brean, Herbert (Ed). *The Mystery Writer's Handbook* New York: Harper & Bros. 1956.

Burack, A. S. (Ed). *Writing Detective & Mystery Fiction* Boston: The Writer Inc. 1967.

Busby, Ian. *Bloodhounds of Heaven* Harvard: Harvard University Press. 1976.

Butler, Wm. Vivian. *The Durable Desperadoes* London: Macmillan. 1973.

Cameron, Ian. *A Pictorial History of Crime Files* London: Hamlyn. 1975.

Chandler, Raymond. *The Notebooks of Raymond Chandler* London: Weidenfeld & Nicolson. 1976.

Chandler, Raymond. *Pearls are A Nuisance* London: Penguin. 1950.

Charles Rarebooks. *Catalogue* Buntingford: Charles Rarebooks. 1955.

Chesterton, G. K. *The Defendant* London: J. M. Dent & Sons Ltd. 1901.

———. *Crimewave* 75 London: Michael Joseph. 1971.

Craig, Patricia and Cadogan, Mary. *The Lady Investigates* London: Victor Gollancz Ltd. 1981.

Freeman, Lucy (Ed). *The Murder Mystique* New York: Frdk. Ungar. 1982.

Green, Roger Lancelyn. *Tellers of Tales* London: Edmund Ward. 1946.

Greene Paulette. *Mystery Detective & Science Fiction Catalogue 5* New York: Paulette Green. 1983.

Gross, Miriam (Ed). *The World of Raymond Chandler* London: Weidenfeld & Nicolson. 1977.

Haining, Peter. *Agatha Christie Murder in Four Acts* London: Virgin Books. 1990.

Hart, Anne. *The Life and Times of Hercule Poirot* London: Pavilion Books Ltd. 1990.

———. *The Life and Times of Miss Jane Marples* London: Dodd, Mead & Co., Inc. 1985.

Haycraft, Howard (Ed). *The Art of the Mystery Story* New York: Simon & Schuster. 1946.

Haycraft, Howard (Ed). *Murder for Pleasure* London: Peter Davies. 1942.

Henderson, Lesley (Ed). *Twentieth-Century Crime and Mystery Writers,* 3rd Edition Chicago: St. James Press. 1991.

Highsmith, Patricia. *Plotting and Writing Suspense Fiction* London: Popular Press. 1983.

Keating, H.R.F. (Ed). *Agatha Christie First Lady of Crime* London: Weidenfeld & Nicolson. 1977.

———. *Crime Writers* London: B.B.C. 1978.

———. *Murder Must Appetize* London: Lemon Tree Press. 1975.

———. *Whodunnit?* London: Winward. 1982.

La Cour, Tage and Mogensen, Harold. *The Murder Book* London: Book Club Association. 1971.

Lane, Margaret. *Edgar Wallace* London: The Book Club. 1939.

Lofts, W.O.G. and Adley, D. J. *The Men Behind Boys' Fiction* London: Howard Baker. 1970.

Luhr, William. *Raymond Chandler and Film* New York: Ungar Publishing. 1982.

Mandel, Ernest. *Delightful Murder* London: Pluto Press. 1984.

Maugham, W. Somerset. *The Vagrant Mood* London: Wlm. Heinemann Ltd. 1952.

McCleary, G. F. *On Detective Fiction and Other Things* London: Hollis & Carter. 1960.

Melling, John Kennedy. *Alchemy of Murder: A Clinical Survey of Crime Writers* London: 1993.

———. *Gwendoline Butler—The Inventor of the Women's Police Procedural* London: 1993.

———. *Murder Done to Death* London: 1979.

———. *Planning Murder Parties* London: 1995.

Morgan, Janet. *Agatha Christie (A Biography)* London: Collins. 1984.

Narcejac, Thomas. *Un Machine a Lire: Le Roman Policier* Paris: Denoel Gonthier. 1975.

O'Brien, Geoffrey. *Hardboiled America* New York: Van Nostrand Reinhold. 1981.

Pate, Janet. *The Book of Sleuths* London: New English Library. 1977.

———. *The Book of Spies and Secret Agents* London: Galley Press. 1978.

Quayle, Eric. *The Collector's Book of Detective Fiction* London: Studio Vista. 1972.

Ramsey, G. C. *Agatha Christie Mistress of Mystery* London: Collins. 1967.

Raymond, John. *Simenon in Court* London: Hamish Hamilton. 1968.

Reed, J. D. *Mistress of Murder* New York: Time Magazine. 1986.

Routley, Erik. *The Puritan Pleasures of the Detective Story* London: Victor Gollancz Ltd. 1972.

Ryan, Elizabeth Bond and Eakins, William J. *The Lord Peter Wimsey Cookbook* New York: Ticknor & Fields, USA. 1981.

Sayers, Dorothy L. *Unpopular Opinions* London: Victor Gollancz Ltd. 1946.

Scott-Giles, C. W. *The Wimsey Family* London: New English Library. 1977.

Snelling, O. F. *A Report by 007 James Bond* London: Panther. 1964.

Stafford, William T. (Ed). *Modern Fiction Studies* West Lafayette, Ind.: Purdue University. 1983.

Steinbrunner, Chris and Penzier, Otto. *Encyclopaedia of Mystery and Detection* London: Routledge & Kegan Paul. 1976.

Stewart, R. F. *. . . And Always a Detective* Newton Abbot: David & Charles. 1981.

Symons, Julian. *Bloody Murder* London: Faber & Faber. 1972.

———. *The Detective Story in Britain London:* Longmans, Green & Co. 1962.

———. *The Great Detectives* London: Orbis. 1981.

Tani, Stefano. *The Doomed Detective* Carbondale, Ill.: Southern Illinois University Press. 1984.

Tanner, Lt.-Col. William. *The Book of Bond* London: Pan Margaret Flash. 1966.

Thoorens, Leon. *Qui Etes Vous Georges Simenon* Brussels: (Belgium) 1959.

Turner, E. S. *Boys Will Be Boys* London: Michael Joseph. 1948.

Usborne, Richard. *Clubland Heroes* London: Hutchinson. 1953 (1974).

Watson, Colin. *Snobbery With Violence* London: Eyre Methuen. 1971.

Winn, Dilys. *Murder Ink* New York: Westbridge Books. 1977.

———. *Murderess Ink* New York: Westbridge Books. 1979.

Index

Abbott, Anthony, 46, 131–132
Ace Crawford, Private Eye, 213
Adams, Samuel Hopkins, 131–132
Adams, Tom, 175
Adler, Bill, 195
Aldini, Carlo, 249
Aldridge, Michael, 219, 224
Alington, Adrian, 58
Allen, Steve, 35
Alleyn, Roderick, 7, 32–33, 140, 142, 165
Allingham, Marjorie, 8, 18, 24, 29, 35–36, 61, 80, 134, 180
Alphaville, 213
Ambler, Eric, 45, 106
Ameche, Don, 237
American Dream, 213–214
Ames, Delano, 29–30
Amis, Kingsley, 137–138, 180, 189
Anderson, James, 138–141
Anderson, Loni, 108
Antony, Peter, 49, 253
Any Roads to Murder, 202
Appleby, Sir John, 55, 84, 117, 140, 165
April Robin Murder, The, 169, 183
Archer, Lew, 79, 122, 145
Arden, Eve, 92
Aristotle, 34, 152, 154, 211
Arlen, Michael, 22, 168, 184
Armstrong, Anthony, 128–129
Arnold, Dorothy, 48, 102

Arnold, Thomas, 1
Arsenic and Old Lace, 214, 221–222, 257
Arthur, Gwynfil, 135
Asdell, Phillip T., 131
Ashcroft, Peggy, 240
Asher, Jane, 207
Asimov, Isaac, 7, 113, 189–190, 193
Askey, Arthur, 216–217, 223
Astaire, Adele, 217
Astaire, Fred, 217
Astor, Mary, 28, 215
Atkinson, Alex, 58
Attenborough, Richard, 249
Auden, W. H., 37, 100–101
Austen, Jane, 18
Austin, Bliss, 57
Avelone, Mike, 53, 59
Avengers, The, 109, 214–216

Babson, Marian, 74, 140, 141–142, 147, 185, 186
Bacall, Lauren, 141
Bailey, H. C., 8, 18, 24, 61, 67, 249
Baines, Carfax, 8
Baker, Sam S., 27
Baker Street, 245
Ball, Brian, 142–143
Band Waggon, 217
Band Wagon, 216–217
Band Wagon, The, 217
Bankhead, Tallulah, 143
Banks, Leslie, 182

Bantock, Neil, 190
Barker, Ronnie, 68, 256–257
Barnard, Robert, 36–37, 54, 130, 186
Barnett, James, 37
Barnum, Phineas T., 5
Barr, Robert, 11
Battle, Superintendent, 120, 201
Baxt, George, 59, 143
Baxter's Last Case, 218
Beach, Vernon, 8
Beatty, Clyde, 149
Beef, Sergeant Matthew, 117
Beef, Sergeant William, 115–118, 123
Bel Geddes, Barbara, 249
Bel Geddes, Norman, 217
Bell, Daisy, 8
Bell, Dr. Joseph, 43, 91, 172
Bell, Roger T., 75, 172
Bellem, Robert Leslie, 136
Belmondo, Jean-Paul, 221, 233, 257
Bennett, Alan, 30
Bennett, Arnold, 75
Bennett, Dorothea, 143
Bennett, Olive, 48
Benny, Jack, 54
Bentley, E. C., 8, 46, 60, 87, 133–134, 163–164
Beresford, Tommy, 67, 118–120
Beresford, Tuppence, 67, 118–120
Bergerac, 187
Bergman, Andrew, 89, 143
Berkeley, Anthony, 14, 18, 24, 45, 49–50, 51, 61, 127–128, 129–130, 133–134, 138, 144, 163–164, 249
Biederman, Jerry, 93
Big Enchilada, The, 166
Big Noise, The, 235
Biggers, Earl Derr, 8, 112, 181

Bingham, John, 45, 89
Binyon, T. J., 89, 144
Birns, Margaret, 61
Biter Bit, The, 12
Black Bird, The, 218
Black, William, 83
Blackshirt (Richard Verrall), 79, 184
Blaise, Modesty, 109–110
Blake, Nicholas, 37, 87, 149, 195
Blake, Sexton, 8, 31, 41–42, 54, 112, 124, 134–135, 180, 184, 253
Blakeney, Sir Percy, Baronet, 18, 211
Blakeney, T. S., 147
Bland, C. Maurice, 211
Bleak House, 7
Bloch, Robert, 192
Block, Lawrence, 144–145
Blume, Wilhelm, xiii, 43–44
Blumenthal, John, 61
Blyton, Enid, 196
Bogart, Humphrey, 28, 48, 59, 75–76, 89, 91, 107, 143, 215, 225, 226, 246, 258
Bognor, Simon, 80–81
Boileau-Narcejac, 20, 26, 97, 110, 130
Bolton, Guy, 255
Bond, James, 27, 68, 73, 74–75, 78, 89–90, 95, 109, 110, 138, 143, 172–173, 180, 189, 220–221
Borges, Jorge Luis, 11, 16, 72–73
Borsalino, 213
Boston Quackie, 218
Boucher, Anthony, 49, 79, 150
Bowman, Lee, 249
Boyer, Charles, 221, 259
Bradley, Dame Beatrice L'Estrange, 127–128
Brahms, S. J., 22, 23, 176–177

Index

Bramah, Ernest, ix, 145–146
Branch, Pamela, 21
Brand, Christianna, 64, 128
Brandon, John G., 134, 252–253
Breen, Jon L., 2, 61, 94, 112–114, 184, 190
Breslin, Jimmy, 62
Brett, Dixon, 8
Brett, Simon, 60, 63–64, 65, 114–115, 146, 190
Brooks, Edwy Searles, 25, 134
Brown, Father, ix, 8, 9, 39, 67, 70, 116, 118, 123, 212
Browning, Robert, 34, 152
Brownrigg, Nurse, 47
Bruce, Jean, 89, 248
Bruce, Leo, 115–118
Bruce, Nigel, 161
Brumpton, Keith, 189
Brunt, Thomas, 159
Buchan, John, 8, 30, 61, 172, 182
Buchanan, Jack, 217
Bulldog Jack, 219
Bullshot, 219
Bullshot Crummond, 219
Burke, James, 208
Burr, Raymond, 181, 258
Busby, Ian, 71
Bush, Christopher, 116, 163
Butler, Ellis Parker, 75
Butler, Gwendoline, 6, 39–40, 45, 57, 68–69, 109, 125, 146–147, 162, 163, 178, 188, 208, 211, 243
Butler, Ragan, 147
Butler, William Vivian, 38, 65–66, 180–181
Butterworth, Michael, 64, 147

Cadfael, Brother, 166–167
Cagney, James, 59, 68, 230
Cain, James M., 134
Caldicott and Charters, 223–224

Calling All Detectives, 207
Campbell, R. T., 30–31
Campion, Albert, 18, 24, 29, 35–36, 61, 81, 116, 180, 184
Canning, Elisabeth, 47
Cannon, Jo Ann, 137
Capone, Al, 48, 81, 148, 178, 242, 248
Cargill, Patrick, 24, 25, 139
Carmichael, Ian, 18, 24, 127, 224
Carnell, Jennifer, 64
Carr, John Dickson, 8, 31, 37–38, 44, 67, 82, 113, 117, 123, 128, 137–138, 189
Carrados, Max, ix, 145
Carroll, Amy, 190
Carry on Laughing, 220
Carter, Lynda, 108
Carter, Nick, 68
Carter, Philip Youngman, 180
Cartier, 45
Cartmell, Cleve, 170
Caruso, Enrico, 166
Case for Mickey Slain, A, 220
Case of the Dead Flamingo Dancer, 243
Case of the Oily Levantine, The, 220, 259
Cashman, John, 45
Casino Royale, 220–221
Caspary, Vera, 44
Cat and the Canary, The, 212, 214, 221–222, 229, 232, 245
Cecil, David, 39–40
Cecil, Jonathan, 39–40
Chambers, Peter, 147–148
Chambrun, Pierre, 113
Chan, Charlie, 7, 32, 62, 82, 112–113, 181, 184, 249
Chance, John Newton, 135, 142
Chancellor, John, 128–129
Chandler Raymond, 8, 9, 19, 27, 31, 33, 61, 62, 65, 67, 75, 76,

89, 91, 93, 114, 123, 148, 155, 157, 161, 165, 175, 183–186, 199, 225, 232, 233, 243, 246, 250, 257
Charisse, Cyd, 217, 256
Charles, Nick, 27, 30, 41, 82, 238
Charles, Nora, 27, 30, 41, 119
Charlie Chan and the Curse of the Dragon Queen, 223
Charlie's Angels, 216
Charteris, Leslie, 18, 38–39, 65–66, 89, 148
Chase, James Hadley, 20, 148, 223, 244
Chastain, Thomas, 181, 195
Cheap Detective, The, 224–225, 238
Chenevier, Charles, 48, 96
Chesterton, G. K., ix, 8, 9, 31, 37, 39, 51, 58, 60, 66–67, 129–130, 133, 138, 148, 171, 249
Cheyney, Peter, 198, 201, 213
Christie, Agatha, 8, 16, 18, 21, 24, 32, 33, 39, 49, 64, 67–68, 80, 82, 104, 112, 114–115, 118–120, 123, 129–130, 133–134, 136, 138, 139, 140, 141, 148, 153, 159, 162, 163–164, 175–178, 185, 186, 189, 193, 201, 205, 206, 210, 220, 226–227, 233, 236, 237, 240, 241, 245, 249, 250, 253, 254–255, 257, 259
Chung Apana, 181
Churchill, Winston, 38, 70, 104, 139, 177, 244
City of Angels, 214, 220, 243
Clark, Mary Higgins, 126
Cluedo, 200, 201–202, 203, 204, 208–209
Clues, 10, 19
Clyde, Derek, 8
Cochrane, Molly, 126

Coffin, Commander John, 146–147
Coghill, Professor Neville, 39
Colbert, Claudette, 132
Cole, George, 220, 237
Collins, Max Allan, 126, 148, 178
Collins, Michael, 18
Collins, Wilkie, 6, 7, 12, 13, 38, 41, 49, 61
Colosimo, Big Jim, 154
Colt, Thatcher, 132
Connell, Brian, 182
Connolly, Cyril, 68, 87–88, 101
Conquest, John, 144, 165
Conquest, Norman, 25, 77
Conti, Tom, 214
Conway, Tom, 170, 184
Cooper, J. W., 42
Copper, Basil, 148–149, 151, 235
Corbett, Ronnie, 68, 256–257
Cork, Captain Jeremy, 168
Cory, Desmond, 120–121
Courtneidge, Cecily, 219, 223
Coward, Noël, 44, 150, 213
Cracks, 225
Creasy, John, 8, 112, 181
Crimewatch, 207
Crimmins, Alice, 44
Crippen, Dr. Harvey, 156
Crispin, Edmund, 31–32, 39–40, 55, 68–69, 94, 126, 140
Crocker, Superindendent Charles, 42, 103
Crofts, Freeman Wills, 118, 128–129, 133, 134, 179, 249
Cronin, Michael, 128
Crosse, David, 120
Crowley, Aleister, 101
Crowley, Francis ("Two Gun"), 48

D'Agneau, Marcel, 69–70
Dale, Martin, 8

Index

Dali, Salvador, 161
Daly, Elizabeth, 48, 180
Dane, Clemence, 129–130, 133
Dane, Colwyn, 8
Daniels, Chief Superindendent Charmian, 147
Daniels, Paul, 194, 204
Darbon, Leslie, 120
Dard, Frederick, 26
Dare, Stanley, 8
Davenport, John, 37, 100–101
Davies, Joan, 142
Davis, Bette, 60, 161, 215, 226
Day, Doris, 54
Dead Men Don't Wear Plaid, 225–226
Dead Reckoning, 226
Death Beat, 226–227
Death at Broadcasting House, 217
Death to Slow Music, 212–213
Deathtrap, 227–228
d'Eaubonne, Françoise, xii, 43–44
de Castera, Dr. Bernard, 4
Dee, Dr. John, 75, 89, 172
de Ford, Miriam Allen, 196
de la Torre, Lillian, 150, 152
Demarco, Gordon, 150–151
de Monaghan, Hélène, 25, 37
Denver, Paul, 27
Derleth, August, 4, 121–122, 149, 151–152, 157, 186, 190, 235
Detection Club, 9, 14, 15, 21, 39, 50, 51, 55, 56, 57, 60, 118, 125, 126, 127–128, 134, 163–164
Detective, 213
Devil Met a Lady, The, 161
Dew, Inspector, 156, 176–177
Diamond and the Goose, The, 245
Dibdin, Michael, 152–153
Dick Tracy, 160, 180, 227

Dickens, Charles, ix, 7, 12, 13, 41, 44, 70–71, 115, 116, 122, 139–140, 147, 170, 173, 212
Dickinson, Peter, 153
Die Abenteuer GMBH, 118
Dillinger, John, xi, 46, 48
Dime, Mike, 154–155
Dinesen, Isak, 153
Ding Dong Dead, 227
Dircks, John H., 153
Disorder in Court, 227
Doctorow, E. L., 153–154
Doody, Margaret, 152, 154
Dorothy and Agatha, 163–164
Doyle, Arthur Conan, 6, 43, 62, 72, 83, 124, 149, 151, 172, 176, 177, 194
Dragnet, 227
Drake, Kerry, 8
Drat! The Cat, 227
Drawbell, James Wedgewood, 129
Dream Squence Always Rings Twice, The, 228
Drew, Nancy, 107, 108, 178–179
Drummond, Bulldog, 92, 95, 118, 172, 181–182, 184, 219
Dudeney, Henry Ernest, 191
Dupin, Chevalier, 5, 99, 151, 157–158
Durrenmatt, Friedrich, 71–72

Eakins, William J., 48
Eberhardt, Walter, 200
Ecke, Wolfgang, 191
Eco, Umberto, 10, 72–73, 166
Edalji, Case, 43, 194
Eden, Matthew, 149–150
Edge, 122
Edward, Prince, Duke of Windsor, 36
Edson, J. T., 103–104
Eldershaw, M. Barbara, 131
Elwell, Joseph P., 46, 102, 132

Erskine, John, 131–132
Evans, Frank Howel, 178
Evans, Gwyn, 74, 135
Evans, Nick, 240
Exbrayat, 20, 25

Face on the Cutting Room Floor, The, 86–88
Fairlie, Gerard, 181–182
Fairman, Paul W., 75
Falcon, the, 22, 82, 92, 168, 170, 184, 257
Falcon Takes Over, The, 257
Fantoni, Barry, 154–155
Far East, 228
Farjeon, Joan Jefferson, 249
Farleigh, Runa, 166
Farrar, Geraldine, 166
Fatal Attraction, 229
Fathom, 229
Fearing, Kenneth, 40
Fen, Gervase, 8, 32, 39–40, 68–69, 126, 172
Fennedy, Andrew J., 75
Ferndale Housing Estate Townswomen's Guild Dramatic Society Murder Mystery "Murder at Checkmate Manor," 228–229
Ferrars, Elizabeth, 40, 76, 128, 150
Ferrer, José, 217
Fickling, G. G., 76–77
Field, Inspector, 7, 70, 173
Fiendish Plot of Dr. Fu Manchu, The, 229
Fish, Robert L., 50–51, 53, 77, 151
Fisher, John, 15, 194, 203, 231
Fitzgerald, F. Scott, 46, 102
Fleming, Ian, 59, 75, 89, 138, 172, 220–221
Fleming, Joan, 48, 128, 161
Fletcher, J. S., 199–200

Flynn, Errol, 161
Fontaine, Joan, 45
Ford, Corey, 94
Ford, Kenyon, 8
Forde, Nigel, 3
Fort Worth Museum, 205
Fortune, Dr. Reggie, 18, 24, 61, 81, 116
Four Plays for Coarse Actors, 229–230
Fowler, Graeme, 187
Fox, Gordon, 8
Francis, Dick, 112, 208
Franken, K., 191
Franklin, Benjamin, 40, 156–157
Franzen, Nils-Olsen, 77–78
Fraser, Antonia, 45, 57, 106
Freeman, Dr. R. Austin, 8, 40, 118, 151, 249
Fruttero, Carlo, 122
Fu Manchu, Dr., 124, 151, 249
Fuller, Timothy, 78
Further Adventures of Wonder Woman, 210

Gable, Clark, 46, 59, 132, 161
Gadda, Carlo Emilio, 137
Gallo, Joey, 62–63
Gallo, Larry, 44
Galloway, David, 107
Gamadge, Henry, 180
Gangbusters, 160, 202
Gardner, Erle Stanley, 8, 43, 76, 123, 131–132, 181, 192
Garland, Judy, 161
Garrison, Roger, 169
Gautier, Inspector Jean-Paul, 156
Gay Desperado, The, 230
Gem, 39, 124
Gerard, Francis, 55, 117, 181–183
Gershwin, George, 160
Get a Load of This, 244
Get Smart, 230–231

Index

Ghost Breakers, The, 212, 221–222, 245
Ghost Train, The, 222–223
Gideon, Commander George, 138, 180–181
Gielgud, John, 19, 30, 51
Gielgud, Val, 51, 164, 198, 217
Gifford, Thomas, 155
Gilbert, Anthony, 128
Gilbert, Michael, 126, 172, 182
Gill, B. M., 51–52
Gill, Bartholomew, 78
Gilman, George G., 122
Girtin, Tom, 78–79
Godard, Jean-Luc, 213
Goddard, Paulette, 221–222
Godwin, William, 5
Gordon, A. C., 191
Gordon, Gordon, 155
Gordon, Mildred, 155
Gordon, Dr. Richard, 155–156
Gores, Joe, 53, 232
Gorski, Dr. Walter, 9
Goulart, Ron, 79
Gracie Allen Murder Case, The, 94, 231
Graeme, Bruce, 79–80, 184
Graham, Caroline, 156
"Grange Hill Street Blues," 231
Grant, Alan, 7
Grant, Cary, 45, 214, 226, 252
Gray, Eve, 118, 249
Graydon, R. M., 135
Grayle, Panther, 8
Grayson, Richard, 156
Green, Horatio, 212
Green, Nigel, 216
Green, Roger Lancelyn, 4, 151
Greenberg, Martin H., 210
Greene, Paulette, 47, 173
Greenstreet, Sydney, 28, 45, 66, 76, 106, 215, 225, 230–231, 258
Greenwood, Harold, 44, 259

Gribble, Leonard R., 199
Grosse, Detective Inspector Alfred C., 191
Grossmith, George, 18, 211, 255
Gubb, Philo, 8, 75
Guinness, Alec, 104, 234, 238
Gumshoe, 202
Guyler, Deryck, 206
Guzik, Jake ("Greasy Thumb"), 178
Gymslip Vicar, 232

Hale, Robert, 57
Hall, Andrew, 80
Hall, Robert Lee, 40, 156–157
Halliday, Brett, 52–53
Hamilton, Charles, 41, 124, 179, 196, 211
Hamilton, George Heber, 135
Hammer, Mike, 61, 90, 122, 165, 179, 238
Hammett, 232
Hammett, Dashiell, 8, 27, 28, 41, 45, 53, 61, 75, 91, 113, 161, 165, 215, 232
Hamnet, Nina, 30–31
Hannay, Major General Richard, 30, 172
Hardwicke, Cedric, 45, 259
Hardy, Robert, 104
Hardy Boys, The, 178–179
Harker, Gordon, 206
Harris, Charlaine, 52
Harris, Timothy, 157
Harrison, Michael, 151, 157–158
Harsent, Rose, 47
Hart, Frances Noyes, 142
Hartswick, F. Gregory, 192–193
Hastings, Captain, 18, 39, 119, 175
Haunted Through Lounge and Recessed Dining Nook at Farndale Castle, The, 232
Haven't a Clue; or Murder at Withering Heights, 232–233

Hawk, John, 37
Hawke, Dixon, 8
Haycraft, Howard, 5, 23, 45, 57, 81, 83–84, 101, 102, 116, 181, 221
Haydon, Percy Montague, 38
Head, Edith, 54, 226
Heald, Tim, 80–81, 125
Heath, Eric, 37
Hecht, Ben, 81
Hellman, Lillian, 41
Helm, Matthew, 8
Henry, O., 81
Here Lies . . ., 205
Hill, Headon, 81
Hilton, John Buxton, 158–159
Hitchcock, Alfred, 19, 45, 89, 143, 168, 190–192, 223–224, 236
Hoch, E. D. 53–54, 59, 81–82, 112, 159, 163
Hodgson, Judith, 195, 198
Holm, Ian, 240
Holmes, Sherlock, 8, 9, 10, 11, 23, 31, 43, 47–48, 51, 58, 62, 69–70, 72–73, 81, 84, 90–92, 95, 97, 102, 116, 118–119, 122, 124, 134, 138, 142, 145, 149, 151, 152, 153, 159, 160, 163, 168, 171–177, 180, 183, 184, 188, 190, 198–199, 205, 212, 245, 249, 256
Hope, Bob, 46, 54, 212, 221–222, 237, 242, 245–246, 254
Horler, Sydney, 20, 206
Hornung, E. W., 124, 151, 183
Hornleigh, Inspector, 199, 206
Horton, Mileson, 192
Hoskins, Percy, 42
Houdini, Harry, 154
How to Destroy the Reputation of the Greatest Secret Agent, 233
How to Host a Murder, 203

Howard, Clark, 82
Hughes, Rupert, 131–132
Hulbert, Claude, 219
Hulbert, Jack, 115, 219, 223
Hume, David, 128–129
Hume, Fergus, ix, 82–83
Hunter, Tab, 54
Huston, John, 28, 221
Huxley, Aldous, 44, 259
Hyams, Joe, 54
Hylton, Jack, and His Band, 217

Icicle Twist Dinner Party, 202
If I Were You, 255
In Search of Blandings, 211
Innes, Michael, 32, 40, 55, 83–84, 94, 101, 117, 141
Inspector Scott Investigates, 206
It Could Be Any One of Us, 233
It's a Crime, 202

Jack the Ripper, 10, 86, 124, 155, 186, 188, 202, 216
Jacquemard-Senecal, 159
Jeeves, 18, 123, 176, 211
Jeffers, H. Paul, 159–160
Jeffry, Lord Francis, 1
Jepson, Edgar, 129–130
Jepson, Selwyn, 129
Jerome, Jerome K., 11, 86
Jesse, F. Tennyson, 128–129, 194–195
Johns, Stratford, 215
Johnson, Dr. Samuel, 5, 34, 96, 150, 152
Jones, Average, 132
Just Ask for Diamond, 233
Justus, Helen, 183
Justus, Jake, 183

Kai Lung, 145–146
Kakutani, Michiko, 16
Kaminsky, Stuart M., 34, 160–161

Index

Karloff, Boris, 38, 99, 214
Kaye, Danny, 54
Keating, H. R. F., 8, 9, 16, 21, 57, 93, 121, 125, 136, 146, 152, 160–161, 204, 208, 239
Kellerman, Faye, 162–163
Kennedy, Milward, 87, 127–128, 129–130, 133–134
Kenworthy, Superindendent Simon, 159
Kesselring, Joseph, 214
King, C. Daly, 196
Knox, Ronald A., 15, 133–134, 163–164
Kojak, 16, 25, 26
Kurland, Michael, 163
Kyd, Thomas, 157

Lacey, Ronald, 215
Lady Molly of Scotland Yard, 18, 108
Lady Vanishes, The, 223–224
La Guardia, Fiorello, 160
Lambert, Constant, 22, 114
Lamm, Herman K., 151
Larchman, Robert, 17
Larsen, Gaylord, 163–164
Last of Sheila, The, 234
Last of the Midnight Gardeners, The, 207
Late Show, The, 234
Latimer, Jonathan, 8, 23, 26, 54, 64
Laurel and Hardy Murder Case, The, 234–235
Lawrence, T. E., 149
Leacock, Stephen, 4, 84
Le Carré, John, 21, 69
Lee, Gypsy Rose, 22, 168
Lee, Nelson, 8, 109
Lehmann, Rudolf Chambers, 11
Leitch, Thomas M., 50
Lellenburg, Jon L., 124
Le Queux, William, 95

Levant, Oscar, 217
Le Vine, Jack, 89, 143
Levine Philip, 216
Lewis, Jerry, 54, 222
Lewis, Joseph Everglades, 46
Lewis, Norman, 164
Life and Times of Al Capone, The, 244
Lindbergh, Charles, 150–151
Lingle, Jake, 148, 178
Link, Abel, 8
Linscott, Gillian, 84–85
Lloyd, Jeremy, 85, 90, 214
Locke, Ferrers, 8, 124
Lofts, W. O. G., 124
Lorac, E. C. R., 128
Lord Peter Wimsey and the Bergholt Bells, 235–236
Lorre, Peter, 59, 78, 106, 215, 225, 230–231, 246, 258
Love, Jason, 8
Lovesey, Peter, 4, 41, 85–86, 126, 150, 164
Loy, Myrna, 41
Luce, Henry, 40
Lucentini, Franco, 122
Luciano, Lucky, 48, 164
Lugosi, Bela, 99, 222, 245
Lynn, Jonathan, 208
Lynn, Ralph, 24, 211, 255

MacArthur, Douglas, 161
McBain, Ed, 112, 113, 125, 153, 169, 183
MacCabe, Cameron, 16, 86–88
McCloy, Helen, 78
Macdonald, Gregory, 126
MacDonald, J. D., 79, 89, 112
Macdonald, Ross, 25, 62, 79, 89, 112, 122, 145, 157
McGerr, Patricia, 35
McGuffin, 236
McGuire, R. J., 26
McGurr, Machine-Gun Jack, 178

McKay, Randle, 15, 194
McMein, Neysa, 141
McShane, Mark, 88
Madden, Owney, 160
Magnet, 39, 124
Magnum, 214, 233–234
Maigret, Superintendent Jules, 7, 42, 78, 88, 96–99, 122, 175
Mainwaring, Marian, 164–165
Malone, Bugsy, 218–219
Malone, John J., 168, 183
Maltese Falcon, The, 28, 45, 66, 106, 122, 151, 215, 218, 225, 226, 232, 233, 237, 250
Mandel, Ernest, 7
Mansell, Jonathan
Manley, Alfred, 56
Marlowe, Dan J., 144
Marlowe, Derek, 144, 165
Marlowe, Philip, 16, 17, 19, 27, 31, 61, 62, 65, 74, 76, 77, 82, 88–89, 92, 96, 107, 114, 122, 143, 144, 151, 154, 157, 165, 175, 183–184, 226, 239, 243, 250, 253, 257
Marple, Miss Jane, 67–68, 104, 106, 109, 175, 184, 233, 256, 257
Marquand, John P., 78
Marsh, Ngaio, 7, 8, 32–33, 141
Marston, William Moulton, 107–108
Marx Brothers, 22, 95, 114, 161, 225, 243
Mascott, R. D., 90
Mason, A. E. W., 138, 249
Mason, Francis Van Wyck, 196–197
Mason, James, 234
Mason, Perry, 7, 23, 76, 132, 165, 181
Masquerade, 237
Masterpiece of Murder, A, 237
Masur, Harold Q., 123

Mathieson, Theodore, 90
Maugham, W. Somerset, 19, 121, 139, 212
Maxwell, Elsa, 141
Mayfair Mystery, The, 206
Melville, Jennie, 39, 147
Meredith, Hal, 134
Meredith, Sir John, 55, 117, 182–183
Merlini, The Great, 33, 192
Messac, Regis, 4, 250
Meyers, Richard, 126
Meynell, Lawrence, 128
Mickey Mouse, 180
Mike Hammer: More Than Murder, 238
Millar, Margaret, 25
Miller, Barbara, 24, 96, 167, 208, 223, 256–257
Milne, A. A., 4, 163–164
Minder on the Orient Express, 237–238
Miss Lizzie, Detective, 170
Mitchell, Gladys, 127–128
Modern Fiction Studies, 50
Modern Language Studies, 137
Monk, M. J., 90
Monkhouse, Bob, 194, 244
Montespan, Père, 1
Moody, Susan, 109
Moore, Roger, 89, 220
Moore, Will G., 40
Moran, George ("Bugs"), 48, 254
Morice, Anne, 56
Morse, L. A., 165–166
Morton, Guy, 90–91
Morton, J. B., 61
Moto, I. O., 32, 78
Mower, Patrick, 207
Mulligan's Last Case, 238
Murder à la Carte, 203–204
Murder Among Friends, 204
Murder, Anyone?, 202

Index

Murder At Garsington Manor, 238
Murder At The Vanities, 244–245
Murder by Death, 238–239
Murder by Magic, 204
Murder by Misadventure, 239
Murder by the Book, 239–240
Murder Game, The, 240
Murder in a Mist, 241
Murder in the Fifth Position, 240–241
Murder Machree, 180
Murder Observed, 181
Murder of Rover Ackroyd, The, 8
Murder on the Metropolitan Line, 241–242
Murder, She Wrote, 256
Murderer, 241, 259
Murdoch, Richard, 217, 223
murder weekends, 185–188
Murder, Norman, 18, 211
Murphy, Warren, B., 122, 126
Murray, Robert, 135
Musical Comedy Murders of 1940, The, 242
My Favorite Brunette, 246
Mystery of the Thirteenth Guest, The, 246

Name of the Rose, The, 10, 72–73, 166
Nash, Captain, 147
Nash, Captain Charles, 44
Nash, Jay Robert, 45
Nation, Terry, 215
Nesbit, Evelyn, 154
Newall, Patrick, 216
Next Stop Murder, 246–247
Nichols, Beverley, 212–213
Night Train to Murder, 247
Nitti, Frank, 148
Nolan, Williams F., 91
Norman, Frank, 91–92
Novak, Kim, 54

Oakie, Jack, 245, 255
O'Brien, Geoffrey, 201
O'Connor, Monsignor John, 39
O'Connor, Thomas ("Terrible Tommy"), 48
O'Connor, Vincent, 88
OCork, Shannon, 52, 105
O'Donnell, Peter, 109
O'Hare, Jeff, 189
Oldham, Peter, 40, 69
Old Man in the Corner, 18, 118–119
Oliver, Ariadne, 49, 119, 120, 140, 141, 240
Oliver, Edna May, 92
Oliver, Vic, 244
O'Malley, 247
On the Spot, 248
On Your Toes, 248
Onyx, The, 159–160
Opaenheim, E. Phillips, 58, 75, 95
Orczy, Baroness, 18
OSS 117, 89, 248
Ostrander, Isabel, 249
Over My Dead Body, 241

Palmer, Bill, 126
Palmer, Karen, 126
Palmer, Stuart, 5, 92, 168
Papazoglou, Orania, 55
Paramount on Parade, 248–249
Paris, Charles, 63–64, 146
Parker, Dorothy, 143
Parker, Robert B., 27, 89, 144, 183–184
Parkinson, Dr. C. Northcote, 123, 171, 176
Pate, Janet, 182
Paul, Barbara, 166
Paul, Elliott, 21–22, 92–93, 147
Pearson, Edmund, 46
Pagler, Alan, 207–208
Pembroke, Thomas, 192

Pentecost, Hugh, 113
Penzler, Otto, 197
Perelman, S. J., 93
Perowne, Barry, 124, 135, 151, 183
Pertwee, Jon, 192
Peters, Elizabeth, 55
Peters, Ellis, 166–167
Peters, Toby, 160–161
"Philadelphia", 195, 198
Phillips, C. N., 135
Pilkey, Dav, 189
Pinero, Arthur Wing
Player, Robert B., 167
Plomley, Roy, 167–168
Poe, Edgar Allan, ix, 5, 12, 14, 44, 99–100, 154, 157
Poirot, Hercule, 24, 25, 32, 35, 40, 49, 70, 90, 116, 118–119, 120, 122, 123, 139, 141, 162, 165, 175, 184, 201, 212, 220, 226–227, 240, 243, 256–257
Poisoned Pen, 22, 70, 76, 97, 104, 122, 128, 130, 131, 132, 146, 165
Police Hall of Fame, 205
Police Squad, 249–250
Pons, Solar, 121–122, 124, 149, 151, 190, 235
Potts, Jean, 47
Powell, William, 41, 46, 238, 249
Pratt, Anthony, 201
Preiss, Byron, 184
Preiss, H. J., 192
Priestly, J. B., 58
Private Dick, 250
Priwin, Hans, 206
Prize, Matthew, 197
Pronzini, Bill, 93, 136, 145, 177
Punch, 58
Pushing Murder, 180
Puzo, Mario, 44
Pyne, Parker, 8

Queen, Ellery, 1, 7, 15, 33, 52, 53, 55, 57, 77, 82, 112, 113, 122, 123, 124, 137, 151, 157, 165, 175, 184, 192, 249
Queen, Ellery, Jr., 179
Quentin, Patrick, 123, 198
Quin, Harley, 8

Race, Colonel, 120
Radford, Basil, 223–224
Radnor, Alan, 192
Rafferty, S. S., 168
Raffles, A. J., 124, 138, 151, 183
Raft, George, 148, 221, 230
Ramsey, C. C., 119
Randisi, Robert J., 126
Ransord, Sherlock, 193
Rasp, Fritz, 24
Rasp, Renate, 24, 139
Rathbone, Basil, 62, 160–161, 177
Rawson, Clayton, 33, 52, 53
Raymond, John, 97
Real Inspector Hound, The, 250
Reed, Rod, 110
Reeder, J. G., 42, 103–104
Regester, Seeley, 120
Reilly, Helen, 198
Rhode, John, 38, 61, 127–128, 138
Ribblesdale, Lady, 141
Rice, Craig, 21, 22, 92, 168–169, 170, 183
Richards, Frank, 24, 124, 179, 196
Richardson, Ralph, 104, 219
Ridley, Arnold, 222–223
Rinehart, Mary Robert, 44
Ripley, H. A., 192–193
Ripley, Mike, 94
Robbins, Alan, 197
Roberts, Arthur, 4
Robinson, Robert, 94–95
Roi, 250–251
Rolfe, Guy, 216
Roosevelt, Eleanor, 34–35, 161

Index

Roosevelt, Franklin D., 131–132, 148, 178
Ross, Clarissa, 169
Rothstein, Arnold, 45–46, 102
Rovin, Jeff, 169
Roxie Hart, 251
Runyon, Damon, 45–46, 58, 102, 148, 212, 242–243
Rutherford, Margaret, 104, 120, 233
Ryan, Elizabeth Boyd, 48

Saint, the, 18, 38, 65–66, 82, 89, 169, 181, 184, 220, 233
Samuel, Jopseh, 95
Sanders, George, 22, 168, 169–170, 184, 257
Satterthwaite, Walter, 170
Saumaurez, John, 127–128, 129
Savalas, Telly, 10, 25
Sax, Agaton, 77–78, 179
Sayers, Dorothy L., 5, 8, 11, 12, 18, 20, 24, 33, 41–42, 45, 47–48, 60, 67, 93, 94, 115, 125, 127–130, 133–134, 135, 138, 139, 163–164, 210–211, 220, 224, 235–236, 250
Schorr, Mark, 214
Schultz, Dutch, 154
Scott-Giles, C. W., 47
Secret Drawer, The, 251–252
Sefton, John, 9
Segal, George, 218
Selwyn, Francis, 170–171, 176
Sewart, Alan, 56
Shaffer, Antony, 49, 220, 241, 253, 259
Shakespeare, William, 34, 162–163
Sharpe, Tom, 95
Shaw, George Bernard, 149, 163
Shayne, Mike, 33, 52, 122, 181, 246, 257
Shea, Douglas, 95

Shelley, Mary Wollstonecraft, 5, 6
Shelley, Mike, 96
Sheringham, Roger, 18, 50, 127–128
Shore, Jemima, 106
Siegel, Bugsy, 48, 16
Silberkleit, Tom, 193
Silent House, The, 252–253
Silver, Maud, 165
Silvers, Phil, 224
Sim, Alastair, 206
Sim, Sheila, 249
Simenon, Georges, 20, 42, 96–99, 175, 193, 211–212
Simon, Caryl, 22, 23, 176–177
Simon, Neil, 123, 165, 224–225, 238–239
Simpson, Dorothy, 42
Simpson, Helen, 48, 127–128, 129, 133
Sims, George, 171–172
Sims, George R., 2, 99
Sinatra, Frank, 46
Sinclair, Andrew, 99–100
Singing Detective, The, 253
Sitwells, 31, 101
Sjöwall, Maj, 20
Skelton, Red, 54, 255–256
Skene, Anthony, 135
Skin O' My Tooth, 18
Slater, Oscar, 43
Slesar, Henry, 210
Sleuth, 241, 253, 259
Slung, Michele B., 109, 110
Smith, W. K., 74
Smollett, Tobias, 5
Snelling, O. F., 172
Sobol, Donald J., 193
Some Like It Hot, 254
Something's Afoot, 245
Sothern, Ann, 255
Spade, Sam, 17, 26, 59, 61, 76, 82, 96, 122, 157, 165, 215, 218, 232, 233

Spain, Nancy, 100
Spenser, 27, 89, 144
Spider's Web, 206, 254–255
Spillane, Mickey, 56, 90, 179, 238
Spilsbury, Bernard, 156, 177
Spirit, 74
Spoof, 4
Spurrier, Ralph, 133, 197
Stafford, Frederick, 89
Starrett, Vincent, 5
Stephenson, Maureen, 173
Stevens, Christopher, 74
Stevenson, Robert Louis, 57, 212, 216
Stewart, R. F., 116, 130
Stewart, Vivianne, 57
Stout, Rex, 53, 123
Strang, Professor Lord, 40, 68–69
Strange, Earl, 135
Strangeways, Nigel, 37, 149
Stratemeyer, Edward L., 178–179
Streetlife, 202
Stubbs, Jean, 173–174, 178
Summer Lightning, 255
Super-Sleuth, 255
Swift, Fallon, 8
Swift, Joy, 185
Symons, Julian, 4, 21, 39, 72, 87, 101, 102, 105, 107, 146, 149, 167, 174–175, 253

Tandy, Jessica, 259
Tanner, William, 172
Taylor, Professor Alfred Swaine, 40
"Teddy Bear Who Knew Too Much, The", 256–257
Teed, G. H., 135
Ten Little Niggers, 159, 208, 245
Tey, Josephine, 7, 47
That Man from Rio, 233, 257
Thatcher, John Putman, 22
Thaw, Harry Kendall, 154
Theatre of Film Noir, 257

Thin Man, 41, 238–239
Thin Man, The, 245
Things As They Are, 5
Thomas, Donald, 175–176
Thomas, Dylan, 37, 100–101
Thomson, Sir Basil, 21
Thomson, June, 205
Thoorens, Leon, 97
Thorndyke, Dr., 119, 151, 153
Three Stooges, The, 227
Tierney, Gene, 120
Time to Kill, 257
Tomb with a View, A, 257
Too Many Crooks, 257
Top Secret, 202
Torquemada, 8, 193
Tower of David Museum, 205
Track, Martin, 8
Traubel, Helen, 123
Travers, Ben, 24
Treasure, Mark, 22, 104
Treat, Larry, 53, 193–194
Trivial Detective, 202
Trow, M. J., 176–177
Truman, Margaret, 35
Turner, Ethel, 131
Twain, Mark, 4, 69, 102, 124, 183

Uhnak, Dorothy, 44, 109
Underground, 237, 257–258
Ustinov, Peter, 40, 223

Vail, Laurence, 102
Valentine, Lewis J., 160
Vance, Philo, 7, 8, 15, 18, 31, 33, 46, 87, 89, 94, 112, 132, 161, 231, 249
Van Dine, S. S., 15, 18, 46, 62, 87, 94, 102, 112, 131–132, 194, 231
Verity, Sergeant William Clarence, 170–171
Very, Pierre, 20
Vestris, Madame, 2

Index

Vivement Dimanche, 258
von Hoffman, Nicholas, 148, 178

Waddington, 200
Wahlöö, Per, 20
Wallace, Edgar, 8, 18, 20, 33–34, 42, 103–104, 117, 182, 192, 195, 248, 249
Wallace, Penelope, 33–34, 42, 103, 182
Walpole, Hugh, 61, 133–134
Ward, Christopher, 102
Warmington, S. J., 206
Watson, Colin, 24, 29, 30
Watterson, Bill, 74
Wayne, Naunton, 223–224
Weaver, William, 137
Weiman, Rita, 131–132
Weinkauf, Mary S., 67–68
Welles, Orson, 60, 215, 217, 221
Westlake, Donald, 6, 22, 64, 104, 222
Wheatley, Dennis, 169, 196, 198
Where There's a Will, 258
Whistling in the Dark, 255–256
White, Stanford, 154
White, Valerie, 128
Whitechurch, Victor L., 8, 129–130
Whitecuffe, Harry, xii, 43–44
Whiteman, Paul, 160
Whitney, Phyllis A., 179
Who Did It?, 166
Who Done It?, 258
Whodunnit?, 207, 259
Who Killed Agatha Christie?, 218
Who Killed Henrietta?, 204
Wild West Weekly, 112, 180
Wilde, Oscar, 43, 163, 170, 177
Wilde West, 170
Williams, Charles, 36
Williams, David, 22, 39–40, 64, 104, 106, 130

Williams, Emlyn, 30
Williams, Thomas E., 19
Williams, Valentine, 121, 128–129
Willing, Basil, 78
Willing Dead, The, 202
Wilson, Colin, 6, 13, 43–44, 172, 173, 178, 193, 195, 225
Wilson, Joy, 13
Wilson, Sandy, 28, 76, 237
Wilson, Stanley, 56
Wimsey, Lord Peter, 7, 18, 20, 24, 33, 41–42, 47–48, 60–61, 85, 87, 94, 116, 123, 127–128, 135, 138, 140, 165, 172, 173, 184, 211, 216, 220, 224
Wise, Ernie, 208
Withers, Hildegarde, 5, 92, 168
Woddis, Roger, 207
Wodehouse, P. G., 18, 20, 23, 24, 25, 38, 65, 76, 116, 123, 127, 136, 139–140, 156, 224, 255
Wolfe, Gary, 104–105
Wolfe, Nero, 7, 8, 27, 90, 137, 144–145, 165, 175, 240
Wolff, Camille, 118, 199
Woman's Vengeance, A., 259
Wonder Woman, 107–108, 210
Woollcott, Alexander, 44, 46, 107
Woolf, F. X., 196
Wooster, Bertie, 18, 24, 123, 127, 139, 211, 224, 255
Working Murder, 180
Wren, Lassiter, 15, 194

Yates, Dornford, 30, 95, 172
Yonge, Charlotte, 146
Yorio, Carlos A., 166

Zaharoff, Basil, 45
Zangwill, Israel, 105
Zebra Books, 194

About The Author

JOHN KENNEDY MELLING is an English author, broadcaster, critic, and historian. He has specialized in nineteenth-century subjects and the medieval guilds of Europe; has written a standard paperback, now in its fifth edition, on the guilds; another on antiques; and has studied particularly police, crime, and crime and detective fiction. A former member of the committee of the Crime Writers' Association of Great Britain, he edited their *Practical Handbook,* receiving a special award in 1989. He has presented lectures in many venues, including the ocean liner Queen Elizabeth II.

He has contributed to police and crime magazines in England and America. He is a member of the National Association of Chiefs of Police (NACOP), USA Drug Task Force, is an Honorary International Life Vice President of the American Federation of Police, and has received the Knight Grand Cross of NACOP in 1985. He is a member of American and British learned societies, including the British Academy of Film and Television Arts; is a Fellow of the Royal Society of Arts; and is a chartered accountant.

He is an authority on the history of the theatre, as critic, playwright, and historian. He was the first editor, for five years, of the Chivers Black Dagger series of crime classics.

His next book will be *Scaling the High C's,* cowritten with John Brecknock, about Brecknock's career as an operatic tenor; it will be published by Scarecrow Press.